Rebels with La Causa

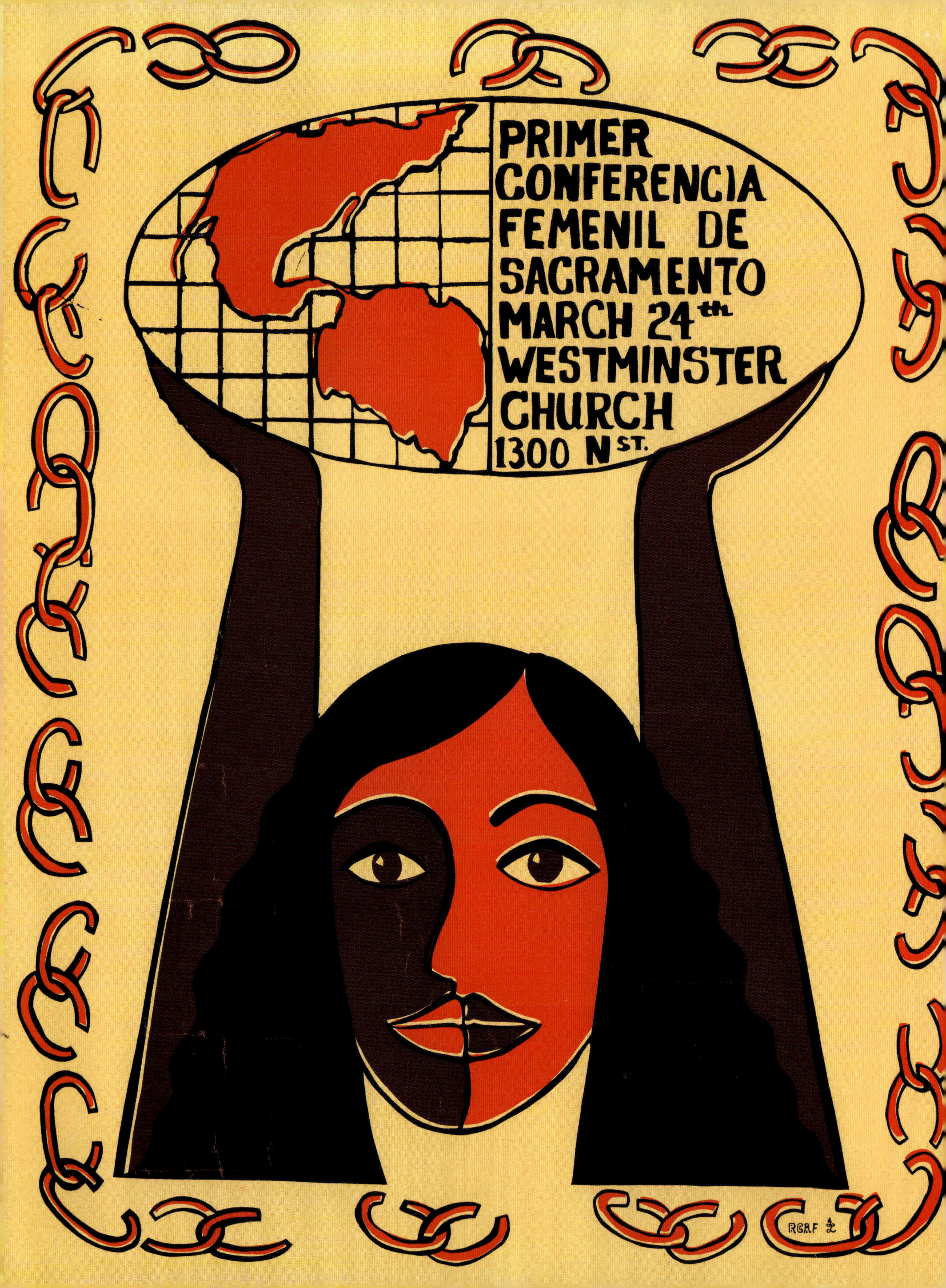
PRIMER
CONFERENCIA
FEMENIL DE
SACRAMENTO
MARCH 24th
WESTMINSTER
CHURCH
1300 N ST.
RCAF

Rebels with La Causa

Royal Chicano Air Force Art and Activism 1970–1990

SCALA

Crocker Art Museum
In association with
Scala Arts Publishers, Inc.

Published in conjunction with *Rebels with La Causa: Royal Chicano Air Force Art and Activism, 1970–1990*, organized by the Crocker Art Museum, Feb 22–June 28, 2026.

First published in 2026 by
Scala Arts Publishers, Inc.
c/o CohnReznick LLP
10th floor, 1301 Avenue of the Americas
New York, NY 10019, USA
www.scalapublishers.com
An imprint of B. T. Batsford Holdings Ltd.

In association with Crocker Art Museum

ISBN 978-1-78551-623-8

Edited by Susan Higman Larsen
Designed by Matt Avery, Monograph
Printed in China
Library of Congress Control number: 2025031364

Scala is represented in UK and Europe by Abrams & Chronicle Books, 1 West Smithfield, London, EC1A 9JU and 57 rue Gaston Tessier, 75166 Paris, France.

10 9 8 7 6 5 4 3 2 1

Frontispiece: Irma Lerma Barbosa (born 1949), *Primer Conferencia Femenil de Sacramento* (detail), 1973. Screenprint, 35 × 23 in. Royal Chicano Air Force Archives, CEMA 8, University of California, Santa Barbara Library.

Front cover: Rudy O. Cuellar (born 1950), Luis C. González (born 1953), and José Montoya (1932–2013), *José Montoya's Pachuco Art, A Historical Update* (detail), 1977. Screenprint, 31 × 13 in. Collection of Luis C. González.

Back cover: Harold Nihei (born 1939), *RCAF Accidentally Joins a Parade in Woodland*, 1976. [Esteban Villa, José Montoya, Ricardo Favela, and Pedro "Pete" Hernandez]. Collection of Harold Nihei.

Contents

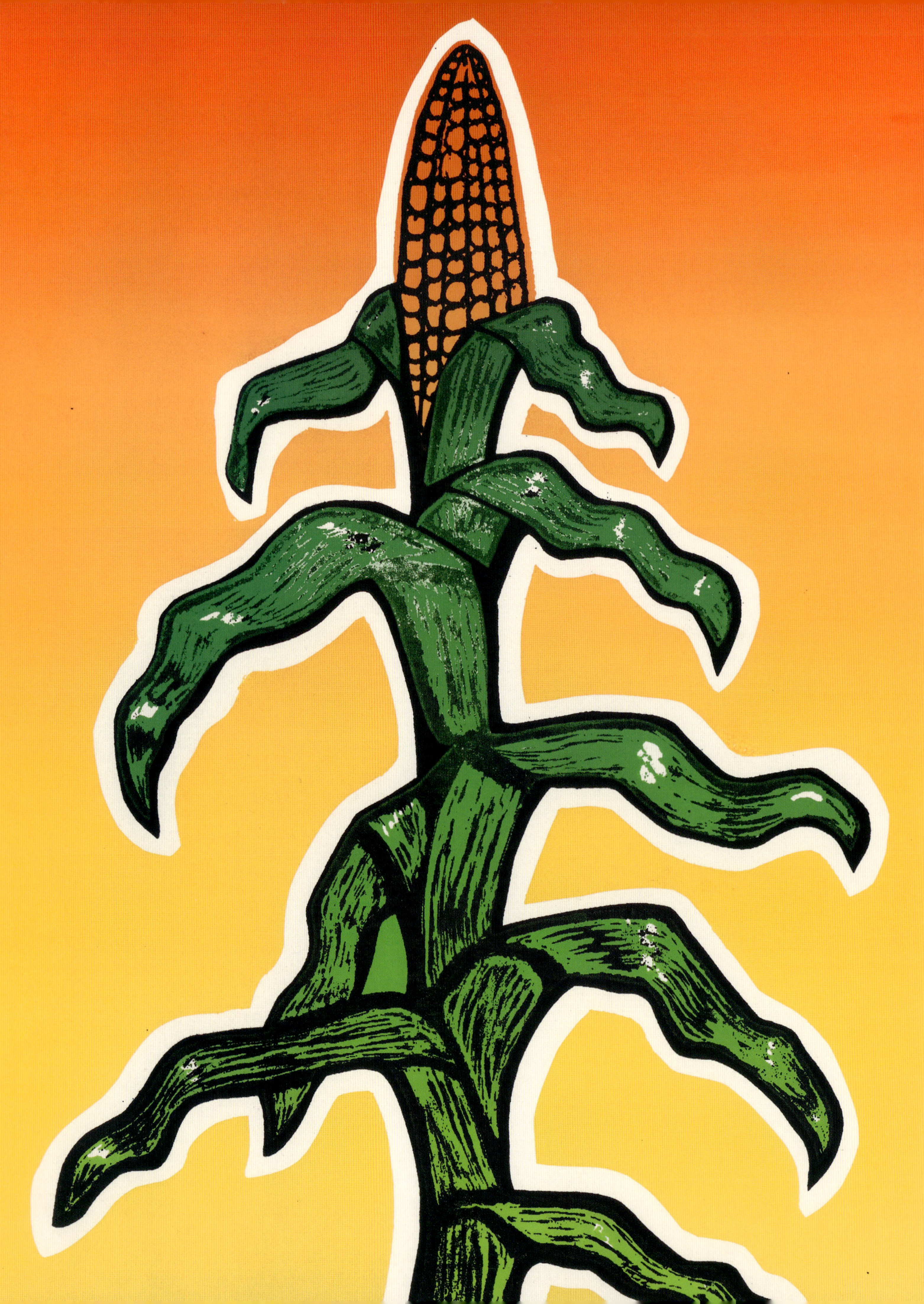

Acknowledgments

Beginning in 1970, students and other professional artists coalesced around Sacramento State art professors José Montoya and Esteban Villa. The group would go on to become the Royal Chicano Air Force (RCAF), one of the Chicano Movement's most prolific and impactful artist collectives. They produced individual artworks and group murals, as well as posters for numerous educational, cultural, and political activities of Chicana/o students, faculty, and community members. They also began their long-standing support of the United Farm Workers (UFW), which morphed into a key tributary to the national civil rights movement. After the collective moved off-campus and established the Centro de Artistas Chicanos in 1973, it grew as artists were joined by other creatives, professors, community members, and political activists.

The RCAF's transformation into a broader collective not only initiated an explosion of Chicano art exhibits, theater productions, concerts, and cultural celebrations in the community, but also promoted civic engagement and political activism. While RCAF posters served as announcements for these wide-ranging events, they are also examples of the artists' aesthetic experimentation and unique contributions to Chicana/o art history and the history of American graphic arts. *Rebels With La Causa: RCAF Art and Activism, 1970–1990* explores the creative production and expansive output of the RCAF in its first two decades, and this exhibition and publication position the collective as an integral protagonist in the larger history of poster/print production in the United States.

This important project was a multiyear endeavor that came to fruition through the efforts and support of many contributors. First and foremost, we extend our gratitude to the Chicana/o artists and activists of this seminal collective. They enacted an artistic, cultural, and political renaissance that continues to reverberate in the Sacramento region and beyond. The work featured in this catalogue includes prints and photos by Juan Carrillo, Juan Cervantes, Armando Cid,

Rudy O. Cuellar (born 1950), *Fiesta de Maíz* (detail), 1977.

Rudy O. Cuellar, Ricardo Favela, Eva Garcia, Kathryn Garcia, Max Garcia, Lorraine García-Nakata, Bill Gee, Luis C. González, Irma Lerma Barbosa, José Montoya, Juanishi Orosco, Stan Padilla, Celia Herrera Rodriguez, Raul Suarez, and Esteban Villa, along with photographs by Rodolfo Cuellar Sr., Alfred "Freddy" González, Héctor González, Harold Nihei, and additional items from José Arenas and Taller Arte del Nuevo Amanecer (TANA), Luzmaria Espinosa, Evelyn Jenkins-Cronn, Enrique Ortiz Villegas, Guadalupe Portillo, and Dr. Arnaldo Solis. Many artists not only contributed their posters and photographs but also assisted with research documenting their significance.

The exhibition would not have been possible without the artists and families who generously lent artwork or facilitated photography for this catalogue. They include: Juan Carrillo, Rudy O. Cuellar, Tina Favela and Clara Cid, Alfred "Freddy" González, Héctor González, Luis C. González, Harold Nihei, Elicia Powell, Phil Serna, Rene and Nathan Villa, and Enrique Ortiz Villegas. Though no longer with us for this well-deserved recognition, the exhibition and catalogue serve as a tribute to Juan Cervantes, Armando Cid, Rodolfo Cuellar Sr., Ricardo Favela, Eva Garcia, Max Garcia, Evelyn Jenkins-Cronn, José Montoya, Juanishi Orosco, and Esteban Villa. A special *ofrenda* featured in the exhibition and these pages honors their and RCAF activists' contributions.

The exhibition was aided tremendously by the assistance of our colleagues at institutional collections, through both loans and photography: Angel Diaz at the University of California, Santa Barbara's California Ethnic and Multicultural Archives (CEMA); Brianna Loughlin and Sarah Allison at California State University, Sacramento's Gerth Special Collections and University Archives; Sue Tyson and Kristi Powell at the California History Section, California State Library; and Emily Smith at the Oakland Museum of California. We are also grateful to David Rasul for lending key prints, as well as Stacy Paragary for the loan of an iconic José Montoya painting.

The Crocker Art Museum's staff was also instrumental in the realization of this multifaceted project. We are especially grateful to Curatorial Projects Coordinator Mariah Briel, whose in-house project management was indispensable to the success of the exhibition and catalogue. Indeed, this project would not have come to fruition but for her. Ted and Melza Barr Chief Curator and Associate Director Scott A. Shields, Ph.D., helped to conceptualize the project and extended the invitation for Terezita Romo to curate the show. Lial A. Jones, the former Mort and Marcy Friedman Director & CEO, championed the project from its inception. The collaborative spirit of the Museum's Director of Education, Javier Plasencia, and Education Manager, Houghton Kinsman, provided the exhibition with interpretive insight and programming support.

Also at the Crocker, photographer Gerard Vuilleumier produced beautiful reproductions of many of the posters featured in this book, and Max Garcia, Héctor González, Alfred "Freddy" González, Harold Nihei, and Phil Serna supplied additional key images. Matthew Isble, Brian Suhr, and Tyler Turner captured the colorful, collaborative spirit of the RCAF in the exhibition and its accompanying collateral. The Crocker staff broadly, along with the ever-supportive Co-Trustees, supported this project from the beginning.

For their role in creating such an important and scholarly catalogue, we thank an esteemed group of contributors. Art historian and professor Tatiana Reinoza's essay provides insight on Luis C. González's unique concrete poetry within an international movement that began in the 1950s. Artist and professor Jesús Barraza discusses Chicana/o *Indigenismo* (a pivotal tenet of the RCAF), as well as the collective's influence on him as an artist and activist. Professor Ella Maria Diaz's utilized the concept of "mural environs" to document existing and destroyed RCAF murals, reflecting on notions of public art's permanence and representation. Historian and professor Lorena Márquez posits the RCAF as a grassroots organization exemplified by the activism of its non-artists members and the collective's connections to the social issues of Sacramento's *la gente* (the people).

At Scala Arts Publishers, Inc., Jennifer Norman, Director of Publications, and her team, including Beth Holmes, senior editor; Susan Larsen, editor; and Matt Avery, designer; created this beautiful and important catalogue. They, like the scholars, lenders, supporters, families, and, especially, the artists listed above, sought to celebrate the RCAF and create a lasting testament to the collective's legacy. This publication, like the exhibition it was created to accompany, acknowledges the RCAF's accomplishments within the field of American graphics, public art, and concrete poetry, as well as its pivotal contributions to Chicana/o cultural reclamation, civic engagement, and multicultural solidarity.

Agustín Arteaga, Mort and Marcy Friedman Director & CEO, and Terezita Romo

Note to the Reader

Throughout this catalogue, authors have chosen to use the term Chicana/o to refer to the artists and community members who identify as being of Mexican American heritage in the United States during the period of this exhibition. Chicano is used to refer to the historical Chicano Movement (*el Movimento*) and its participants, and as an identifier for both the Royal Chicano Air Force (RCAF) and its institutions. Alternate spellings, such as Chicana and Xicanx, and Spanish language names and words are spelled according to individual author or artist preferences.

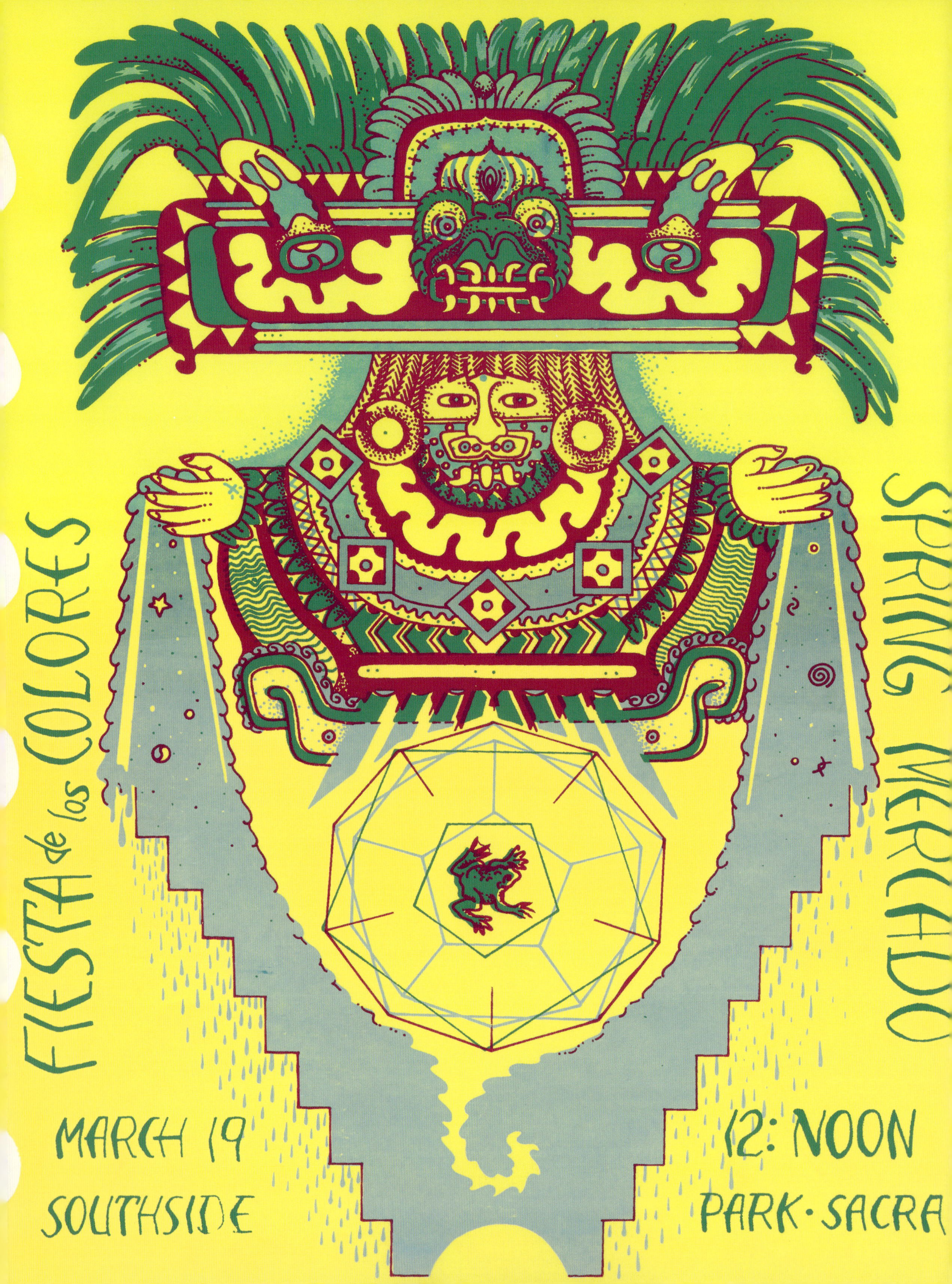
FIESTA de los COLORES
SPRING MERCADO
MARCH 19
12: NOON
SOUTHSIDE
PARK · SACRA

TEREZITA ROMO

RCAF Poster Art, Activism, and Ceremonia, 1970–1990

As cultural-political strategy, artists assumed that the undermining of entrenched artistic hierarchies would create apertures for questioning equally rooted social structures.

TOMÁS YBARRA-FRAUSTO

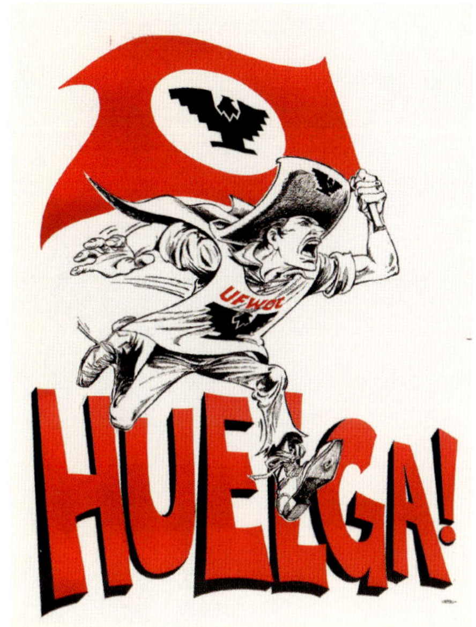

Fig. 1. Andrew Zermeño (born 1935), *Huelga!*, 1966. Offset lithograph on paper, 24 × 18½ in. Smithsonian American Art Museum, Gift of the Margaret Terrazas Santos Collection, 2019.52.1.

During the 1960s and 1970s, politically conscious Mexican Americans from different generations and regions of the US came together as "Chicanos" to confront educational disparities and racial discrimination, as well as decry the subhuman working conditions of farm workers and the high fatality rate of Mexican Americans in the Vietnam War.[1] Artists became key protagonists in the Chicano Movement, and as art historian E. Carmen Ramos notes, the "proliferation of visual works beginning in the 1960s inundated Chicano communities with imagery and references that contested their social invisibility and assigned value to their culture."[2] In fact, scholars cite Andrew Zermeño's posters in support of the United Farm Workers (UFW) union in 1965 as the beginning of Chicana/o art (fig. 1). Many artists formed collectives to coordinate artmaking in service to the larger *Movimiento* and to connect to their local communities, while also providing a creative environment for the production of individual and collective artworks.

Within Chicana/o art history, collectives are not rare.[3] In fact, many Chicana/o artists rebuked the mystique of the individual artist pursuing a successful solo career and even denounced the creation of "art for art's sake" as a "ludicrous fantasy" within the nation's volatile political climate during the civil rights movement.[4] Instead, an important goal was to eliminate barriers between artists and the community and democratize the artmaking process. Devoid of the "high" and "low" hierarchies of Western European art history, Chicana/o collectives also exposed the community "to a pluralistic rather than a monolithic aesthetic," becoming a "Chicano alternative art circuit [that played] a central and commanding role in nurturing a visual sensibility in the barrio."[5] Within a collective

Stan Padilla (born 1945), *Fiesta de los Colores*, 1978 [Plate 63].

setting, artists could be mutually supportive, which allowed them to experiment and create art that was not only cultural affirming but also reflective of their lived experiences, including art training and popular culture. Among Chicana/o collectives, Sacramento's Royal Chicano Air Force (RCAF) is unique in its longevity and membership.

Focused on the first two decades of the group's work, *Rebels with La Causa: Royal Chicano Air Force Art and Activism, 1970–1990* features posters from one of the Chicano Movement's most prolific and impactful artist collectives. It provides an artistic survey of the range of aesthetics embodied by the multigenerational RCAF as expressed through their mastery of screenprinting techniques and their experimentation within graphic arts overall. Moreover, with their confluence of bicultural (Mexican and American) aesthetics, iconography, and strategic incorporation of subversive humor, RCAF posters and prints refuted definitions of Chicana/o art as solely political, "ethnic," or folk art. In their blurring of what constituted a political statement, announcement poster, and art print, they also contributed to Chicana/o graphics' distinct tributary into American art history.

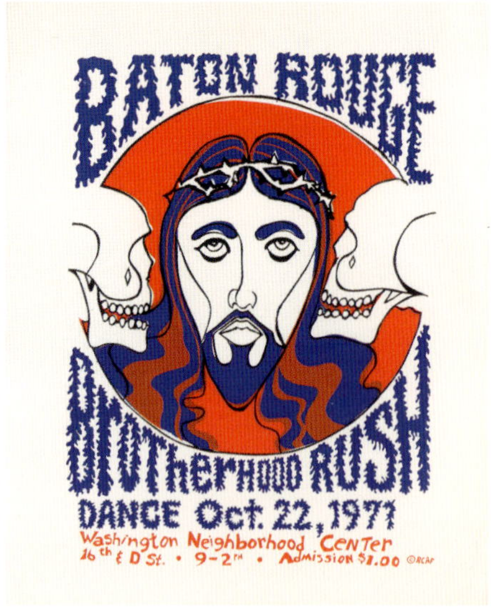

Fig. 2. Max Garcia (1942–2020), *Baton Rouge*, 1971 [Plate 5].

An early example of the RCAF's wide-ranging aesthetics is Maximino "Max" Garcia's *Baton Rouge* (1971; fig. 2) poster for a rock concert at the Washington Neighborhood Center (WNC), a multiservice facility located near downtown Sacramento in one of the city's oldest barrios. The composition is dominated by a red circle in which a disembodied, Christ-like head with a blue beard, long wavy hair, and a crown of thorns confronts the viewer. On either side, the profiles of two skulls turn toward the head, as if to whisper in his ears. The fuzzy, prickly, hand-drawn lettering, rendered in different sizes and in a seemingly random selection of upper and lower cases, adds to the edgy visual effect. Garcia's three-color print incorporated Pop and psychedelic art styles that were prevalent in concert posters of the 1970s. His composition is a juxtaposition of Christian religious iconography and ancient Mesoamerican death symbology. The skulls also recall the promotional art and "Deadhead" persona of the rock group The Grateful Dead, as well as the *calaveras* (skeletons) of the Mexican master printmaker and political illustrator José Guadalupe Posada.[6] The divergent imagery also evokes Susan Sontag's declaration that posters can claim "attention—at a distance" by being "visually aggressive," an important attribute for an announcement poster. [7] However, Garcia's print for American rock bands performing in a Chicana/o barrio also elucidates his ability to meld divergent artistic sources and, as in this case, appeal to audiences who did not know it was "Chicano art."

In addition to foregrounding RCAF artists' aesthetic experimentation, *Rebels with La Causa* also explores their activities as a multidimensional community group fomenting a cultural renaissance and fostering political activism. The exhibition begins with their formation at Sacramento State (officially California State University, Sacramento) as the Rebel Chicano Art Front, a collective comprising two art instructors, their aspiring art students, and professional artists. It transformed into the Royal Chicano Air Force and grew to include poets and writers, as well as cultural anthropology, government, and communications professors.

The exhibition chronicles the RCAF's establishment and the evolution of their nonprofit organization Centro de Artistas Chicanos, which allowed them to increase their community membership with the inclusion of local musicians, dancers, actors, mental health professionals, culture bearers, and UFW union activists. The RCAF also expanded to encompass the nonprofit organizations Breakfast for Niños (BFN) and La Raza Bookstore, later becoming La Raza Galeria Posada (LRGP), and members of the Alkali Flat Project Area Committee (Alkali PAC), which increased the collective's activities and impact. Of note is their formation of the Cultural Affairs Committee, an internal body that facilitated the production of yearly exhibitions, literary presentations, civic events, and the initiation of community *ceremonias* (Indigenous-based ceremonies).[8] In fact, the exhibited posters, photographs, and ephemera underscore the multidisciplinary collective as an antecedent of "community art" in contrast to a current gentrified social practice.

Rebels with La Causa includes a component related to La Raza Bookstore and LRGP's exhibitions of RCAF artists. As the only organization of its kind, LRGP had a pivotal role in the region. The bookstore promoted Chicana/o and Native American literature, music, and theater programming, as well as Spanish-language publications. The gallery, which exhibited Chicana/o, Latino, and Native American artists, was a crucial venue filling a void in the Sacramento region, especially in its barrios. The exhibition also highlights the RCAF's political activism and solidarity. Along with their well-documented support of the UFW union with their production of numerous posters, flags, and lawn signs, RCAF members participated in marches and food drives, and served as security guards for the union's leader, César Chávez. Artists also created posters in support of the American Indian Movement, prison reform, and Central American wars against dictators. Ultimately, the exhibition serves as a tribute to a collective, with its genesis during the Chicano Movement, that transformed into a multifaceted community group whose artistic experimentation, cultural revitalization, and political activism continue to resonate.

From Rebel Chicano Art Front to Royal Chicano Air Force

In the fall of 1969, high school art teachers and *compadres* José Montoya and Esteban Villa reunited at Sacramento State. Montoya was a participant in the Mexican American Education Project (MAEP), a statewide initiative that supported students pursuing undergraduate and master's degrees in the social sciences. Based on Montoya's recommendation, Villa was contracted by the MAEP as an art consultant.[9] Each brought their unique artistic talents and a long personal association that extended back to the late 1950s as students and graduates of the California College of Arts and Crafts in Oakland (now California College of the Arts in San Francisco). In 1968, Villa co-founded the Mexican American Liberation Art Front (MALAF), one of the earliest documented Chicana/o artist collectives.[10] The Oakland-based group, which included René Yañez, Manuel Hernández-Trujillo, and Malaquias Montoya (José's brother), formed "for the purpose of organizing Chicano artists who are interested in integrating art into the Chicano social revolution sweeping the country."[11] It lasted for a year and a half, holding weekly meetings that provided opportunities for discussions on the philosophy and definition of Chicana/o art.[12] José was a frequent participant at these gatherings in which, as Villa recalled, "At first, our group was composed mainly of painters and we would bring our work and criticize it. Discussions were heated, especially the polemics on the form and content of revolutionary art and the relevance of murals and graphic art."[13]

In March 1969, MALAF invited other artists, including José, to participate in an exhibition at East Oakland's La Causa Center, located in the city's Mexican American Fruitvale neighborhood. In the written statement for the exhibition, *New Symbols for La Nueva Raza* was described as "an effort to present in visual form an artistic account of the Chicano movement."[14] The featured artworks also represented a rejection of an imposed Western European aesthetic and the revival of an art reflective of "*el hombre nuevo* (the new man): the Chicano who had emerged from the decolonization process."[15] The exhibition included posters and prints, which, given their accessible technology, portability, and cost-effectiveness, became a popular medium for disseminating a nascent Chicana/o aesthetic. These attributes also made them the favored artistic medium for the promotion of the movement's political ideology as well as cultural reclamation, especially during the 1960s and 1970s. "It was like a call went out to all Chicanos," declared (José) Montoya. "Artists had their mandate—to pictorialize the struggle … and the posters were our newsletters."[16]

This seminal period of Montoya and Villa's artistic activism, along with their backgrounds as farm workers, educational experiences, and personal ties, influenced them greatly. They were also inspired by the Chicano Movement's overall mandate regarding the role of the artist. As stated in the pivotal manifesto *El Plan Espiritual de Aztlán*, it was incumbent on Chicana/o "writers, poets, musicians, and artists [to] produce literature and art that is appealing to our people and relates to our revolutionary culture."[17] MALAF, along with its articulation of a postcolonial Chicana/o art, advocated for artists to create art *with* and not *for* the community. This commitment to *artivism*, along with Villa and Montoya's cultural imagery and egalitarian teaching styles, became a magnet for some Sacramento State Chicana/o art students and independent artists, their affiliation altering their lives and careers.

In addition to Montoya and Villa looking like them and sharing their culture, the aspiring Chicana/o art students were drawn to their professors' status as professional artists. Montoya and Villa became mentors, often meeting with students after class and encouraging them to create art from their experiences and including their Mexican heritage as subject matter. This relationship provided a counterbalance to the Art Department's Western European focus as well as the students' exposure to graffiti, commercial billboards, psychedelic rock posters, and comic books. The students learned about Mexican art, including the murals of José Clemente Orozco, Diego Rivera, and David Alfaro Siqueiros, which

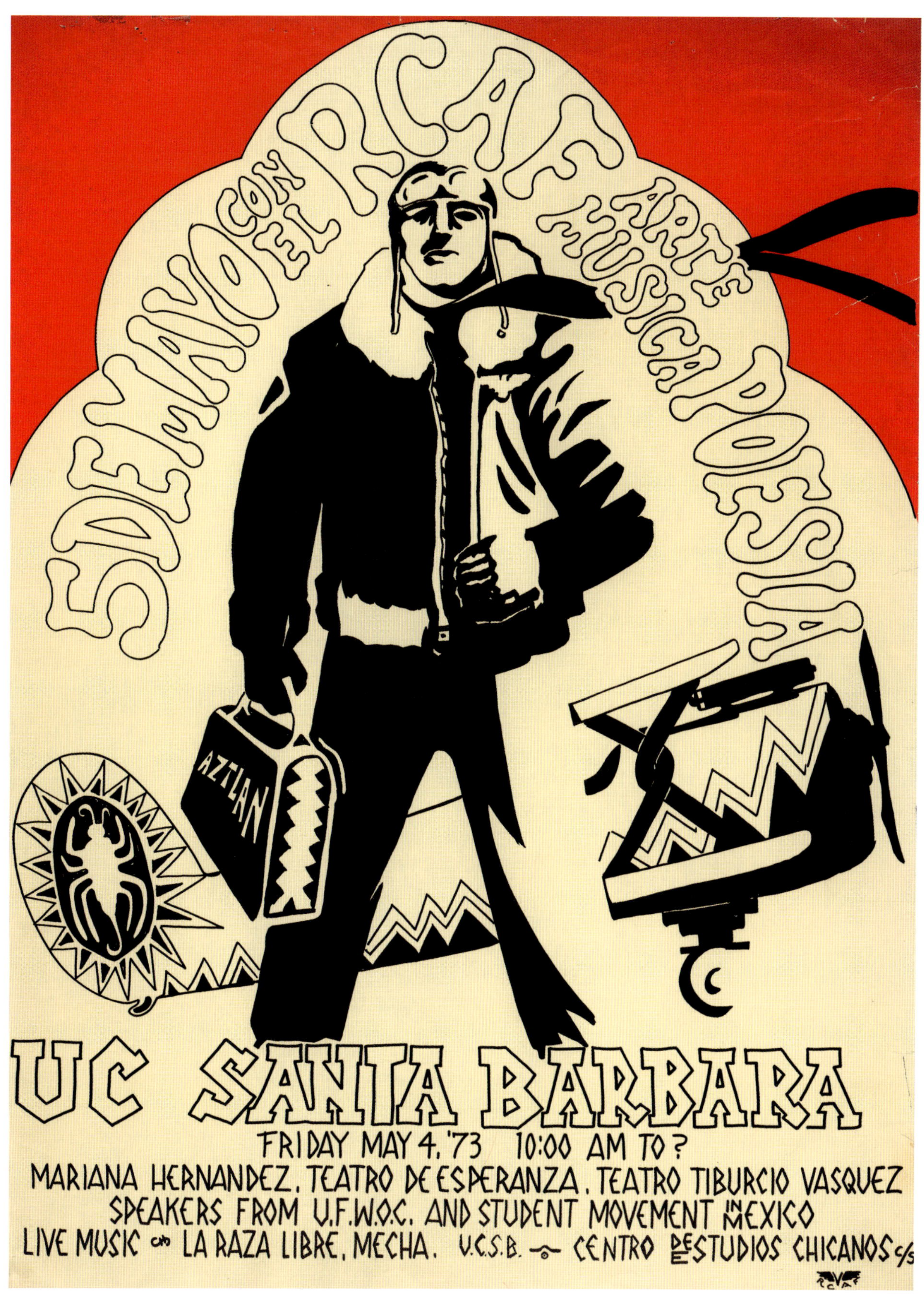

Fig. 3. Esteban Villa (1930–2022), *5 de Mayo con el RCAF*, 1973 [Plate 14].

Montoya and Villa had seen while traveling in Mexico. They were introduced to Posada's graphic work and Mexico City's Taller de Gráfica Popular, a print collective active since 1937.[18] In the spring of 1970, with the intent of exposing their art students to "the work of major Chicano artists, both professional and teachers from colleges and universities throughout the state," Villa organized an exhibition, *Arte de la Jente* [*sic*] (Art of the People; pl. 7), that was sponsored by MALAF.[19] It is not clear if there was an intent to revive Villa's former collective; however, by 1971, Montoya, Villa, and the students had formed their own group, which included Armando Cid, Juan Cervantes, Rodolfo "Rudy" Cuellar, Ricardo Favela, Kathryn Garcia, Luis "Louie the Foot" González, Héctor González, Irma Lerma (Barbosa), Juan "Juanishi" Orosco, Enrique Ortiz Villegas, and MAEP graduate fellow Juan Carrillo, along with artists Max Garcia and Stan Padilla.[20] They called themselves the Rebel Chicano Art Front in homage to MALAF and adopted their revolutionary nomenclature as a means "to establish a cultural front that was different from the mainstream art world."[21] Together, they were involved in campus activism, mainly through the Movimiento Estudiantil Chicano de Aztlán (MEChA; Chicano Student Movement of Aztlán) and community support for the burgeoning UFW's boycotts and picket lines.[22]

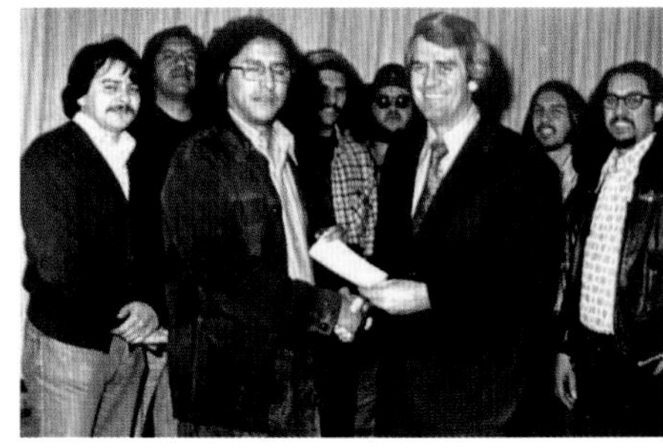

Fig. 4. Rodolfo Cuellar Sr. (1927–2008), *Sacramento County Supervisor Ted Sheedy handing a check to Centro de Artistas Chicanos founding director Max Garcia*, 1973. L-R (back row): Armando Cid, Esteban Villa, Juanishi Orosco, Ricardo Favela, Rudy Cuellar, and José Montoya. Collection of Rudy O. Cuellar.

Within a couple of years, the "Rebel Chicano Art Front" became the "Royal Chicano Air Force," after their initials were confused with the Royal Canadian Air Force.[23] "People would come up to us and ask, 'Do you guys have something to do with the Royal Canadian Air Force?' After a while, we started saying, 'No, we're the Royal Chicano Air Force.'"[24] According to Montoya, "The name went along with the whole notion and not only of an air force, but of an 'air farce,' with its ironic sense of making fun of ourselves."[25] This can be seen in Villa's announcement poster, *5 de Mayo con el RCAF* (1973; fig. 3), in which an aviator in full military garb, including leather jacket, flight cap, and goggles with an "AZTLAN" briefcase, faces the viewer. A World War II biplane with Indigenous symbols and an image of a scorpion, denoting Villa's family roots in the Mexican state of Sinaloa, fill the background. The discernable yet loosely defined figure and plane were created through the strategic placement of black ink on beige paper. The composition was augmented by a red sky in the top corners. As was true of most RCAF posters, the image dominates with the text rendered in thin letters condensed at the bottom.

The adoption of "Air Force" in their name, military clothing and regalia, and the integration of flight imagery in their murals and posters also allowed the RCAF to employ humor as a form of activism. Military phrases were also incorporated internally for group activities, with references to RCAF trips as "reconnaissance missions," "solo flights," and the occasional threat of a "court martial," which served as coded communication and playful bantering. It should be noted that Villa's poster's description of the RCAF's presentation of "arte, musica, poesia" also conveyed its multidisciplinary membership. This elastic membership and its move into the community would further expand the RCAF beyond its origins as an artist collective.

Centering the Community: The Centro de Artistas Chicanos

In January 1972, the collective moved off campus and formally incorporated the following year as the Centro de Artistas Chicanos (Centro), a nonprofit organization.[26] In early 1973, their first director, Max Garcia, secured city and county funding that allowed the group to rent a former furniture shop at 3210 Folsom Boulevard (fig. 4). According to Montoya, "There was a need for this [Chicana/o art center]. Chicano art wasn't being taught anywhere," and there was even a belief among art professors that 'there was no such thing as Chicano art.'"[27] The large space housed a small screenprint studio and also hosted exhibitions, screenprinting and mural classes for youth, and film showings.[28] Though located near Sacramento State, they collaborated with the BFN, La Raza Bookstore, Alkali PAC, Washington Community Council, WNC, and Sacramento Concilio, organizations in Mexican and Chicana/o–dominated neighborhoods near downtown Sacramento. At the same time, Montoya and Villa remained as art professors, and the artists continued to produce posters for Chicana/o events on campus and sponsor exhibitions that provided opportunities for RCAF as well as non-RCAF artists (fig. 5).[29] However, it was the physical space in the community that accelerated their transformation into a multidimensional, community-based collective.

Along with on-site programming, the Centro sponsored events at other community venues. Irma Lerma Barbosa, a painter and performer, organized the Primer Conferencia Femenil de Sacramento (First Women's Conference, 1973) at a local

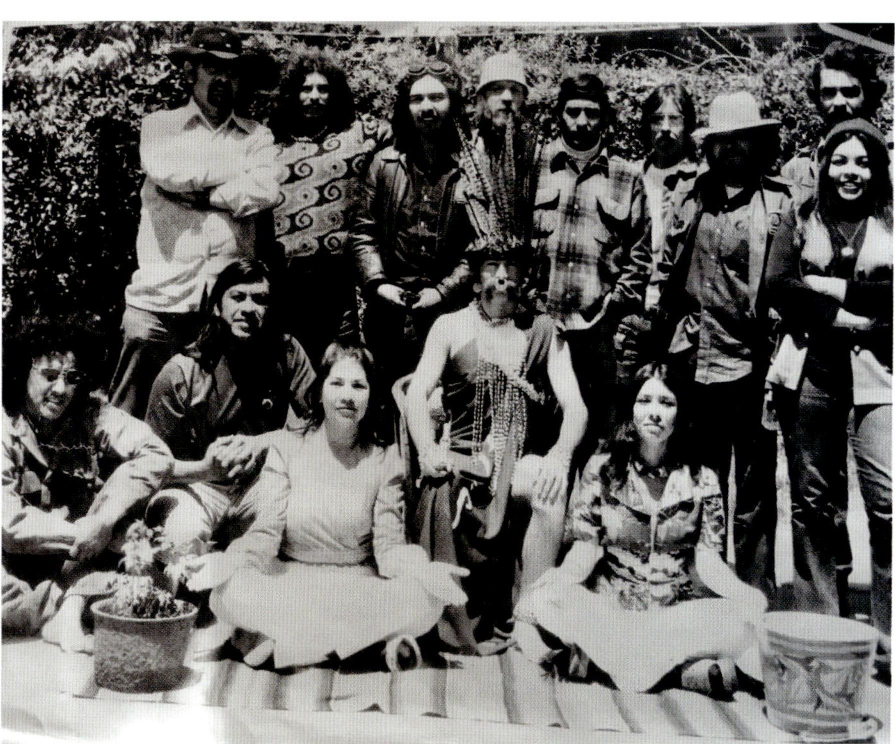

Fig. 5. Rodolfo Cuellar Sr. (1927–2008), *RCAF artists and supporters at Sacramento State during an exhibition reception*, 1972. Collection of Rudy O. Cuellar.

church. The conference focused on Chicana artists, who participated as speakers and exhibiting artists. According to Lerma Barbosa, "Local Chicana artists and artist wives of the RCAF were invited to attend. It was not easy for these women to participate because most of them were responsible homemakers who had sublimated their art to support their husbands and raise the kids and keep the family together."[30] Lerma Barbosa had traveled to Cuba as part of the Venceremos Brigade in 1972 to harvest sugarcane and was exposed to Cuban graphics, which can be seen in her poster promoting the conference (fig. 6).[31] The flat forms become a woman's face with long hair and arms holding up an oval sphere that contains the announcement text alongside a borderless map of North and South America. With her frontal gaze and powerful arms, the overall image is one of strength. Forming a frame, the broken chains signify Chicanas' power to break free of patriarchy and racial oppression. As noted by artist and curator Amalia Mesa-Bains, "The cultural production of the women artists of our community is embedded in the intracultural struggle for equality and respect. Artistic and cultural work defined under the early Movement emphasized an ethnic identity that superseded issues of gender."[32]

By also including an image of the entire Americas, Lerma Barbosa was "focusing on lifting up all Latino Americano, Spanish-speaking women who share cultural issues."[33] Her female figure dominates a composition in which the effective use of space and the intentional "off registration" appearance of the chain links soften the flatness of the central graphic elements. Her use of two colors (black and red) on bright yellow paper is also an example of how, even with minimal ink colors, RCAF artists were able to generate a strong visual impact.[34]

Unfortunately, unstable financial support forced the Centro to move out of the building on Folsom Boulevard after only two years. However, in 1975, the Centro and BFN were invited to move into classrooms at the former Holy Angels School building near Southside Park, another neighborhood with a large concentration of Mexican Americans. The Centro adapted one of their two rooms for screenprinting and the other became a dedicated space for poster design and layout, as well as for meetings and gatherings.[35] During their three years in the subsidized space, they increased their general operations budget with additional grants from the City and County of Sacramento, California Arts Council, and National Endowment for the Arts. Most significantly, they acquired funds from the Comprehensive Employment and Training Act (CETA) to hire five artists to teach classes on poster design, screenprinting, and sculpture, as well as produce posters for the community.[36] They were also able to purchase better quality screens, ink, paper, large drying racks, and additional equipment, including a light table, a copy camera for film positives and negatives, an exposing unit for burning photo stencils, and a four-color garment printer for T-shirts.

That same year, their director, Ricardo Favela, produced *El Centro de Artistas Chicanos* (1975), a visual play on the "business-card" format (fig. 7). In hand-drawn lettering, the Centro's name is clearly seen at the top, with the contact

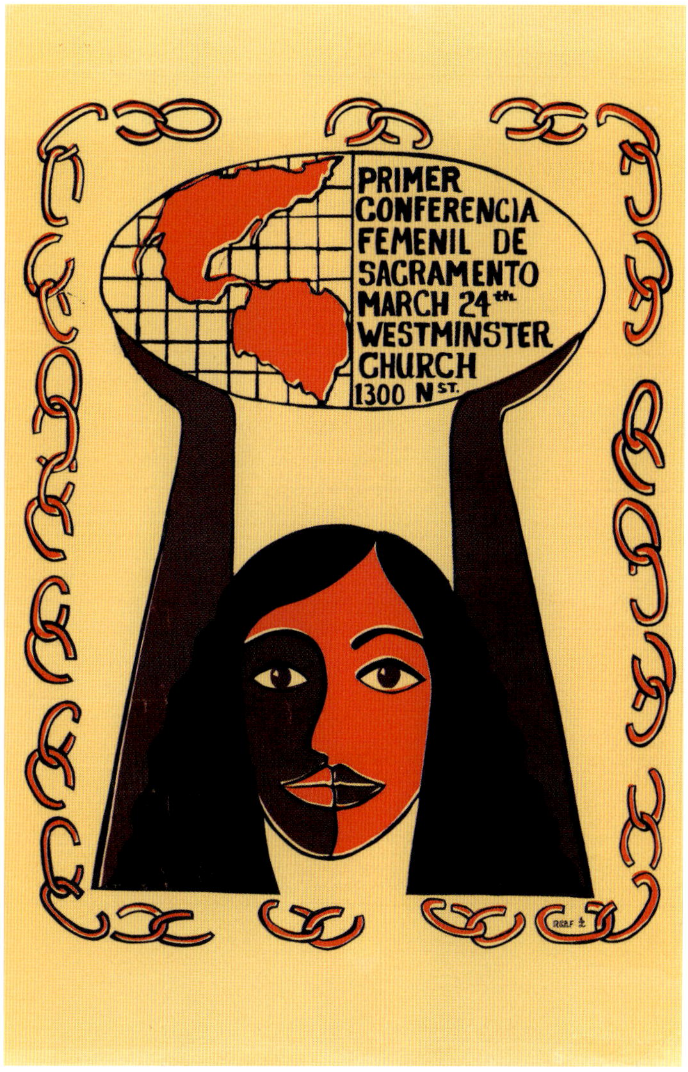

Fig. 6. Irma Lerma Barbosa (born 1949), *Primer Conferencia Femenil de Sacramento*, 1973 [Plate 12].

information wrapped around the edges, acting as a frame. In a nod to their Chicano Movement roots, their location is cited as "Sacra, Califas," instead of the city's official name. On both sides, Favela added the UFW logo. At the bottom their services were listed bilingually: "posters, *murales y clases de arte para la gente*" (art classes for the people). Favela embellished the RCAF logo at the bottom with extended, stylized wings on each side, which became another design element that artists would emulate to varying degrees.

Like other RCAF artists, Favela favored a composition in which the image—predominantly, figures—dominated and included readable but not sizable text. In this poster, the central image serves as a humorous portrayal of two of the Centro's staff artists, Rudy Cuellar (left) and Luis González (right), wearing his signature wool cap. They are depicted as whimsical *calaveras* engaged in a heated

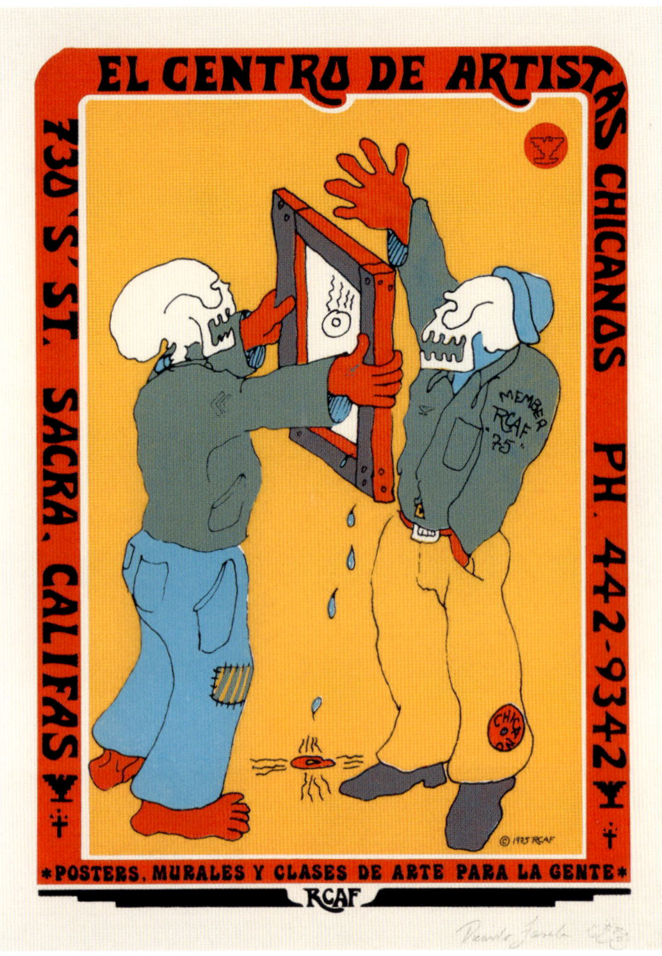

Fig. 7. Ricardo Favela (1944–2007), *El Centro de Artistas Chicanos*, 1975 [Plate 8].

conversation as Cuellar holds a screen up to the sun, revealing a tear that renders it unusable. A favored image, skeletons filled Favela's sketchbooks, doodles, and posters, many times in scenes reminiscent of Posada, a major influence on him and other Chicana/o artists.[37] In their joint master's thesis, "Posada: The Man and His Art," which included examples of Favela's work, Juan Carrillo and José Montoya declared, "Posada reflected the times and the society in which he lived. Chicano artists are doing the same."[38] Produced as penny broadsides (low-cost, tabloid-style newspapers), Posada depicted the daily life of Mexico's rural and urban residents, many times as a theater of the absurd. He also rendered the elite class and political figures as skeletons, exposing their corruption as well as ridiculing their inability to escape death, the same fate that befell poor and powerless Mexicans. Favela admired Posada's use of *calaveras* to reflect human nature, but especially his incorporation of humor as a powerful tool for communication. Not surprisingly, Favela's *calaveras* also appeared frequently on his ceramic pieces and collaborative murals.

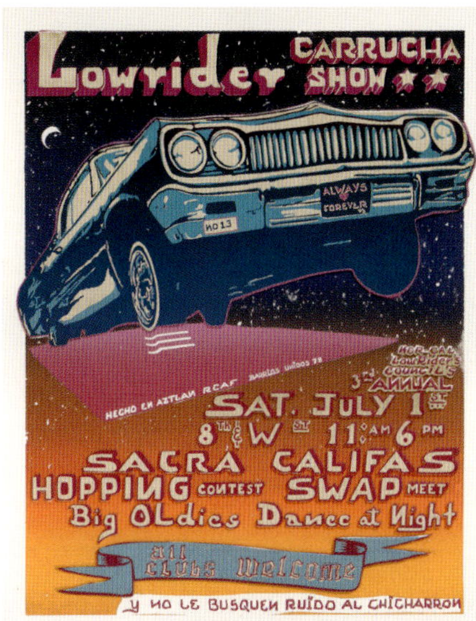

Fig. 8. Rudy O. Cuellar (born 1950), *Lowrider Carrucha Show*, 1978 [Plate 29].

The Centro's additional equipment, operational funding, and CETA-funded positions allowed the artists to produce greater quantities of posters for the community. More important, it afforded them financial stability and dedicated time to experiment with iconography, composition, and more complex printing techniques, such as photo-based screenprinting. While some of the staff artists taught classes, most spent their time producing posters or painting murals. Cuellar and González became the Centro's most prolific printers of announcement posters, while also assisting other artists, many times as named collaborators.

Though not intentionally, Cuellar became the de facto poster artist for the Sacramento region's active lowrider scene through his relationship with members of the lowrider club based at the WNC who had provided security for several RCAF events. In 1978, Cuellar received a request from the Nor Cal Lowriders Council for a poster to promote their third annual car show and dance. The surrealistic composition of *Lowrider Carrucha Show* is dominated by an image of a 1964 Chevy Impala against a dark night sky filled with stars and a crescent moon (fig. 8). Viewed from the front, the car is depicted in a "hopping" elevated motion that seems to propel it out of the picture plane. Though drawn from a photograph, Cuellar's reinterpretation features the soft shading of monochromatic colors and an accentuated front grille. A pink protruding shape that resembles a floating platform provides the car—and the viewer—with a visual grounding. It also functions as a graphic division from the lower half containing the event details, which are set against a gold background with further allusions to its cosmic setting. "I've always been a space head," recalled Cuellar. "My dad used to take us out at night to the outer side of Roseville when it was still country and wait for the meteor showers."[39] Night skies filled with stars would form an important element in many of his signature posters.

Evident in the seamless transition between various colors in *Lowrider Carrucha Show* is the RCAF print artists' mastery of the "split-fountain" screenprinting technique. Cuellar also incorporated aspects of political activism and humor into his design. This can be seen in the inclusion of a "no on [Proposition] 13" bumper sticker below the grille along with *Hecho en Aztlan*, a Chicana/o variation on the "Made in Mexico" label on the platform. A popular Mexican saying referencing pork rinds at the bottom loosely translates as "Don't cause any trouble."[40] With its integration of an artistically complex composition, personal references, and playful text, Cuellar's event announcement is elevated into a visually compelling and futuristic-tinged print.

Though initially a poet, González, through observation and experimentation, became a skillful screenprint artist with an ingenious visual vocabulary, using photography, flat graphic images, and cultural symbols as well as painterly backgrounds that mimicked abstract painting. His bold color palette and combinations were informed by bicultural sources, including American candy wrappers and Mexican blankets.[41] In 1976, he created multiple posters in support of the UFW's efforts to pass California's Proposition 14.[42] *Viva la Huelga* features an abstract background of expansive green in the lower portion with handwritten letters that spell out the phrase (fig. 9). At the top are two quadrants; one is sky blue and the other is orange-red with black foliage-like forms containing a barely discernable sign stating "Boycott Gallo," referencing the wine producer. In the center is a black and light blue figure of Montoya on a picket line with a UFW flag. The photograph was taken by his brother, Héctor, who also attended Sacramento State from 1970 to 1973 and took a class with Montoya (fig. 10).[43] At the bottom, white block letters on black entreat the viewer to vote "Yes on 14" and "Help the Farmworkers." Its bright colors and photo-derived composition are reminiscent of Pop Art, yet it also incorporates a painterly background consisting of abstract elements. With González's inclusion of a direct appeal to the viewer, the image is an example of the way RCAF posters blurred art and politics, existing "somewhere between the unique art object and the mass media."[44]

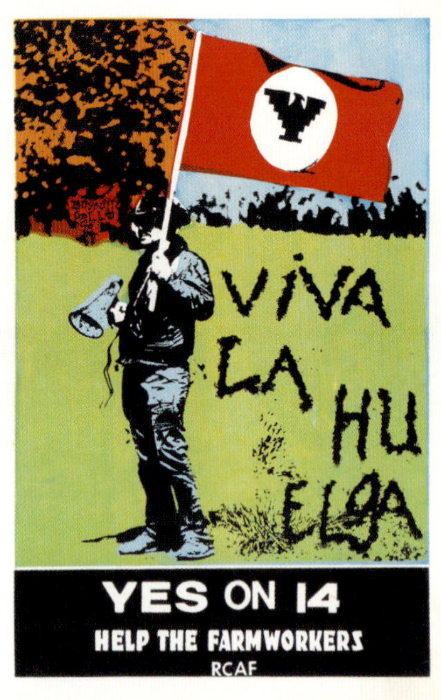

Fig. 9. Luis C. González (born 1953), photograph by Héctor González, *Viva la Huelga*, 1976 [Plate 72].

La Cultura Cura: The Cultural Affairs Committee

The Chicanos are like the corn and our roots are deep in this land. The water that feeds us is our culture, our fruit is the reawakening generation of the future. . . . Beginning as a group of concerned artists and community individuals, we have now developed into a vital component known as the Cultural Affairs Committee.

CULTURAL AFFAIRS PROJECT, CALIFORNIA ARTS COUNCIL, OCTOBER 15, 1976

The physical proximity to the BFN provided the Centro with administrative support and the grant-writing skills of its director, Rosemary Rasul. It also became a meeting place for the RCAF's organizations and groups, along with interested community activists. Weekly meetings were held to share information and discuss joint projects, including those with other neighborhood organizations. These included the joint sponsorship of the annual Mexican civic celebrations at Southside Park that attracted thousands of attendees. These events provided the RCAF with the opportunity to integrate the Mexican *fiestas patrias* with Chicana/o speakers and performers, bringing different segments of Sacramento's community together. As event co-sponsors, the RCAF's artists were free to incorporate a Chicana/o perspective in their announcement posters. Armando Cid's exuberant composition for *Cinco de Mayo* (1976; pl. 43) is replete with recognizable cultural and political imagery spanning centuries. It includes Mesoamerican figures and glyphs, a portrait of Mexican Revolutionary icon Emiliano Zapata, and the UFW's logo, along with calls for the boycott of Gallo wine and Coors beer. Prominently located in the center, an eagle devours a snake atop a cactus, the potent national symbol on Mexico's flag. Visually, the stark change from bright yellow to dark blue and the jagged border between them provides a dramatic pictorial contrast. At the bottom, Cid's text with its seemingly random placement and font sizes creates an arresting visual effect, drawing the viewer's attention equally to the images and event information. Ostensibly created for an event celebrating the Mexican army's defeat of Napoleon's much larger forces at Puebla

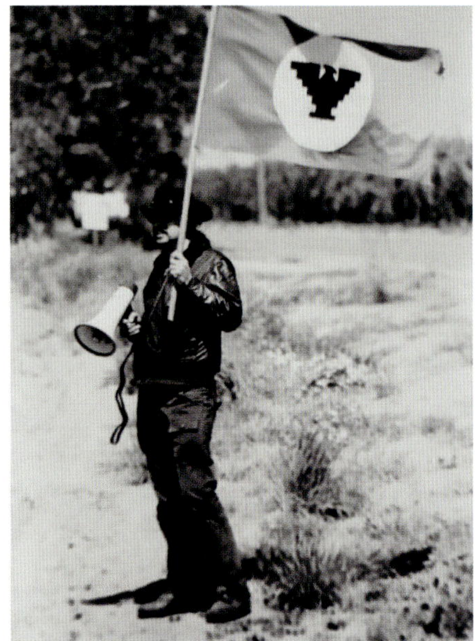

Fig. 10. Héctor D. González (born 1945), *José Montoya at a United Farm Workers strike in Yuba City*, 1973. Collection of Héctor D. González.

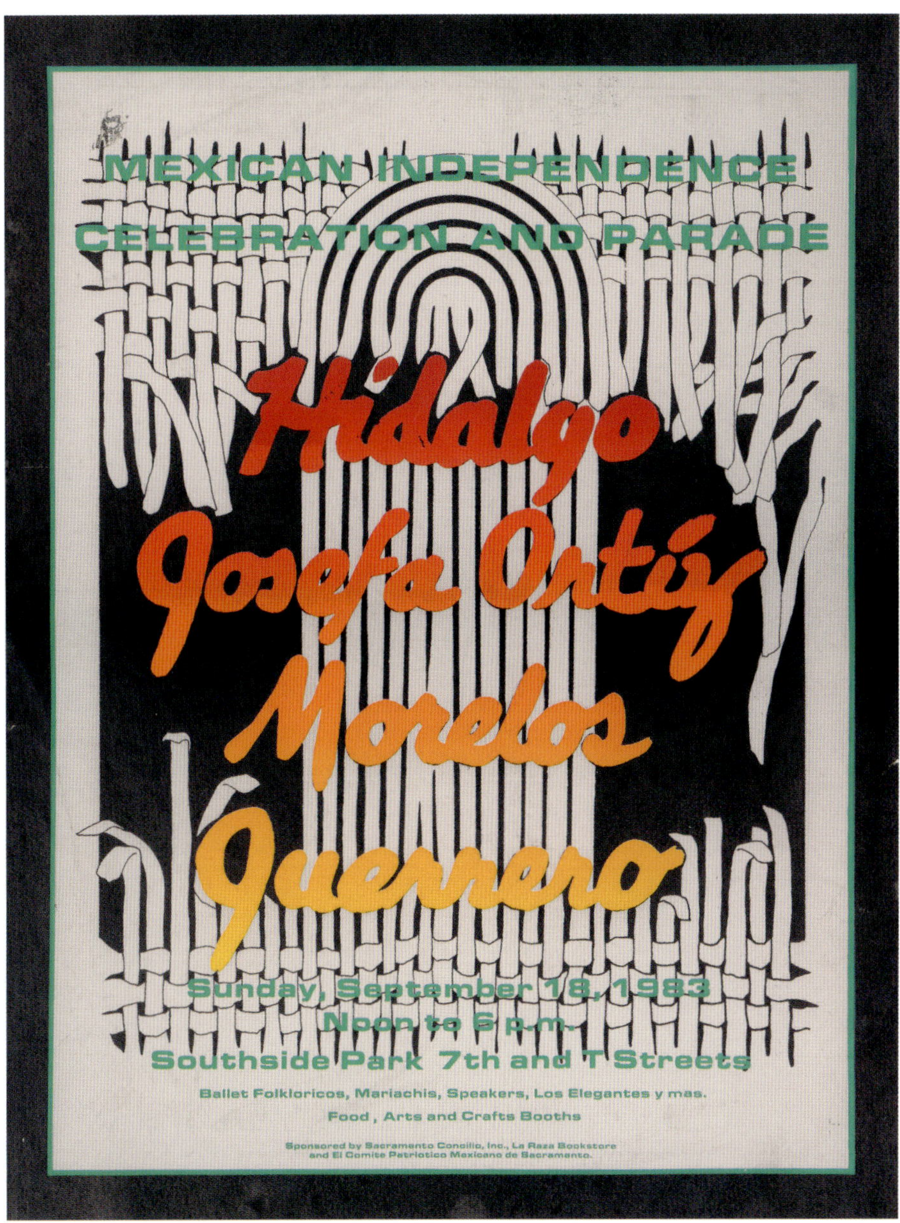

Fig. 11. Lorraine García-Nakata (born 1950), *Mexican Independence Celebration and Parade*, 1983 [Plate 47].

in 1862, Cid's print visually connected the Chicana/o resistance in the US to its Indigenous roots and through Mexico's history of wars against their internal and external tyrants.

Lorraine García-Nakata's *Mexican Independence Celebration and Parade* (1983; fig. 11) offers a Chicana-centered viewpoint on Mexico's independence movement, focusing on its multiracial and female leaders. The composition is dominated by a weaving design in which the names Hidalgo, Josefa Ortiz de Domínguez, Morelos, and Guerrero are written across the center threads.[45] Father Miguel Hidalgo y Costilla, José María Morelos, and Vicente Guerrero are well known in Mexico and to many Mexicans in the US. However, few are aware of Guerrero's African and Indigenous heritage. Ortiz de Dominguez, another key protagonist in

Mexico's fight for independence, is not widely recognized in the US. With her depiction of the weaving's broken strands, García-Nakata sought to graphically communicate the "complex history and cultures comprised in our Indigenous, colonial Spanish, African [lineages and] acknowledge the strength of their contributions to the historical trajectory [embodied by the] September 16th moment in time."[46] García-Nakata studied ceramics at Sacramento State, and she later mastered drawing and painting. Her skill in various mediums is apparent in the poster's replication of a three-dimensional weaving pattern and clean lines of the typeface. With the painterly strokes of the brightly colored, handwritten names in the center, she not only added a visual counterpoint to the gray and black background but also enhanced its aesthetic appeal with the neon-like lettering.

In 1975, several RCAF artists, culture bearers, and staff members of the Sacramento Concilio's community mental health program came together, motivated by a shared conviction that "in addition to the understanding of Chicano psychology and the experience of Chicanos with oppressive behavior, there needs to be an understanding of our spiritual aspect."[47] They believed that connecting to Mexico's and Chicanas/os' Indigenous heritage and spiritual values would counteract the negative effects of colonization and racial discrimination. The RCAF members were also enacting the Chicano Movement's call for reclamation of cultural and spiritual traditions. Their goal was to recover Chicanas/os' pride in an Indigenous heritage through community *ceremonias* (spiritual ceremonies), which would not only support individual mental health by fostering a sense of belonging but also engender community cohesion through participation within a communal setting.

The first of these *ceremonias* was the Día de los Muertos (DDLM) observance held that year. Some RCAF members had experienced the Mexican traditions of home altars and family visits to the cemetery. Others had attended San Francisco's Galería de la Raza's observance, which along with Self Help Graphics & Art in Los Angeles had transformed the personal rituals into a public observance in 1972.[48] There was also an acknowledgment by RCAF members that the Mexican DDLM, with its Indigenous roots and adoption by the Catholic Church, was a potent *ceremonia* that could appeal to various segments of the community. Held at a cemetery, their commemoration emphasized personal and familial remembrances of recently deceased loved ones and the honoring of ancient ancestors.

Sacramento's DDLM observance on November 1st began with a procession spanning seven blocks from Hiram W. Johnson High School to St. Mary's Cemetery (fig. 12). The procession continued inside and ended at the site of a permanent altar that over the years became a community *ofrenda* (altar).[49] There, a Catholic Mass was held in recognition of All Saints Day and as a "holy day of obligation." The observance ended with an Indigenous ceremony honoring the ancestors and dance offerings by Capitana Generala Angelbertha Cobb's Aztec dance group, Danza Quetzalcoatl, which was later led by RCAF member Jesse "Chuy" Ortiz as Danza Quetzalcoatl-Citlalli.[50] Not surprisingly, Favela created the poster, which

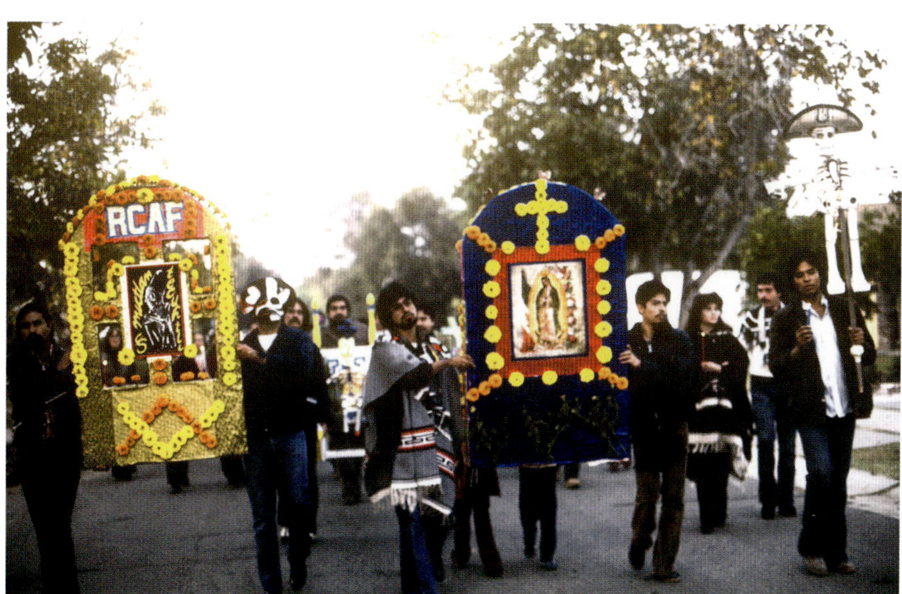

Fig. 12. Alfred "Freddy" González (born 1955), *Día de los Muertos Procession*, 1979. Collection of Alfred "Freddy" González.

featured a skeleton with a hat and a border of bones (pl. 54). However, with its depiction of the figure with a bull's-eye on its back posting the announcement on a wall, he crafted a humorous and clever "poster within a poster" composition. His posters for subsequent years depicted skeletons happily skipping in the cosmos gathering floating skulls (1976) and a skull posing with a gold tooth for the viewer (1977). Over the fifty years of the annual observance, multiple artists have continued to create DDLM posters incorporating a wide range of iconography, from depictions of Mictlantecuhtli (Aztec god of death) and military skeletons to contemporary *ofrendas.*

In 1976, the second *ceremonia*, Fiesta de Maíz, was held at Zapata Park, a small, newly created outdoor space adjacent to public housing in the Alkali Flat neighborhood (fig. 13).[51] Subsequent celebrations were moved to Southside Park to accommodate the strong community interest. Juan "Juanishi" Orosco, a co-founder of the *ceremonias*, created the poster for the 1979 Fiesta de Maíz, which continued his personal exploration of imagery derived from a long-standing interest in Indigenous spirituality (pl. 61). It had even earned him the nickname of "Ishi," which was later combined with his first name to become Juanishi.[52] The ornate composition mimics a *nicho*, an enclosed space for a statue within a church. It is both notable in its imagery as well as in Orosco's technical proficiency, with multiple colors that required precise color registration, accurate hand lettering, and a seamless transition of the background from light to dark blue that extended into the outer band to form a frame. In the center, a young woman walks toward the viewer, holding a platter with green corn. She represents the Aztec goddess of corn, Xilonen, and the young girl that personifies her within the *ceremonia*.[53] She is wearing a traditional *quechquemitl* (blouse) and a *falda* (skirt) with a stylized Mesoamerican corn glyph in blue at the bottom. Above and around her head are images of doves and moons eclipsing the sun, forming a halo. A faint pyramid can be seen behind her. The poster brings

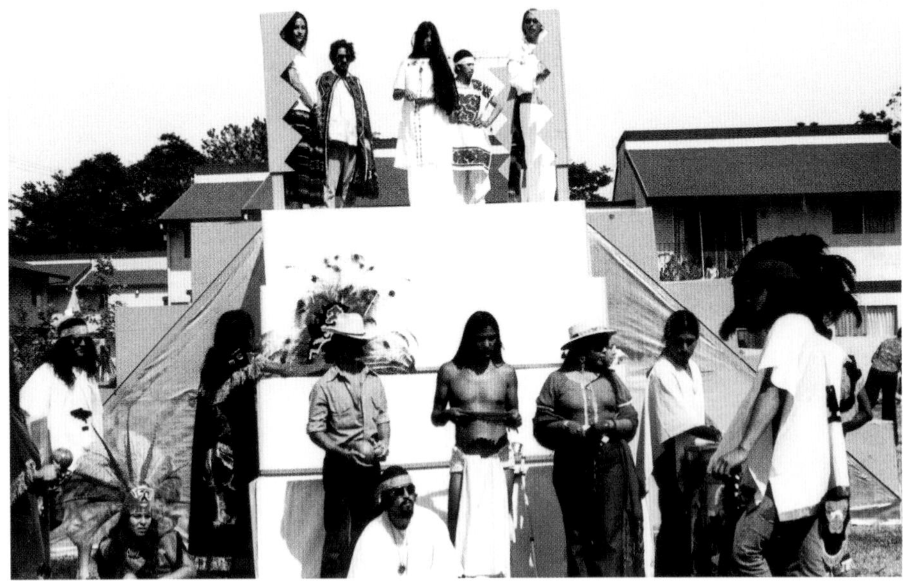

Fig. 13. Rodolfo Cuellar Sr. (1927–2008), *First Fiesta de Maíz ceremony, Zapata Park*, 1976. Collection of Terezita Romo.

together the colors of the sky, sun, and corn with Indigenous symbols, effectively capturing the basic elements of the celebration of a young woman coming of age. Orosco's imagery derives from his interpretation of an ancient goddess personifying corn and its enduring role as physical sustenance and symbol of spiritual resilience for Mexicans and Chicanas/os.

The need for a formal administrative and programmatic infrastructure to support the burgeoning community activities as well as sustain the RCAF's "growing awareness of the necessity to preserve, maintain, and revitalize our important cultural traditions" led to the formation of the Cultural Affairs Committee (CAC).[54] In 1977, Centro director Favela and BFN director Rasul submitted a joint application to the County of Sacramento for ten additional CETA positions and funds to launch the CAC as an ambitious multiyear project. With the supplemental positions and funding, they not only continued the annual civic events and *ceremonias* but also dedicated a staff position to research and document its activities. Importantly, the CAC served to formalize the RCAF as an intergenerational collective of multidisciplinary artists and community activists and strengthen the bond among its organizations.

A key component of the CAC proposal was the continuation of the two existing *ceremonias* and the addition of a third. In Stan Padilla's announcement poster for the inaugural *Fiesta de los Colores* in 1978 (pl. 63), he adapted a figure found in several murals at the ancient site of Teotihuacán in central Mexico.[55] Known as the "Great Goddess of Teotihuacán," she is depicted in the original mural mainly in red and some yellow with a bird-like face surrounded by elaborate plumage and jewelry. In Padilla's composition, the goddess wears the mask of the rain god, Tlaloc, on her face and in the center of an ornate plumed headdress. Water also flows from her outstretched hands, becoming steady streams that form a stepped

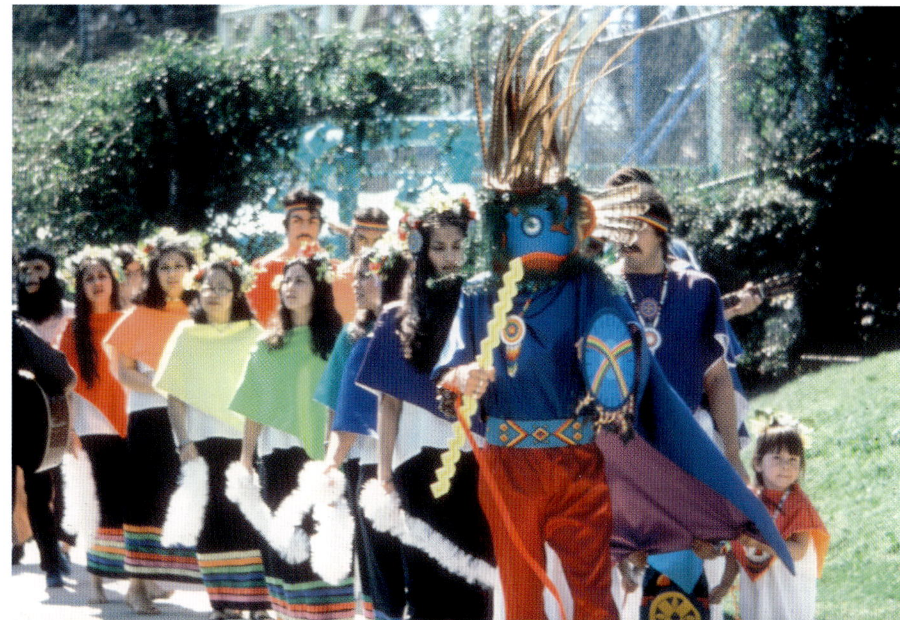

Fig. 14. Alfred "Freddy" González (born 1955), *Fiesta de Colores*, 1979. Stan Padilla leading procession at Southside Park Royal Chicano Air Force Archives, CEMA 8. University of California, Santa Barbara Library.

vessel at the bottom of the picture frame. Enveloped in this enclosed space is a circular form created by several additional circles with a frog in the center, a symbol of spring and its reliance on water. Padilla used mainly yellow and green with red accents to transmit a feeling of spring. "I chose lime green to represent new growth, and the yellow is the sun, sunlight, both which contribute to the renewal of nature. In our Fiesta, [it is] the renewal of our culture."[56] The rich yellow background is rendered with visual undulations at the edges, creating a sense of movement like water spilling out toward the sides.

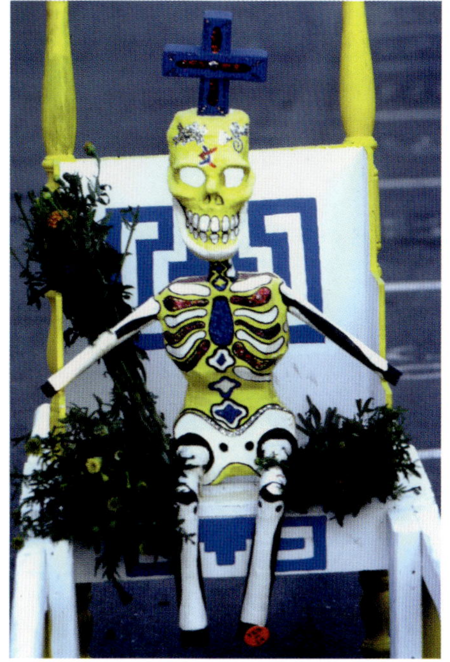

Fig. 15. Alfred "Freddy" González (born 1955), *Armando Cid's God of Death on his throne*, late 1970s. Collection of Alfred "Freddy" González.

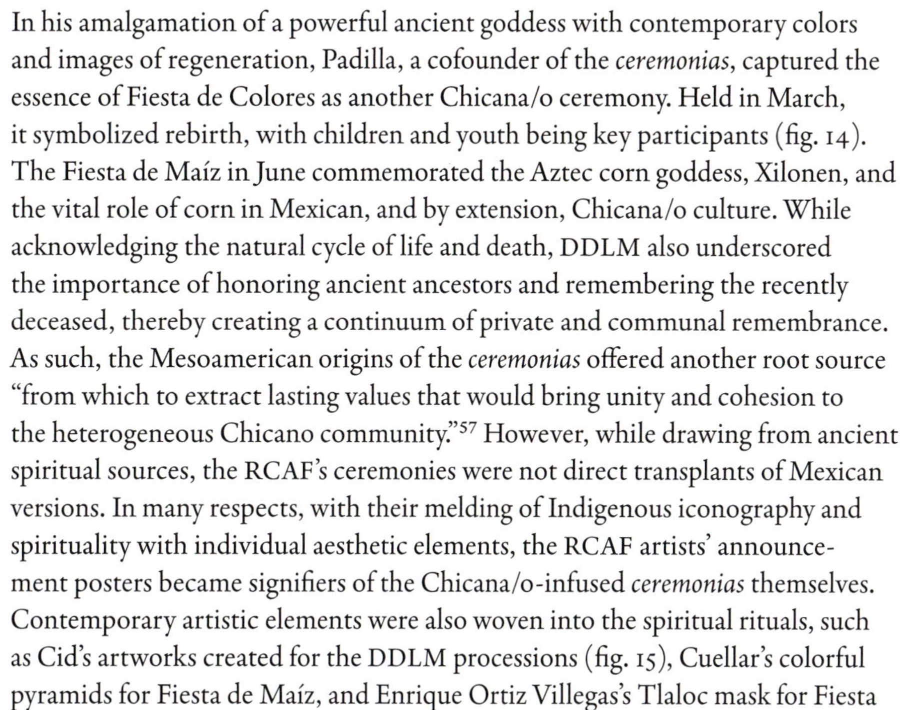

In his amalgamation of a powerful ancient goddess with contemporary colors and images of regeneration, Padilla, a cofounder of the *ceremonias*, captured the essence of Fiesta de Colores as another Chicana/o ceremony. Held in March, it symbolized rebirth, with children and youth being key participants (fig. 14). The Fiesta de Maíz in June commemorated the Aztec corn goddess, Xilonen, and the vital role of corn in Mexican, and by extension, Chicana/o culture. While acknowledging the natural cycle of life and death, DDLM also underscored the importance of honoring ancient ancestors and remembering the recently deceased, thereby creating a continuum of private and communal remembrance. As such, the Mesoamerican origins of the *ceremonias* offered another root source "from which to extract lasting values that would bring unity and cohesion to the heterogeneous Chicano community."[57] However, while drawing from ancient spiritual sources, the RCAF's ceremonies were not direct transplants of Mexican versions. In many respects, with their melding of Indigenous iconography and spirituality with individual aesthetic elements, the RCAF artists' announcement posters became signifiers of the Chicana/o-infused *ceremonias* themselves. Contemporary artistic elements were also woven into the spiritual rituals, such as Cid's artworks created for the DDLM processions (fig. 15), Cuellar's colorful pyramids for Fiesta de Maíz, and Enrique Ortiz Villegas's Tlaloc mask for Fiesta

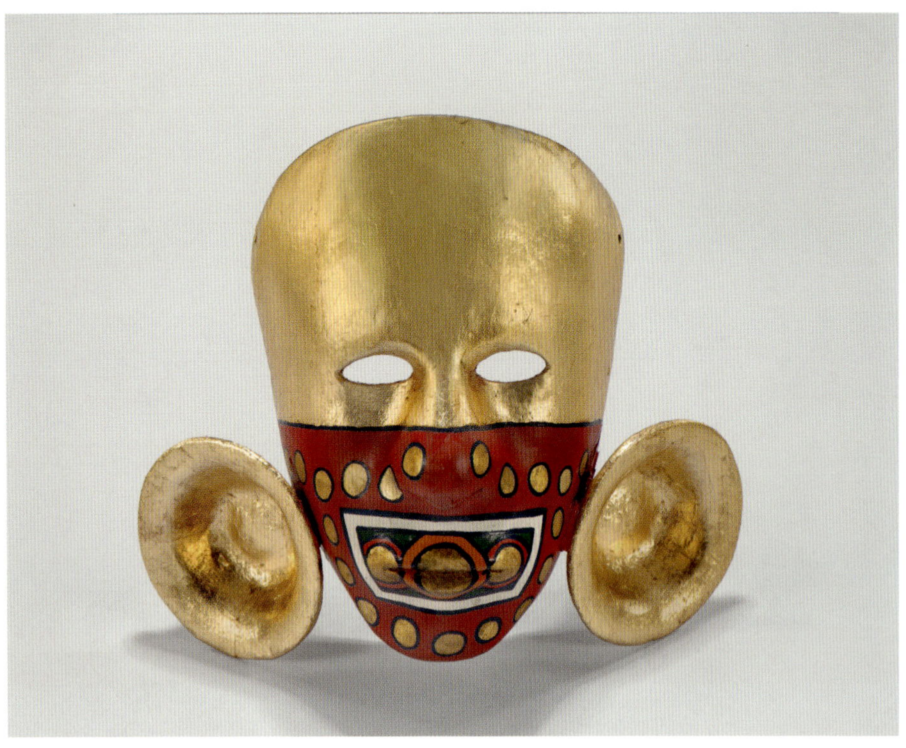

Fig. 16. Enrique Ortiz Villegas (born 1944), *Tlaloc Mask from Fiesta de Colores*, 1979; restored 2024. [Plate 65].

de Colores (fig. 16). As descendants of ancient cultures, the RCAF's CAC artists and community members respectfully reinterpreted spiritual practices and imagery associated with Mexican Indigenous rituals and offered them to the community as Chicana/o *ceremonias*. Decades later, these ceremonies not only continue in Sacramento but have also been adopted by other communities in California.

Exhibiting La Raza

The RCAF's La Raza Bookstore (LRB) was founded in 1972 by Sacramento State students Philip "Pike" Santos, Juan Gutierrez, Luis González, and Pedro "Pete" Hernandez, with the support of MEChA. It was initially located at 1228 F Street in the Alkali Flat neighborhood (fig. 17). As noted by Santos and González, "We could have called it the Chicano Bookstore. But we didn't. We called it La Raza Bookstore so as not to leave anybody out. 'La Raza' is all-inclusive of peoples from this continent."[58] During its first decade, the volunteer-run LRB expanded its Chicana/o offerings to include Spanish language and Native American books and records, along with posters and merchandise from El Taller Grafico, the UFW's merchandising arm. In 1975, it was incorporated as a nonprofit organization and in 1979 expanded into an adjacent building.

With a grant from the California Arts Council, the original LRB space became a gallery, opening with a traveling exhibition of Posada's broadsides from the Centro Cultural de la Raza in San Diego. The exhibition was fortuitous, not only in its timing but also because of Posada's impact on several RCAF artists. For the announcement poster, Cuellar and González incorporated a drawing

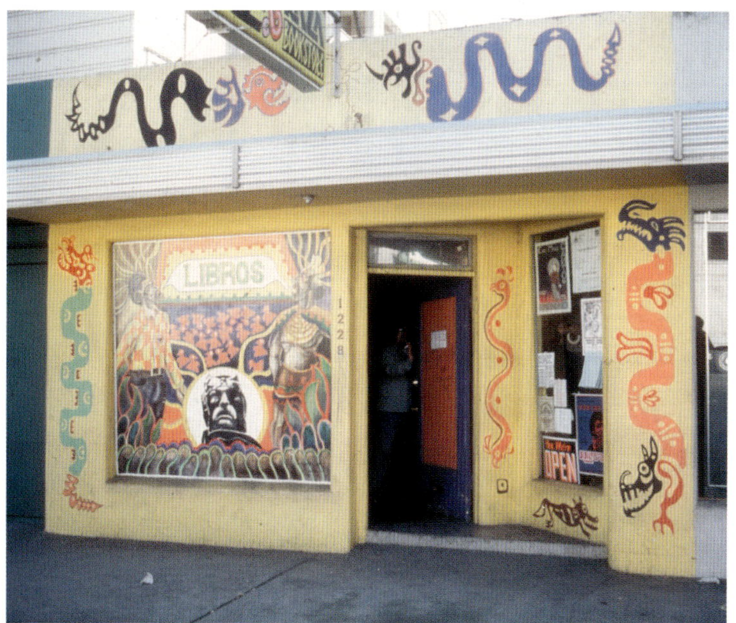

Fig. 17. *La Raza Bookstore*, 1973. Royal Chicano Air Force Archives, CEMA 8, Department of Special Collections, University Libraries, University of California, Santa Barbara.

based on a photograph of Posada and his son along with the figure of his iconic fashionably dressed female skeleton, La Catrina (fig. 18). At the bottom, hand-drawn, gold lettering adds to the vibrancy of the black and white figures on a dark red background. Two years later, the organization became La Raza Galeria Posada, keeping "La Raza" in its name to honor Chicanas/os' Indigenous roots as a mixed-race people and adding "Galeria Posada" in honor of the influential Mexican printmaker.[59]

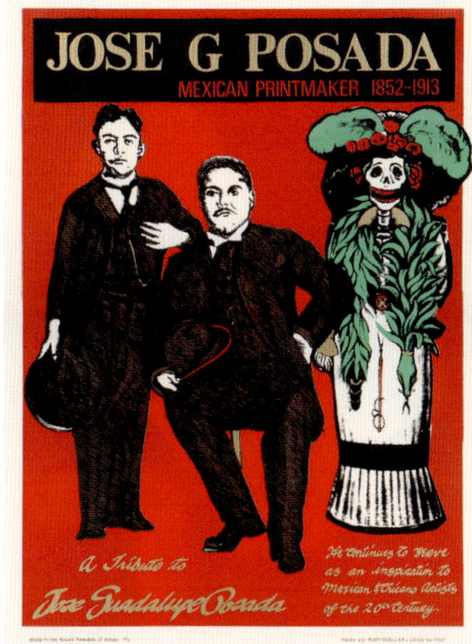

Fig. 18. Rudy O. Cuellar (born 1950) and Luis C. González (born 1953), *José G. Posada*, 1980 [Plate 93].

The lack of interest in the work of RCAF artists and Chicana/o art in general by commercial art galleries in Sacramento and museums more broadly demonstrated the need for a community exhibition space with a mission to exhibit Chicana/o, Latina/o, and Native American artists. LRGP provided opportunities for local and national artists and writers to share their work with the community and with each other. During the 1980s, it also hosted the first major exhibitions of several RCAF artists: González (1980), Villa (1981), Cid (1983; fig. 19), Padilla (1986), and Orosco (1987). RCAF artists were featured in the group exhibitions *What We Are Now* (1980) and *Winging It: In Flight Retrospective of RCAF Posters* (1984; fig. 20).[60] Cid, Eva Garcia, García-Nakata, and Celia Herrera Rodriguez were included in *Personal Reflections: Masks by Chicano and Native American Artists in California* (1983), and Cid participated in *Ofrendas* (1984).[61] In 1987, Santos and Cid curated *La Raza's Quinceañero*, an exhibition of screenprints commissioned to celebrate LRGP's fifteenth anniversary.[62] In addition to providing exhibition opportunities and catalogues, LRGP's programming integrated RCAF members within its Chicana/o, Latina/o, and Native American poetry readings, writers' workshops, music and theater performances, and scholarly symposiums. LRGP also participated in the CAC's ongoing programs, events, and *ceremonias*. In fact, it assumed the sponsorship of the DDLM observance after the Centro and BFN closed, augmenting it with an annual exhibition and related workshops at its facility.[63]

Imprint of a Legacy

People say the Movement is in pieces, but the way we look at it, the pieces have movement. And that's who we are.

LUIS "LOUIE THE FOOT" GONZÁLEZ

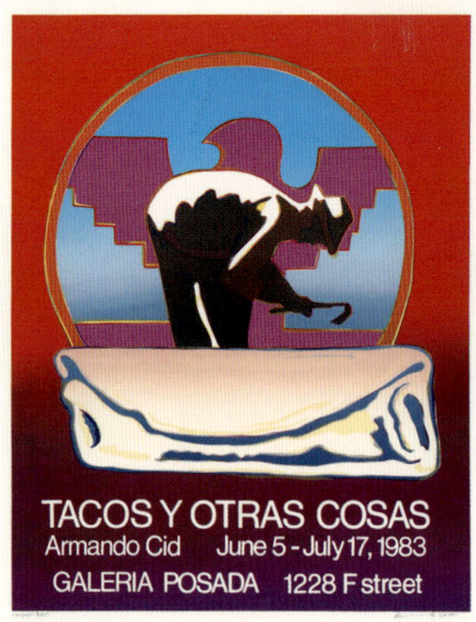

Fig. 19. Armando Cid (1943–2009), *Tacos y Otras Cosas*, 1983 [Plate 98].

Citing the need to upgrade the building, the Centro and BFN were evicted from the former Holy Angels School in 1978 and received temporary administrative space at the Alkali PAC offices. The Centro artists took refuge at a woodshop owned by fellow artist Sal Yniguez. "Those were tough days," noted González, "half of our shop didn't have a roof, so wintertime was very hard. It's difficult [to screenprint] when your paper expands on you."[64] However, it was the elimination of the Centro's, BFN's, and CAC's CETA positions the following year that forced major changes. In 1981, Cuellar and González established a small business, Centro Screen Print, near downtown Sacramento, where they designed and produced posters and prints for individuals, organizations, and commercial clients and offered framing services. There, they revitalized their solo and collaborative exploration of screenprint techniques and experimentation. González's brother, Alfred "Freddy" González, opened Crystal Clear Printers next door and provided printing services to the artists and LRGP. Favela, Orosco, Villa, Montoya, and Garcia established the RCAF Graphics and Design Center on Franklin Boulevard in south Sacramento. Along with providing graphic services, they offered mural, theater, and Danza Azteca classes to the community. In 1981, the Design Center was awarded a grant from the California State Department of Mental Health to design and produce graphics that promoted mental wellness in the community. Their project, "La Cultura, Cura: Respeto, Familia, Hermandad, Salud," included individually named posters by Favela, Montoya, Orosco, and Villa that targeted veterans, youth, and intergenerational families.[65] Villa, Orosco, and Padilla were also able to collaborate on major mural projects throughout Sacramento. As Favela, the director, noted in a multipage article in the *Sacramento Union*, "We're very much like a spider plant. We send out shoots; they grow and become independent."[66] However, by 1992 the Graphics Center and Centro Screen Print had closed. As RCAF artists embarked on individual careers, several secured teaching positions at area educational and correctional institutions.

One of their major achievements, the RCAF's graphics earned them a place in Chicana/o art history. As event announcements or political statements, each poster manifested bicultural aesthetic choices and multivalent influences in the artist's compositions, iconography, and screenprinting techniques. Their merging of context along with composition and form reflected an "aesthetic of the message," in which the seamless integration of multiple dichotomies—artistic and political, artist and activist, personal and universal—was achieved. While operating in the public sphere, RCAF posters communicated with specific Mexican and Chicana/o audiences and educated others about Chicana/o artistic expression. As noted previously, imagery dominated the composition with the text often relegated to a small area of the poster. Thus, the image was not only a

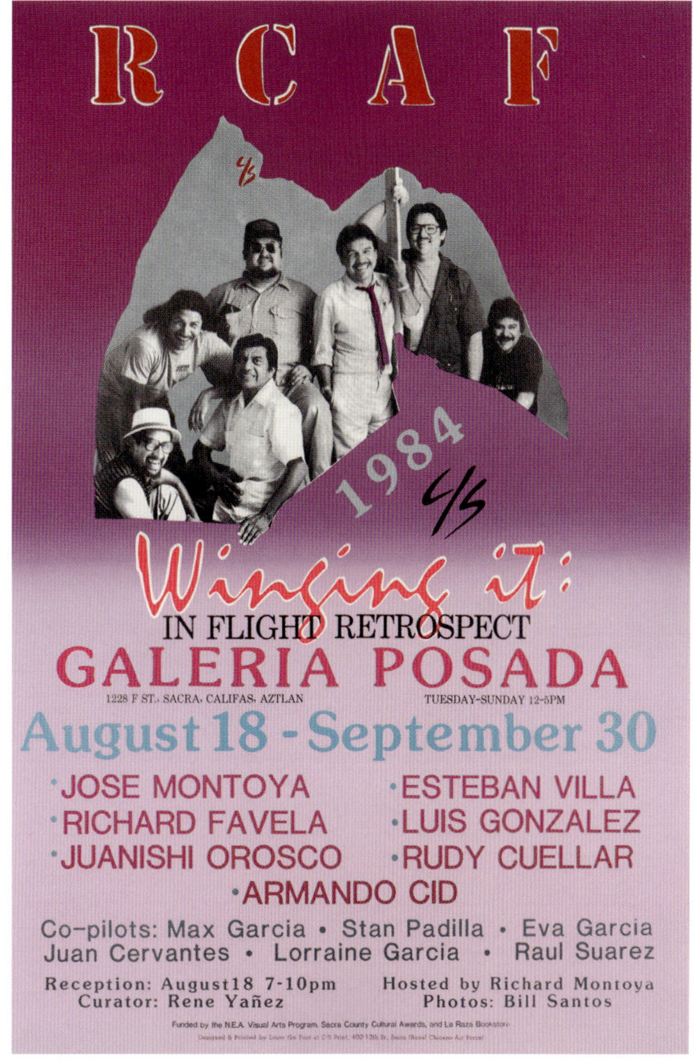

Fig. 20. Luis C. González (born 1953), photograph by Bill Santos, *Winging It*, 1984 [Plate 96].

visual component but also a key aspect of the poster's message, to the point that many were framed and displayed in homes.

The RCAF artists also appreciated the value of the poster's multiplicity. At their core, posters countered the Western European art history canonization of only singular, "original" works possessing artistic value. For the artist, they allowed them to reach a significant number of community members, promoting cultural pride through recognizable Mexican iconography but also expanding their exposure to Chicana/o art. This polygonal approach is apparent in Juan Cervantes's poster *The Singer* (1976; fig. 21). Cervantes joined the RCAF after he transferred to Sacramento State, and his training in illustration is apparent in this playful depiction of a Chicano singer with sunglasses and a microphone strutting on a checkered dance floor in front of a bright red circle. Captured in performance, his face turns to the side and his mouth is open in song. The forward

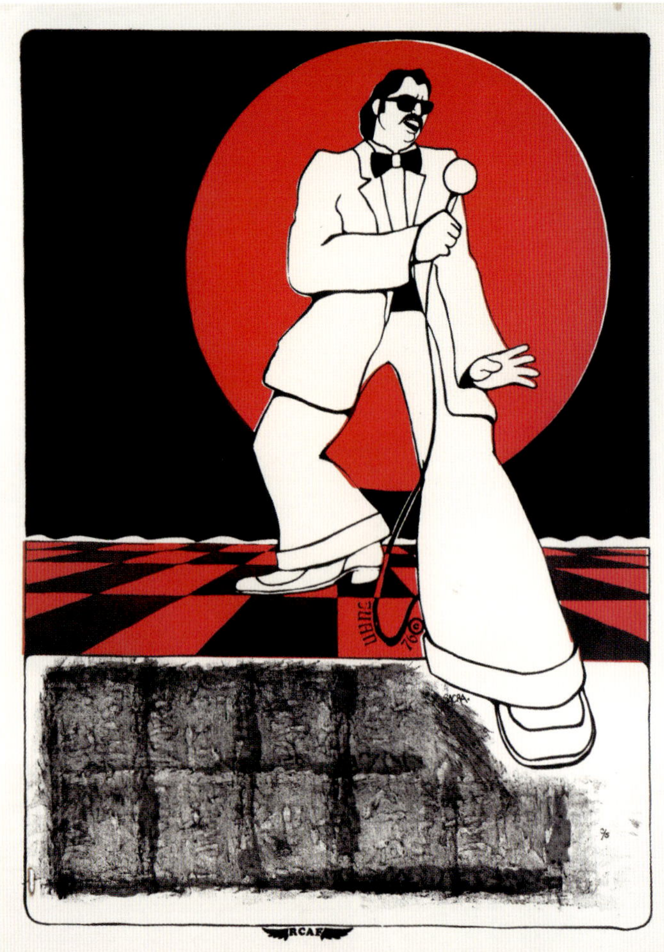

Fig. 21. Juan Cervantes (1951–2014), *The Singer*, 1976 [Plate 28].

movement of the figure's elongated front leg breaks the picture plane, reminiscent of cartoonist Robert Crumb's "Keep On Truckin'" cartoon figure introduced in his counterculture *Zap Comix* (1968), which became popular in the 1970s. Cervantes's strategic use of bold red and black on white paper to delineate the figure accentuates the sense of motion and drama within its one-page comic composition. In addition, his design intentionally created an art print that could become an announcement poster by eliminating the black tile bottom section and inserting text. As such, it underscores how the RCAF poster's aesthetic foundation guided the artists' community-based production overall.

While initially formed on a university campus and primarily composed of Montoya, Villa, and aspiring art students, the group also included professional artists.[67] This diversity of artistic training and aesthetic influences would engender powerful political posters. Even those promoting Mexican civic events provided a uniquely Chicana/o historic and gender perspective. However, other posters refuted the prevalent perception that Chicana/o graphics were solely agitprop. Their compositions consciously incorporated words from multiple languages, including English and Spanish, as well as Pachuco Caló and Chicano Movement nomenclature. As noted by UCLA professor and curator Chon Noriega, this turned "the referential quality of the poster back upon itself, revealing the considerable 'play' that exists in both language and image making," in many ways making the words into objects.[68] The RCAF's humor as a potent form of communication was not only utilized as "a means of resistance or defiance,"[69] but the deft promotion of their military persona also contributed to a multilayered aesthetic.

Equally important was the RCAF's multidimensional membership, which embraced artists, other creatives, and community activists from different professions, generations, and genders. In addition to its nonprofit organizations, it included the Aztlán Dance Company, Teatro de la Calle, and RCAF Band (creators of *XicIndio*, a Chicano rock opera), as well as an auto co-op, Aeronaves de Aztlán. "As you study a particular poster or the work of a particular artist," Montoya instructed, "look beyond and you will see a host of supportive brothers and sisters and community elders that were involved in producing those efforts."[70] As reflected in the exhibition's posters, those "efforts" included the myriad activities in the community sponsored by members of their organizations, groups, and collectively by the Cultural Affairs Committee. Today, RCAF members individually and collectively continue to build their artistic and activist legacy, inspiring younger generations of artists and activists. *Rebels with La Causa* serves as a testament to the power of their inextricable link among artistic practice, community service, and political activism.

Notes

Epigraphs: Quoted in Tomás Ybarra-Frausto, "*Califas*: California Chicano Art and Its Social Background," unpublished manuscript, 43, prepared for Califas Seminar at Mary Porter Sesnon Gallery, University of California, Santa Cruz, April 16–18, 1982; "Cultural Affairs Project," from proposal to California Arts Council, October 15, 1976, possession of author; Luis C. González in *Pilots of Aztlán: The Flights of the RCAF*, produced by Steve LaRosa and Toby Momtaz, aired September 15, 2021, KVIE, https://www.pbs.org/video/royal-chicano-air-force-art-and-activism-pgl7zg.

1 "Chicano" does not have a formal definition and is a self-designated identity. However, according to the slain *Los Angeles Times* journalist Rubén Salazar, "A Chicano is a Mexican American with a non-Anglo image of himself. . . . What, then, is a Chicano? Chicanos say that if you have to ask, you'll never understand, much less become a Chicano." Ruben Salazar, "Who is a Chicano? And what is it the Chicanos want?" *Los Angeles Times*, February 6, 1970. During the Chicano Movement, young politicized Mexican Americans transformed the pejorative term into a badge of pride.

2 E. Carmen Ramos, "Printing and Collecting the Revolution: The Rise and Impact of Chicano Graphics, 1965 to Now," in *Printing the Revolution! The Rise and Impact of Chicano Graphics, 1965 to Now* (Smithsonian American Art Museum, 2020), 36. See also Carlos Francisco Jackson, *Chicana and Chicano Art: ProtestArte* (University of Arizona Press, 2009); and Terezita Romo, "Chicana/o Art: 1965–1975," in *A Companion to Modern and Contemporary Latin American and Latina/o Art*, ed. Alejandro Anreus, Robin Adele Greeley, and Megan A. Sullivan (Wiley-Blackwell, 2001).

3 The late 1960s and 1970s were a fertile period for the formation of artist collectives. In California, along with Oakland's Mexican American Liberation Art Front/MALAF (1968), they included Los Angeles's Mechicano (1969), Asco (1972), and Los Four (1973); San Francisco's Galeria de la Raza (1970), La Raza Silkscreen Center (1971), and Mujeres Muralistas (1973); and San Diego's Artistas del Barrio (1968) and Toltecas en Aztlan (1971). In Texas, San Antonio's El Grupo (1968) became Con Safo (1972), and Austin had Mujeres Artistas del Suroeste (1977). New Mexico's Los Artes Guadalupanos de Aztlán (1970) and La Cofradia de Arte y Artesanos Hispánicos (1978) were in Santa Fe. In Chicago, the Movimiento Artistico Chicano/MARCH (1975) was the first Chicano arts organization in Illinois, though it was originally founded in Indiana as El Movimiento Artístico de la Raza Chicana (1972). In Phoenix, artists formed Movimiento Artistico del Rio Salado/MARS (1978). Richard Griswold del Castillo, Teresa McKenna, and Yvonne Yarbro-Bejarano, "APPENDIX: Catalog of Grupos, Centros, and Teatros," in *Chicano Art: Resistance and Affirmation, 1965–1985* (Wight Art Gallery, University of California, Los Angeles, 1991), 223–24.

4 José Montoya and Juan M. Carrillo, "Posada: The Man and His Art: A Comparative Analysis of José Guadalupe Posada and the Current Chicano Art Movement as They Apply Toward Social and Cultural Change: A Visual Resource Unit for Chicano Education" (master's thesis, California State University, Sacramento, 1975), 39.

5 Tomás Ybarra-Frausto, "The Chicano Movement/The Movement of Chicano Art," in *Exhibiting Cultures: The Poetics and Politics of Museum Display*, ed. Ivan Karp and Steven D. Lavine (Smithsonian Institution Press, 1991), 137.

6 An engraver and illustrator, José Guadalupe Posada in his broadsides used skulls and *calaveras* (skeletons) to satirize politicians as well as depict humorous scenes of the daily life, political travails, and urban traumas of the people of Mexico.

7 Susan Sontag, "Posters: Advertisement, Art, Political Artifact, Commodity," in *The Art of Revolution, Castro's Cuba: 1959–1970* (McGraw-Hill, 1970), vii.

8 I credit RCAF membership for my decision to pursue a career as an art historian and curator as well as an arts administrator. Beginning in 1974, I became a volunteer at La Raza Bookstore, where I later served as an executive and artistic director and as a board member and president. With the support of founding director Santos and a grant from the California Arts Council, I added an exhibition space (1980) and became its curator. Two years later, the board approved the name La Raza Galeria Posada (1982), which maintained its Chicano Movement roots and reflected its expanded artistic role in the community. From 1972 to 1990, LRB directors were Santos, Antonio "Al" Negrete, and Romo; the LRGP, Santos, Romo, Josephine "Josie" Talamantez, and Cid.

9 As noted in their resumes, Montoya had been teaching in Wheatland and Villa in Linden, both in California. According to co-director Duane Campbell, the MAEP "was an attempt to prepare educational change agents to overcome the decades of educational neglect suffered by Mexican American students in schools." Duane Campbell, Mexican American Education Project, *Institute for Democracy and Education*, accessed March 27, 2024, https://sites.google.com/site/democracyandeducationorg/chicano-mexican-american-digital-history-project/mexican-american-education-project. The program consisted of two cohorts, the Experienced Teacher Fellowship Program for graduate students and the Prospective Teachers Fellowship Program for undergraduates. Along with Montoya, other RCAF members involved in the MAEP were graduate student Juan M. Carrillo and undergraduate Irma Lerma (Barbosa). Equally significant, from 1971 to 1973 the campus activism of the MAEP Fellows and the student organization, MEChA, propelled the establishment of the Ethnic Studies Department and Chicano studies programs. It also resulted in Chicana/o professors in various other departments, including cultural anthropology, social science, history, music, literature, communications, and government.

10 MALAF was also humorously known as *mala-f* (with the "f" pronounced in Spanish as "efe."

11 Eva Cockcroft and Holly Barnet-Sanchez, eds., *Signs from the Heart: California Chicano Murals* (Social and Public Resource Center, 1990), 27.

12 Shifra Goldman, *Dimensions of the Americas: Art and Social Change in Latin America and the United States* (University of Chicago Press, 1994), 168.

13 Ybarra-Frausto, "Chicano Movement," 130.

14 Jacinto Quirarte, *Mexican American Artists* (University of Texas Press, 1973), 134.
15 Ybarra-Frausto, "Chicano Movement," 130.
16 Quoted in Victoria Dalkey, "Call to La Causa," *Sacramento Bee*, April 1, 1992.
17 "El Plan Espiritual de Aztlán," in *Aztlan: An Anthology of Mexican American Literature*, ed. Luis Valdez and Stan Steiner (Vintage, 1972), 405. The "Spiritual Plan of Aztlán" was adopted at the National Chicano Youth and Liberation Conference sponsored by Rodolfo "Corky" Gonzales's social service organization, Crusade for Justice (Cruzada por la Justicia), in Denver in March 1969. With contributions from several authors, the Denver artist and muralist Emanuel Martinez wrote the section on the role of artists and writers within the movement. Victor Alejandro Sorell, "The Persuasion of Art—The Art of Persuasion: Emanuel Martinez Creates a Pulpit for El Movimiento," in *Emanuel Martinez: A Retrospective*, ed. Teddy Dewalt (Museo de las Américas, 1995), 27.
18 Villa's class offerings at Sacramento State included "Murals in the Barrio" and "Peoples Poster Art," which were the first classes to include a Chicano focus in the Art Department. Mildred Monteverde, *Chicanos Gráficos … California* (Southern Colorado State College, 1971), 10.
19 "Chicano Art Show at SSC," *State Hornet*, May 22, 1970. "Gente" is spelled correctly in the article.
20 CSUS students Celia Herrera Rodriguez and Kathryn Garcia's sister, Lorraine García-Nakata, met the collective's members in 1974. Raul Suarez joined while an intern at the Centro de Artistas Chicanos.
21 Rene Yañez, interview by author, June 7, 2008.
22 MEChA continues to be active on many US college and university campuses.
23 Like many Chicano artists, RCAF members did not sign their posters, instead choosing to stay anonymous as a rejection of an individual-focused art career.
24 Don Schwartz, "Out Front on the Art Front," *Suttertown (Sacramento) News*, February 14–21, 1985.
25 John Robin Witt, "Outsider Chicano Artists Now Insiders," *Sacramento Bee*, October 24, 1989.
26 According to an article by Charles Johnson, the RCAF "had a room in the Washington Community Council headquarters at 14 and E Streets, as part of Montoya's barrio art program at California State University"; Charles Johnson, "Centro Keeps Low Profile," *Sacramento Bee*, October 30, 1977. However, Cuellar and Orosco's resumes cite the Centro's initial location at 630 9th Street, the former St. Joseph's School. Royal Chicano Air Force Archives, CEMA 8, Box 9, Folder 7, Department of Special Collections, University Libraries, University of California, Santa Barbara.
27 Manuel Valencia, "Storefront Academy For Chicano Artists," *Sacramento Union*, 1973.
28 Charles Johnson, "Color, Corazon Express Life of Chicanos," *Sacramento Bee*, June 10, 1973. The classes were part of Montoya's Barrio Art Program, which he established at Sacramento State.
29 The names of the artists in the Royal Chicano Air Force's first exhibition at Sacramento State in November 1972 were not listed in a campus newspaper article. However, the following year, in an article for the second RCAF exhibition, the names listed were "Jose Montoya, Juan Cervantez [*sic*], Victor Rodriguez, Cathy Garcia, Carlos Lopez, Juan Orozco [*sic*], Armando Cid, Esteban Villa, Rudy Cuellar, Ron Andrade, Henry Ortiz, David Tafoya, Richard Lucero, Elma Hernandez, Irma Lerma, David De Leon, Jose Feliz [*sic*], Simona Juarez, Richard Favella [*sic*], and Max Garcia. It is sponsored by the Centro de Artistas Chicanos." Linda Solley, "Second Annual Royal Chicano Art Show—A Real Treat," *State Hornet*, May 16, 1973. The list includes non-RCAF artists.
30 Irma Lerma Barbosa, email to author, August 14, 2024. She credits artist Simona (Juarez) Hernandez for the idea and for securing the conference space.
31 Irma Lerma Barbosa, email to author, October 9, 2024. With its flat composition and bold colors, the poster is reminiscent of Felix René Mederos Pazos's graphics. This influence is more apparent in her poster for a slide presentation on her trip to Cuba when she returned in 1972. For more information regarding the impact of Cuban posters on Chicana/o artists, see Terezita Romo, "*¡Presente!* Chicano Posters and Latin American Politics," in Russ Davidson et al., *Latin American Posters: Public Aesthetics and Mass Politics* (University of New Mexico Press, 2006).
32 Amalia Mesa-Bains, "Memory, Cultural Identity, and the Social Imaginary: Art of the Chicano/a Community," presented at the Tenth Annual Ernesto Galarza Commemorative Lecture, Stanford Center for Chicano Research, Stanford University, 1995.
33 Lerma Barbosa email, October 9, 2024.
34 According to Lerma Barbosa, "Simona Hernandez contact[ed] me and ask[ed] why Chicana artists were not recognized nor celebrated. We decided to hold an exhibition." Email to author, August 14, 2024. Kathryn Garcia assisted Lerma Barbosa with this conference and collaborated with her on other posters.
35 Luis "Louie the Foot" González, text to author, November 26, 2024.
36 The Centro hired Cuellar, Favela, González, Orosco, and Arturo Singh, who was a sculptor. CETA's crucial role within the arts is detailed in Mirasol Riojas, *The Accidental Arts Supporter: An Assessment of the Comprehensive Employment and Training Act (CETA)*, report no. 8 (UCLA Chicano Studies Research Center, 2006). According to Riojas, "Although it was not conceived as an arts program, CETA proved to be one of the most substantial sources for federal funds in addition to the NEA." Riojas, *Accidental Arts*, 5. Unfortunately, this reliance destabilized many arts organizations after its elimination in the early 1980s.
37 Posada's *calaveras* also served to remind viewers of death as the great equalizer among rich and poor, beautiful and ugly, young and old. One of his iconic figures was La Catrina, a well-dressed, female skeleton who was Posada's critique of Mexico's high society and became associated with the Día de los Muertos in Mexico and the United States.
38 Montoya and Carrillo, "Posada: The Man and His Art," 2.
39 Rodolfo "Rudy" Cuellar, email to author, July 5, 2023.
40 The literal translation is "Don't look for noise in a pork rind."
41 Luis "Louie the Foot" González, text to author, January 8, 2025.
42 The ballot summary for this measure included new appointments to the Agricultural Labor Relations Board (ALRB) and "access for union organizers to property of employers for certain periods." Accessed November 27, 2024, https://ballotpedia.org/California_Proposition

_14,_Agricultural_Labor_Relations_Board _Initiative_(1976).

43 Héctor González, text to author, November 8, 2024.

44 Chon Noriega, "Postmodernism or Why This is Just Another Poster," in *Just Another Poster? Chicano Graphic Arts in California* (University Art Museum, University of California, Santa Barbara, 2001), 23.

45 Ortiz de Domínguez is included in Mexico's annual "Grito de Dolores," which commemorates Father Hidalgo's speech on September 16, 1810. García-Nakata's inclusion of her name in the poster was meant to bring attention in the US to Ortiz and her contributions.

46 Lorraine García-Nakata, email to author, June 9, 2024.

47 "Desdoblamiento," ca. 1978, document in author's possession. It presents a concise case for Chicano Mental Health, including its origins, theory, and methodology. A key proponent was Dr. Arnaldo Solis, a psychiatrist and clinical director of the Sacramento Concilio's La Olotera mental health unit. Solis, La Olotera counselors David Rasul and Terezita Romo, Sra. Cobb, Cid, Orosco, Padilla, Gina Montoya, and Guadalupe "Lupe" Portillo represent the unique confluence of Indigenous spirituality, psychology, art, and family observance of cultural traditions within the RCAF's initiation of the Día de los Muertos observance.

48 Chicanos introduced the US to the public-oriented observances of Día de los Muertos that are now ubiquitous. Sacramento's is the third oldest observance in the country. For more information regarding the DDLM in California, see Terezita Romo, ed., *Chicanos en Mictlán: Día de los Muertos in California* (Mexican Museum, 2000). For a detailed analysis of the observance in Mexico and US, see Regina Marchi, *Day of the Dead in the USA: The Migration and Transformation of a Cultural Phenomenon*, 2nd ed. (Rutgers University Press, 2022).

49 In the first year, Portillo, who learned altar-making from her grandmother and mother, undertook and continues the creation of the community *ofrenda* at the cemetery, now with her daughters and granddaughters. *Ofrendas* are altars constructed for the DDLM (November 1 and 2) to honor and remember deceased loved ones. Along with their picture(s), water, flowers (especially, *cempaxochitls*/marigolds), and candles, the *ofrenda* includes the loved one's favorite food, drinks, and personal items. Though traditionally created in Mexico at home and/or at cemetery plots, artists during the Chicano Movement introduced the DDLM altars in the US as public *ofrendas*, some as art installations. Beginning in 1977, the DDLM procession included stopping to recognize the four cardinal directions as well as at the cemetery's veterans' section.

50 Angelbertha Cobb, phone call with author, March 30, 2025. Ortiz studied Danza Azteca under Sra. Cobb and was a member of Danza Quetzalcoatl before being entrusted with the group. His group was also known as Grupo Xitlalli.

51 While the first was called "Fiesta del Maiz," subsequent ones became "Fiesta de Maiz." Pictured in the photograph on the pyramid: Gloria Rangel, José Montoya, Maria Paiz (Xilonen), Arnaldo Solis, and Stan Padilla. Bottom: Danny Valdez, (unidentified), Frederico Vuittonet, Enrique Ortiz, Willie Chacon (kneeling), Joe Rivera, Juanita Polendo Ontiveros, Jesse "Chuy" Ortiz, and Richard Rodriguez.

52 Ishi (ca. 1861–March 25, 1916) was proclaimed to be the last member of the Yahi tribe in Northern California when he was discovered in Oroville in 1911. He spent the last five years of his life as a living specimen at the University of California, Berkeley.

53 The Aztecs held the festival of Xilonen in the summer, typically in July. A young girl, symbolizing fertility and renewal, would dance in the annual ritual. In the RCAF's *ceremonia*, she received advice from female elders.

54 "Cultural Affairs Project" proposal.

55 While the poster cites "Fiesta de los Colores," in subsequent years it was "Fiesta de Colores."

56 Stan Padilla, interview by author, May 28, 2024.

57 Ybarra-Frausto, "*Califas*," 57.

58 Santos and González, phone call with author, March 2, 2024. Evicted by the landlord to make room for an apartment complex in 1986, LRGP moved to the former (Benny) Barrios Gallery on 15th and G Streets, where it remained until 1991. The larger two-story building allowed it to expand its Chicana/o, Latina/o, and Native American bookstore items and public programming, as well as increase its gallery space.

59 As with La Raza Bookstore, LRGP incorporated Native American artists in exhibitions and related programming. Along with invited guest curators, a curatorial committee was formed that included Native American artists, curators, and scholars. The organization's Native American inclusion was eliminated by the early 2000s.

60 Curated by García-Nakata, *What We Are Now* included Patricia Dunsmore de Carrillo, Eva Garcia, Kathryn Garcia, Lorraine García(-Nakata), and Celia Rodriguez. *Winging It* was curated by Rene Yañez, the co-director of the Galeria de la Raza in San Francisco, and featured Cid, Cuellar, Favela, González, Montoya, Orosco, and Villa.

61 In the *Ofrendas* exhibition, Cid created an altar to honor Posada, Carmen Lomas Garza to Frida Kahlo, Amalia Mesa-Bains to Dolores del Rio, and Rene Yañez to the "Unknown Artist." The artists in *Personal Reflections* were David Avalos, George Blake, Eduardo Carrillo, Yreina Cervantez, Sal Garcia, Zarco Guerrero, Ester Hernandez, Frank LaPena, Carmen Lomas Garza, Gilbert Lujan, Ralph Maradiaga, Emmanuel Montoya, Ernest Palomino, Richard Rios, Patricia Rodriguez, Javier Sandoval, and Linda Vallejo. Romo curated both exhibitions. San Francisco's Mexican Museum educators, Bea Carrillo Hocker and Nora Wagner, designed the installation of the *Personal Reflections* exhibition.

62 The commissioned artists were Carrillo, Cid, Cervantes, Cuellar, Favela, González, Lerma Barbosa, Montoya, Padilla, Orosco, and Villa. During the first decade, Santos and Cid organized other exhibitions as well.

63 According to Portillo, who continues to co-organize the RCAF's Día de los Muertos, LRGP's support ended in 2012 when the director began her own DDLM event. Author correspondence with Portillo. In 2024, ten years after it ceased to exist, the RCAF's LRGP was revived to conduct research and present programming centered on the RCAF's history, contributions, and legacy, including the DDLM observance.

64 Ruthe Thompson, "Centro Screenprinting: Architects of the Chicano Renaissance," *ScreenPrinting* (August 1987): 115.

65 Orosco contributed the suite's cover, *There is a Tomorrow,* as well as the poster, *Sus Consejos Valen (Your Advice Matters).* Favela's poster (with Héctor González's photograph of Favela's ceramic homeboys) was titled *Veteranos*; Montoya's, *Familia, Cultura, Familia*; and Villa's, *Hazlo [Do It] For Better Mental Health.* Images and titles can be found at the Royal Chicano Air Force Online Archive of California, https://calisphere.org/collections/18781/?q=&sort=a.

66 Michael Ackley, "Chicanismo: Thriving Artists Draw from Mexican/Indian Roots," *The Sacramento Union*, September 12, 1983. Ackley also included La Raza Galeria Posada as one of the "shoots."

67 Ella Maria Diaz, *Flying Under the Radar with the Royal Chicano Air Force: Mapping a Chicano/a Art History* (University of Texas Press, 2017), 11–12. Max Garcia was a commercial graphic designer with a degree from the Art Center College of Design in Pasadena. Cid received art training there as well. Padilla held BFA and MFA degrees from the San Francisco Art Institute.

68 Noriega, "Postmodernism," 22.

69 Carlos Francisco Jackson, *Chicana and Chicano Art: ProtestArte* (University of Arizona Press, 2009), 148.

70 José Montoya, *In Search of Mr. Con Safos: RCAF Retrospective Poster Art Exhibit*, exhibition brochure, Lankford & Cook Gallery, Rancho Cordova, CA, 1989, n.p.

JOSE MONTOYA'S
PACHUCO
EL RALPH
RIFA POR VIDA
ART
LA VERDAD
RCAF c/s
A HISTORICAL UPDATE
OPEN RING ART SPACE
1223 J. ST. SACRA.
ACROSS FROM THE CONVENTION CENTER
TEATRO, MUSICA Y LOCURAS
DEC. 9
7:30 11:00 P.M.
THRU
JAN. 7 1978

JOSÉ MONTOYA

The Anatomy of an RCAF Poster

Shortly after the *Chicano Art: Resistance and Affirmation (CARA)* exhibition at the Wight Art Gallery in Los Angeles, I received an offer from a major corporation expressing a desire to buy my *Pachuco Art* poster, "*¡El Ralph Rifa Por Vida!*" There was no specified sum mentioned, but the inference that I could name my own price was clearly implicit. Since producing posters during the Chicano Movement was never done with marketing in mind, I ignored the offer. But subsequent interest in the poster, and its frequent reproduction in articles and books about Chicano art, did compel me to reexamine the piece. Rather than try to establish any aesthetic impact, I want simply to recall what exactly was happening at the time we produced the poster and perhaps even write it all down as part of Sacramento lore that had been building around the RCAF: The Rebel Chicano Art Front (aka, The Royal Chicano Air Force) and its fabled squadron of adobe airplanes (fig. 1).

The poster was created for my 1977 exhibition, *Pachuco Art, A Historical Update*. It demonstrates how the RCAF managed the concept of a collective to its fullest and most creative potential in producing a poster when time and manpower were of the essence, given the myriad tasks and responsibilities we had all assumed as committed cultural workers in those days of the Chicano Movement. *El Frente Rebelde de Arte Chicano* in Sacramento wasn't only about painters, muralists, and commercial artists. It included in its ranks students, educators, historians, poets, *teatristas*, and community organizers, all operating within the constructs of struggle and resistance to utilize the impulse of pure creative energy in all aspects of organizing. If a given situation called for *locura*, it was creative madness—*la locura cura* was the RCAF's favorite mantra. If it was about demonstrations or picket

This essay is based on the keynote lecture Montoya delivered on the occasion of the opening of the exhibition *Just Another Poster? Chicano Graphic Arts in California*, on January 12, 2001, at University of California, Santa Barbara. The lecture was titled, "*La Palabra*—Spread It! The Chicano Poster."

Fig. 1. Rudy O. Cuellar (born 1950), Luis C. González (born 1953), and José Montoya (1932–2013), *José Montoya's Pachuco Art, A Historical Update*, 1977 [Plate 36].

lines, it was creative picketing and demonstrating. Thus, every aspect of our political involvement was predicated on being as dramatic and as outlandish as was deemed necessary to pull off the mission, which ultimately was to use art as an organizing tool.

One vital area of interest for young Chicana and Chicano students in the fledgling days of Chicano studies at California State University, Sacramento (CSUS) was researching the true history of Chicano youth in previous epochs. They were beginning to get historical perspective from their ethnic studies professors quite different from what they were used to seeing depicted in the media. It was different from what they had gotten in their public school education from historically biased textbooks and from insensitive and, worst of all, indifferent teachers. They began with a focus on media coverage of the Southwest, in general, and California, in particular. The plan was to disseminate the revised information back to the Chicano community.

One of our earliest confrontations on campus was to force the *State Hornet*, CSUS's school newspaper, to relinquish column space and a desk for Chicanos to air their opinions. This was one of the first of many victories at CSUS, coordinated by the students and carried out by the collective efforts of faculty, students, and barrio-based organizations, including the Brown Berets and the local office of the United Farm Workers Organizing Committee. A young graduate student in anthropology named Jaime Vigil from East LA began a series of columns specifically on *pachucos*. His writings included articles on the Sleepy Lagoon trials and the so-called Zoot Suit Riots of the 1940s. Both students and faculty were encouraged to submit material and even to be featured guests for the *Pachuco* column. This began an entire body of knowledge and research that was to become an integral part of the Chicano studies curriculum at CSUS. My contribution as a faculty member in the Art Department was to mount an art exhibit of my *pachuco* art production and include a narrative of *pachuco* history. Due to the volume of information or, better stated, the misinformation that was mounting, the exhibition expanded in scope to include a photo essay, *teatro* and music, and even a car show of vintage *ranflas* of that epoch.

As it turned out, this refocusing on the history of *Pachuquismo* launched me on a journey in time that went back far beyond the heady days of *La Causa* and the RCAF and the Chicano Movement in Sacramento. I was flung, hurtling back, back in time, past the jitterbug and the Palomar Ballroom in Fresno; back to Telegraph Avenue in Berkeley and art school in Oakland (California College of Arts and Crafts) and the GI Bill, and hooking up with the other Chicanos there, including Esteban Villa, Salvador Torres, and other Korean War vets. And, most importantly, to that perfectly timed encounter with a young intellectual who was to become our ideological mentor and navigator who got us through the murky waters of academia—El Ralph Ornelas: *pinto* poet revolutionary, and accomplished thief and scholar. This is [the] same Ralph whose memory I was posthumously honoring in the *Pachuco Art* poster. But the journey back in time couldn't stop in Berkeley. To appreciate the entire history, it would be necessary to go all the way back to the forties and to the events affecting the lives of Mexican American youth at that time.

Having grown up in the barrios of Albuquerque and around Fresno, I was quite familiar with the earliest manifestations of the *pachuco* phenomenon. As a paperboy and gopher for Gus's shine parlor on Central Avenue in Albuquerque, I was awed by the sharp and classy *vatos* getting their double-soled *calcos* spit-shined. And their *jainas*, in their short skirts and pompadours, also oozing style and glamour, were indeed a sight to behold. By virtue of having lived and gone to school in most of the barrios of Albuquerque, I had known these young Chicanos. I hung around with their younger siblings, regularly being rapped on the side of the head for wanting to tag along, yet getting *feria* for being *alcahuetes* delivering notes to our older sisters. Because there were no laws prohibiting child labor, or if they existed they were never enforced, we would work after school and on weekends. The types of jobs were limited to low-paying menial tasks, such as dishwashers and bus boys in the big hotels downtown. But every *vatito* secretly nursed aspirations to be old enough to make it as a waiter or, better yet, the top *jales*: a bellhop! Within that milieu, I had always seen these dudes as hard workers. Mopping floors and working the sculleries of hospitals, we younger *vatitos* looked with admiration at how young Chicanas worked hard in the kitchens and as nurses' assistants in starched uniforms, caring for sick people and emptying bedpans. I didn't see the dirty, lazy, reefer-smoking, draft-dodging Mexicans that the newspaper headlines and the media talked about. I never saw any gun molls or girls of loose morals. It took hard work to pay for tailor-made drapes, spiked high heels, and webbed stockings—too hard to be shiftless and lazy. And, as a matter of fact, I recall these same "aberrations" standing in long lines at the draft boards enlisting to go fight in World War II.

I had always suspected the media of giving Chicano youth of that era a bum rap, particularly in the coverage of the so-called Zoot Suit Riots. The research for the show clearly exposed the media hype mounted by Randolph Hearst and the *Herald Express*. Unfortunately, the only Spanish language newspaper, *La Opinión*, simply translated the xenophobic headlines expressed in the Hearst papers. Hearst even tried to connect the *pachucos* to some clandestine, fifth column conspiracy involving the *Sinarquistas* of Mexico, a right-wing syndicate that sided with the Axis during World War II. Hearst was upset with President Lázaro Cárdenas for expropriating the property of foreign industrialists in Mexico. Unleashing the US Navy and the Marines in violation of their own Uniform Code of Military Justice to round up and viciously strip and beat up *pachucos* was all he managed to accomplish. Mexican youth were the scapegoats caught in the crossfire of war hysteria.

The US media wasn't the only source of negative coverage regarding Chicano youth. In the fifties, Octavio Paz had come out with *The Labyrinth of Solitude*, where he made the *pachucos* appear like buffoons, *payasos*, resorting to outlandish "costumes" in an effort to get attention and acceptance. My *compadre*, Esteban Villa, and I had traveled to Mexico City in 1964 with the misguided idea of hooking up with José Luis Cuevas. It was a pipe dream from the gate. We began hearing about this enfante terrible when we were in art school. On Telegraph Avenue in Berkeley, Cuevas was being talked about in all the coffeehouses. His series of drawings for Kafka had everyone ecstatic. And how he was being written up in the *Evergreen Review* as a rebel against traditional culture, and particularly Mexican art, sure made him sound like a young, antiestablishment, nonconformist Chicano to us. The naive notion of even getting close to locating Cuevas fell through when we discovered that our art school connection in Mexico City had unexpectedly left town and was painting lewd religious murals in San Miguel de Allende. We were close to being broke and, to add to our plight, we managed to get out-hustled by a couple of aging beatniks. We had to resort to talking a US Marine guard at the American Embassy out of a few dollars for gas after the Mexican American staff threatened us for embarrassing them. The way we were dressed was insulting, they claimed, adding, "It's guys like you that give us a bad name!" We hopped in our old VW van and headed for San Miguel de Allende.

San Miguel turned out to be a trendy colonial contradiction best known as an "art colony," mainly for Sunday painters from Iowa and Scandinavia. We did, however, link up with our Mexico City connection, who was managing a bookstore that was the favorite hangout for Europeans and arty types from the US, all discussing *The Labyrinth of Solitude*. After an altercation or two over Paz's views, we were asked to leave San Miguel, not by the Mexicans, but by intellectuals who accused us of being ashamed of our origins.

Needless to say, when the opportune time to set the record straight presented itself in Sacramento in the seventies, we were eager to employ every available resource in order to give our side of that history. But not the version that had even convinced some of our own folks that the entire *epoca de los pachucos* had been an embarrassment to the Mexicans in the US. Some pseudo-radicals even accused us of being reactionaries. The *Movimiento* needed revolutionary symbols. The idea of romanticizing *pachucos* and depicting those decadent times had no redeeming social value. That is precisely why it became important to present more than an art show.

It soon became apparent that the logistical implications were going to require beyond what the RCAF packed in its arsenal. It was, however, an opportune time to incorporate and test fly the umbrella scheme Chicano studies had insisted on initiating at CSUS in the formative years of ethnic studies. The plan was called *El Concepto de la Comuniversidad*. It stipulated that all Chicano courses were to hold at least one class in the barrio. This immediately increased the woman/manpower necessary to handle the cultural and historical aspects of the proposed production the *pachuco* exhibit had become.

The RCAF already had barrio art classes in the inner city. Professor Esteban Villa had silkscreening and poster-making classes in the barrio (fig. 2). Professor Eduardo Carrillo had his mural painting classes in the Gardenland barrio in Northgate. I had art and education majors facilitating after-school arts and crafts

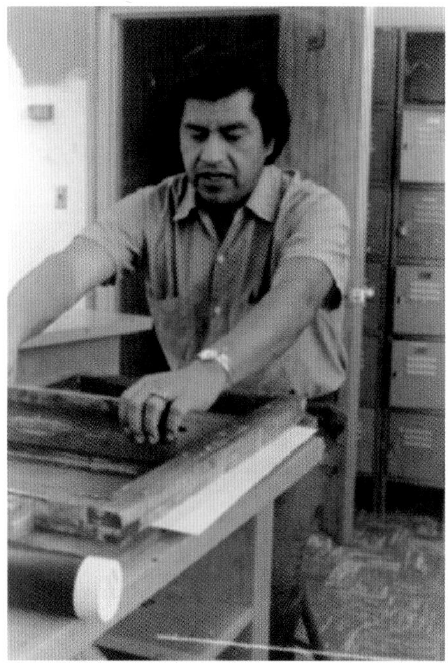

Fig. 2. Héctor D. González (born 1945), *Esteban Villa screenprinting at Sacramento State*, 1972. Collection of Héctor D. González.

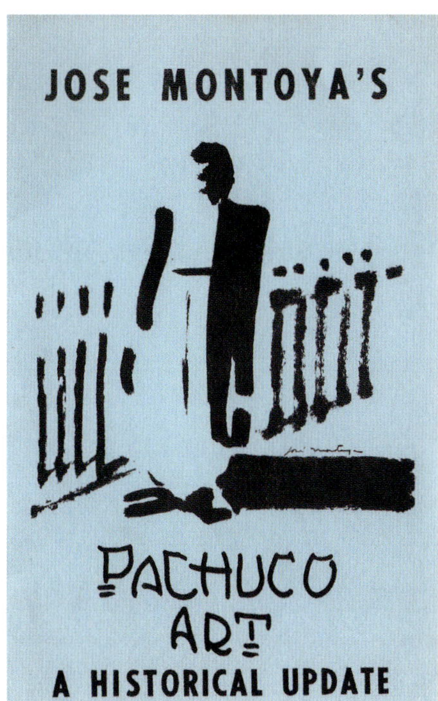

Fig. 3. Cover of *José Montoya's Pachuco Art, A Historical Update* exhibition booklet, 1977. Collection of Terezita Romo.

activities in the Washington and Alkali barrios downtown that included three age groups: preschool to age thirteen at the Washington Neighborhood Center; high school students, for whom we had negotiated class credits from their respective schools, at the Washington Community Council; and adults and senior citizens with activities at the Washington Plaza, a low-rent housing complex for the elderly in the barrio. Two of the components would become invaluable to the success of the show: the high schoolers were given the task of raiding their family photo albums for snapshots of the forties to be blown up for the show. One enterprising young *cholo*, Mike "Mad Dog" Escobedo, uncovered a bonanza of material in the archives of the State Library and a most cooperative state librarian eager to help. Other high school students had to learn to dance the jitterbug, while others scoured the racks at Goodwill outlets and the Salvation Army for baggy slacks and sport coats, which the adults and senior students would re-tailor into twelve-inch, tapered-bottom zoot suits and fingertip coats. Short skirts, high-heeled *poraps*, and webbed stockings were not as hard to come by. And there were enough older ladies in the classes who could still rat an outrageous pompadour.

As a result of the collective commitment of all involved, the entire and incredible undertaking—except for the actual installation of the artwork—was completed two whole weeks before the opening. The stepped-up frenzy of activities had been necessary because the RCAF had a previous commitment to do some work for the UFW during those two weeks, and all the artists would be going to La Paz. With everything ready in Sacramento, we could fulfill our obligation to the union and be back in plenty of time to install the show and tie down the loose ends before the opening date (fig. 3). We were elated. We were celebrating! Then we remembered that we had overlooked the most important aspect of the entire effort: The Poster! *La palabra!* The word! That most decisive conveyor of the information crucial in inviting a community to attend an important presentation regarding the historical truths of an earlier epoch had ironically been overlooked. In fact, the oversight was discovered at the *parranda* we were having at the Reno Club celebrating both the exhibition's accomplishments and our departure. Without panic and without breaking the mood of the celebration, we set up an emergency session away from the bar—not that far—and before too long we had flight plans for both missions.

In the beginning, I was to design the poster. All I had were rough sketches and different layouts in my sketchpad. That was the extent of it. But I did have notes of what I wanted the poster to include beyond the regular venue information. One was to honor José Guadalupe Posada by using a *pachuco calaca* and doing a four-color woodcut. The other was to dedicate the poster to Ralph Ornelas, the young and astute intellectual who had been our mentor in Berkeley and who had instilled in us the power inherent in uncovering the true history of Chicano people and exposing the lies.

The plan for the woodcut was scrapped, but not altogether. Rudy Cuellar had some pieces of linoleum in his van and a few cutting tools. All the scraps were ten inches wide and the lengths varied. I wasn't too happy with the narrow format, but we were in a bind. I began drawing the image directly on the linoleum with a felt marker. I got the porkpie hat, the skull, and the arms just below the belt line. On another piece I got the hands, and on another scrap I got the rest of the drapes and the shoes. Time was running out. If we didn't get our planes in the air soon, we would never get into La Paz by morning. By now the proverbial straws had been drawn and "Louie the Foot" [González] and Rudy were going to stay behind and pull the prints. I started with the cutting tools and managed to complete the figure. We had to start our engines. Rudy and Louie had all the information that still had to be fitted into the design. My instructions were stated and repeated back by the two: all the information had to be accommodated; there were to be at least two color separations, and the vertical format was not to exceed twenty-eight inches high. A tall order, the *pachuco* figure had already eaten up nineteen inches. Louie and Rudy assured us everything would be taken care of and we were off.

I called Sacramento a couple of days later and the progress wasn't going well. They had forgotten to put the word "art" after "*pachuco*," but not to worry. I asked if the word "truth" had been accommodated. "The what word?" Rudy asked. More problems: pulling the prints was going too slow—rolling on the ink, burnishing, and pulling. And the color plates still had to be cut and the process repeated. But, hey, no sweat, we have all the high school students helping, Rudy chirped. I was amazed at Rudy's and Louie's assurances not to worry. I took their word for it.

Rolling into Sacramento back from La Paz we convinced the DP (Designated Pilot) to get off on Florin Road and onto Franklin Boulevard for a six-pack. Once on Franklin we began to notice what appeared to us to be colorful announcements on telephone poles and storefronts. At first we thought they were posters for some *conjunto* but the narrow verticality and the flashy colors made them appear more like bullfight posters. At the intersection of Franklin and Fruitridge, the image of the *pachuco* was unmistakable. *¡El Ralph rifa, por vida!* The guys and gals had pulled it off.

Rudy and Louie had gotten Freddy at Crystal Clear Printers to shoot a positive of one of the linocut prints, then burned it onto a screen. They had found a stack of pre-cut lawn-sign color stock, a horrible yellow left over from some political campaign job. The size was perfect: thirteen by thirty-one inches. They taped off a ten by twenty-eight-inch area and poured down a split-fountain rainbow of colors, lined up the registration marks, and with one pull of the squeegee laid down the entire colorific background for the poster. After that it was just a matter of printing the photo-stenciled linoleum cut outline in black. And, in fact, they even had time to do a third and a fourth color run, like finely placed signatures: white for the bony *calaca*, the artist's name, and the date, and a golden brown for the hat and the zooter drapes. And that very offensive yellow color of the chipboard had made it all possible with, of course, the genius of two impudent young pilots *de la RCAF*—Little Rudy and Th' Foot.

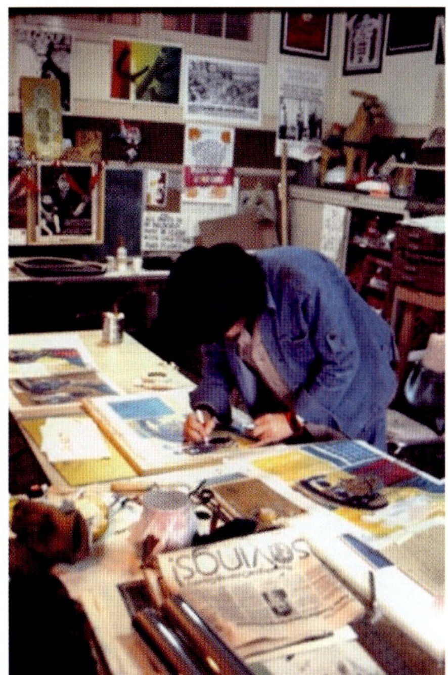

Fig. 4. Héctor D. González (born 1945), *José Montoya signing his screenprint for* La Historia de California *calendar* (1977), 1976. Collection of Héctor D. González.

So there we have it. What is the history of Chicano posters? I have given the history of just one poster. Imagine how many histories exist just in this exhibition alone, histories that should be shared with young people who may not be aware of what went on or, for that matter, even be aware of what is going on today. We certainly know what is going on. The issues have changed, yet the issues remain the same, or worse, for our youth in these times. Randolph Hearst is gone. But the hysteria and the violence are still here, and the prisons are here. Who is spreading the word, *la palabra*? Computers? Can cyberspace replace duct tape and staple guns for getting the word out to all parts of the barrios and to the labor camps? Have museum and gallery walls replaced the walls of the barrios? Malaquias Montoya, the well-known Chicano poster artist, has always maintained that the only exhibition space we should consider for posters has to be the space in the streets and the alleys of the community. Is that possible once the art writers, the reviewers, and the curators (both mainstream and *Raza*) become the ones who call the shots? One writer has written about the RCAF as a has-been Chicano artist group from the old days of the Chicano Movement. We never went anywhere. We're still doing posters and teaching young people the process (fig. 4).

Perhaps the only way to end this discussion regarding the history of Chicano posters is to end by asking the question, what is the future of Chicano posters? And we need to separate the question from what is the future of Chicano art. I think money has already settled that question.

Personally, regarding the young Chicana and Chicano artists, I feel *cariñosamente*, very reassured by what I see as I travel around the country. They definitely have a huge respect for the poster and they utilize it very effectively to air their opinions. And they continue to hone their skills, prompted, no doubt, by the political climate in this country. Recent legal actions directly affecting *Raza*, in general, and youth, in particular, have politicized them in a way very reminiscent of the early days of the old Chicano Movement. It is precisely that strong reaffirmation and a commitment to change that makes me hopeful. But I am also cognizant of the fact that the attitude of a much larger number of Chicano youth is totally apolitical. That makes the efforts of the committed few far more difficult than it was for us in the old days, when political involvement wasn't hampered by drugs and gang affiliations. And we didn't have to deal with the divisive specter of Hispanicization robbing us of our indigenous roots. But those few, the ones who are spreading the word today, they are the ones who give this old *ruco* the hope I refer to above. They have embraced the silkscreen process as creatively as the old timers, and they are computer savvy to the max. The T-shirt is their way of spreading the word regarding the plight of our people, yet they recognize the power of the poster and particularly appreciate the economical advantage of producing multiples for large distribution. They also know enough Aztec high tech to understand that cyberspace doesn't always get out of the labor camps or to certain parts of the barrio. But a poster does.

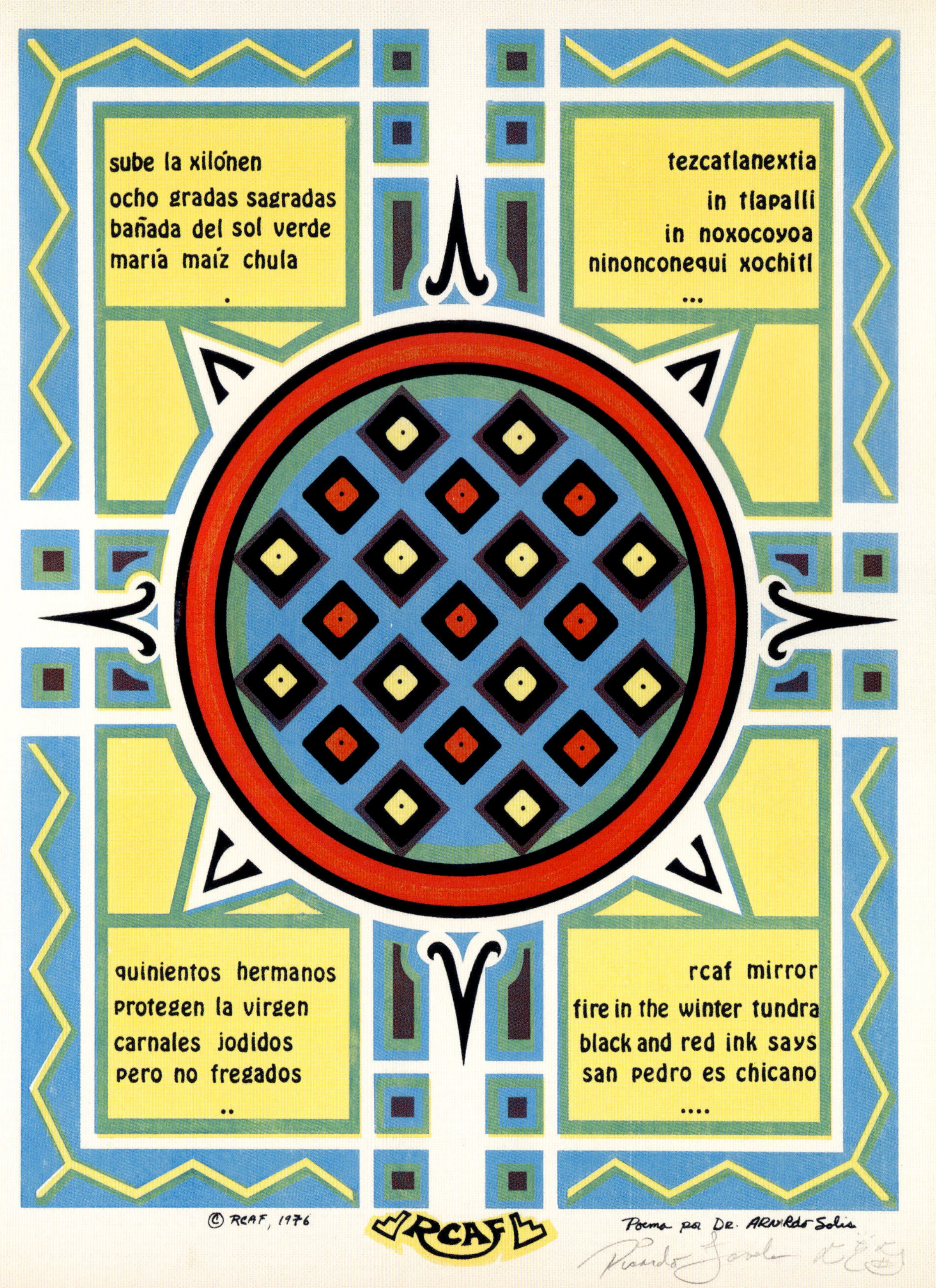

Ricardo Favela (1944–2007), *Sube La Xilónen*, 1976. Poem by Dr. Arnaldo Solis [Plate 60].

Sube La Xilónen

Dr. Arnaldo Solis
1976

sube la xilónen
ocho gradas sagradas
bañada del sol verde
maría maíz chula
.

quinientos hermanos
protegen la virgen
carnales jodidos
pero no fregados
. .

tezcatlanextia
in tlapalli
in noxocoyoa
ninonconequi xochitl
. . .

rcaf mirror
fire in the winter tundra
black and red inks says
san pedro es chicano
. . . .

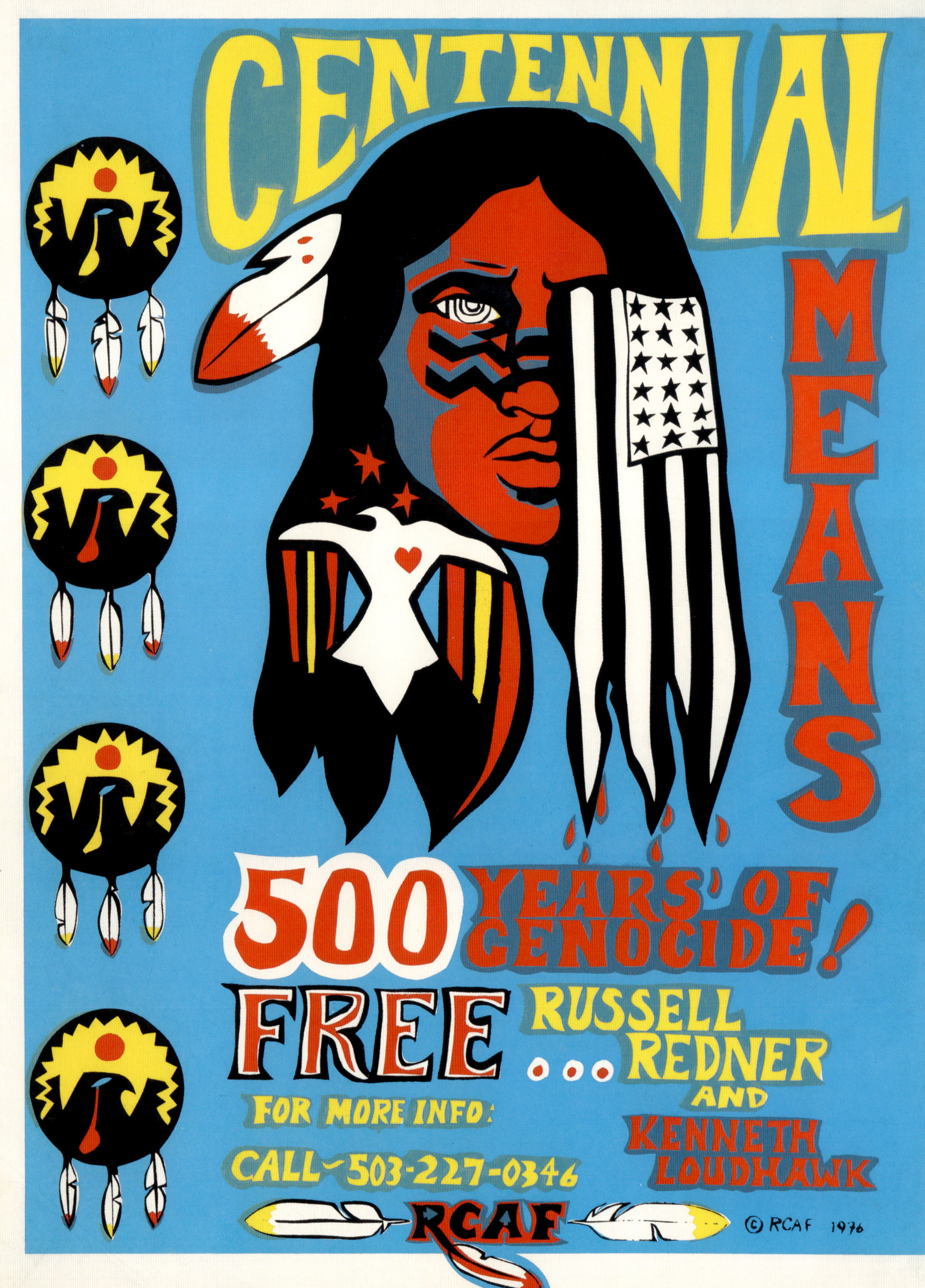
CENTENNIAL
MEANS
500 YEARS OF GENOCIDE!
FREE ... RUSSELL REDNER AND KENNETH LOUDHAWK
FOR MORE INFO:
CALL ~ 503-227-0346
RCAF
© RCAF 1976

JESÚS BARRAZA

Ancestral Lineage: The Indigenous Solidarity Posters of the Royal Chicano Air Force

As an artist I have been fortunate to meet and learn from Chicano Movement artists throughout my life. While learning printmaking at Mission Gráfica in San Francisco, I worked with its director, Juan R. Fuentes, who taught me his process of creating posters. More importantly, he passed down a history of printmaking that helped me to become a part of an artistic lineage, carrying on the traditions of those who came before me and passing them down to future generations. In this essay, I explore this lineage and its relationship to the posters of the Royal Chicano Air Force (RCAF), specifically those made in solidarity with Native communities in the United States. These posters can also be seen as an embodiment of Gloria Anzaldúa's concept of "spiritual activism" and its "ethics of interconnectivity," which reaches beyond the internal wounds of colonization to bring about connection with others.[1] As part of this artistic lineage, I have also come to understand the RCAF's politics of solidarity within my own practice and through co-founding Dignidad Rebelde, an Oakland-based graphic arts collaborative that uses art to highlight community struggles and support global Indigenous and people of color movements.

Like many young Mexican Americans, I struggled at school while growing up. It was not until my older sister introduced me to the student activism within the Chicano Movement that I felt excited to learn. She brought home many books from college that opened up a whole new world for me to explore, but it was the catalogue from the exhibition *Chicano Art: Resistance and Affirmation (CARA)* that set my mind on fire. Its essays and artworks revealed a history of resistance I was never taught in school, and the posters impressed me the most, especially *José Montoya's Pachuco Art, A Historical Update,* created by the RCAF's Rodolfo "Rudy" Cuellar and Luis "Louie the Foot" González. The colorful poster featured RCAF-member José Montoya's *calaca pachuco* dressed up in his zoot suit, and it represented another world that I wanted to join (pl. 36).

Ricardo Favela (1944–2007), *Centennial Means 500 Years of Genocide!*, 1976 [Plate 83].

A decade later, posters became my medium of choice, and I began to study the prints of the RCAF. In 2006, I met Rudy, Juan "Juanishi" Orosco, and Esteban Villa at the opening of the *Chicano* exhibition at the de Young Museum in San Francisco. Later, I visited with Rudy and Louie at their studio, and I listened to their stories of screenprinting in the 1970s. Rudy recounted the collaborative nature of the process, given the many roles that were part of their production methods, from holding the screen up, positioning paper, and running the squeegee, to racking the posters to dry.[2] For me, it not only demonstrated the collective spirit of the RCAF but also demystified the idea of the artist as a lone creator. I developed a deeper appreciation for their methodology and, especially, their posters.

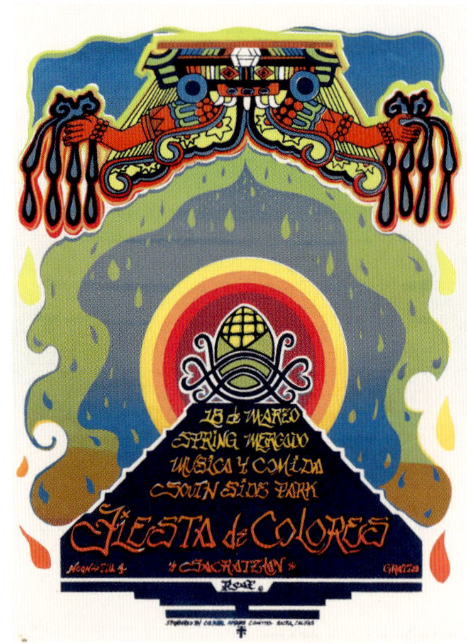

Fig. 1. Juanishi Orosco (1945–2023), *Fiesta de Colores*, 1979 [Plate 64].

As a young printer studying Chicana/o poster history, I was inspired not only by the RCAF's powerful posters for the *Movimiento* and its collective approach, but also by the group's prolific poster production for the Chicana/o community. I wanted to be like them, to print as many posters as humanly possible; to make art that inspired *la comunidad*, the people. Most importantly, I wanted to make artwork where people could see themselves represented. As a poster artist, I reflected on the aesthetic power and activist role of the RCAF's posters and those of many other artists created in the 1970s. The RCAF's huge archive of prints also allowed me to trace their lineage toward a practice defined by their politics of solidarity with Native peoples.

Influenced by the Bay Area's Third World internationalist history, I was drawn to posters created in support of sociopolitical struggles.[3] As a mentor, artist, and activist, Fuentes had also shown me that internationalist solidarity had a similar cultural and political trajectory. As part of the Movement's call for pride in an Indigenous heritage, Chicanas/os began to ask questions and to learn about where their Indigenous ancestry came from in Mexico. What resulted from this process was a Chicana/o consciousness documented through the art of the Movement and through new images that reflected *La Nueva Raza*.[4] Beginning in the early 1970s, the RCAF interpreted this key moment with posters that served as visual representations and documentation of their Indigenous ceremonies and helped to trace the ways Chicanas/os were reconnecting with their Indigenous ancestry.

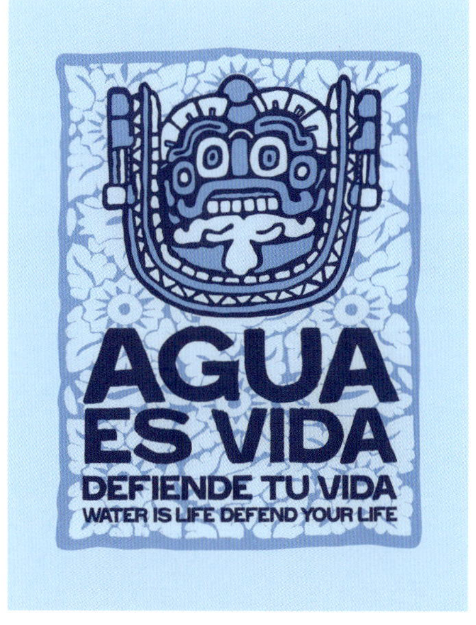

Fig. 2. Jesús Barraza (born 1976), *Agua es Vida, Defiende Tu Vida*, 2012. Screenprint, 26 × 20 in. Collection of the Artist.

The RCAF's posters also exemplified the art of *La Nueva Raza* by incorporating contemporary interpretations of ancient iconography into their work. As such, the RCAF's ceremony posters represented an aesthetic return to an Indigenous spirituality as well. In college, I started going to various Bay Area ceremonies and later discovered the posters. They made me realize these events had been part of the Chicana/o community for decades and by participating, I felt like part of an intergenerational historic movement. For example, Juanishi's poster for the *Fiesta de Colores* (1979; fig. 1) influenced my *Agua es Vida, Defiende Tu Vida* (2012; fig. 2) print, and specifically the image of the Aztec rain god, Tlaloc. Through examples like this, RCAF artists' Mesoamerican iconography moved me to work with images of other Aztec gods and goddesses, and my work became a link helping to sustain the spirit of the RCAF and the *Movimiento* through the generations.

Some of the RCAF's most impactful posters were announcements for their Día de los Muertos and other Danza Azteca–related ceremonies, which helped me understand how the modern Xicanx *Indigenismo* I embraced had its roots in the 1960s and 1970s, as Chicanas/os reconnected with their Indigenous ancestry. Thus, in the 2000s, when I saw Ricardo Favela's *Centennial Means 500 Years of Genocide!* (1976; pl. 83) poster online, it reinforced a connection I recognized between Xicanxs and Native peoples who both struggle for liberation from the colonial confines that work to strangle us together. I saw RCAF posters as a way to create both a bridge of solidarity between Native American communities and enhance Anzaldúa's "spiritual activism": "We need artistic expressions and efforts that heal and inspire, that generate enough energy to make a difference in our lives and in those of others. We must create new art forms that support transformation."[5] Through the solidarity shown in their posters, RCAF artists gave voice to a shift in the consciousness within the Chicana/o and Native American communities toward working together and seeing each other as relatives in a mutual struggle for decolonization.[6] Ricardo's poster is an example of this lineage, a thread that runs from the 1960s to today.

During the height of the Movement, Chicanas/os were also making artistic and activist connections with Native American communities, creating posters in support of their cultural heritage and political struggles for self-determination. An early example is the RCAF poster *Native American Indian Alliance Culture Days* (1975; fig. 3), which was a collaboration between Celia Herrera Rodriguez, Rudy, and Louie.[7] Celia was asked by Nomtipom Wintu artist and Sacramento State (officially California State University, Sacramento) Professor Frank LaPena to produce a poster promoting the Alliance's annual Culture Days on campus. She attributed much of the poster's design to her experiences in LaPena's classes and his ability to provide an historical "grounding of California and see art not just as something that started with all the Western European methodologies, but to see basketmaking, carving as well as [Native] music and dance traditions not as folk art, but as art forms that were much older."[8] This comes through in her melding of California Native iconography and Mesoamerican stamp patterns, creating a sense of solidarity through imagery. The two-layer design made it quick to produce, while the use of a three-color split-fountain in the background provided an economical way to add multiple colors behind the text and graphics. The second layer is hand drawn, made before the days of computer-aided design, with text created using Letraset rub-on letters or by a typesetter. In this instance, Celia designed her type, creating three different styles for the poster: the primary text with sharp corners resembling basket designs; the secondary type face with a more rounded look; and the third, a simplified version of the first with its own flourishes.

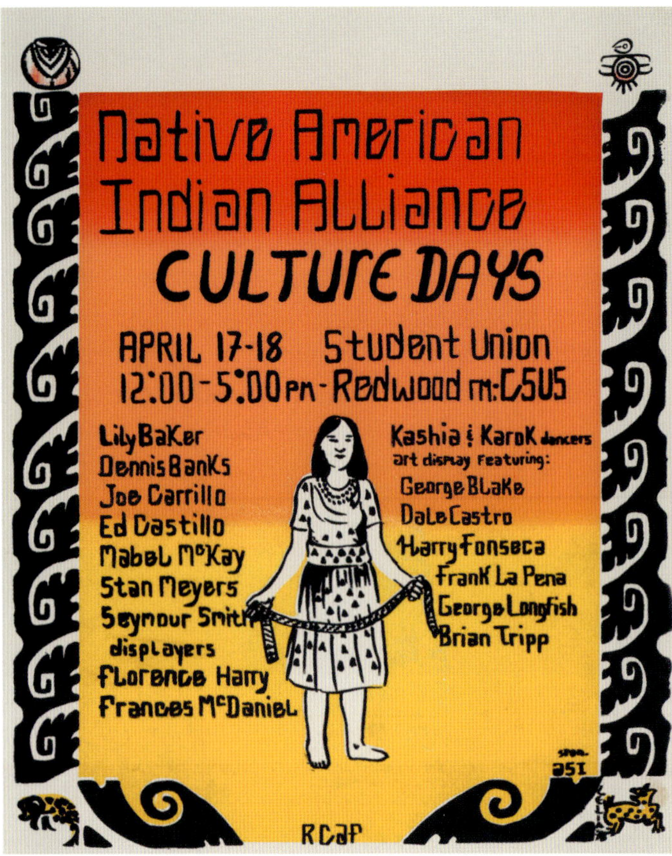

Fig. 3. Celia Herrera Rodriguez (born 1952), Rudy O. Cuellar (born 1950), and Luis C. González (born 1953), *Native American Indian Alliance Culture Days*, 1975 [Plate 81].

Celia's composition features a Northern California Native dancer with a long ribbon in her hand participating in a ceremony, rocking her arms and moving the ribbon to the beat of the clapper sticks being played by musicians. This style of ceremonial dance is shared by many of the state's northern Indigenous groups and provides an inter-tribal perspective that is also reflected in the poster's list of participants, including artists, who represented various Indigenous groups. The four corners of the poster include small symbols of a basket, eagle, deer, and salmon, all cultural markers that Celia incorporated "from the story telling I was experiencing in Frank LaPena's classes ... [and] the symbols that were being shown there."[9] Three sides of the border design have a Mexica stamp pattern taken from Jorge Enciso's 1953 book *Design Motifs of Ancient Mexico*, which Celia included to represent her Chicana culture and heritage.[10] She had studied symbols from ancient Mexican pottery, weavings, and baskets and felt that "these are the same things, we're just looking at the displaced or decontextualized symbols that [Enciso] found in the cultural remains. So, I wanted to use them."[11] For Celia the stamp patterns offered a sense of connection between Native Americans and Chicanas/os, a type of solidarity that asks to be seen as relatives.

She also noted that during the 1970s there was collaboration between the groups within the Ethnic Studies Department that generated joint programming, such as the annual "Third World Writers and Thinkers" symposium (pl. 9). She believes that this camaraderie also made it possible for Chicana/o students to create a poster for a Native American event.[12]

I have used this same perspective to forge solidarity between Xicanx and California Native people in the San Francisco Bay Area, specifically the Lisjan (Ohlone) and their Sogorea Te Land Trust. Created in consultation with these groups, my graphics incorporate aspects of their iconography, including spiritual and cultural imagery. I see this regional solidarity as another example of the lineage of Chicanas/os and Indigenous peoples working together to dismantle the colonial system that oppresses us across the continent.

Other connections made between Xicanxs and Northern Indigenous people during the 1970s helped solidify the bond that came with the mutual recognition of Chicana/o Indigeneity. The American Indian Movement's (AIM) spiritual leader Leonard Crow Dog (Oglala Sioux) invited a group of Chicanas/os to attend the Sun Dance ceremony at his home, Crow Dog's Paradise, in South Dakota. This brought Lakota spiritual practices, including the sweat lodge and the ceremonies from the Native American Church, to the Chicana/o community.[13] I started attending the sweat lodge ceremonies in college, and I now reflect on the impact this knowledge had with other Chicanas/os from California. For example, Danza Quetzalcoatl-Citlalli's leader Jesse "Chuy" Ortiz participated in the Sun Dance ceremony in South Dakota, and he, along with other RCAF members, incorporated the sweat lodge ritual as part of their preparation for the community ceremonies.[14]

In addition to their documentation of important ceremonies, I was inspired by the role RCAF posters played in Indigenous political activism, with their messages against the genocide of Native Americans and the US government's continued discrimination against Native peoples. In José Montoya's *Dennis Banks* (c. 1976; fig. 4) poster, the high-contrast portrait of the Ojibwe AIM leader was created in the artist's trademark sketching style, an aesthetic continued throughout the design. The poster exemplifies what can be visually achieved with three layers, including a split fountain that creates a sense of a light focused on Banks's face. In his expression we see a longing for liberation, for the freedom of his people from the constraints of colonialism and an end to the persecution he faced as an Indigenous person who stood up to the government's horrific mistreatment of his people. Around his neck, Banks wears a medallion with the United Farm Workers (UFW) eagle, a sacred bird for Chicanas/os and the Ojibwe, visually linking the Chicano Movement with the AIM. The bottom features the text "Stop His Extradition," the process that the State of South Dakota demanded from California for Banks's participation in the Wounded Knee Occupation. California Governor Jerry Brown denied the extradition request on the grounds

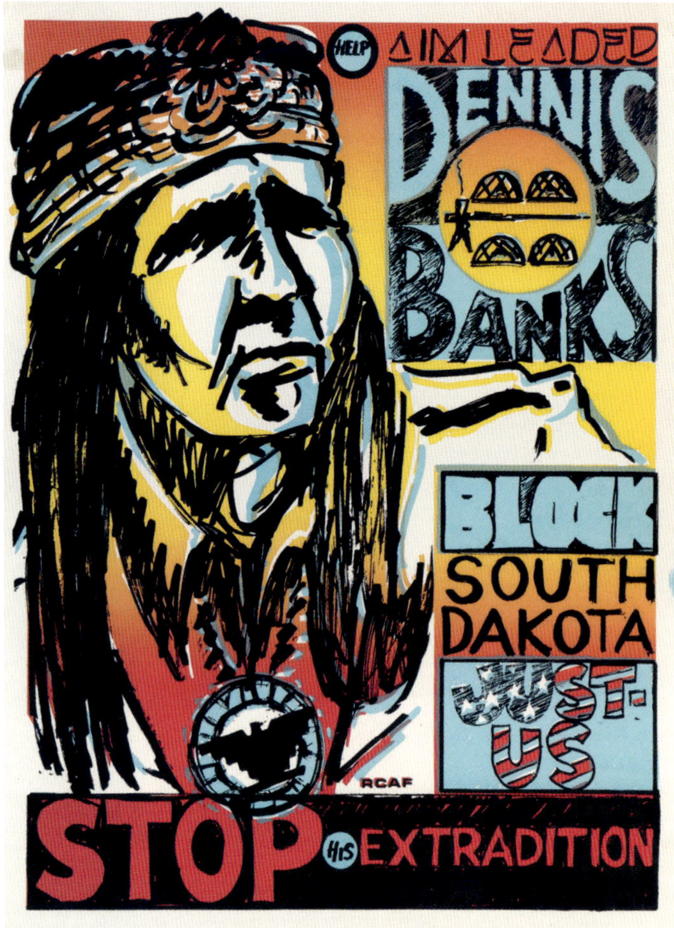

Fig. 4. José Montoya (1932–2013), *Dennis Banks*, c. 1976 [Plate 84].

that surrendering Banks could endanger his life.[15] Thus, the plea in José's poster to help the AIM leader contributed to a wider, cross-cultural campaign to help Banks remain a free man.[16]

José's poster can also be a reminder of a time when social justice activists were actively and publicly pursued by the government, such as the cases against Angela Davis and Assata Shakur. Like José, I have also created posters that feature individuals who have been labeled as criminals for defending their communities against the United States' unequal interpretation of "Just-US," as noted in his poster. "We struggle to decolonize and valorize our worldviews," noted Anzaldúa, "views that the dominant cultures imagine as other, as based on ignorance."[17] My print of Captain Jack (Kintpuash) of the Modoc (1837–1873) is based on a drawing of the leader made while he was jailed by the US military as an "enemy of the state" for defending his people and their land (fig. 5). I tried to capture the essence of an Indigenous man persecuted for seeking the liberation of his people. Captain Jack's legacy depends on one's positionality or perspective,

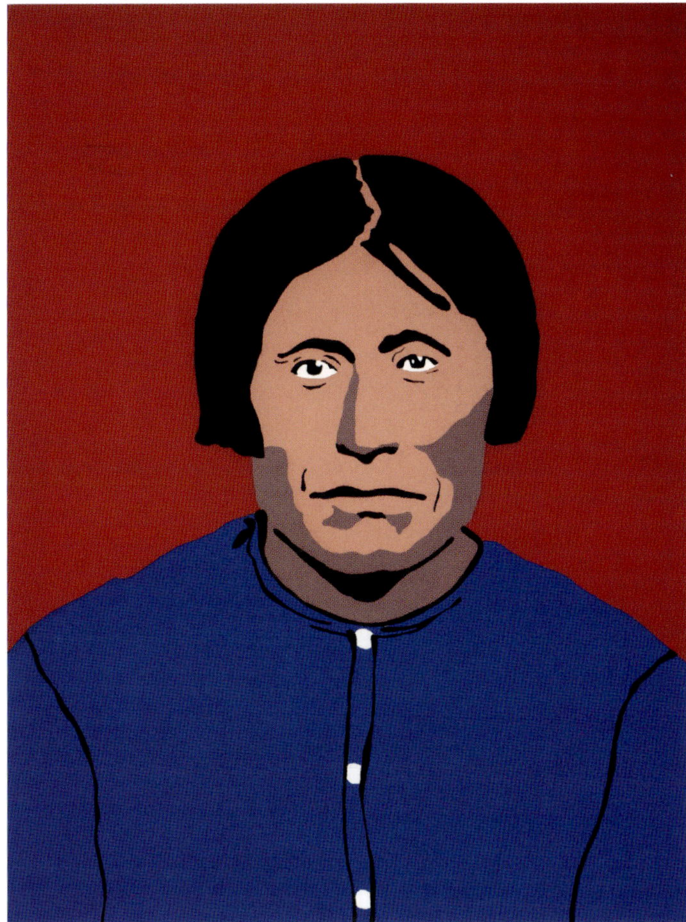

Fig. 5. Jesús Barraza (born 1976), *Capt. Jack*, 2001. Screenprint, 30 × 22 in. Collection of the Artist.

and as a Xicanx *Indigena* I see him as a hero, while the dominant society of the time saw him as an enemy.

Ricardo's *Centennial Means 500 Years of Genocide!* (1976; pl. 83) poster stands in solidarity with AIM members Russell Redner and Kenneth Loud Hawk, demanding their freedom after the pair were arrested in Oregon. Like many other AIM members, Redner and Loud Hawk were seen as enemies of the state for their defense of Lakota sovereignty at the Pine Ridge Indian Reservation in South Dakota. Acting on FBI information, Oregon state police officers stopped Redner and Loud Hawk's car while looking for Dennis Banks and Leonard Peltier.[18] When the police did not find who they were looking for, they arrested Redner and Loud Hawk for illegally possessing firearms and explosives, charges that were dismissed in 1988 after thirteen years of pretrial.[19] The primary text of Ricardo's poster connects Redner's and Loud Hawk's imprisonment not only with the US's second centennial in 1976 but also a genocide that began in 1492 with Columbus's arrival in the Caribbean. In so doing, it condemns the racist

US legal system that has persecuted Indigenous peoples fighting to protect their land from settler colonialism. However, the poster looks beyond the colonial history of the US, tying the plight of contemporary Indigenous people with a genocide that occurred throughout Abya Yala at the hands of multiple colonial entities.[20] As such, the poster serves as an indictment of all colonial enterprises that have led to the oppression and death of Indigenous people.

The central figure in Ricardo's poster confronts the viewer with a defiant stare. This is a man standing up to the history of US violence against Indigenous people, most recently in the incarceration of Redner and Loud Hawk and the persecution of other AIM members. The man's face is partly obscured by a black-and-white US flag dripping blood onto the text below, which reads "500 Years of Genocide." Thus, the blood represents not only the Indigenous lives murdered in the name of Manifest Destiny but also those taken throughout Abya Yala by the violence of colonialism. To the left of the face, an eagle feather appears from behind his head. I've been taught that these feathers hold special significance to Native Americans because eagles fly the highest of any bird in the sky, getting as close as possible to the Creator. As we follow his hair down his shoulder, we see an eagle with a red heart, with three stars above its head and its wings spread. I consider the eagle's sacred significance here as a blessing and in contrast to the death emanating from the US flag. The eagle seems to soar through the sky with a freedom for which Indigenous people yearn. On the left is a series of four eagle shields, representing the four cardinal directions and the four elements (water, fire, earth, and air). In Ricardo's composition, the shields adorned with eagle feathers may signify protection for the figure in the poster, and symbolically with Redner and Loud Hawk, as they face the colonial violence of the carceral system.

The act of solidarity as expressed through artmaking attempts to make connections between people. In Ricardo's *Centennial* poster, he connected Chicanas/os with Native peoples living through state violence. In this manner, the RCAF solidarity posters strive to transform society and to demonstrate how, as relatives, Chicana/o oppression is bound with that of Native peoples. These posters reflect a politics of solidarity and self-determination, along with a demand for a rejection of this country's colonial ideas of justice and a recognition of the history of genocide in the Americas.

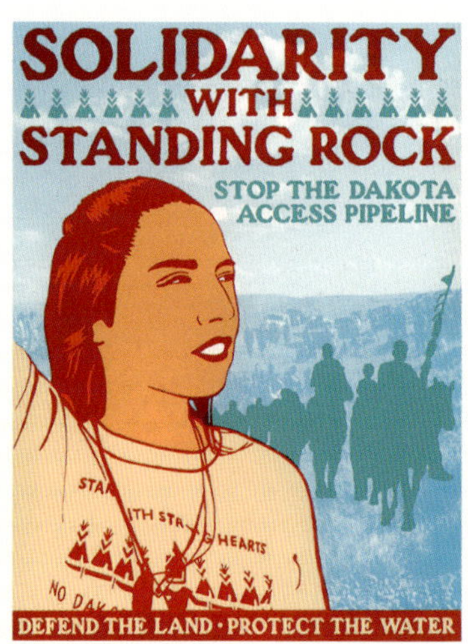

Fig. 6. Jesús Barraza (born 1976), *Solidarity with Standing Rock*, 2018. Screenprint, 26 × 20 in. Collection of the Artist.

Support of Indigenous activism has been an important part of my art practice as well. In 2016, I created *Solidarity with Standing Rock* to express Xicanx solidarity with North and South Dakota's Standing Rock Sioux Tribe's demand for sovereignty and right for self-determination as expressed in their rejection of an oil pipeline on their lands (fig. 6). The RCAF's solidarity posters helped me to understand my role as a cultural worker in a decolonial struggle. It is this lineage of resistance that I continue in my work.

In her book *Flying Under the Radar with the Royal Chicano Air Force*, Ella Maria Diaz connected Rudy's *Día de la Raza* (1975; fig. 7) poster with the *Indian Land*

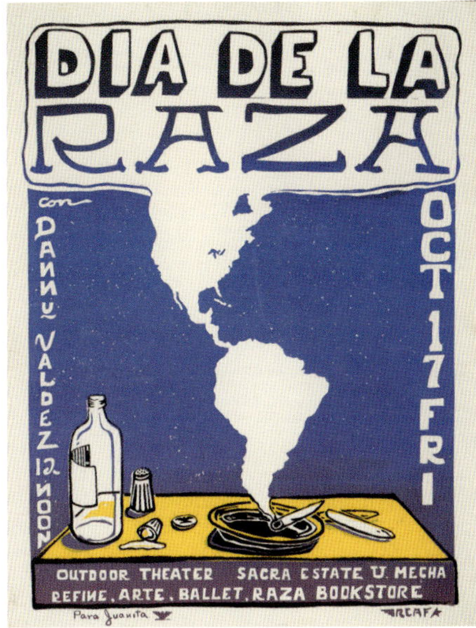

Fig. 7 Rudy O. Cuellar (born 1950), *Día de la Raza*, 1975 [Plate 21].

(2004; fig. 8) print designed by Nancy Hernandez and me, asserting that my depiction of Abya Yala without the lines of modern borders demonstrated a continuation of a "decolonial message."[21] Rudy's poster depicts a kitchen table with a bottle; shot glass; salt; UFW button; and an ashtray with a joint, the smoke of which wafts up to form a map of the Americas against the cosmos in the background. As Diaz points out, both maps are liberated from colonial borders to show a unified Abya Yala, one that looks forward to a future in which Indigenous people have autonomy over their ancestral lands. At the time, Rudy did not consider these Indigenous politics within his poster. His intention was to make a still life, which he thought was a neglected genre in Chicana/o art. His depiction of the continent as smoke coming out of the joint was also his attempt to capture the "beauty of how smoke is sensual."[22] Yet in Rudy's poster a visual connection is made between the borderless Americas and the celebration of Día de la Raza, which was the Chicana/o rebuttal to Columbus Day and a recognition of a mixed-race heritage that included Indigenous blood. My *Indian Land* poster supports the Land Back movement, which reminds us that as Xicanxs our liberation is bound with that of Indigenous people throughout Abya Yala.[23] It is also a Xicanx call for a return of ancestral land to its rightful caretakers. Even with different intentions, both posters reflect a vision of the Americas without colonial borders.

Rudy created his poster in 1975, the year before I was born. Twenty-nine years later, I produced *Indian Land* as a fundraiser to be sold at the annual Indigenous People's Day sunrise ceremony at Alcatraz Island. Thus, both posters were made for the same holiday, completely by coincidence. Done almost thirty years apart, I believe these posters share a Chicana/o perspective that is grounded in Indigenous solidarity and together are a continuation of a methodology that has been passed down through the generations. Through this practice one comes into a consciousness that creates new perspectives and ways of understanding the world. In the words of Anzaldúa, "*Te entregas a tu promesa* to help your various cultures create new paradigms, new narratives."[24] In this manner, posters created in solidarity with Native American people challenge dominant ways of seeing the world and offer a decolonial perspective. I see the RCAF artists' solidarity posters representing this challenge to the US empire, which I continue almost fifty years later as an artist. It is a lineage that I am proud to carry from the artists who came before me and for the Xicanx artists who will come after.

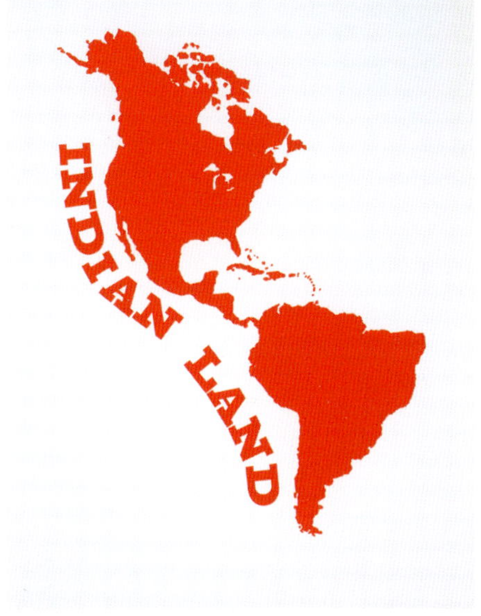

Fig. 8. Jesús Barraza (born 1976) and Nancy Hernandez (born 1980), *Indian Land*, 2004. Screenprint, 23 × 17½ in. Collection of the Artist.

Notes

1 Gloria Anzaldúa, *Light in the Dark/Luz en lo Oscuro: Rewriting Identity, Spirituality, Reality*, ed. Ana Louise Keating (Duke University Press, 2015), xxiii.

2 Rodolfo "Rudy" Cuellar, conversation with author, June 2015.

3 To learn more about Bay Area Third World internationalist history, see Jason Ferreira, "With the Soul of a Human Rainbow: Los Siete, Black Panthers, and Third Worldism in San Francisco," in *Ten Years that Shook the City: San Francisco 1968–1978*, ed. Chris Carlsson (City Lights Foundation Books, 2011).

4 I am referencing Malaquias Montoya's poster *New Symbols for la Nueva Raza* (1969), made for the Mexican American Liberation Art Front (MALAF) exhibition of the same name. A co-founder of the Oakland-based MALAF, Montoya stated in an interview, "Up to that first exhibition we talked about how many of us had felt about who we were, *el indio, la india, el negrito*, those names we were called and how terrible we felt. And all of a sudden, we're discussing what beautiful people we are [and how] we have to create images of ourselves we are proud of." I see the idea of "La Nueva Raza" as a people who are proud of who they are and use art to express a sense of pride in themselves and their ancestors. See *Visions of Aztlán*, directed by Jesús Salvador Treviño (Barrio Dog Productions Inc., 2010).

5 Anzaldúa, *Light in the Dark*, 92.

6 I am using the word "relative" as in the Lakota concept of Mitákuye Oyás'iŋ or "All Are Related," a sense of interconnectedness between all living things.

7 For the poster, Celia created the artwork and selected the colors, while Rudy and Louie screenprinted it.

8 Celia Herrera Rodriguez, telephone interview by author, December 2, 2024.

9 Celia Herrera Rodriguez, telephone interview by author, November 21, 2024. Celia also credits her experiences with professors José Montoya and Esteban Villa as important to her formation as an activist, thinker, and artist.

10 Jorge Enciso, *Design Motifs of Ancient Mexico* (Dover Publications Inc., 1953), 23.

11 Herrera Rodriguez telephone interview, November 21, 2024.

12 Celia Herrera Rodriguez, telephone interview by author, December 11, 2024.

13 Celia Herrera Rodriguez, interview by author, February 26, 2016.

14 Gina Montoya, telephone interview by author, October 2, 2024. Gina and Ortiz were two of the founding members of the Cultural Affairs Committee, a collaboration among the RCAF's Centro de Artistas Chicanos, Breakfast for Niños, La Raza Bookstore/La Raza Galeria Posada, and community groups and members.

15 Governor Brown refused to extradite Banks to South Dakota. In a letter to South Dakota Governor Richard F. Kneip, he wrote that he had "probative information, including sworn statements, that raise a substantial question of the likelihood of danger to Mr. Banks if he were returned." See "California Bars the Extradition of Dennis Banks," *New York Times*, April 20, 1978.

16 Members of the RCAF were involved at Deganawidah-Quetzalcoatl University, also known as D-Q University, a Chicana/o and Native American Tribal College located in Yolo County, California. At the culmination of ten months of "political, legal, and social agitation" to establish D-Q University, a Victory Day celebration was held on the site of the future campus. The celebration included "Native and Chicano leaders, scholars, and activists," music by Paul Ortega, and an exhibition organized by José Montoya and Esteban Villa of their artwork. See Joshua Frank-Cardenas, "The Rise and Fall of D-Q University: Foundations," *Tribal College Journal of American Indian Higher Education* 31, no. 2 (Winter 2019), https://tribalcollegejournal.org/the-rise-and-fall-of-d-q-university-foundations. According to Ella Maria Diaz, in 1971 a "Chicano Art" class taught by Montoya and Villa was listed in the D-Q University newspaper. Ella Maria Diaz, *Flying Under the Radar with the Royal Chicano Air Force: Mapping a Chicano/a Art History* (University of Texas Press, 2017), 53. Rodolfo "Rudy" Cuellar, *The Country Workshops (DQU)*, ca. 1970s, and Luis C. González, *DQU Benefit*, ca. 1970s.

17 Anzaldúa, *Light in the Dark*, 90.

18 Leonard Peltier was wanted for the killing of two FBI agents on the Pine Ridge Indian Reservation in 1975. See "Former Indian Leader Sentenced to Probation," *New York Times*, March 9, 1988.

19 Kenneth S. Stern, *Loud Hawk* (University of Oklahoma Press, 2002), viii.

20 Abya Yala is the Indigenous name given to the Americas in the Kuna language and has been adopted by many Indigenous communities as a rejection of the colonial name that was given by Europeans to the land. I chose to use Abya Yala as an alternative to the "Americas" and as a way for me to ascribe to a "decolonial message" that looks beyond borders and the 532 years of colonial history.

21 Diaz, *Flying Under the Radar*, 6.

22 Rodolfo "Rudy" Cuellar, interview by author, December 8, 2024.

23 Land Back is a contemporary movement that calls for "reclaiming Indigenous spheres of influence and sovereignty and extending our values to result in better stewardship of ecological, political, and economic systems." See N. A. Pieratos, S. S. Manning, and N. Tilsen, "Land Back: A Meta Narrative to Help Indigenous People Show Up as Movement Leaders," *Leadership* 17, no. 1 (2021): 47–61.

24 The Spanish translates as "You commit to your promise"; Anzaldúa, *Light in the Dark*, 138.

Yo Soy Chicano

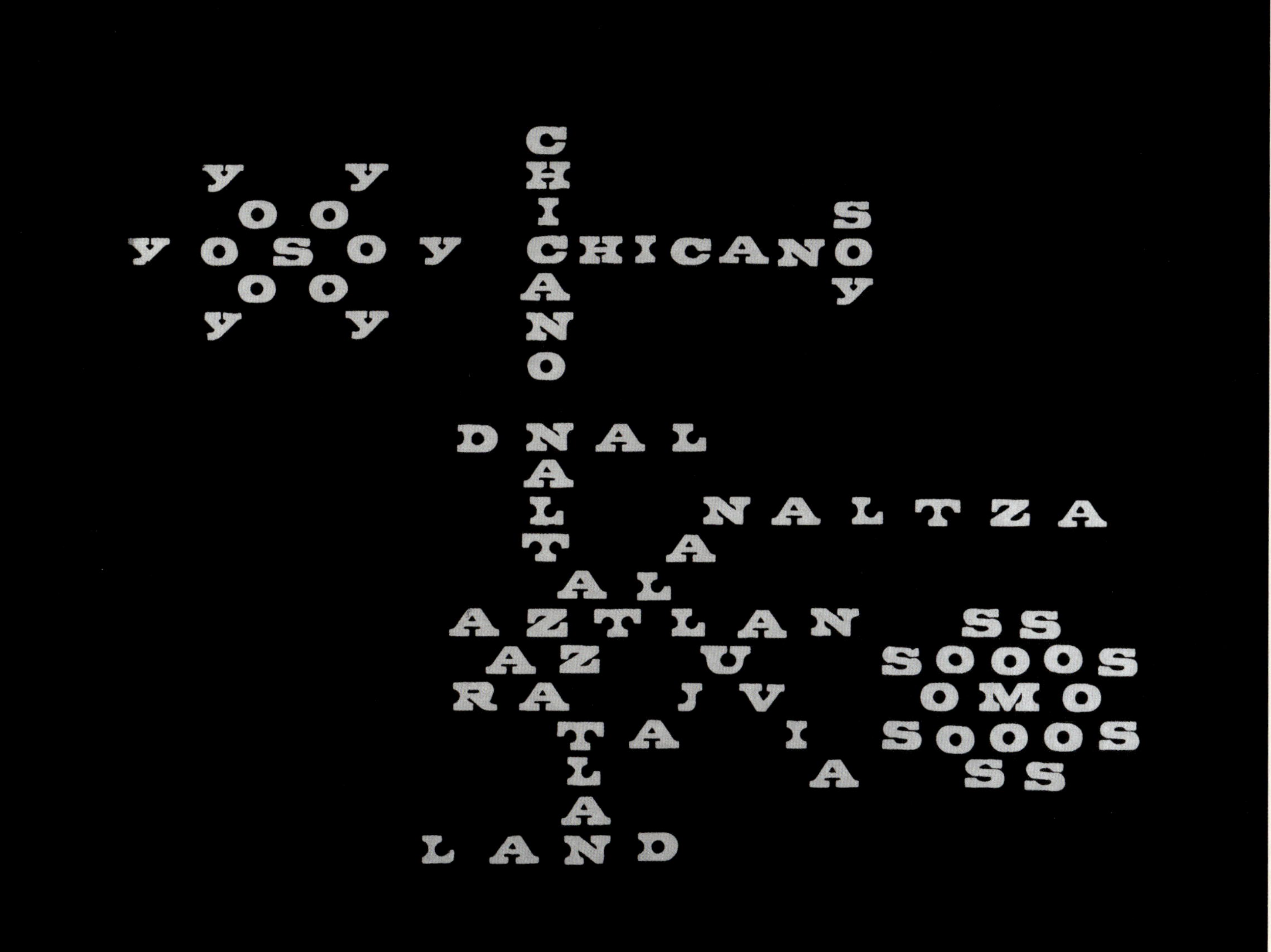

Luis C. González (born 1953), *Yo Soy Chicano*, 1975 [Plate 32].

c r
c s r
c i r
c m r
c o e r
c o n a m o r t l r
c c e l a r o a r
o i a m o r a z a
n c m a z a r o m a
t a c o s e r a
s c o n r l
a c o r e
f c z r a p t
o o c a r e z
s a m o r o m a s
z e r a c o o
t p a r z c f
e r o c a
l r n o c s
a r e s o c a t
a m o r a z a m c n
a z a r o m a i c o
a r a o r a l e c c
r l t r o m a n o c
r e o c
r m c
r i c
r s c
r c

telaraña(másomenos)chicana

TATIANA REINOZA

Louie the Foot's Poetic Abstractions of Aztlán

In 1974, the artist-poet Luis Carlos González created the concrete poem "telaraña (másomenos) chicana," a rarity in the corpus of Chicana/o art and literature (fig. 1).[1] There were many poets and artists in the heyday of the Chicano Movement, but few of them combined their skills into the interdisciplinary practice of concrete poetry whereby letters, words, and phrases are arranged into a visual composition. To create the structure for this concrete poem, González, who is better known by his moniker "Louie the Foot," placed diagonal lines of "r"s and "c"s to form an X at the center. The black background and blue lettering add a celestial dimension reinforcing the cosmic nature of the piece, while the poem's shape also alludes to a spiderweb, with the lettering doubling as linework. In this dynamic textual composition, the viewer is encouraged to read and seek meaning in various directions as the eye moves across, down, and backward. By doing so, the reader enters into an intellectual game that conjures the words and utterances of what being Chicano means to the poet: "con safos," "simón," "tacos," "órale," until we reach the center and the words "razón" and "amor." Through this playful gesture, González reminds us that the reason he calls himself Chicano is from a place of love—love for himself, for his family, for his ethnic heritage—in a society intent on destroying and disparaging what he holds dear.

Concrete poetry was an international movement with origins in Latin America and Europe that developed in the early 1950s. By the time González enrolled at Sacramento State College (later California State University, Sacramento, and popularly known as Sacramento State) in 1971, concrete poetry was a worldwide phenomenon recognized in the publication of anthologies and major exhibitions such as the *International Concrete Poetry* (1966) exhibition at Galería Universitaria Aristos of the National Autonomous University of Mexico (UNAM) in Mexico City, and the Stedelijk Museum's *Sound Texts, Concrete Poetry, Visual Texts* (1971) in Amsterdam.[2] As an English and history double major, who was already coming into his own as a poet, González spent time at the college's library studying the

Fig. 1. Luis C. González (born 1953), *telaraña (másomenos) chicana*, from the book *Concreto y con safos*, 1974. Screenprint, 11 ¾ × 9 in. Collection of Luis C. González.

work of the trend's foremost exponents, particularly the Brazilian Noigandres Group (Décio Pignatari, and the brothers Augusto and Haroldo de Campos).[3] Their poems were visual objects, much like the posters his friends in the Rebel Chicano Art Front (later known as the Royal Chicano Air Force, or RCAF) were making in support of the United Farm Workers (UFW), but in his case language was the subject matter and the medium with which to construct a composition. González was drawn to concrete poetry for two reasons: the movement was multilingual and spoke to a utopian interconnected world, and it offered unparalleled freedom from the rules of art and language.

This essay focuses on González's numerous experiments with concrete poetry, most of which took place in 1974 and 1975 and resulted in the production of poems, posters, chapbooks, and anthologies. First, I will delve into González's early years in Sacramento and explore how these experiences became the foundation of a practice based on humor and code-switching. Then I turn to the importance of poetry in the Chicano Movement. As a young poet and activist, González was politicized by the *Movimiento* but also found within its cultural spheres a life of letters that held a liberatory potential. However, he did not follow the paths established by such canonical figures as Alurista, Juan Felipe Herrera, and José Montoya. González broke ground within this cultural intelligentsia by creating concrete poems that went beyond the confines of Chicana/o literary nationalism. I further contextualize González's concrete poems within this global network of artists whose playful experiments with art and language created multisensory experiences. I argue that González's concrete poetry harnessed this tension between the local and the global as a way to internationalize and give visual form to poetic abstractions of Aztlán.

Coming of Age as a *Poeta*

In the realm of Chicana/o poets and artists, González stands out for having been born in Mexico and raised fully bilingual. His parents had emigrated from Jalisco to Sacramento in the late 1940s to work in the canneries. His dad, a former bracero, never learned to speak English. Out of necessity, his bilingual mother took on the role of being the public face of her family. González explained, "She was as *Mexicana* as they come, so you couldn't bullshit her in either language."[4] When his mother was pregnant with him, his grandmother, who lived in Mexico City, fell deathly ill, and they made the trip back to care for her. The first six months of his life were spent there with extended family. Returning to Sacramento, he grew up in a home with his parents, siblings, and *tias* where language and code-switching became a way of life, and an entry point into lightness and humor. González's witty and clever wordplay came from this bilingual, bicultural environment: the Spanish of home coming through in a term of endearment or during a night watching Cine de Oro films with Mexican movie stars like Cantinflas and Tin Tan, the Spanglish he spoke with his siblings, and the official English of the school day.

By the age of fourteen, González was beginning his writing practice and was growing more conscientious of the overarching struggle for civil rights. He joined the Junior Brown Berets, a pro-Chicana/o paramilitary group that modeled itself after the Black Panther Party.[5] In their meetings and through their minister of information, the youth affiliated with the Brown Berets discussed issues of police brutality, inequities in education, and labor rights for Mexican Americans. After moving to the south side of Sacramento, he attended Luther Burbank High School, where the school newspaper provided the young writer a venue for reflection. He likewise began to experiment with poetry as an expression of his Chicanismo, the cultural and political movement that emerged in the 1960s calling for self-determination for Mexican Americans, and through the Brown Berets he would go on to meet the acclaimed artist-poet José Montoya and the painter Esteban Villa.[6]

Protests and public actions likewise shaped his revolutionary fervor. On August 29, 1970, the Los Angeles Chicano Moratorium brought together a broad-based coalition of more than twenty thousand people in one of the largest anti-war protests in California history. Police responded with brutal force, and the murder of *Los Angeles Times* journalist Ruben Salazar ignited a series of protests and civil disobedience actions. González was seventeen years old when he heard the news and decided to drive to East Los Angeles with a group of Brown Berets, as well as Montoya and Villa. On September 16, 1970, the annual celebration for Mexican Independence Day, González found himself in the middle of a large-scale protest. He was attacked by LAPD officers wielding batons and was subsequently saved by other protesters.[7] The event ignited something in him, and Chicanismo offered a language in which to articulate this desire for justice.

González's creative education came from inside and outside the academy. He enrolled at Sacramento State and declared both English and history as his majors. A number of influential professors helped him to develop political awareness and hone his craft. He took courses like "History of Mexico" and "The Mexican Revolution" with Joseph Pitti and Leslie J. Royal, "Chicano Literature" with Olivia Castellano, government courses with Joe Serna Jr., and often visited Kadema Hall to dabble in art with Montoya and Villa.[8] In addition to this important coursework, a great deal of his sentimental education came from his work in the community, where he was beginning to take on the persona of a poet. Along with Philip "Pike" Santos, MEChA (Movimiento Estudiantil Chicano de Aztlán) President Pedro "Pete" Hernández, and Juan Gutierrez, González co-founded La Raza Bookstore in 1972 to fill a void in the market for Chicana/o and Mexican literature.[9] Chicano Organization for Political Awareness (better known by the acronym COPA), a political action group led by Serna Jr., offered its meeting space at 1228 F Street in downtown Sacramento to house the store, with a month of prepaid rent. The ethnic studies faculty at Sacramento State likewise supported the cause by asking, and sometimes requiring, their students to buy their textbooks at La Raza Bookstore.

Visualizing Poetry

González dedicated the next two years of his life to ensuring the bookstore kept its doors open, and while there, he was often writing, filling dozens of notebooks with words and images. For some of these early experiments, González began using old stamps for food processing that his father had brought home from the cannery. In *Hand Led* (c. 1972; fig. 2), one of these notebook compositions, we see the image of a guerrilla fighter in fatigues, perhaps an homage to the leaders of the Cuban Revolution or a reference to the paramilitary dress code of the Brown Berets. Upon closer inspection, one realizes the entire image is made of stamps: one says "trimming," another "led," and a numerical one that reads "300." The effect it produced—an image made of words—was a lightbulb moment for the young poet-artist.[10]

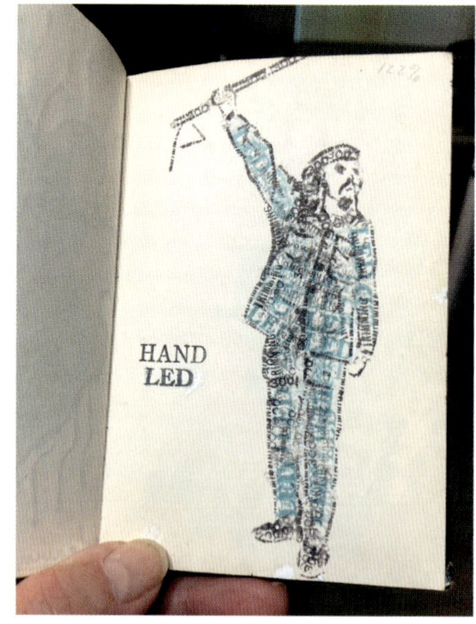

Fig. 2. Luis C. González, *Hand Led*, artist notebook, c. 1972. Collection of Luis C. González.

At the time, González was also immersed in the itinerant poetry workshops, Taller de Poesía, hosted by local writers. These were *tertulias* where poets would gather to read and critique each other's work (fig. 3). The Taller would go on to publish *Poemasomenos de Sacra* in 1973, which included the writings of González, Ricardo Torres, and Lupe Castellano, as well as illustrations by three RCAF artists: Max Garcia, Ricardo Favela, and Juan Cervantes.[11] A poem by Lupe Castellano from this collection titled "A Fear" shows an interest in typesetting the text in diagonal, vertical, and horizontal patterns that illustrate the words at hand. González included love poems, *Movimiento* poems, and one early concrete poem titled "love *ciegamente*," which broke down the word love into a quadrant composition moving clockwise. The poem captures the viewer visually with characteristic power; as art historian Jennifer Josten describes them, "as advertisements or posters, concrete poems seek maximum efficiency with minimal words."[12] Critic Manuel Valencia reviewed the book in *The Sacramento Union*, noting that the poets were forming a positive definition of the Chicana/o experience through images, metaphors, and symbols, and he called González's ode to the movement a "Chicano magnificat."[13] Yet he also mentioned that this Chicana/o poetry renaissance was tinged with madness: "How else can one explain the action of three Chicano poets who sold their blood to the local blood bank twice weekly for six weeks in order to raise the money needed to publish their poems?"[14] The humorous observation contemplated the precarity in which these artists and writers were operating and the absolute freedom that came from self-publishing their own work.

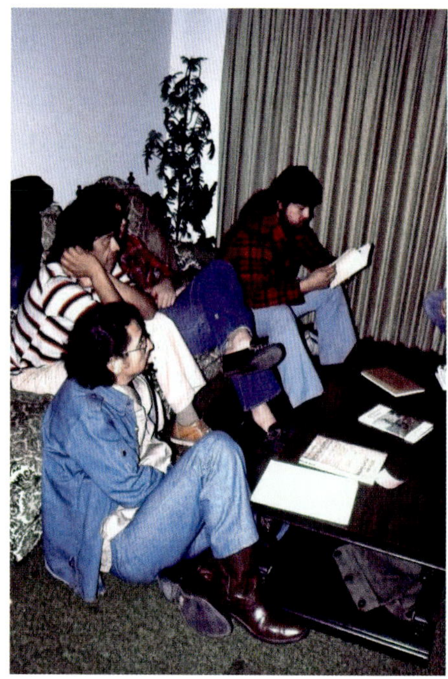

Fig. 3. *Gathering of the Taller de Poesía at González's family home in Sacramento*, 1972. L–R: José Montoya, Esteban Villa, Ricardo Torres, and González. Photograph courtesy of Luis C. González.

Reflecting the socialist ethos of the movement, independent publishing took on a new role in terms of controlling the means of production and providing a platform for Chicana/o poets. The literary critic Randy Ontiveros has noted, "The printed word was [the Chicano Movement's] most vital instrument because print was accessible, and because print allowed creator and audience to imagine themselves as part of a Chicano/a nation."[15] This understanding of the Chicana/o press, which included a plethora of community-based newspapers, magazines, pamphlets, journals, chapbooks, and manifestos, aligns with

Benedict Anderson's concept of "imagined communities," whereby national identities emerge from cultural products of collective imagination. But Chicana/o nationalism was a form of cultural nationalism with a vexed relationship to the nation-state, one characterized by internal colonialism and the redrawing of borders after the Treaty of Guadalupe Hidalgo in 1848, when Mexico lost more than half its northern territories.

For many Chicana/o poets, Aztlán, the mythical homeland of the Aztecs, would become the symbol of this lost and reclaimed land that was foundational for their collective identity.[16] However, while this held true for much of the poetry produced at the height of the *Movimiento*, González's experiments with concrete poetry placed Aztlán as symbol, metaphor, and myth within an international framework that held a supranational character. As Jamie Hilder has noted, "Concrete poetry is affected by the language and material conditions of everyday life of its time, and ... it did not develop in isolation, but through engagement with the work done by poets and artists in other nations."[17] This transcendence of the cultural nationalism of Chicanismo was a result of the global aesthetics of the genre.

To return to the concrete poem "telaraña (másomenos) chicana" (1974; fig. 1), González generally based it on the language of his everyday life and local environment, but on a formal level he was most likely drawing on the work of Brazilian poet Augusto de Campos. Words such as "órale" expressed approval, "simón" indicated a slang form of "yes," and "tacos" represented a staple food in any Chicana/o household. These were utterances of everyday life for the poet, his family, and his friends. The poem was published in a chapbook *Concreto y con safos* (1974; fig. 4), whose dedication page reads: "These RCAF concrete poems are dedicated to the believers of con safismo." The phrase "con safos," often marked as C/S, is a Chicana/o term that seeks safety and respect for the work. For the artist, it was an everyday phrase that Chicana/o artists could use as "a sort of spiritual protection for our creations."[18]

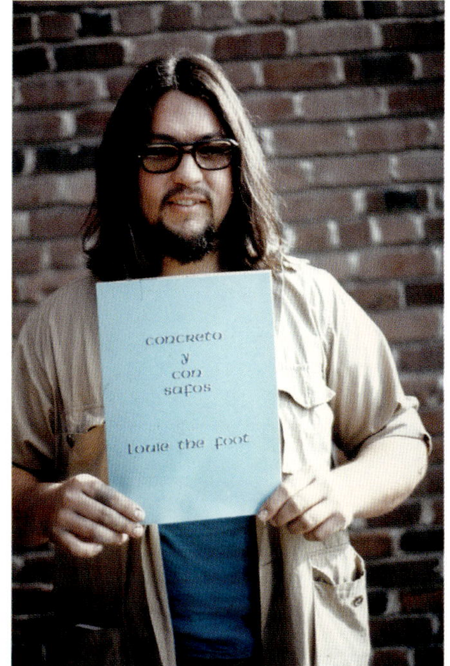

Fig. 4. Héctor D. González (born 1945), *Luis C. González holding his recently published book* Concreto y con safos, 1974. Collection of Luis C. González.

The formal composition of his spiderweb poem, however, owed a great deal to the visual word play of de Campos, particularly his well-known poem "terremoto" (1956; fig. 5). The poem is in five stanzas and shaped like a crossword puzzle descending diagonally across the page. In the poem, de Campos reflected on the effects of an earthquake, perhaps a recent occurrence in his life, that invoked the words "fear, "death," "meter," and "thermometer" and yet also had a cosmic dimension. Not only were the words arranged in the form of constellations over a blue background, but they also directly addressed the sun and the stars. To decode the poem, the reader had to engage in this form of play in order to make connections that would suggest that what happens on Earth corresponds to a larger cosmos that is interdependent. The visual component was dynamic and, most importantly, nonrepresentational.

The structure of "telaraña" is built by two intersecting lines of "r"s and "c"s that reference the concept of *raza cósmica*, popularized by the Mexican philosopher

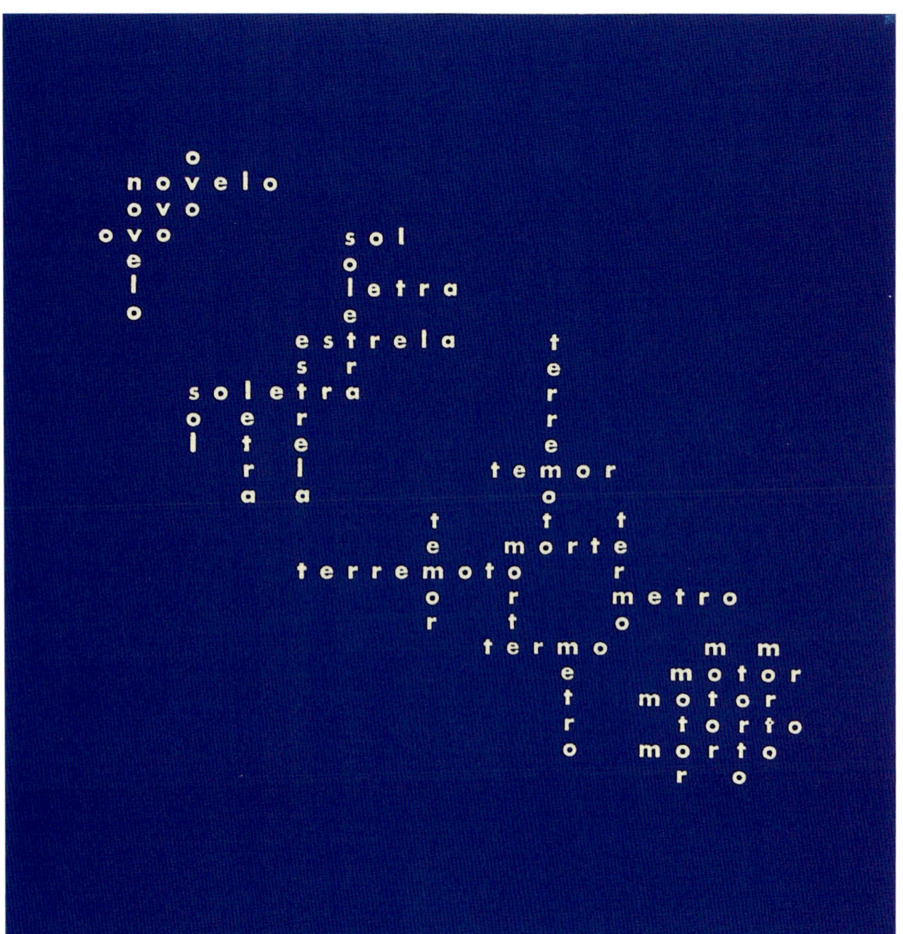

Fig. 5. Augusto de Campos (born 1931), *terremoto*, 1956. Ink on paper. Published in Mary Ellen Solt, *Concrete Poetry: A World View* (1968).

José Vasconcelos. Vasconcelos came to prominence as the minister of education in a postrevolutionary 1920s Mexico, where he enlisted prominent artists and writers to contribute to the formation of a national identity. In 1925, he published a book that railed against Anglo-European dominance and the privileging of whiteness by positioning the racial mixtures of Mexico and Latin America, which make up the image of the mestiza/o, as superior and "more capable of true brotherhood and of a truly universal vision."[19] As literary critic Rafael Pérez-Torres has noted, the concept was embraced by Chicana/o poets in the early 1970s because "the discourse of a cosmic race was an attempt to convey a pride in the mestizo heritage of Chicano identity."[20] González's poem conveys this pride in racial and ethnic identity as a form of self-love that challenges the self-hatred and shame experienced by Mexican Americans as a result of everyday forms of racism. But "telaraña" is not solely about race. The poem positions bilingual wordplay, integral to Chicana/o culture, as a form of joy that exceeds the contours of the single-language national poetries in Mexico and the United States. Furthermore, it focuses on an identity that is relational rather than individualistic, hence the visualization of a web.

This focus on collectivization is likewise present in González's poem "Yo soy Chicano" (1975; see page 51). The poem begins with a circular structure that diagonally reads "Yo soy" or "I am," which is mirrored diagonally on the right by "Somos," or "we are." From these circles, the viewer is summoned to read along vertical and horizontal axes the crossword form "I am Chicano," or "We are Chicano Aztlán." The shift from first person to a collective "we" pronoun is a deliberate act to suggest an identification with a larger group identity and its origin site in Aztlán. The poem appeals to the eye and likewise uses words that evoke imagery and sound, such as multitudes in "Raza"; lost and reclaimed territories in "Land"; the feel of water in "Lluvia"; and the sonic jubilee of a Mexican *grito*, such as "Ajúa." To be Chicana/o, therefore, suggests a rootedness in a homeland, Aztlán: a geography, a people, a space for enactment. "Yo soy Chicano" demonstrates the tension between the local aims of Chicana/o nationalism in Sacramento to identify with their land, their peoples, and their joys, but to do so from the vantage point of a global modern aesthetic. These dynamic designs generated poetic abstractions of Aztlán, as word, image, and myth that could resonate with international audiences. For example, one might walk up to "Yo soy Chicano" and think of Mathias Goeritz's mural poem "Pocos cocodrilos locos" (1967), a sonic concrete poem that was literally cast out of concrete on the facade of a restaurant in Mexico City. Goeritz's simple three-word poem, the words of which are playfully rearranged across the space of five lines, requires similar audience engagement. To decode, one must read aloud, listen to the syncopated rhythm, visualize the crazed crocodiles, and delight in what feels like a tongue twister.

This turn toward abstraction, performance, and visualization was gradual for González, but took on a new significance when he left the bookstore and began volunteering his time at the Centro de Artistas Chicanos.[21] In an interview he added, "As a volunteer I helped in the production of posters without any idea that someday I would be doing a lot of that stuff. . . . Before long something clicked and I saw that silkscreen was a form of publication. So I decided to publish some of my poetry. . . . I used to draw with words, give them shapes, spirals, angles."[22] He was part of what scholar Karen Mary Davalos calls the "sweat equity" of Chicana/o institutions and would later be hired as a staff member at the Centro through funds provided by the Comprehensive Employment and Training Act (CETA).[23] According to fellow RCAF artist Rodolfo "Rudy" Cuellar, the Centro began with grants from the City and County of Sacramento, and he and González were hired to work in the screenprinting shop.[24] This was the era of Governor Ronald Reagan, and Centro artists were encouraged to produce work in the service of community organizations, while also enacting subversive resistance to the current regime.

In her groundbreaking article "A Public Voice: Fifteen Years of Chicano Posters," art historian Shifra Goldman wrote about the importance of the Centro as a site of poster production that involved community members, students from Sacramento State, and RCAF artists. The article prominently featured González

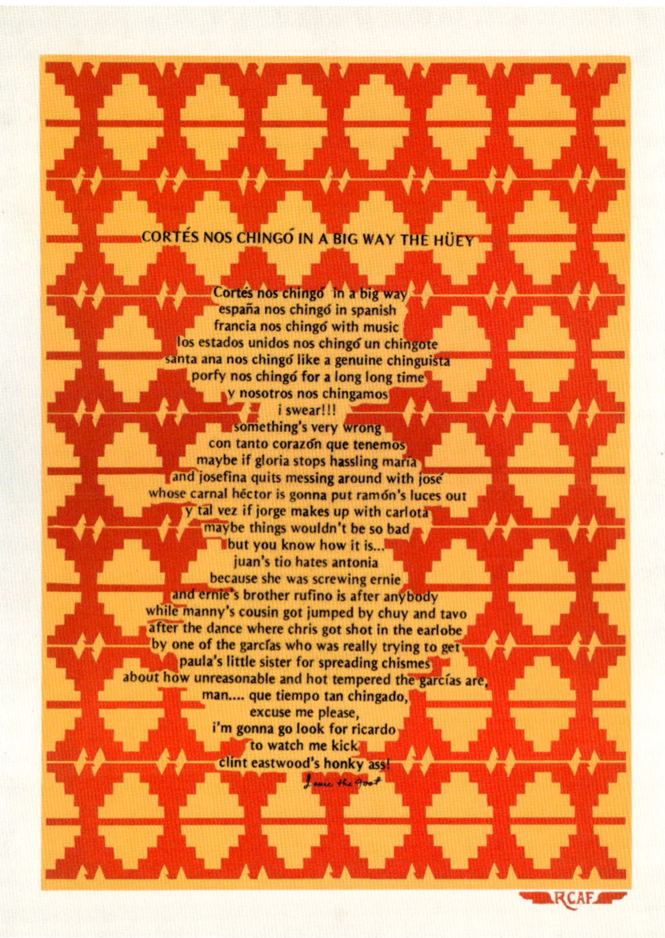

Fig. 6. Luis C. González (born 1953) and Ricardo Favela (1944–2007), *Cortés Nos Chingó in a Big Way The Hüey*, 1976 [Plate 34].

and Ricardo Favela's collaborative poster *Cortés Nos Chingó in a Big Way The Hüey* (1976; fig. 6), noting how this use of screenprinting in the service of poetry was "an ingenious idea when one has little access to the publishing industry, which for years rejected Chicano manuscripts."[25] *Cortés Nos Chingó* became one of González's most well-known works, in large part because of the poem's use of humor to discuss the violence of colonialism. The expletive title directs the reader to Hernán Cortés who "screwed us" in a big way, while the first stanza speaks to colonial incursions by Spain, France, and the US. But the light-hearted tongue-in-cheek tone likewise invokes a self-deprecating humor to address the *Movimiento*'s struggles with infighting, which the artist-poet viewed as a divide-and-conquer strategy.[26] While the eagle of the UFW is patterned and mirrored to frame the poem, this was not a concrete poem, as it did not follow the basic tenets of the genre to use words, letters, and phrases as a basis for the visual composition. González was working in various genres simultaneously, while quickly adopting screenprinting for publishing.

The use of screenprinting techniques led to an interesting breakthrough for González, and he started his series of typewriter poems, which were also an established part of the concrete poetry genre and held a particularly modern aesthetic as examples of objects that mimicked machine language.[27] Of these works, *Hasta La Victoria Siempre* (1975; fig. 7) stands out as among the most successful integrations of concrete poetry with cutting-edge graphic design. The poster was a collaboration with González's brother Héctor, a photographer and schoolteacher, who documented local marches and protests. Héctor had recently photographed José Montoya with a bomber jacket and hat, holding a megaphone and bearing a UFW flag during a strike in Yuba City.[28] González used the photograph to create a silhouette stencil of the "General," which he printed using a split-fountain technique with a vibrant red on the flag and a dark ocher toward the bottom. Then he superimposed the silhouette over a full-page concrete poem that repeated the phrases "viva la huelga" (long live the strike) and "viva la mañana" (long live tomorrow), in precise patterning over a high-key

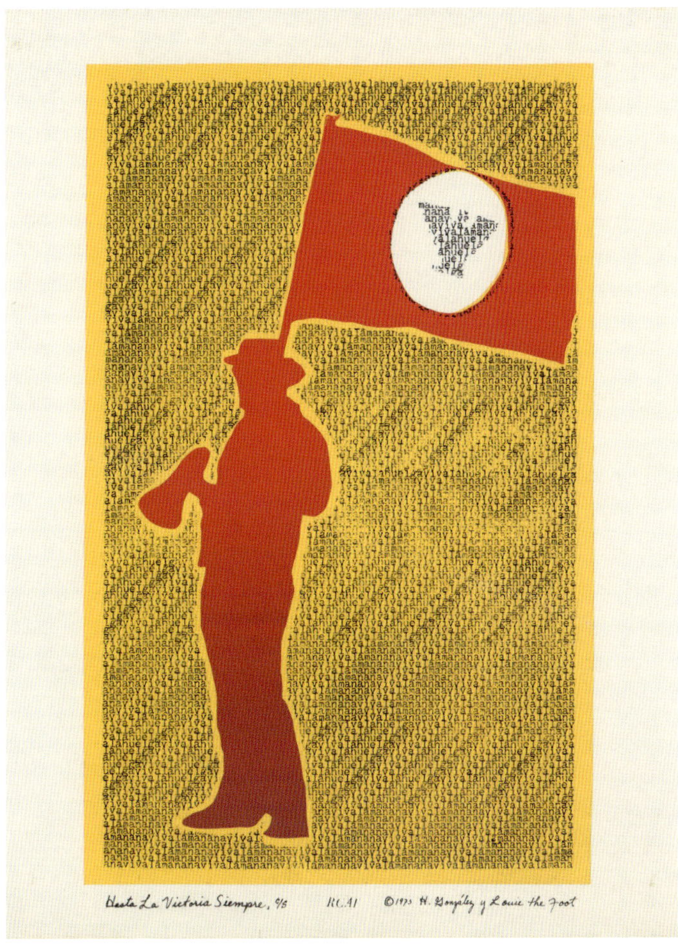

Fig. 7. Luis C. González (born 1953) and Héctor D. González (born 1945), *Hasta La Victoria Siempre*, 1975 [Plate 33].

yellow. The red gradient of the silhouette captured viewers' attention, while the poem created a sonic landscape, one that seemingly could reverberate the chants and slogans emanating from that bullhorn. Interestingly, even the eagle of the UFW logo was constructed from these words, as if poetry could encapsulate the aspirations of the labor movement. Cultural critic Ella Maria Diaz has noted, "Such sayings were part of the verbal-visual architecture of the Chicano Movement because, like the poster, they transformed the space in which Chicanas/os lived, worked, and moved into a shared political vision for the future."[29] This was indeed the most Chicana/o futurist work to emerge from this productive period for González. The print reflected on multiple generations of activism that coalesced to create a different future for Chicanas/os. However, *Hasta La Victoria Siempre* would mark the tail end of his experiments with concrete poetry. We can observe that his subsequent poster, *Viva la Huelga* (1976; pl. 72), reproduces the photograph for a political campaign in a Pop Art–style, four-color poster that shifts to more representational work.[30] González would never abandon poetry, but the poster production at the Centro demanded that he create more easily recognizable imagery that could effect change.

Globalizing Aztlán

While the impetus for taking part in the international concrete poetry movement was to break the rules of art and language, González achieved much more. The genre allowed him to solidify his stature as a Chicano poet, to be recognized for visual compositions whose materiality was based in language, and to develop his characteristic trademarks of code-switching and humor. He learned to self-publish his work through his innovative use of the screenprint medium and became an active producer of culture at the height of the Chicana/o press movement. He was also published in important anthologies, such as Tino Villanueva's *Chicanos: Antología histórica y literaria* (1980), printed by the Fondo de Cultura Económica in Mexico City.[31] And perhaps unbeknownst to him, he created some of the most evocative poetic abstractions of Aztlán in visual poems, whereby his readers took pride in their Chicana/o identities and became global subjects through this international style. But breaking the rules came at a price. By the time González was actively publishing concrete poetry, the international trend was waning. Concrete poets had succeeded at "becoming unbound by [the] linguistic borders" of nations, and yet their strengths in internationalism and interdisciplinary work were also their weaknesses, as they suffered from scholarly neglect and criticism.[32] For González, who was linked to a working-class labor movement through his production with the RCAF, the problem was especially acute. The utopian possibilities of international concrete poetry seemed remote to a political movement clamoring for basic human rights. In that context, González's concrete poetry could easily be misunderstood as bourgeois, apolitical, or overly intellectual. And yet, it was none of those things.

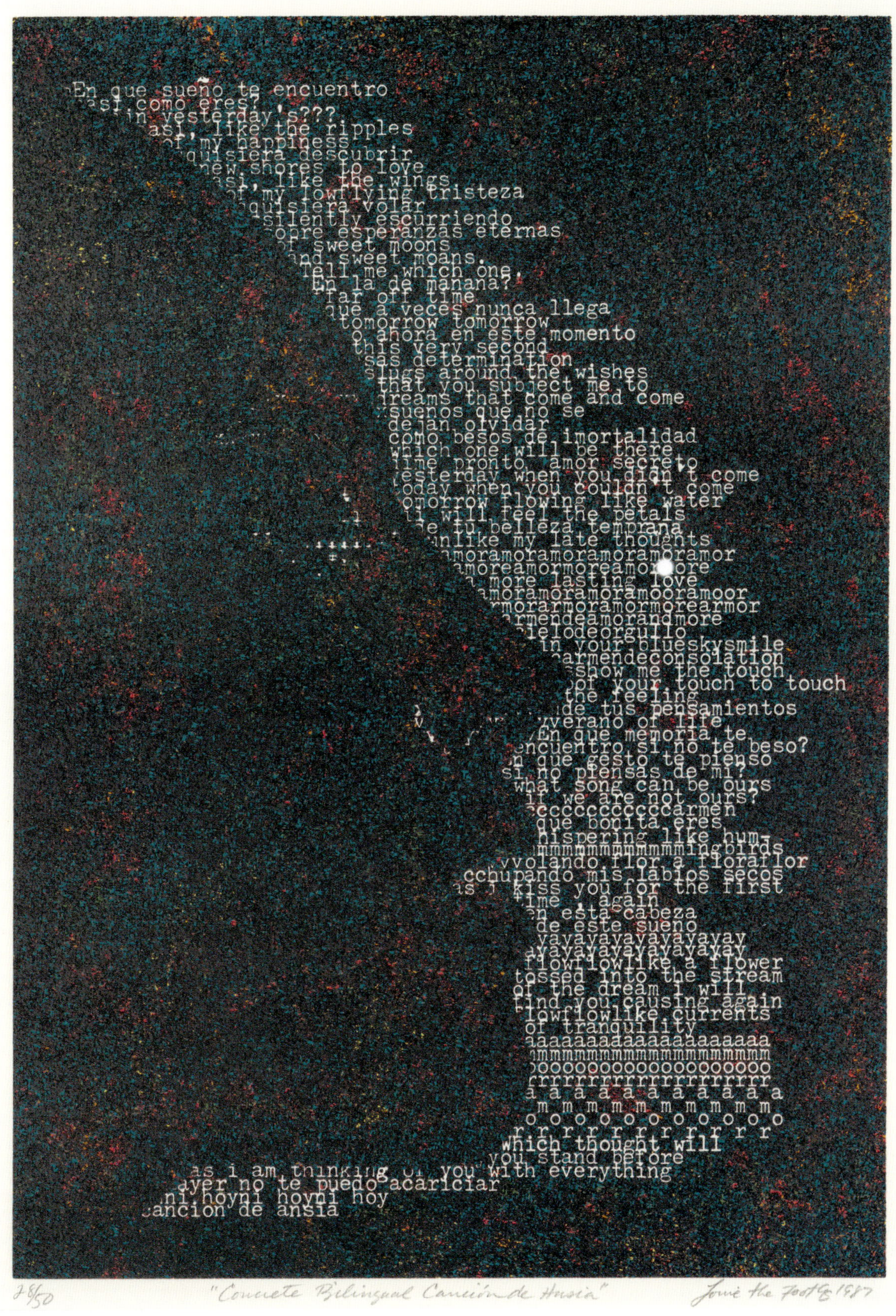

Fig. 8. Luis C. González, *Concrete Bilingual Canción de Ansia*, 1987. Screenprint, 25 × 19 in. Crocker Art Museum Purchase, 1993.10.7.

In 1987, González revisited one of his concrete poems from 1975 titled "Palabras que me causas. (pl. 35)"[33] What had initially been a simple typewriter composition, the line work of which revealed the profile of a woman's face printed in rudimentary pattern, had now become an impeccably printed screenprint composition. The background is stipple-brushed with blue, red, yellow, green, and black, and the typewritten poem is printed boldly in contrasting white. As one reads, the face of the figure emerges from the darkness. The love poem speaks of desire—"in what dream can I find you as you are?"—but also nostalgia—"dreams that cannot be forgotten."[34] *Concrete Bilingual Canción de Ansia* (1987; fig. 8) marks a return to this productive period in González's life, signaling its importance for the writer and for the movement at a time when poetry held limitless potential. The title translates to "Bilingual Concrete Song of Longing," and while this poem speaks to a particular lover, we should also see it as a melancholic return to a time when González used words to visualize a multilingual, multiracial community whose storied land was earnestly part of a much larger world.

Notes

1 Few Chicana/o poets experimented with this genre in the 1960s and 1970s. One notable example is Cecilio García-Camarillo, whose concrete poems can be found in *La Voz Poética del Chicano*, ed. Herminio Rios and Octavio Romano, El Grito Quarterly Book Series (Quinto Sol Publications, 1974), 40–45.

2 Some of these anthologies include Stephen Bann, ed., *Concrete Poetry: An International Anthology* (London Magazine, 1967); Mary Ellen Solt, ed., *Concrete Poetry: A World View* (Indiana University Press, 1968); Eugen Gomringer, *The Book of Hours, and Constellations*, trans. Jerome Rothenberg (Something Else Press, 1968); Pierre Garnier, *Spatialisme et poésie concrète* (Gallimard, 1968); among others.

3 Luis C. González, phone interview by the author, February 15, 2023. In this interview, González spoke about how the work of the Brazilian poets was instrumental for him in seeing language transformed into visual poetry. He remarked, "They blew my mind." He likewise commented on how the experiments of E. E. Cummings inspired him to play with syntax, and how the electric typewriter (both his sister's and the IBM typewriter at Sacramento State's Educational Opportunity Program office) provided a modern aesthetic for his concrete poems.

4 Luis C. González, interview by the author, September 7, 2023.

5 Terezita Romo, "The Visual Poetry of Luis Gonzalez," in *The Second Coming of Con Safos*, exhibition brochure (C.N. Gorman Museum, 1993). For more on the Brown Berets, see David Montejano, *Sancho's Journal: Exploring the Political Edge with the Brown Berets* (University of Texas Press, 2012).

6 Montoya and Villa had recently moved to Sacramento. Villa was an art consultant in the Art Department, while Montoya was a graduate student with a fellowship in the Mexican American Education Project at Sacramento State. Villa had previously co-founded the Mexican American Liberation Art Front (MALAF, 1968) in Oakland, and Montoya had attended many of their weekly meetings. For more on MALAF, see Terezita Romo, *Malaquias Montoya* (UCLA Chicano Studies Research Center Press, 2011), 46.

7 González interview, February 15, 2023.

8 González interview, February 15, 2023. While these professors played an influential role in his formation, González also encountered racist professors who were hostile to his research and creative writing. Frustrated with their disparaging comments, he would eventually abandon his studies prior to completion. Coursework was verified by transcripts in his artist papers.

9 Terezita Romo, correspondence with Philip "Pike" Santos, August 23, 2024. In 1974, Romo became a volunteer and expanded the book list to include Native American publications. Also see Mike Torres, "Serving the Community," *State Hornet*, May 19, 1972.

10 During the Brazilian dictatorship, artists and poets also used rubber stamps to parody the bureaucratic process of official documents. See Mari Rodríguez Binnie, *The São Paulo Neo-Avant-Garde: Radical Art and Mass Print Media in Cold War Brazil* (University of Texas Press, 2024), 72–76.

11 The book was printed by Alfred González, Luis González's brother, and distributed by La Raza Bookstore. At the time, Favela spelled his name Fabela. See Ricardo Torres, Lupe Castellano, and Luis C. González, *Poemasomenos de Sacra* (Taller de Poesía and RCAF, 1973). The title of the collection references the twentieth anniversary of Augusto de Campos's book *Poetamenos* (Minuspoet) from 1953.

12 Jennifer Josten, "Goeritz y la poesía concreta," in *Artecorreo* (RM Editorial, 2011), 2.

13 Manuel Valencia, "Poemas o Menos de Sacra," *The Sacramento Union*, July 1, 1973.

14 Valencia, "Poemas o Menos de Sacra."

15 Randy Ontiveros, *In the Spirit of a New People: The Cultural Politics of the Chicano Movement* (New York University Press, 2014), 39.

16 Amalia Mesa-Bains, "Spiritual Geographies," in *The Road to Aztlan: Art from a Mythic Homeland*, ed. Virginia Fields and Victor Zamudio-Taylor (Los Angeles County Museum of Art, 2001), 332–41.

17 Jamie Hilder, *Designed Words for a Designed World: The International Concrete Poetry Movement, 1955–1971* (McGill-Queen's University Press, 2016), 22.

18 Debra J. Belt, "A Conversation with Louie the Foot Gonzalez," *Artweek* 24, no. 3 (February 4, 1993): 21.

19 José Vasconcelos, "The Cosmic Race," reprinted in *Modern Art in Africa, Asia, and Latin America: An Introduction to Global Modernisms*, ed. Elaine O'Brien (Wiley-Blackwell, 2013), 408.

20 Rafael Pérez-Torres, *Movements in Chicano Poetry: Against Myths, Against Margins* (Cambridge University Press, 1995), 41.

21 The Centro de Artistas Chicanos was founded in 1972. For more on the workshop, see Terezita Romo, "Aesthetics of the Message: Chicana/o Posters, 1965–1987," in *Printing the Revolution! The Rise and Impact of Chicano Graphics, 1965 to Now*, ed. E. Carmen Ramos (Smithsonian American Art Museum, 2020), 86–88.

22 Belt, "A Conversation," 21.

23 Karen Mary Davalos, "Centro de Arte Público/Public Art Center," *Aztlán* 36, no. 2 (2011): 171–78.

24 Rodolfo "Rudy" Cuellar, phone interview by author, July 24, 2024.

25 Shifra M. Goldman, "A Public Voice: Fifteen Years of Chicano Posters," *Art Journal* 44, no. 1 (1984): 50–57.

26 Randy Ontiveros comments on this tendency as a result of what he calls "movement exceptionalism," noting "the effects of presentism ... deepened their isolation from a rich tradition of cultural and political activism, leaving them more vulnerable to infighting and sabotage"; Ontiveros, *In the Spirit of a New People*, 26. The RCAF was not immune to such infighting: professional jealousy, romantic triangles, and friend breakups created friction within the group.

27 A prominent anthology of this subgenre was published as *Typewriter Poems*, ed. Peter Finch (Something Else Press, 1972).

28 Ella Maria Diaz, *Flying Under the Radar with the Royal Chicano Air Force: Mapping a Chicano/a Art History* (University of Texas Press, 2017), 37. Diaz has also written about the performance politics of developing the air force persona as a way to protect the community from physical violence and to protect Chicano art from vandalism. See Ella M. Diaz, "The Necessary Theater of the Royal Chicano Air Force," *Aztlán* 38, no. 2 (2013): 41–70.

For more on the aesthetics of militarism and its projection of sovereignty, see Frances Negrón-Muntaner, "The Look of Sovereignty: Politics and Style in the Young Lords," *Centro Journal* 27, no. 1 (Spring 2015): 4–33.

29 Diaz, *Flying Under the Radar*, 38.

30 California Proposition 14, Agricultural Labor Relations Board Initiative, was a 1976 ballot initiative that would have allowed union organizers to enter places of employment, appoint new members to the board, and allow the board to make determinations about unfair labor practices. The measure was defeated.

31 Five of González's concrete poems were included in the anthology: "Nueve vidas de sed," "Dancing," "Yo soy Chicano," "telaraña (másomenos) chicana," and "Hasta la victoria siempre."

32 Hilder, *Designed Words*, 94.

33 "Palabras que me causas" was a stream of consciousness poem, and the silhouette of the female face came from an advertisement. González interview, September 7, 2023.

34 Excerpts translated by the author.

Southside Park

Lyrics and music by Esteban Villa, c. 1985
Performed by El Trio Casindio

Southside Park
After dark, in the moonlight
Southside Park
A summer day, in the sunshine

Children come and play all day
Mama dreams the hours away
Yeah, yeah, yeah, yeah
Yeah, yeah, yeah, yeah, yeah

Pretty faces shinin' bright
Everything's gonna be all right
Yeah, yeah, yeah, yeah
Yeah, yeah, yeah, yeah, yeah

Daddy likes to play handball
Those of you who hate the Mall
There's el Southside
Aqui en Sacra

Gettin' tired
Of bein' fired
Aqui en Sanjo
En el Southside

Gettin' high
Gettin' higher
Aqui en Santa

Southside Park
A summer day in the sunshine Southside Park
A summer day in the sunshine

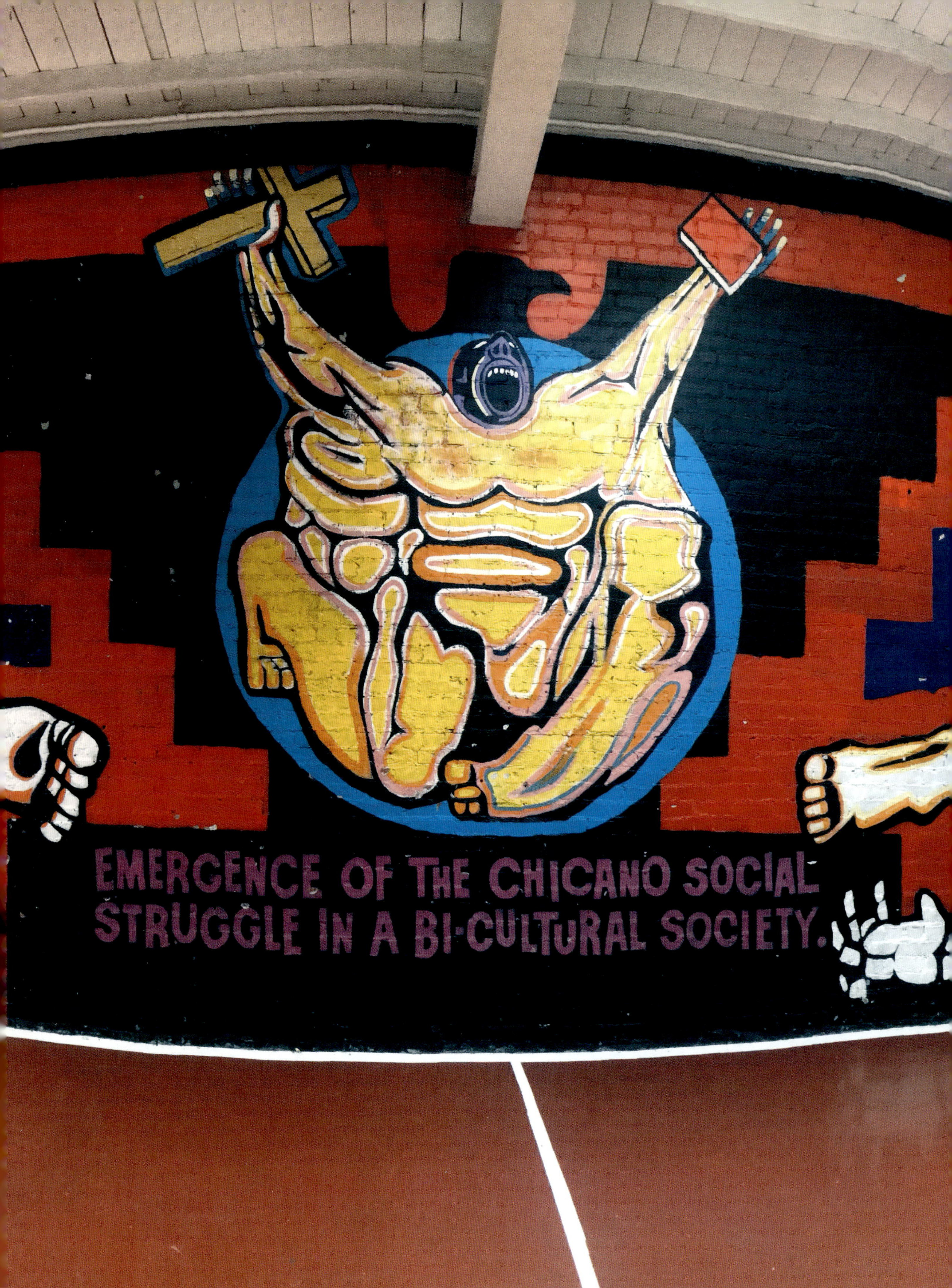
EMERGENCE OF THE CHICANO SOCIAL
STRUGGLE IN A BI-CULTURAL SOCIETY.

ELLA MARIA DIAZ

The Royal Chicano Air Force's Mural Environs: Chicana/o Public Art History's Digital Future

The end of the twentieth century in the United States witnessed a war on public art as a (mis)representation of the nation's history and cultural values, expressed through a coded language of public safety that circumvented discussions of race, ethnicity, gender, and sexuality. Debates over the potential of "terrorist" attacks with George Sugarman's sculpture *Baltimore Federal* (1977) continued in the polarized receptions to Maya Lin's *Vietnam Veterans Memorial* (1982). The removal of Richard Serra's *Tilted Arc* (1981) from the New York Federal Building Plaza in 1989 posed additional questions about public art and its relationship to the built environment for which it was created.[1] While Royal Chicano Air Force (RCAF) murals were not made with materials traditionally used for monuments (e.g., iron, steel, stone), they, too, were cause for controversy in Sacramento, California, regarding access to walls supervised by various government agencies. But the public art negotiations, battles, and victories of the RCAF are missing from the history of public art amid the culture wars of the late twentieth century. When the RCAF's murals are moved to the center of that history, they suggest that the controversies in the 1980s and 1990s were an extension of the sociopolitical demands for visibility, representation, and inclusion made by Chicana/os during the Chicano Movement of the 1960s and 1970s. Chicana/o artists expressed these demands through the community murals they created in the places where they lived, worked, and struggled for inclusion in real and symbolic spaces of US history and dominant culture.

In the twenty-first century, the RCAF's murals offer a deeper understanding of the shared legacy of Chicana/o art in Sacramento and the nation. In addition to work in California's capital city, RCAF artists created murals at Chicano Park in San Diego's Barrio Logan and for the Idaho Migrant Council in Boise. In this essay, I draw on art historian Guisela Latorre's idea of the "mural environment," with which she analyzes historical locations of Chicana/o murals made in close proximity, and expand her concept to a "mural environs," offering a wider lens

Esteban Villa's mural, *Emergence of the Chicano Social Struggle in a Bi-Cultural Society* (detail), 1970. Photograph by Jocelin Hernandez.

for viewing RCAF murals made beyond Sacramento.[2] The relationship between RCAF murals within and beyond Sacramento may seem too large in scope for Latorre's concept; she asserts that mural environments are not "seen as single works of art, but rather their position and iconography [is] understood in function of the surrounding murals and in relation to the space in which they reside."[3] Digitized records of RCAF public art, however, create a "mural environs," connecting the murals to the creative dialogues, collaborative methods, and visual vocabulary that RCAF artists created with each other and artists of color during the 1960s and 1970s US civil rights era.

The RCAF's online mural environs also brings together murals made by the artists over six decades, bridging two centuries, further suggesting that the artists maintained a collective approach to artmaking across the decades of their muralism, despite art historical interpretations of the impact that official funding and commissions made on activist artists of color.[4] Thus, the RCAF's mural environs reveals that the artists did not work with regard to art historical periodization that distinguishes 1960s and 1970s murals from those of the 1980s, 1990s, or twenty-first century. While periodization of community murals made prior to government funding and now, corporate sponsorship, is important for understanding the nuances of exclusion and censorship of divergent and nonconforming representations of US history, it often fails Chicana/o art because it elides the ways in which RCAF artists maintained a Chicana/o visual vocabulary and collaborative methods to decenter Western notions of beauty and individual genius in single works of art.

The RCAF's mural environs further produces relational knowledge of the collective's historical legacy and currency of Chicana/o visual vocabulary in contemporary murals.[5] Their 1970s murals intervened in the cultural, historical, and political absence of Chicana/o and Indigenous peoples in the building(s) of California and the nation. In turn, RCAF murals in the 1980s and 1990s fortified the structure of Chicana/o cultural representation with renovations to earlier works and new murals in the early 2000s. In the second decade of the twenty-first century, individual artists, through corporate sponsorships and neoliberal enterprises, like Sacramento's "Wide Open Walls," build on the visual vocabulary and sociopolitical architecture of RCAF murals—both the content and form as well as their public art infrastructure.[6] In this essay, however, I center the RCAF's legacy of impact on public art history by focusing on their mural environs created by digital access to their murals over the first two decades.

La "Primera Epoca"

In the 1970s, RCAF artists created Chicana/o signs, symbols, and text across Sacramento's built environments.[7] Their visual vocabulary reflected Chicana/o expressions of power and solidarity, often conveyed through the concept of Aztlán—a homeland within the southwestern United States. "Chicano/a artists," Latorre writes, "took to the streets not to search for Aztlán, but instead to *re-create* it with the aid of the public mural."[8] Marking barrio space with Chicana/o murals included the interior walls of preexisting buildings like the Washington Neighborhood Center (WNC) in the Alkali Flat. By the late 1960s, this Sacramento neighborhood had changed from a wealthy suburb (in the late nineteenth century) to an impoverished one that served local Mexican, Chicana/o, and working-class families.[9] "We held classes there with a lot of the young kids," RCAF co-founder and artist Esteban Villa recalled.[10] Asked to paint a mural for a summer youth study program at the WNC,[11] Villa explained the informality of his mural's genesis: "I'd bring my students and start. [I asked] 'Don't I need permission? Papers to fill [out], insurance, money, paint?' [They said,] 'No, just start.'"[12] Villa brought supplies from "the Art Department, without them knowing about it," referring to the Art Department at Sacramento State (officially California State University, Sacramento), where he participated in the Mexican American Education Project (MAEP) as an art consultant in 1969 and, shortly thereafter, as faculty.[13]

The RCAF was germinating in 1969–70, and Villa's mural *Emergence of the Chicano Social Struggle in a Bi-Cultural Society* reflects the collective's creative genesis (fig. 1). Several RCAF artists and students provided the "manpower" in the "only place in Sacramento that let us use their backyard, so to speak, to establish social and community organizations to improve people's lives." Villa added, "It was a huge difference in those early years, you know in 1968 to '69, and [the mural is] still here."[14] These years are significant to Villa because they convey that *Emergence* is part of a "graphic *testimonio*"—a shared history of the Chicano Movement and government-sponsored education programs that led Villa and several of the RCAF's founding members to live and work in Sacramento.[15]

The mural's "graphic *testimonio*" also includes aesthetic influences from the Black Arts movement and transnational encounters, which are missing from art historical discourse on Chicana/o public art in the United States. Prior to initiating the WNC mural, Villa had heard of the 1967 *Wall of Respect*, the first community mural created on Chicago's South Side by the Organization for Black American Culture, AfriCOBRA, and local residents.[16] Representation was key to the community mural movement, as a creative response to civil rights actions in the 1960s and 1970s. It encompasses early Chicana/o public art and was the impetus for the evolution of visual vocabularies that communicated counternarratives to the dominant cultural ones.

Emergence is a foundational example of the visual vocabulary specific to Chicana/o artists because of its transnational influences. On a trip to Mexico in 1964 with his art school friend and future RCAF cofounder José Montoya, Villa was inspired by the murals he toured. The experience prompted him to bring students from the Sacramento State Art Department to paint one in the WNC. John Pitman Weber identifies the "late Siqueiroesque graphic style" in the central figure of *Emergence*, referring to the Mexican artist David Alfaro

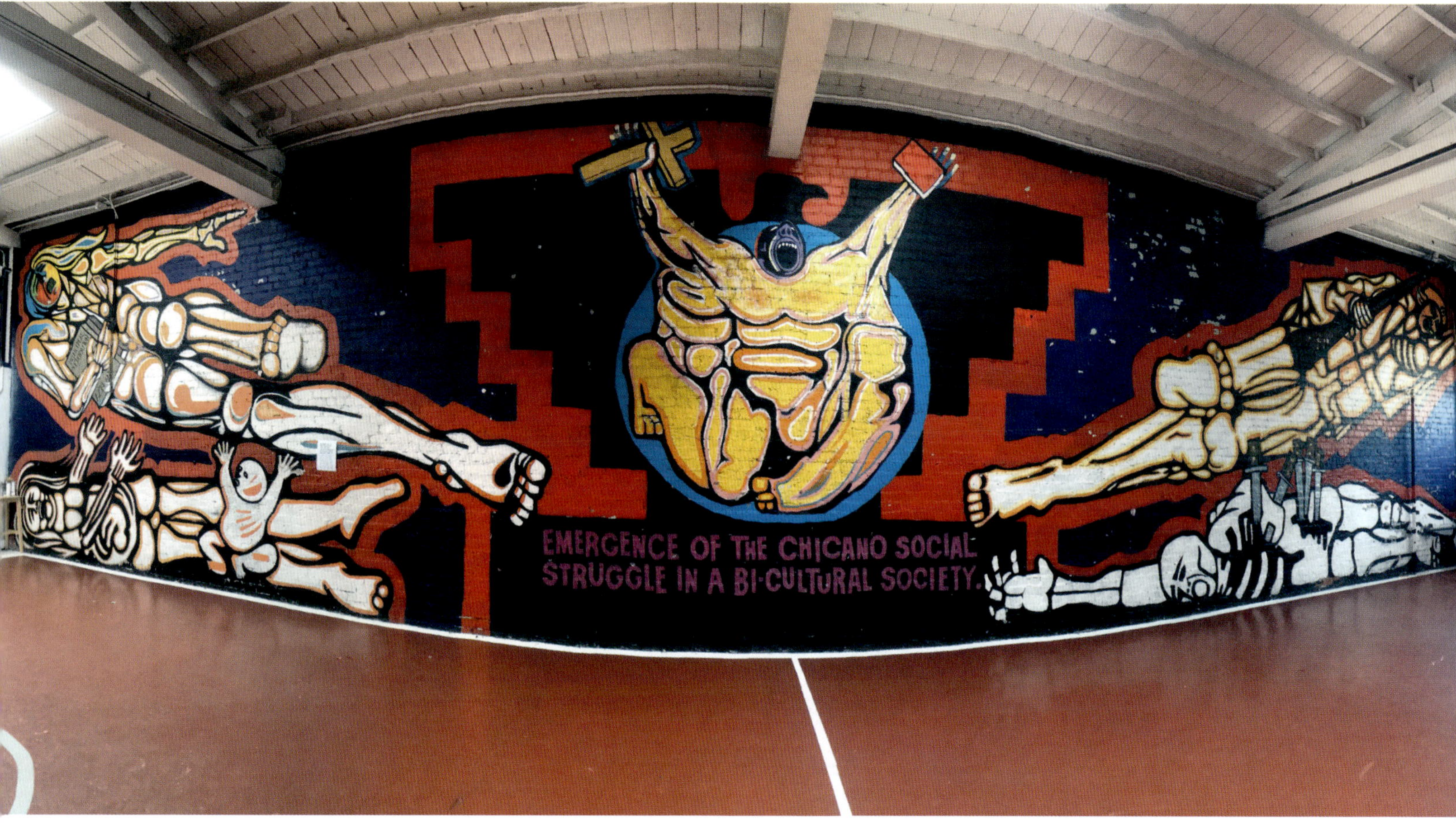

Fig. 1. Esteban Villa's mural, *Emergence of the Chicano Social Struggle in a Bi-Cultural Society*, 1970. Photograph by Jocelin Hernandez.

Siqueiros's emphasis on muscles, bodies, and hands in many of his later works.[17] Villa's design of four large scenes that spring forth from the central figure further invokes Diego Rivera's mural *Man at the Crossroads*, created in 1933 and destroyed in 1934, which Rivera recreated in *Man Controller of the Universe* (1934).[18]

The site-specific design of *Emergence* evokes José Clemente Orozco's murals *Prometheus* (1930) and *The Epic of American Civilization* (1932–34), which incorporate large-scale and partially nude human figures in specific architectural confines to articulate epic struggles of man against self, society, and nature—classic themes of Western culture. The central male in *Emergence* nearly touches the ceiling with his fingers, and Villa's attention to the WNC's architecture is similar to Orozco's placement of *Prometheus* in the arc of the dining hall's ceiling at Pomona College.

In *Gods of the Modern World*, a panel from Orozco's *The Epic of American Civilization*, a skeletal woman gives birth. A similar scene reappears in *Emergence*, but with a different outcome for the WNC's BIPOC viewers. While Orozco's scene includes academic faculty presiding over skeletal newborns wearing graduation caps and trapped under glass display cases, in Villa's mural a child reaches toward a woman holding foundational journals and documents of the Chicano Movement: *El Grito* and *Principles of Education: Aztlán*, the latter of which is a combination of *El Plan Espiritual de Aztlán* (1969) and *El Plan de Santa Barbara* (1969).

The integration of readable signs, symbols, and text in RCAF murals with attention to a location's preexisting architecture continued in surrounding works, many of which no longer exist. Between 1976 and 1977, RCAF artist Armando Cid and students created *Para la Raza del Barrio* at 12th and D Streets in the Alkali Flat (fig. 2).[19] The mural bordered the parking lot of a local bar on which Cid continued the vivid work, marking the building with readable signs for the Chicana/o community. Cid's public-facing mural exemplified the political, cultural, and creative intersections of RCAF artwork as the tavern became a hub for RCAF-sponsored Chicana/o poetry readings in the 1970s.[20]

With *Para la Raza del Barrio*, Cid exemplified the RCAF's method of collaborative artmaking, which worked in opposition to the idea of artistic genius being solely the realm of the individual artist.[21] Cid's mural team comprised students from a city-supported neighborhood youth program.[22] As part of the nation's community mural movement, the work aligns with the student mural "brigades" and artist groups that created murals as cohesive compositions. But Cid (and all RCAF artists) did not focus on unified visions via aesthetic uniformity. Rather, he integrated students into the creative processes, providing direct learning experiences for young, aspiring artists.[23]

One of the most striking features of Cid's mural was the text that announced the building as a space for local people, specifically Chicanas/os—with a code-switch to "la Raza." Using paint to visually imitate street art, the lettering is reminiscent of bubble letters, outlined with a darker color and surrounded by symbols and graffiti, including a cross and Mexican flag. The mural also includes ethereal

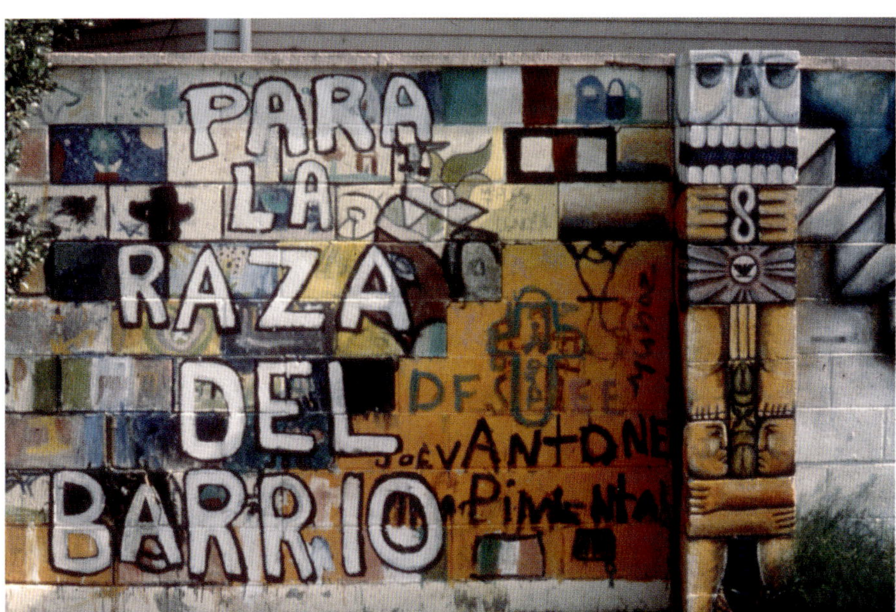

Fig. 2. *Para la Raza del Barrio* (detail), c. 1976. Royal Chicano Air Force Archives, CEMA 8, Department of Special Collections, University Libraries, University of California, Santa Barbara.

scenes of farmworkers hearing calls from otherworldly sirens, perhaps a visual pun on both the political call of the Chicano Movement and the Chicana/o search for Aztlán in pre-Conquest cultural recovery work. This is further supported by the feathered serpent, which is an amalgam of the Mesoamerican deity Quetzalcoatl and the United Farm Worker's eagle symbol that radiates above the worker. Coupled with Villa's *Emergence*, Cid's mural was a decolonizing expression—an alternative architecture in Sacramento's Alkali Flat because it reclaimed "*physical* space on behalf of the Chicana/o community," Latorre writes, and "asserted *metaphorical* spaces for said population."[24]

Art in Public Places

In the second edition of *Toward a People's Art*, historian Ben Keppel recalls the Chicana/o murals that "appeared" to him in Sacramento during the 1970s, a phrasing that obscures the administrative labor involved in the creation of public art.[25] RCAF murals did not simply appear; they resulted from collective groundwork put in place over several decades. By 1979, the RCAF had created approximately fifteen murals in Sacramento, and Keppel must have seen many of them, including Cid's murals *Ollin* and *Sunburst* (c. 1976; fig. 3).[26] A resident of the Alkali Flat in the 1970s, Cid worked with local Chicana/o youth to create murals on the front and rear facades of the Washington Square Apartments, which were built during a major redevelopment phase in downtown Sacramento. These murals were made possible through money secured by a community action group, the Alkali Flat Project Area Committee, as well as the Sacramento Concilio, a social services organization for the Spanish-speaking community.[27] Both murals were colorful tile mosaics of a pre-Conquest symbol—a readable sign for Chicana/o viewers in the 1970s.

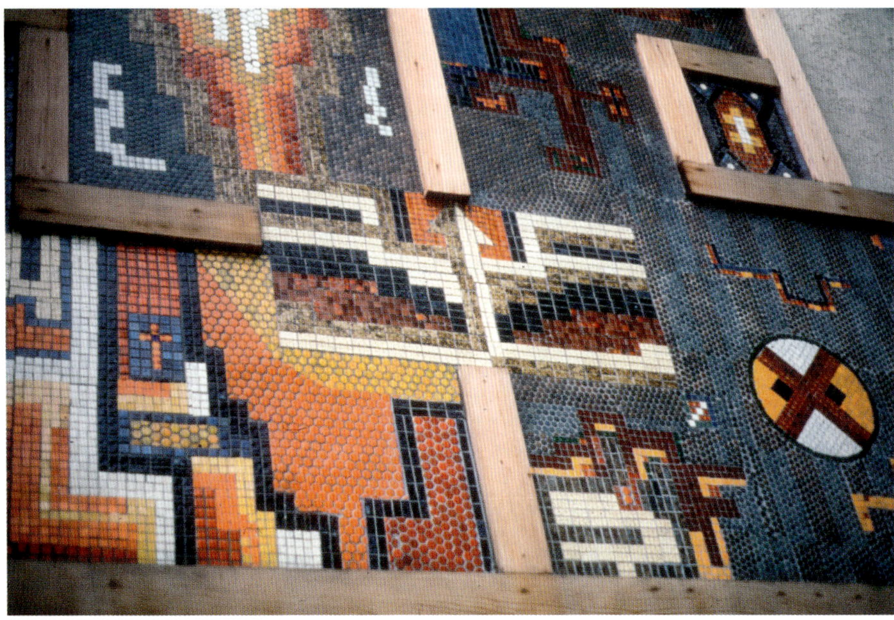

Fig. 3. *Ollin* (detail), 1976–77. Royal Chicano Air Force Archives, CEMA 8, Department of Special Collections, University Libraries, University of California, Santa Barbara.

Ollin means "movement" in Nahuatl, an Indigenous language spoken in Mexico and commonly referred to as the language of the Aztecs in the United States. Cid selected the symbol to honor the Aztec sun deity Ollin Tonatiuh, or "Movement of the Sun," visually communicating the Chicana/o search for Aztlán and situating a pre-Conquest past as the context for community activities in the adjacent Zapata Park. Thus, Cid's use of the Ollin symbol commemorated real changes brought about by the movement of people against political and economic forces of urban redevelopment in Sacramento.

These murals further illuminate the administrative work of RCAF members who built infrastructure to support RCAF murals in Sacramento and which benefited all public art in California. *Ollin* and *Sunburst* preceded the Art in Public Places (APP) ordinance in Sacramento, implemented in 1977 and allocating two percent of construction budgets on public land to public art.[28] The murals were a critical precedent (if not blueprint) for the Sacramento Metropolitan Arts Commission (SMAC), which came into existence around the time of the APP ordinance. The RCAF artists used their preexisting public art infrastructure through the Centro de Artistas Chicanos (Centro), founded in 1972, as a hub for art production and community organizing, as well as a clearing house for arts funding, commissions, and grants.[29]

Following Cid's murals, the RCAF entered a new phase of Chicana/o muralism by negotiating public art in Sacramento through the city's official channels. Their first APP award was for *Metamorphosis*, a sixty-five-foot-long, four-story mural, proposed by the Centro to adorn the east wall of a new parking structure bordered by K, L, 3rd, and 4th Streets (fig. 4).[30] SMAC approved the design in 1978, and Villa, Juan "Juanishi" Orosco, and Stan Padilla began the project alongside a crew of their adult children, students, and other RCAF members. The butterfly mural features cosmic imagery but is land-based, connecting local Indigenous histories to the modern built environment, including Rancho Seco, a decommissioned nuclear power plant.[31]

Completed by 1980, *Metamorphosis* is seemingly benign in comparison to earlier RCAF murals because it lacks the Chicana/o visual vocabulary of the earlier era.[32] Scholarly discourse on community murals made after the US civil rights era typically contends that government funding neutralized the political content of Chicana/o and other BIPOC murals in the 1980s, reflecting a multicultural turn in such art amid the rise of institutional collections and exhibitions of "ethnic" art.[33] Reaction from local Chicana/o viewers was also mixed. "Up to that time," Padilla recalled, "so-called Chicano murals had to have a certain iconography: you know, a huelga bird, a pyramid, Aztec calendars—the old Mexican grocery store calendars and stuff. If it didn't have that, well then it wasn't Chicano."[34]

But *Metamorphosis* was (and is) very much a Chicana/o mural in two important ways. First, the RCAF maintained its radical tradition of collaboration in each stage of its creation, communicating the importance of consciousness-raising

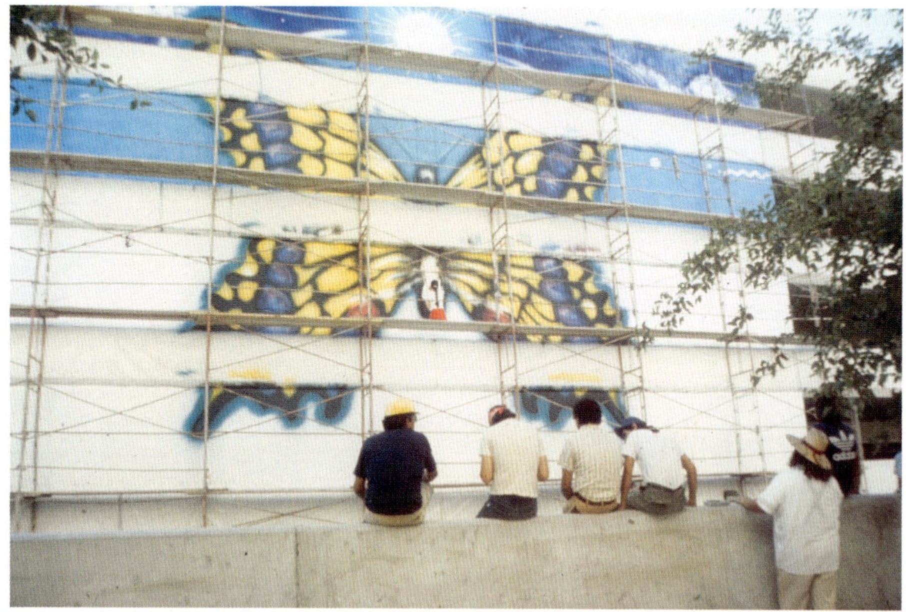

Fig. 4. *Metamorphosis*, 1980. Royal Chicano Air Force Archives, CEMA 8, Department of Special Collections, University Libraries, University of California, Santa Barbara.

as a shared process with their large mural crew and to the people witnessing its creation. An original roster of participants involved in the public art commission lists the names of seventeen people.[35] Reflecting on the planning stages of *Metamorphosis*, José Montoya recalled resistance from city officials over the size of the mural team. "Even after we got them to OK our work," he explained, "the restrictions were really detrimental to what we were trying to do [which] was, first of all, to get young people to understand the importance of art in general."[36]

The RCAF also intervened in Sacramento's official public space by requesting an important location of Chicana/o history in their proposal. Montoya revealed that *Metamorphosis* honors the site of Ernesto Galarza's first home in Sacramento.[37] In *Barrio Boy* (1971), Galarza recalls his childhood experiences in Sacramento: "418 L St, our refuge in a strange land.... my mother and I began to take short walks to get our bearings.... we noted by the numbers on the posts at the corners that we lived between 4th and 5th streets on L."[38] *Metamorphosis* is well named; the mural honors what was once the "lower part of town" in Sacramento's West End, where first-generation and immigrant communities worked and lived during the early twentieth century.

On the heels of *Metamorphosis*, the RCAF began inquiring with SMAC about the nearby K Street tunnel, adjacent to their butterfly mural, where police had prevented Villa from painting a mural with his students in 1978.[39] Connecting K Street to the city's riverfront district, the underground walkway was created by the Interstate 5 on-ramp constructed in the 1960s. City officials began razing and redesigning the riverfront district after it fell into disrepair and urban blight.[40] Moving through a thirty-year redevelopment plan, city officials turned their attention to the Alkali Flat district, the West End, and reconstruction of the

Capitol Mall area that included the parking structure on which *Metamorphosis* remains.

The historical backdrop of the RCAF's tunnel mural, *LASERIUM*, which stands for *Light Art in Sacramento, Energy Resources In Unlimited Movement*, was the US culture wars, which included a backlash against multicultural trends in public art funding (fig. 5).[41] The culture wars impacted nationally touring Chicana/o art shows like *Chicano Art: Resistance and Affirmation (CARA)*, queer and women performance and visual artists, as well as the design of *LASERIUM*. Comprising two murals that span the length of both sides of the pedestrian tunnel, *LASERIUM* was designed by RCAF artists Orosco and Villa. Orosco's plans for the mural's south wall were initially rejected by SMAC and city officials in the early 1980s because of his use of identifiable Indigenous figures and pyramids, as well as his design of site-specific art. Orosco wanted to replicate "the serpent shadow" that appears on the pyramid of El Castillo at Chichén Itzá during the spring and fall equinoxes by incorporating the tunnel's architecture. Thinking about space and time three-dimensionally, Orosco planned a suspension system on its ceiling that would hold two large crystals on "two overhead shafts, which were water spillways from the overpass." When light would hit the suspended glass prisms, they would produce a rainbow at "sunrise, from the east, and then around 3:00 p.m., from the west."[42]

The desired effect made by the crystals was more than aesthetic novelty, however. It rethought the function of public space as well as the experience of time by paying homage to pre-Conquest architectural design. In thinking about *Energy Resources In Unlimited Movement*, Orosco wanted to recognize an alternative history of technology, one that considered the resource management of Indigenous

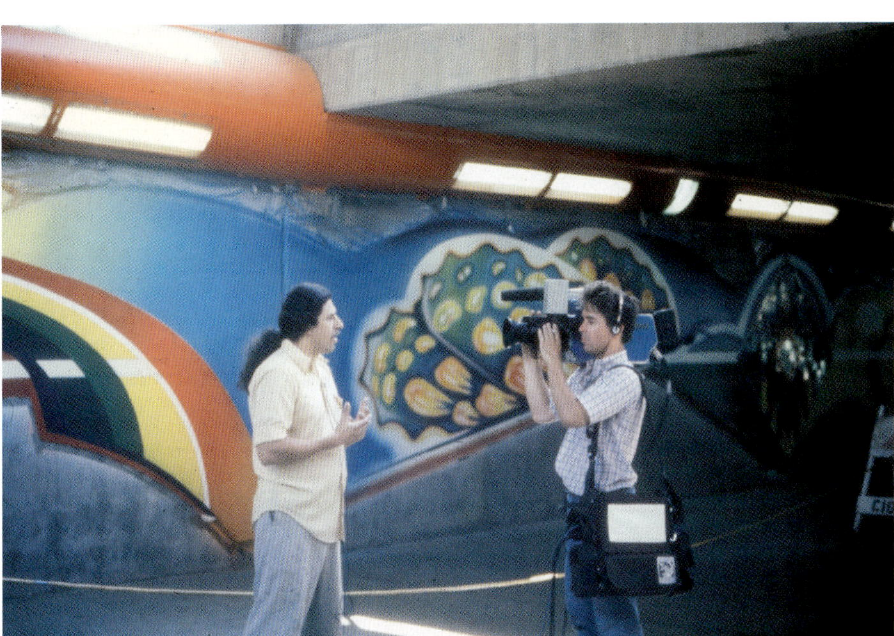

Fig. 5. Progression of *LASERIUM* Mural, 1983–84. Royal Chicano Air Force Archives, CEMA 8, Department of Special Collections, University Libraries, University of California, Santa Barbara.

civilizations, which more than likely was informed by his representation of Sacramento's nuclear power plant in *Metamorphosis*. After his original design was dismissed by SMAC, he resubmitted his plans to move forward with the RCAF's public art commission. Completed by 1984, *LASERIUM* was renovated in 1999 by Villa and Orosco; but unlike Villa, who had embedded Chicana/o visual vocabulary in his original mural, Orosco created an entirely new mural on the south wall, painting a crystal at one end to further signify the original "Light Art" concept.[43]

Renovation and Recognition

The RCAF's *Southside Park Mural* (1977; fig. 6) is, perhaps, the collective's best known public artwork, especially after the 2001 renovations that restored the mural's vibrancy and a City Council resolution in 2001 that acknowledged the RCAF's contributions to community life in Sacramento.[44] The mural is in a beloved park that has served as a hub for the Chicana/o community for five decades.[45] Indeed, Southside Park remains a significant site for many communities, and the mural is the backdrop for multicultural performances, rallies, and events. Like all RCAF murals in Sacramento, *Southside Park Mural* reflects decades of grassroots and administrative work by RCAF members and community activists in building Sacramento's public art culture.[46] The mural, which also preceded the APP ordinance, is site-specific; the artists reimagined a stage built in the early twentieth century with Chicana/o visual vocabulary that offers cultural, political, and spiritual histories of Sacramento's role in the Chicano Movement.[47]

In 1976, RCAF artist and Centro director Ricardo Favela and RCAF member Rosemary Rasul negotiated with the Southside Park Neighborhood Association and city officials to create the mural. The negotiations, which took place before those for *Metamorphosis*, involved input from Montoya, Orosco, Villa, Padilla, Juan Cervantes, and Lorraine García-Nakata. Each artist painted panels with assistance from their adult children, students, and community members, exemplifying the RCAF's emphasis on artistic collaboration as an act of consciousness-raising that subverts hierarchical notions of singular artistic genius.

Southside Park Mural epitomizes the RCAF artists' distinct styles and free association with different aspects of the Chicano Movement. In the center panel, Villa painted a priest-like figure holding a newborn. The figure is rendered in broad strokes of color with Pop Art references in his integration of images and text: a rosary, a sacred heart, and the word *vida* (life). On the left, Orosco created *ojos de dios* with Hopi influences, representing Chicana/o reclamations of Indigenous knowledge during the Chicano Movement, which sought to reconnect with ancestral and contemporary Native American cultures across geopolitical borders. Padilla also blended Indigenous imagery with a monarch

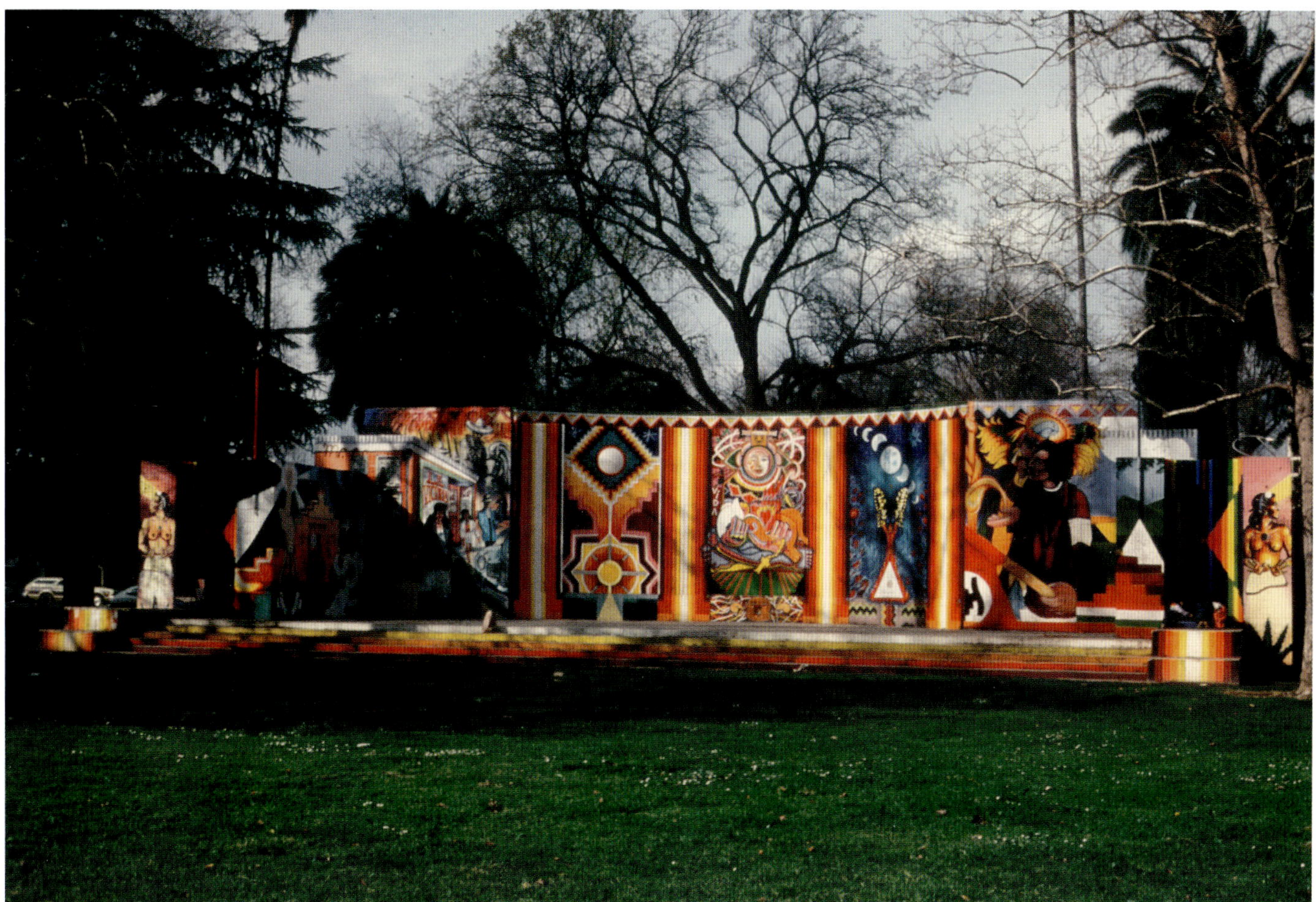

Fig. 6. *Southside Park Mural*, 1977. Royal Chicano Air Force Archives, CEMA 8, Department of Special Collections, University Libraries, University of California, Santa Barbara.

butterfly—a prototype for *Metamorphosis* that he and his RCAF colleagues planned for the parking garage adjacent to what would become *LASERIUM*.[48] In his panel, Cervantes depicted RCAF philosopher Francisco Godina as a "*Huelgista* (Farm-worker striker)," creating a graphic *testimonio* of "the total Chicano movement, banner and petition in hand, determined to be heard," as the pre-Conquest deity Quetzalcoatl whispers in his ear.[49] For RCAF member and Sacramento State Chicana/o Studies professor Sam Ríos Jr., this "good god of the Aztecs" is the "voice of the ancestors, the voice of our *ancianos* (elders,) the voice of people like César Chávez [who] all unite to implore him to non-violence."[50] Appropriate for the site of decades of music, political rallies, and cultural events, Cervantes's panel commemorates historical marches of farmworkers to Sacramento.

On the outer edges of the stage, two massive female figures flank both sides of the mural and recall the performance history of the location. Created by García-Nakata, the women with "outstretched arms and palms opened toward viewers" take "a position of accepting power."[51] In their commanding position, they caution viewers before entering the stage, a message underscored by the size of their hands that equally conjure the "late Siqueiroesque graphic style" that Pitman Weber detects in Villa's *Emergence*.

Renovations to *Southside Park Mural* in 2001 ushered in another phase of new murals and renovations to earlier works.[52] In 2009, Cid's *Sunburst* mural was restored, following his untimely passing and the perseverance of his spouse, RCAF member Josie Talamantez.[53] In 2013, Villa, Padilla, and Orosco, alongside their adult children, created *Eartharium* (2013) in the lobby of the State of California's General Services Department at 16th and L Streets.[54] In 2018, Villa, Orosco, and Padilla completed *Flight*, a three-panel mural installed in the Golden 1 Center in downtown Sacramento.[55] Despite renewed interest in RCAF murals, *Metamorphosis* remains in need of serious repair, as does Cid's original *Ollin* mural.

Toward A Virtual Mural Environs: The RCAF's Digital Future

The legacy of the RCAF's murals is evident in Sacramento's contemporary culture of public art but should be more widely known in US art history. The concept of site specificity in public art became a major counterpoint to the forced removal of monuments and public art installations from official spaces of the United States during the late twentieth century. The concept has been predominantly understood through sculptural objects and permanent materials like stone and metal, which reflect larger questions of access and visibility, such as who can acquire these expensive materials and what do art historians deem valuable (in all senses). Moreover, 1960s and 1970s community murals preceded public monuments by canonical artists like Lin and Serra, as well as the social sculpture of Joseph Beuys, in understanding site specificity as "a critical component of the artwork to the degree that the mural would be incomplete without it."[56]

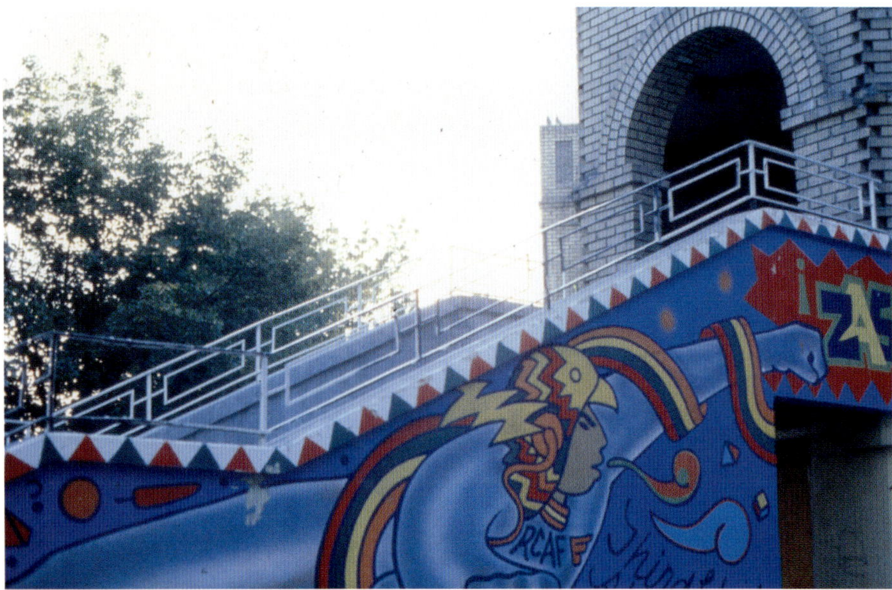

Fig. 7. *Idaho Migrant Council Mural*, c. 1978. Royal Chicano Air Force Archives, CEMA 8, Department of Special Collections, University Libraries, University of California, Santa Barbara.

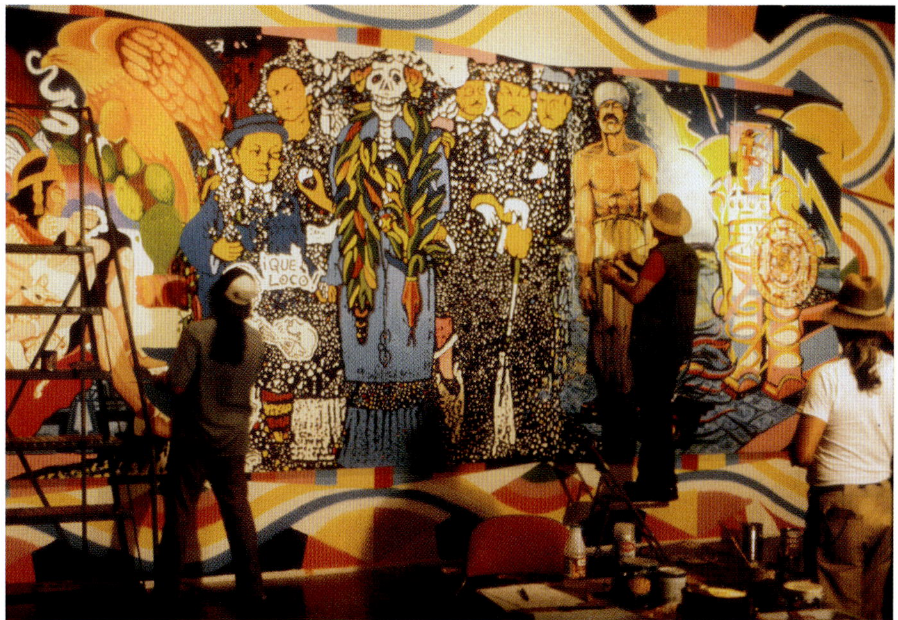

Fig. 8. Poster Exhibition and Work in Progress for *Crystallizing the Chicano Art Myth Mural*, 1983. Royal Chicano Air Force Archives, CEMA 8, Department of Special Collections, University Libraries, University of California, Santa Barbara.

If material choices define the longevity and, thus, value of public art of the late twentieth century, then RCAF murals continue to upend notions of permanence, representation, and memory in the public sphere. The digitization of photographs, slides, and various records of RCAF murals make it possible to see their proximity to one another despite location, date of creation, and whether or not a mural is destroyed. A case in point is evident in digitized images of RCAF murals that several of the artists created in 1975 at Chicano Park in San Diego's Barrio Logan. Available for viewing online, these images reveal the iconographic and architectural conversations in which they engaged with one another and Chicana/o artists across the US Southwest. Further, the RCAF's mural created for the Idaho Migrant Council in Boise extends this conversation beyond California because it includes a fusion of pre-Conquest symbols like speech scrolls with popular culture and Pop Art references (fig. 7).[57] An Indigenous figure punches through the sky with a closed fist, evoking the iconic power-first symbol of the civil rights era as well as a comic-book illustration of the fist's impact: "¡ZAS!"

The relational knowledge generated by the RCAF's online mural environs also includes portable murals, or moveable panels, which leads to the Crocker Art Museum in Sacramento. In 1983, the RCAF's Centro exhibited the *Progressive Mural Installation* in conjunction with a suite of historical RCAF posters (figs. 8 and 9). Favela, Montoya, Villa, and Orosco each painted portable panels for a mural titled *Crystalizing the Chicano Art Myth* to illustrate "the technique, cooperation and collective discipline exemplified by the Centro de Artistas Chicanos."[58] The portable mural also engaged with the RCAF posters on display because it communicated the fusion of several cultural influences on Chicana/o art—a fusion that had solidified over decades of signs, symbols, and text and which continues today. *Crystalizing the Chicano Art Myth* also preceded the latest, perhaps last, RCAF mural, which is a portable mural permanently installed in the

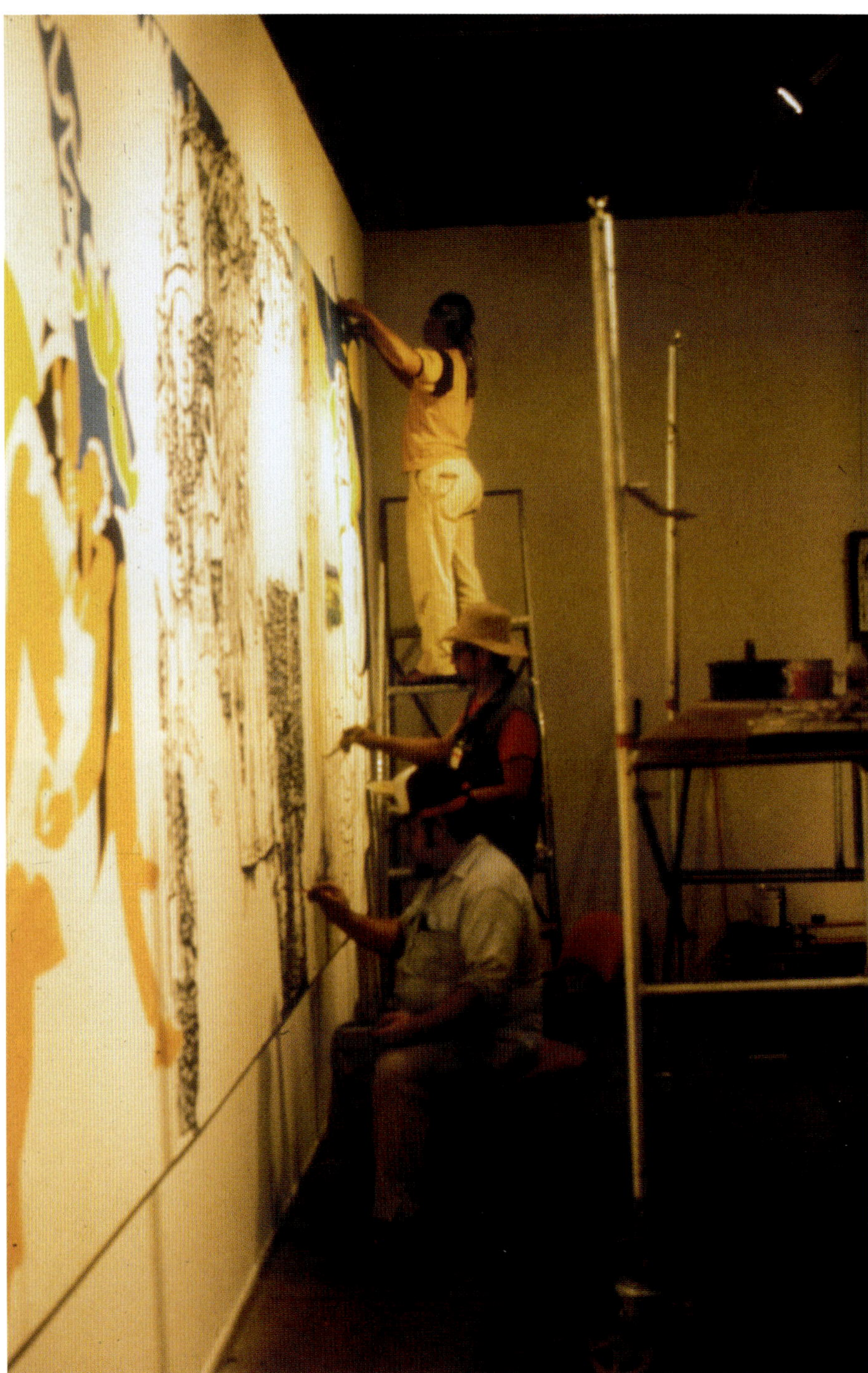

Fig. 9. Poster Exhibition and Work in Progress for *Crystallizing the Chicano Art Myth Mural*, 1983. Royal Chicano Air Force Archives, CEMA 8, Department of Special Collections, University Libraries, University of California, Santa Barbara.

Golden 1 Center. The comparison or, rather, connection between the RCAF artists' portable mural in 1983 and the one made in 2018 recovers an art historical antecedent for the RCAF and Chicana/o art history. It suggests that the artists remained engaged in concepts of public art across decades of their collective productions and as materials and access to space changed. Such an important art historical antecedent and point of analysis is only made possible when exploring the RCAF's mural environs.

Notes

1 Ella Maria Diaz, *Flying Under the Radar with the Royal Chicano Air Force: Mapping a Chicano/a Art History* (University of Texas Press, 2017), 187–88. For a concise history of public art controversy in the United States, see Richard Serra, "Art and Censorship," in *Writings/Interviews* (University of Chicago Press, 1994), 214–23; Harriet F. Senie, *The Tilted Arc Controversy: Dangerous Precedent?* (University of Minnesota Press, 2001); and Marjorie Heins, "Public Art, Censorship, and the Constitution," *Public Art Review* 6, no. 1 (1994): 101–2.

2 Guisela Latorre, *Walls of Empowerment: Chicana/o Indigenist Murals of California* (University of Texas Press, 2008), 142.

3 Latorre, *Walls of Empowerment*, 142.

4 For more on the impact of government funding of community murals and art historical periodization of Chicana/o and African American art in the 1980s and 1990s, see Terezita Romo, "Points of Convergence: The Iconography of the Chicano Poster," in *Just Another Poster? Chicano Graphic Arts in California*, ed. Chon Noriega (University Art Museum, University of California, Santa Barbara, 2001), 92–115; see Michael D. Harris, "Urban Totems: The Communal Spirit of Black Murals," in *Walls of Heritage, Walls of Pride: African American Murals*, ed. James Prigoff and Robin J. Dunitz (Pomegranate Communications, 2000), 24–43.

5 One need only glimpse the monarch butterfly murals across downtown Sacramento, along with the other direct recreations of RCAF posters as murals in south Sacramento, sponsored by the Franklin Boulevard District, to trace the influence of the RCAF's visual vocabulary on contemporary public art in Sacramento.

6 Wide Open Walls, https://www.wideopenwalls.com/about/#board-section.

7 The subsection's title draws on a record of *Emergence* that offers a synopsis of the origins of Chicana/o art titled "Esteban Villa, Summer Youth Study / *Primera Epoca*: The Awareness of the Militant '60s," n.d. Royal Chicano Air Force Archives, CEMA 8, Box 17, Folder 3, Department of Special Collections, University Libraries, University of California, Santa Barbara (hereafter, "RCAF Archives").

8 Latorre, *Walls of Empowerment*, 146. Emphasis in original.

9 William Burg, *Sacramento Renaissance: Art, Music, and Activism in California's Capital City* (History Press, 2013). Alkali Flat was home to several canneries and mills from the late nineteenth to late twentieth centuries. See Steve M. Avella, *Sacramento: Indomitable City* (Arcadia, 2003).

10 Esteban Villa, interview by author, June 23, 2004.

11 See note 7.

12 Villa interview.

13 Diaz, *Flying Under the Radar*, 10–11, 40.

14 Villa interview. While Villa anchors his "start date" for *Emergence* in 1968–69, in an interview with the author, curator Terezita Romo points out that if the mural commenced during a summer youth study program at the Washington Neighborhood Center, then *Emergence* began in the summer of 1970, as Villa was not in Sacramento until fall 1969. Nevertheless, I find the years in which Villa situates his mural to be reflective of the historical context of the Third World Liberation Front strikes at university and college campuses in the San Francisco Bay Area, which led to the rise of ethnic studies and Chicana/o studies programs in particular.

15 Raúl Villa, *Barrio Logos: Space and Place in Urban Chicano Literature and Culture* (University of Texas Press, 2000), 189. Villa saw "graphic *testimonio*" as a visual record of a collective experience, extending the literary genre of *testimonio* to visual culture. This is a critically important lens for (re)considering other modes of cultural production as narrative and, in regard to the genre of *testimonio*, which is described as a "literature of personal witness" involving an interlocutor—a person who listens, responds, and shares a witness's account of historical events with a larger audience—or one beyond the community from which the witness comes forward. See John Beverley, "The Margin at the Center: On 'Testimonio' (Testimonial Narrative)," *Modern Fiction Studies* 35, no. 1 (Spring 1989): 11–28; "*testimonio*" is narrative that shares a collective experience of historical events, typically experiences of historical forces of power beyond one's control. See Ella Maria Diaz, "The Art of Telling: Toward a Genealogy of Testimoniadoras," *Label Me Latina/o* 13 (2023): 1–19.

16 Floyd Coleman, "Keeping Hope Alive: The Story of African American Murals," in Prigoff and Dunitz, *Walls of Heritage*, 10.

17 John Pitman Weber, "Politics and Practice of Community Public Art: Whose Murals Get Saved?" Essay presented at Getty Research Institute and Getty Conservation Institute Symposium, May 16–17, 2003, Los Angeles, https://www.getty.edu/conservation/publications_resources/pdf_publications/politics_community_art.html.

18 Beth Harris and Steven Zucker, "Diego Rivera, *Man Controller of the Universe*," in *Smarthistory*, March 19, 2020, accessed October 22, 2024, https://smarthistory.org/seeing-america-2/diego-rivera-man-controller-of-the-universe.

19 According to Alan W. Barnett, Cid's mural was titled *Por Libre Vida de mi Raza* and not considered two separate murals. See Alan W. Barnett, *Community Murals: The People's Art* (Cornwall Books, 1984), 274–75. In my 2017 book, I read the mural as two separate works, with the one on the building facade titled *Reno's Mural* and the panels surrounding the parking lot as *Para la Raza del Barrio*; Diaz, *Flying Under the Radar*, 200–202.

20 For more on the idea of the political, cultural, and creative intersections reflected in the mural, see Diaz, *Flying Under the Radar*, 199–200.

21 Diaz, *Flying Under the Radar*, 260–61.

22 "Pamphlet for the Washington Barrio Education Center," n.d., and "1978 Summer Schedule," n.d. SCUA-CSU, Sam Ríos Jr. Papers, Box 2, Folder 49.

23 Diaz, *Flying Under the Radar*, 204.

24 Latorre, *Walls of Empowerment*, 141. Emphasis in original.

25 Ben Keppel, Eva Sperling Cockcroft, John Pitman Weber, and James Cockcroft, *Toward A People's Art: The Contemporary Mural Movement*, 2nd ed. (University of New Mexico Press, 1998), xxvii.

26 Diaz, *Flying Under the Radar*, 186.

27 Diaz, *Flying Under the Radar*, 25.

28 Sacramento's 1977 Art in Public Places ordinance designated "2% of eligible City and County capital improvement project budgets be set aside for the commission, purchase, and installation of artworks," Folders for Art in Public Places, Sacramento Metropolitan Arts Commission Archives, 2016.

29 Diaz, *Flying Under the Radar*, 16, 114–18, 182–86.
30 Diaz, *Flying Under the Radar*, 214–16; See also Jane Goldman, "Art Against the Wall," *Sacramento Magazine*, August 8, 1980, RCAF Archives, CEMA 8, Box 27, Folder 33; "This Mural Hopes to Break Down Walls to Communication," *Sacramento Union*, July 17, 1980, RCAF Archives, CEMA 8, Box 29, Folder 1.
31 Diaz, *Flying Under the Radar*, 216.
32 Centro de Artistas Chicanos press release, RCAF Archives, CEMA 8, Box 16, Folder 10.
33 Lucy Lippard, *Mixed Blessings: New Art in a Multicultural America* (Pantheon, 1990).
34 Stan Padilla, interview by author, July 12, 2004.
35 Centro de Artistas Chicanos, "RCAF Inter-City Mural Project," June 16, 1980, CEMA 8, Box 8, Folder 5, RCAF Archive. See also Diaz, *Flying Under the Radar*, 218.
36 José Montoya, interview by author, July 5, 2004.
37 Montoya interview.
38 Ernesto Galarza, *Barrio Boy* (University of Notre Dame Press, 1971), 197.
39 Diaz, *Flying Under the Radar*, 182–86.
40 Burg, *Sacramento Renaissance*, 11.
41 *LASERIUM* was officially completed in 1984, but it could be argued that the tunnel murals began in 1978. For more on this, see Diaz, *Flying Under the Radar*, 182–86.
42 "Internal Memo from Department of Engineering to City Manager's Office," April 1, 1980, Sacramento Metropolitan Arts Commission Files; Juanishi Orosco, interview by author, December 23, 2000. Orosco worked with architect Roger Scott on the prisms. See Diaz, *Flying Under the Radar*, 224.
43 Gilka Romero, "Creativity Unleashed in Tunnel," *Sacramento Bee*, October 21, 1999. For more on Orosco's original design and revision of *LASERIUM*'s south wall mural, see Diaz, *Flying Under the Radar*, 223–26.
44 Resolution, collection of Terezita Romo.
45 Villa, *Barrio Logos*, 189.
46 Solon Wisham Jr., "Memo to Robert Thomas, Dir. Of Parks & Community Services," July 27, 1990, collection of Terezita Romo.
47 The stage was constructed in 1934 and named for "Robert E. Callahan, a former Southside Park resident when it was an Irish neighborhood who later became a community leader, city commissioner and Sacramento county supervisor." Burg, *Sacramento Renaissance*, 96.
48 Diaz, *Flying Under the Radar*, 95.
49 Sam Ríos Jr., "Chicano MURALIST: TOLTECAYOTL EN AZTLAN" 1978, 14, RCAF Archives, CEMA 8, Box 17, Folder 9.
50 Ríos, "Chicano MURALIST."
51 Terezita Romo, "Two Compas on a Mission: The Emergence of the Royal Chicano Air Force," master's thesis, California State University, Sacramento, 1996, 35.
52 In 2001, Esteban Villa and Ricardo Favela designed and created the Joe and Isabel Serna Memorial Fountain, which is a three-dimensional mural of sorts, a public art installation consisting of painted ceramic tiles offering aerial views of the San Joaquin Valley. Matt Wagar, "Fountain Built in Late Mayor, Wife's Honor," *State Hornet*, October 2, 2001.
53 Diaz, *Flying Under the Radar*, 22.
54 Diaz, *Flying Under the Radar*, 273.
55 "'Flight' Soars at the Golden 1 Center," March 2, 2018, https://www.philserna.net/flight-soars-at-the-golden-1-center/.
56 Latorre, *Walls of Empowerment*, 141.
57 The mural was commissioned by the Idaho Migrant Council. Handwritten notes attached to invoices and letters to the council, collection of Terezita Romo. The handwriting is more than likely that of Juanishi Orosco.
58 Dyana Curreri-Chadwick, "Centro de Artistas Chicanos: Progressive Mural Installation and Poster Exhibition (1969–80), Exhibition dates: May 14–June 26, 1983." Exhibition files, Crocker Art Museum.

What is the RCAF???

Luzmaria Espinosa, c. 1981

Salsa y Con Safos
y adobe airplanes.
Muchos hermanos Indio Chicanos,
Mujeres, y abuelos, students and niños,
Working together,
Striving for
CAMBIOS!
Through arte y cultura,
become
mentally
physically
and spiritually healthy,
Work for the betterment of all of humanity.
Completing
the
CYCLE
of our
ANTEPASADOS,
Aztlan is our nation, our language is POCHO,
Invincible AIR FORCE
Jalapeño ES cua DRON
No longer como dijo un Carnal
"Lost in a World of
Con fu SHON."
Somos Astro Pilots of Aztlan, arriving to El Sexto Sol!!

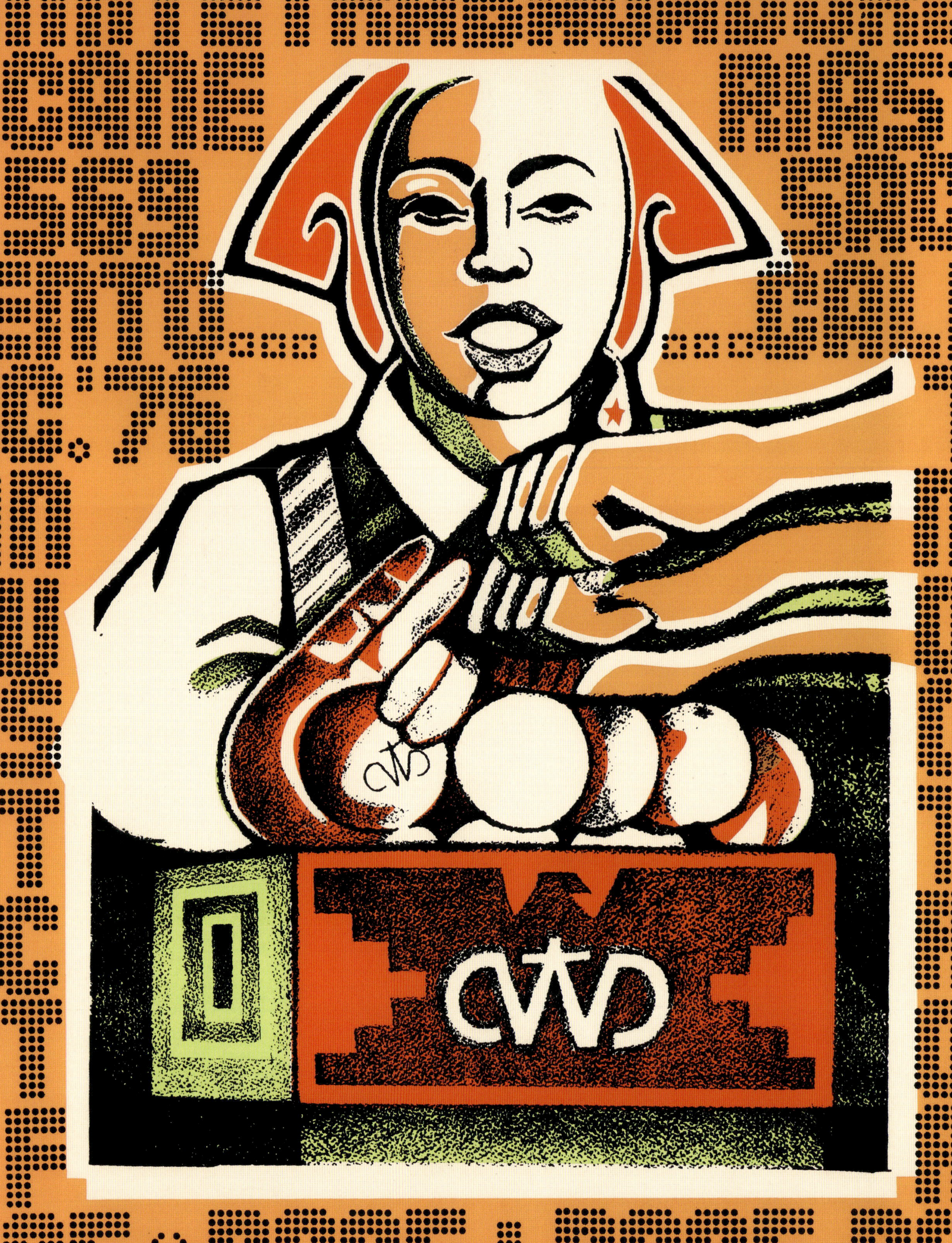

LORENA V. MÁRQUEZ

The Royal Chicano Air Force as a Grassroots Community Model

The Royal Chicano Air Force (RCAF) is one of the most important and well-known Chicana/o art collectives in the United States. Founded by artists in 1970, during the acceleration of the Chicano Movement in Sacramento, California, the RCAF's expansive artistic and activist repertoire would expand during its first decade from "poster making, muralism, poetry, music, and performance, to a breakfast program, community art classes, and political labor activism," and would eventually surpass the longevity, reach, and legacy of most Chicana/o art collectives in the nation.[1] The RCAF's success was due largely to their connections to *la gente* of Sacramento, as the artists came from similar working-class barrios (neighborhoods) and socioeconomic backgrounds. I define *la gente* as "working-class folks, males and females, U.S.-born and foreign-born, documented and undocumented—whose lives were largely governed and anchored in work and the protection of their families."[2] In essence, the RCAF's artists created art for and by *la gente*, including murals and posters, and also offered art classes in the community.

For many members of the RCAF, the art was personal, as it reflected their experiences, history, and commitment to social justice issues. They regularly attended meetings, rallies, and protests, all the while keeping the "creative fire," as described by Stan Padilla, alive.[3] In a 2015 interview, Padilla explained the significance of his involvement in the Chicano Movement: "The art I was dedicated to doing and am doing is for the good of community building and for the betterment of the human condition, not to enhance my life, because I'm a working-class artist. I come from a working-class family and that's how I approach things."[4] For Padilla and many other RCAF members, the needs of the community often superseded their own. In many ways, the community-centered philosophy helped not only attract new recruits to the RCAF but sustain membership over the decades.

While the work of its artists is invaluable, I argue that the RCAF created a grassroots community model through the incorporation of a bottom-up system that addressed economic disparities and social ills through a community-led and

Esteban Villa (1930–2022), *Comite Trabajadores de Canerias* (detail), 1976.

community-centered approach. During the 1960s, this model was adapted by marginalized communities throughout the world.[5] In Great Britain, for example, the Black Panther Party's "grassroots organizing centered on raising awareness of police brutality" and was used to address the oppression of the Black population.[6] Brian D. Christens, Jyoti Gupta, and Paul W. Speer define community organizing as a "process through which residents come together to build social power to investigate and take sustained collective action on systemic issues that negatively affect their daily lives."[7] Likewise, for the RCAF artists and community activists, the ability to come together for a greater good under often harsh and racially hostile conditions created lasting bonds not only among each other but also with the community they represented and served.

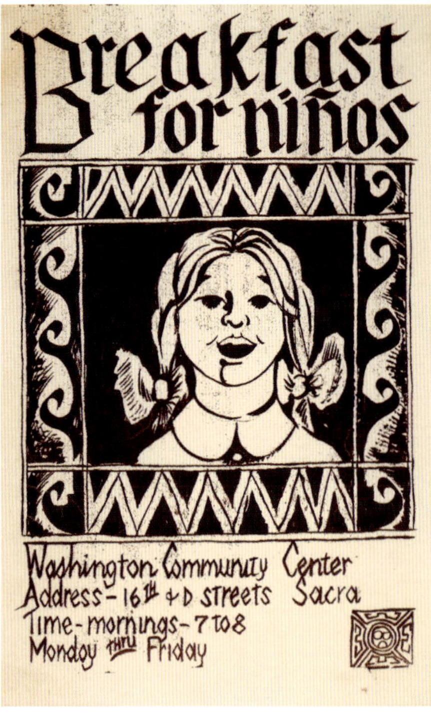

Fig. 1. Esteban Villa (1930–2022), *Breakfast for Niños*, 1969 [Plate 4].

RCAF's nonartist members served a crucial role in expanding their mission of serving *la gente*. In this essay, I will focus on four community members—Joe Serna Jr., Juanita Polendo Ontiveros, Rosemary Rasul, and Tim Quintero—who fought for farmworker rights, political representation, access to childhood nutrition, and affordable housing. The success of the RCAF was due to this unique integration of artists and community activists working together to uplift *la gente*.

One of the most visible examples of the RCAF's activism was Joe Serna Jr., who became a professor of government at Sacramento State (officially California State University, Sacramento), a city council member, and the first Chicano mayor of Sacramento, serving from 1992 to 1999. Others, such as José Montoya, Esteban Villa, and Ricardo Favela, were professors in the art department, while Sam Ríos Jr. taught in anthropology, Joseph Camacho in communication studies, and Frank Godina in ethnic studies. Juanita Polendo Ontiveros became the director of community advocacy, special projects at the Sacramento branch of the California Rural Legal Assistance Foundation, while also heading the Dolores Huerta Support Network in the Sacramento Valley and Northern California.[8] Rosemary Rasul served as the director of the Sacramento Concilio (a consortium of community organizations and social service agencies) as well as the Washington Community Council, where she oversaw the Breakfast for Niños (BFN) program that provided nutritious meals for low-income youth at multiple sites (fig. 1).[9] Tim Quintero served as the director of the federally funded Alkali Flat Redevelopment Project and retired as the area director for Sacramento's Neighborhood Services Department. Numerous other members worked for the City of Sacramento, the State of California, and the US Postal Service, while some became teachers and administrators at local schools and regional academic institutions. In their local, statewide, or national roles, the RCAF members continued to focus on community engagement and advocacy.

RCAF Membership

RCAF members were children of working-class Mexican immigrants who were farm, railroad, and cannery workers; many were also first-generation college students. Membership was loosely governed by a participant's willingness to further the RCAF's goals by demonstrating a commitment to the Chicana/o community. Some of the founding RCAF members were US veterans who were able to use the GI Bill to cover their college tuition. For example, Villa, Montoya, and Ríos Jr. were Korean War veterans. Others served during the Vietnam War, including Armando Cid, Juan "Juanishi" Orosco, David Rasul, Freddy Rodríguez, and Héctor González.[10] They crossed paths on the campus of Sacramento State (then known as Sacramento State College), which became the nexus for Chicano Movement student organizing. In 1967, there were only twenty-five self-identified Chicanas/os on a campus with an enrollment of 14,000—constituting less than one-half of one percent. By 1973, however, there was a 2,000 percent increase in Chicanas/os, accounting for 540 students in a total student body of 18,000—three percent of the total.[11]

The growth of the Chicana/o student body can be attributed, in part, to the founding of the Mexican American Education Project (MAEP), an innovative master of arts and teaching-credential program that ran from 1968 to 1973. MAEP was designed to better prepare K-12 educators to teach Chicana/o students through a culturally sensitive approach.[12] Several of the original RCAF members were recruited to Sacramento State through MAEP or were affiliated with the program, including Montoya, Ríos Jr., Villa, Irma Lerma Barbosa, and Juan Carrillo.[13] The fellowship enticed practicing teachers because it provided up to two years of financial support, including a monthly stipend, educational fees, possible summer study with pay, and an additional $400 allowance for each child/spouse dependent.[14]

The RCAF was a product of the national Chicano Movement and, by extension, a part of the civil rights era. Indeed, the uprisings of multiple sociopolitical campaigns generated unprecedented and energized provocations on college campuses across the nation, especially among marginalized groups. Montoya and Villa's original motivation was to create art that would instill cultural and historical pride as well as promote Chicana/o events on and off campus.[15] The artists' relationship with local activists, labor leaders, and community organizations helped expand the RCAF's influence. In fact, the RCAF became the go-to group for community event posters. Over time, they became one of the best-known Chicana/o art collectives in Northern California and were especially involved in partnerships with the United Farm Workers (UFW) labor union.

Joe Serna Jr. and Sacramento Politics

From very early on, the RCAF artist and nonartist members developed a close working relationship with union labor organizers César Chávez and Dolores Huerta of the UFW and Rubén Reyes of the Cannery Workers Committee in Sacramento. The working relationship and friendship between Chávez and Serna Jr. were noteworthy, and the two retained close ties over the course of their lives. Serna Jr., born to Mexican farmworker parents, labored in the fields as a farmhand when he was young. As migrant workers, the family

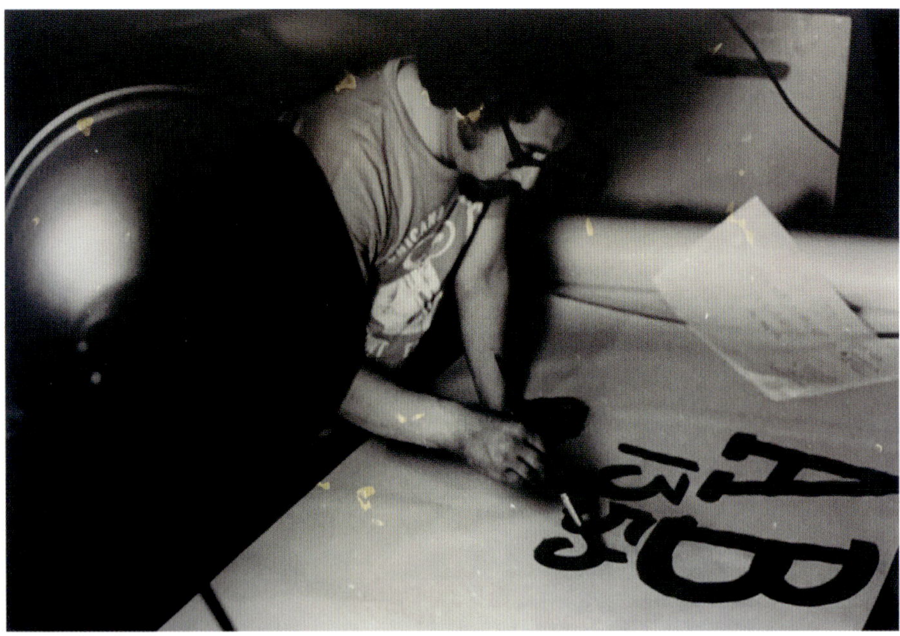

Fig. 2. Max Garcia (1942–2020), *José Montoya in Serna family garage*, early 1970s. Collection of Luis C. González.

followed the crops in the Imperial, San Joaquin, and Santa Clara valleys. In fact, it was a family affair.[16] His sister, María Elena Serna, recalled in a 1992 interview: "My [brother Joe] hated thinning grapes with a purple passion. We knew what field work was like.... When [my mother] told us if we didn't get our diplomas, we'd have to work in the fields, that was enough to put the fear in us."[17] The hard work of pruning, picking, and thinning crops left an impact on the Serna siblings. Similarly, Chávez was a child laborer accompanying his parents while they worked in the fields.[18]

Perhaps it was Serna Jr.'s and Chávez's humble upbringings, their firsthand experience of laboring in California's fields, and their desire to make the world more equitable for families like theirs that helped form their special bond. María Elena and Joe grasped at a young age that education was a vehicle out of the fields. Serna Jr. attended Sacramento City College, then earned a bachelor of arts in social science/government from Sacramento State in 1966, before enrolling in graduate school at the University of California, Davis in political science. He joined the Sacramento State faculty in 1969 as a professor in the government department.[19]

Serna Jr.'s life experiences set him up for a successful career in local politics. Like Chávez, who was a veteran of the US Navy, Serna Jr. was a veteran of the US Army (infantry). He later transferred to the Army Reserves and served from 1962 to 1968.[20] During that time, Serna Jr. joined the Peace Corps along with his first wife, Evelyn, and worked as a community development volunteer at the US Embassy in Guatemala City, Guatemala, in 1962.[21]

Serna Jr. was especially marked by his service in Guatemala. He later expressed this in a letter to voters on March 4, 1983:

Prior to going to Guatemala my life was fairly typical. . . . I worked in the fields as a young boy with my family. I soon went to work as a sheetmetal [sic] *worker and then on to college. There I developed the same cynical attitudes about America and its political institutions that marked that period in our country's recent history.*

But, like many people at that time, I continued to have a desire to be involved and to make things better.

I joined the Peace Corps and was sent to Guatemala.

It was there that my life was changed. It was there that I came to respect our political institutions, our freedom, and our obligation to be involved and make our society a better one.

In Guatemala I saw people walk for days in the mud just to exercise their right to vote. . . . I saw people being killed for speaking out on an issue. . . . I saw my closest friend murdered for standing up for another man's rights. . . . I learned that politics was important and that elections were a sacred act.

When I returned to Sacramento I resolved to get involved, to make our system of democratic government work. . . . I continue to have that desire. . . . I want to be the Mayor [of Sacramento].[22]

This was a watershed moment for Serna Jr. Seeing Guatemalan peasants exercising their right to vote led him to reconsider the importance of American democracy in the world. From that point forward, he committed himself to politics.

When Serna Jr. joined the faculty at Sacramento State, he met and collaborated with student activists, including artists, aligned with the Chicano Movement. He and Evelyn served an instrumental role in the founding of the RCAF, allowing the group to use their garage to set up screenprinting equipment and to print and store posters (fig. 2). Later, RCAF members helped generate publicity for his political campaigns, with the artists making yard signs (fig. 3) and bumper stickers.[23] This helped him win election to the Sacramento City Council, where he served for eighteen years.[24] Serna Jr. was then poised for what would become his highest elected office, mayor of Sacramento.[25]

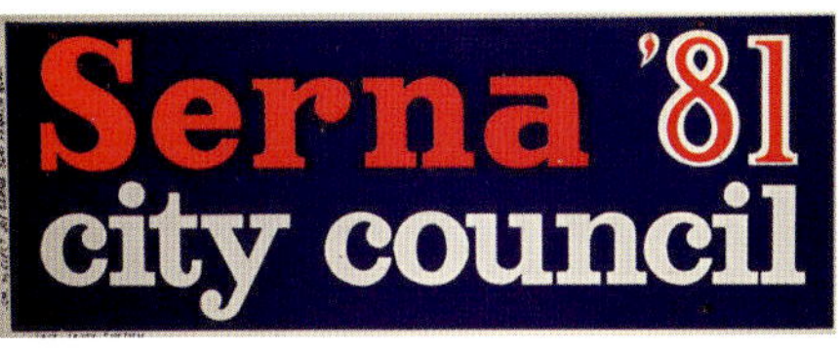

Fig. 3. Evelyn Jenkins-Cronn (1940–1993), *Serna City Council Lawn Sign*, 1981. Screenprint, 12 × 32 in. Serna Family Collection. Photograph by Phil Serna.

In addition to being an inspiring professor, Serna Jr. was also a gifted grassroots community organizer. He founded the Chicano Organization for Political Awareness (COPA; fig. 4), which ran voter registration drives, staffed phone banks, undertook precinct walks, and put Chicanas/os on the ballot. In 1969, for example, COPA, with the help of the RCAF, was instrumental in electing Manuel Ferrales as the first Mexican American member of the Sacramento City Council. Raymond P. Váldez, a COPA member, recalled the impact Serna made on him and other Chicanas/os in a 2015 interview:

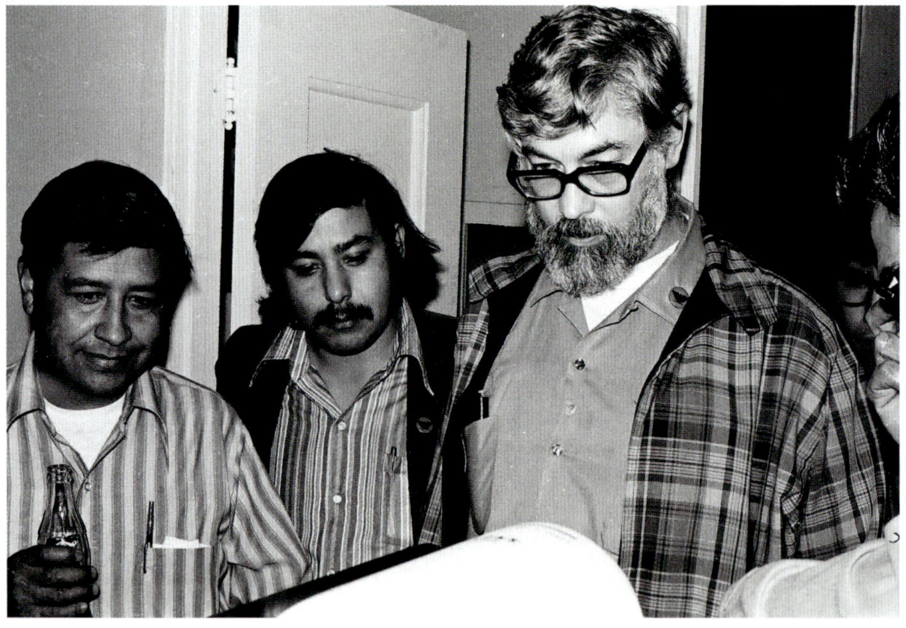

Fig. 4. Héctor D. González (born 1945), *César Chávez, Joe Serna Jr., and Father Keith Kenny observing the printing press at the Chicano Organization for Political Awareness (COPA) office*, 1971. Collection of Héctor D. González.

I got involved with COPA 'cause when Joe Serna started the program ... it was ... right in my neighborhood.... I was involved with that with him and helping him get elected, looking at the things politically because there's also the political aspect of the whole thing. And to me that's one of the most important part[s], politically, 'cause if you have the right people making the right decisions helping the people ... it will help everyone ... to that level where they can do very well in our society.[26]

Serna Jr. was able to recruit college students, including RCAF artists Luis "Louie the Foot" González and his brother Héctor, who was dubbed the photographer of the Chicano Movement in Sacramento, to engage in political and civic action. Héctor recalled, "When I heard him speak about politics, I thought this is the smartest man in the world."[27] With his oratory talent and compelling life story, Serna Jr. was a forceful speaker who motivated audiences. As Serna Jr. ascended in local politics, his and the RCAF's connection to Chávez remained steadfast.

The RCAF and the UFW

The UFW grew to depend on the RCAF as one of its graphic arms, relying on its artists to produce and help distribute posters for rallies and to promote workers' rights, as well as provide images for the grape and lettuce boycotts. Activist Juanita Polendo Ontiveros best captured this relationship in a 2014 interview: "The artists [of the RCAF] were such that, he [César Chávez] understood this, that you couldn't organize whatever movement, whatever cause without the help of the artists because without the artists there are no posters, no buttons, no flags; there is no communication without the artists."[28]

Ontiveros attests to the essential role of the RCAF not only in the farmworker movement but also in the Chicano Movement. She credits the RCAF for effectively communicating to *la gente*.

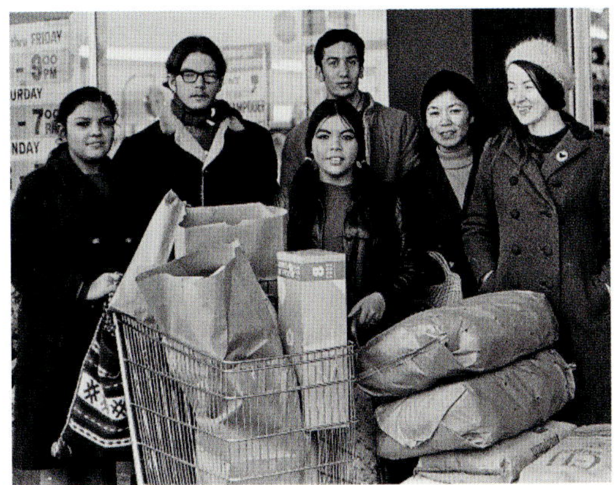

Fig. 5. Héctor D. González (born 1945), *Juanita Polendo Ontiveros (center) leading food drive for UFW*, c. 1968. Collection of Héctor D. González.

The RCAF members were staunch supporters of the UFW's efforts in part because many of them had labored—much like as Chávez and Serna Jr.—in the fields alongside their parents. As Orosco explained:

We were farm workers. Our parents were farm workers, and we knew what the conditions were. So, when the United Farm Workers movement was alive, we jumped in because that was our life experience. I had worked in the fields helping my mother [and] my father, Jesús and Carmen Orosco. They worked hard in the fields all their lives and they raised nine kids and on $100 a month.[29]

This close association with farmworkers and firsthand experience working in the fields enhanced the RCAF's connection with the goals of the UFW. Ontiveros became the UFW's liaison with the RCAF, coordinating picket lines, organizing boycotts at area stores, and arranging for housing and food for farmworkers' rallies at the Capitol as well as a security detail for Chávez while he was in the Sacramento region (fig. 5).

At a young age, Ontiveros had worked as a farmhand and remembered being sprayed with pesticides while in the fields. Supporting the UFW as a student, she has spent her entire adult life working to secure farmworker rights. Ontiveros's commitment to those rights was memorialized in a poster by González, who used a photo by his brother Héctor to create posters for International Women's Year in 1975 (fig. 6 and pl. 70). The image shows Ontiveros in a headscarf, along with Rosalie Souza, a fellow UFW picketer, confronted by the police.

According to Ontiveros, the UFW directed the RCAF to organize farmworkers to graft trees in the Sutter/Yuba area (north of Sacramento). They received clear instructions to organize a peaceful picket line because, as Ontiveros recalled, it was an area "very hostile to people like us." Things quickly became tense when "everybody that had a badge came and immediately started questioning us and booing us." The police asked the two Chicanas for their names and questioned the legality of their assembly. Neither of the women possessed identification, so instead, they gave the officers a fictitious name that Ontiveros stated was from an Indigenous language: "Watachi" (which means "I am me"). "They kept insisting," Ontiveros continued, "'That is not a legal name, everyone has a first and last name.'" To which Ontiveros responded, "No, not everybody. Our people, our ancestors, we have natural names like Wildflower, Crazy Turtle, Crazy Horse. WATACHI." The police grew frustrated and said, "Okay, that does it. I'm taking you in!"[30] Souza and Ontiveros were arrested for not cooperating with police. They were consequently jailed, and the UFW posted their bail shortly thereafter.

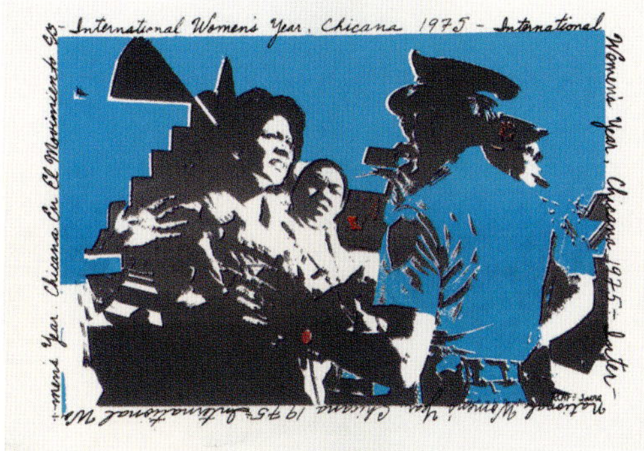

Fig. 6. Luis C. González (born 1953) and Héctor D. González (born 1945), *International Women's Year, Chicana*, 1975. Screenprint, 15 × 22 in. Collection of Luis C. González.

Héctor González, who was photographing the picketers, captured the arrest on camera. The police also threatened him. "They said, 'Hey, stop taking photos! We're going to take that camera away.' I said, 'I don't think you could catch me.' Because you know I had just gotten out of the army. I was faster than them," he chuckled.[31] This relationship between the RCAF and the UFW is memorialized in numerous posters that promoted fundraising events and UFW meetings, as well as California Proposition 14 in 1976 (pl. 71). That measure would have enabled union organizers to enter places of employment to campaign for union elections and allow the state's Agricultural Labor Relations Board to conduct hearings on unfair labor practices, among other things.[32] In spite of the RCAF and UFW efforts, the proposition failed by an overwhelming margin.[33]

The RCAF in *Los Barrios*

The RCAF targeted not only national and statewide matters, but also local issues, including in the Mexican/Chicana/o barrios in Sacramento. Born into a family of cannery workers, Rosemary Rasul had attained a successful career as a buyer for the Macy's department store in Downtown Sacramento before "the spirit of the Chicano Movement struck her heart and she quit."[34] Initially hired as a secretary, Rasul eventually became director of the Washington Community Council (WCC), a social services agency aiding the Washington barrio. There, Sacramento State anthropology professors Sam Ríos Jr. and Senón Valádez introduced her to their Breakfast for Niños (BFN) program. According to Ella Maria Diaz, "Conveyed through its bilingual name, Breakfast for Niños was explicitly a Chicana/o response to a basic need within their community."[35]

The BFN program was modeled on the Black Panther's Free Breakfast for School Children Program that provided breakfast at no cost to inner-city Black youth. Bobby Seale, Black Panther Party co-founder, initially called for volunteers to run the program in Oakland, California, in September 1968, and it was up and running by January 1969.[36] RCAF member Irma Lerma Barbosa learned of the initiative through the Oakland Black Panthers study group. After touring the Black Panther Party's breakfast program, she realized a similar project could be instituted in Sacramento's barrios. She solicited the help of her comrade Mariana Rivera, a Sacramento Brown Beret, to help her recruit volunteers at the Sacramento State campus.

The BFN program was formalized when Lerma Barbosa sought the support of one of her MAEP instructors, Senón Valádez. She recalled, in 1969, "He [Valádez] made it a class for credit called the Community Involvement and Poverty and Education Project at Sac State."[37] By 1972, Professor Ríos Jr. was co-managing the BFN program with WCC director Rasul, and RCAF member Jennie Baca was serving as its coordinator.[38] By offering a class in which students received college credit for serving free breakfast to children at multiple low-income sites such as Washington, Dos Rios, and Stanford Settlement Housing Projects, the program became a model for grassroots community activation.

Rasul provided the leadership and vision necessary to keep BFN in operation. In 1975, BFN was incorporated as a nonprofit and expanded to include "comprehensive youth services ... that would include free breakfast each school morning, cultural and recreational programs, tutoring, parent involvement and to increase the educational achievement level of low-income youth."[39] Key to the BFN's

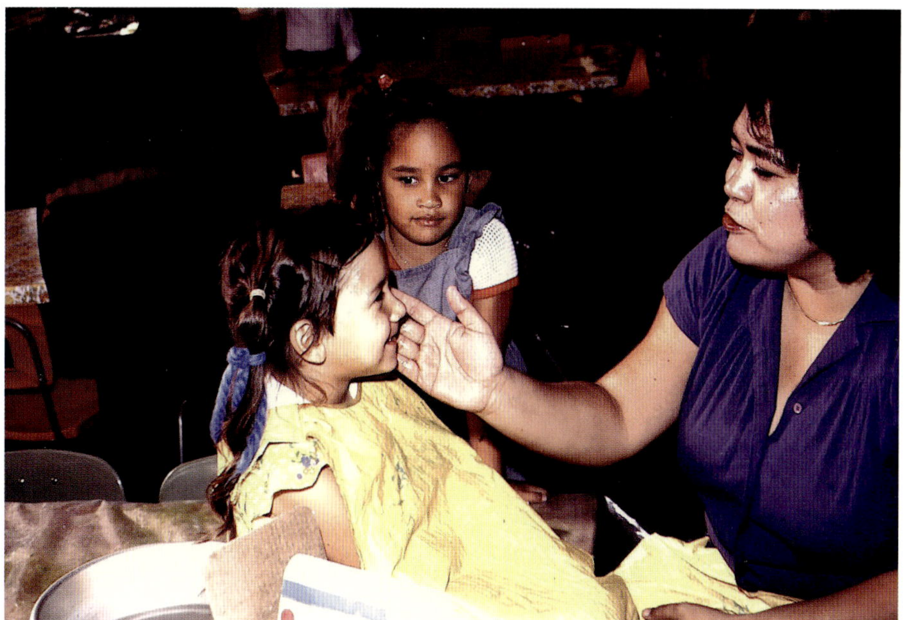

Fig. 7. Alfred "Freddy" González (born 1955), *Rosemary Rasul, Breakfast for Niños director, at mask-making workshop for Día de los Muertos*, late 1970s. Collection of Alfred "Freddy" González.

growth and stability were Rasul's administrative capabilities and grant-writing skills, which she used to secure and grow city and county operational grants as well as Comprehensive Employment and Training Act (CETA) funds to augment staffing. In 1975, Rasul also procured a contract from the Sacramento City Unified School District to "prepare breakfast for elementary K–6 pupils residing in the Washington School attendance area."[40] By securing sizable grants and the commitment from the local school districts, the BFN program reached underserved children on a larger scale.

The BFN's close association with the Centro de Artistas Chicanos allowed for the co-presentation of community cultural programs, most notably the Día de las Madres (May) and Operation Christmas Unity (December) celebrations, which were free for families and held in neighborhood school auditoriums. Día de las Madres provided families with a free dinner along with a music and dance program (pls. 48–50). The Operation Christmas Unity event included refreshments, a large piñata, and a toy giveaway (pls. 51–53). According to BFN program coordinator Melinda Santana Rasul, "We were able to bring those type of activities into their lives, because probably [they] wouldn't have gotten them, considering their family situation. So those type of things that we did, and these are more grassroot things, but they were important. There [are] young people that we worked with that went on to continue their college education" (fig. 7).[41] Thus, Rasul's commitment to the community's children not only impacted their health but also their futures.

Tim Quintero, another longtime RCAF activist, was deeply entrenched in community redevelopment and social service agencies. Born in Sonora, Mexico, Quintero was raised in the Broderick barrio, now West Sacramento, from the age of nine. Drawing from his experiences as a young boy, he was keenly aware and

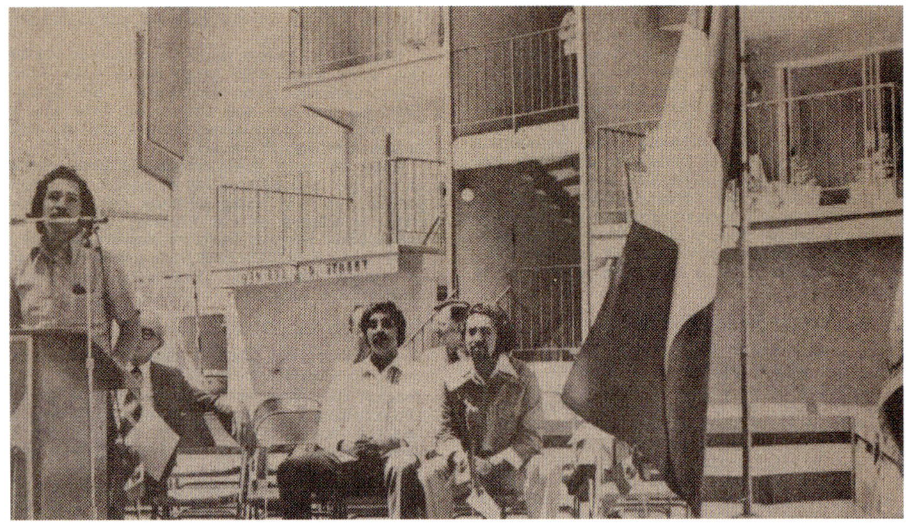

Fig. 8. Rodolfo Cuellar Sr. (1927–2008), *Dedication ceremony for Zapata Park,* August 8, 1975. Left to right: Francisco "Fox" Godina, Bill Aguirre, and Tim Quintero. Collection of Terezita Romo.

sensitive to the multiple economic, social, educational, and health disadvantages faced by families in working-poor communities.[42] Hence, Quintero had worked tirelessly throughout most of his adult life to bring semblances of hope in an often depressed and neglected part of Sacramento's barrios, which, he surmised, had suffered too much for too long. In 1968, he began his career as a fierce social worker and community advocate, volunteering at the Sacramento Concilio after reading about its establishment in a local newspaper. Soon, he was hired in the group's Family Service Center, which he recalled in a recent interview "changed my whole life—for the better."[43]

Quintero's work at the Sacramento Concilio set him on the path for a lifetime committed to change through social service and community redevelopment agencies. Later, he served as director of the Alkali Flat Redevelopment Project and its Project Area Committee (PAC), beginning on January 2, 1973.[44] PAC was a "local, urban redevelopment project located in the northwest section of downtown Sacramento" with approximately 1,500 residents. Its board made "decisions on low-income, senior citizens housing development, rehabilitation of substandard housing structures, rezoning decisions, commercial and industrial development," including the development of park space and other issues affecting Alkali Flat residents.[45] Quintero's work with the Sacramento Concilio and PAC is indicative of a successful career in social service agencies that addressed the needs of *la gente*.

As a member of the RCAF, Quintero was able to merge his interests by establishing and dedicating a Sacramento city park to the Mexican Revolutionary hero Emiliano Zapata. Located on 8th and E Streets, and known by residents as Zapata Park, it is a recreational green space for the Chicana/o communities of Alkali Flat (fig. 8). The park was funded through the Alkali Flat Redevelopment Project, which called for the establishment of parks in inner-city neighborhoods. After the completion of the Washington Square Apartments, the first federally

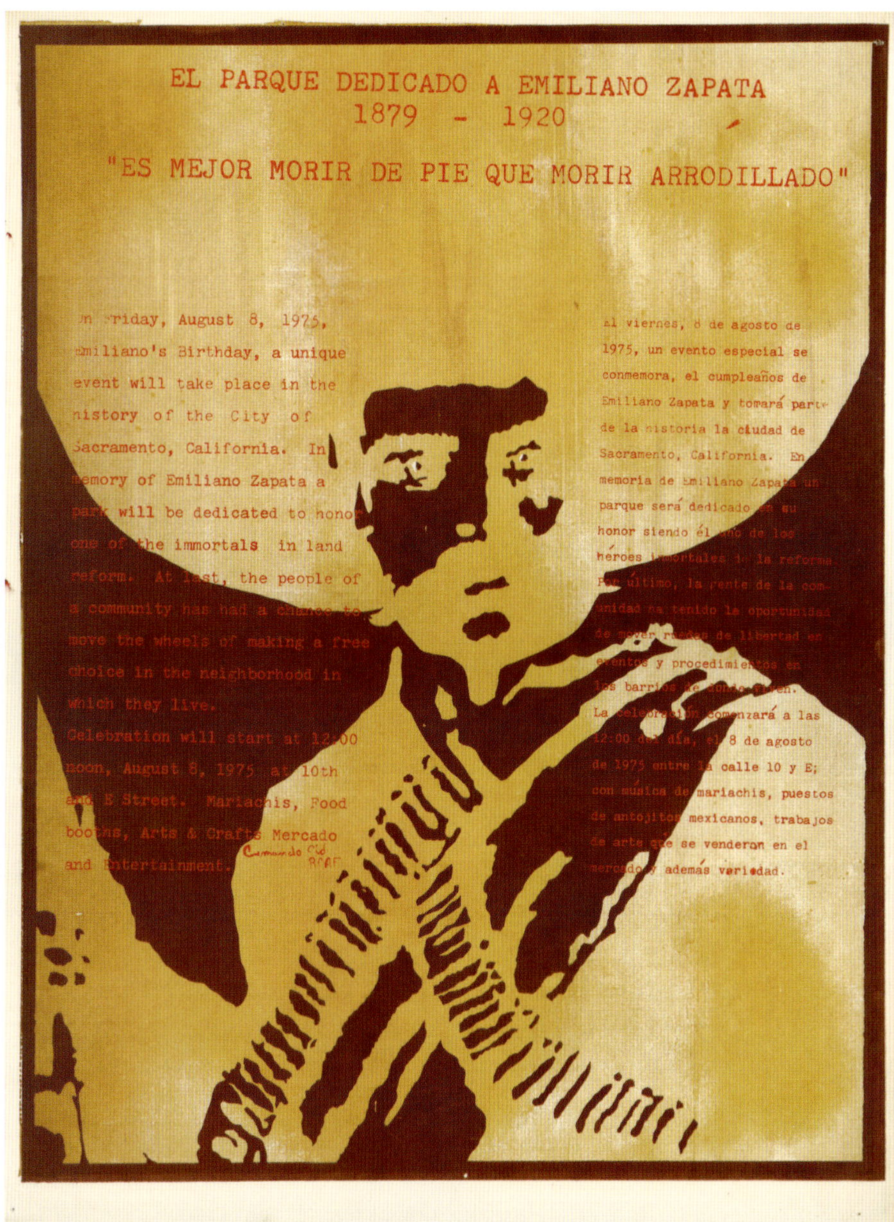

Fig. 9. Armando Cid (1943–2009), *El Parque Dedicado a Emiliano Zapata*, 1975 [Plate 22].

funded, subsidized, family-housing project in Alkali Flat, it made sense to build a park nearby for the residents to enjoy. Quintero recalled that once the park's funding was secured,

The big fight was, "What are we going to name it?"

The City Parks Director . . . said "We're going to name it Vallejo". . . .

"Why do you want to name it that?"

"Wasn't he a Californiano [Californio] and part of the [Chicano] history?"

I said, "No. We're not going to name it that!"

"Well, that's what my recommendation is to the City Council."...

I said, "Our recommendation is we're going to name it after Emiliano Zapata, period."

So he goes to the City Council, he makes his presentation, I go next. I've got Martha Bustamante. I've got all my Chicanos out in the audience at City Hall. We bring candles. It's like a demonstration.

I said, "We didn't want [it] to be named after ... Vallejo, someone who didn't mean anything to the Chicanos. We are Chicanos now. This is our time ... you can see our community is in favor of it because we call ourselves Chicanos.... Emiliano Zapata represents us as revolutionaries for freedom.... We are his descendants, and we want to continue that legacy of Emiliano Zapata."[46]

Luckily, Quintero recalled, the City Council members were progressive and knew of the Chicano Movement, and they voted to name the park after Zapata. According to Quintero, the Cómite Patriótico Mexicano de Sacramento purchased a bronze bust of Emiliano Zapata from Mexico, and Quintero was able to secure additional funding to build the pedestal and fencing around it.

The Chicana/o community, through the leadership of Quintero, won one of many victories during the Chicano Movement in Sacramento. By distancing himself and the Chicana/o community from the historical legacies of Spanish and Californio conquests, and insisting on Zapata as the park's name, Quintero was making a case that Chicanas/os were better aligned with the Mexican Revolutionary hero who stood for *tierra y libertad* (land and freedom). He made a case that the green space stood for more than a simple park; it stood as a symbol of historical pride and empowerment. Zapata Park opened to the public on August 8, 1975 (fig. 9). At its inauguration, RCAF philosopher Francisco Godina stated that the park represented "[un] orgullo para la colonia mexicana como para la comunidad en general" (a source of pride for the Mexican residents as well as the larger community).[47]

The RCAF Legacy

The RCAF forms an important chapter in the national Chicano Movement and Sacramento's history. The group's artistic reach and legacy are memorialized through archival collections and multiple books on Chicana/o art, including Ella Maria Diaz's books *Flying Under the Radar with the Royal Chicano Air Force: Mapping a Chicana/o Art History* and *José Montoya*, as well as artist Carlos Francisco Jackson's *Chicana and Chicano Art: ProtestArte*, among others. Chicana/o scholars consider Chicana/o art a form of resistance and an integral part of the Chicano Movement.

The RCAF comprised not only artists but also community activists who contributed to a grassroots model of activism. These activists left an imprint on the Sacramento landscape, as exemplified by Quintero's leadership with Zapata Park and Rasul's direction of the BFN program that helped hundreds of families. They also played a crucial role in local politics, as noted by Serna Jr.'s political ascendance to become the first Chicana/o mayor of Sacramento. They worked tirelessly for farmworker rights through the UFW, as demonstrated by the crusades of Juanita Polendo Ontiveros. These activists were equally valuable members of the RCAF, yet their contributions are often left out of the art collective's history.

The RCAF's impact in Sacramento remains strong because of its steadfast commitment to the Chicana/o community's struggles for social and economic justice. This is corroborated by multiple interviews of RCAF members, who continuously center the Chicana/o community in their organizing efforts and artistic practices. The RCAF helped originate other community programs that deserve mention, including the Barrio Art Program at Sacramento State and La Raza Bookstore, which became La Raza Galeria Posada. Luis González encapsulated what it meant to be a member of the RCAF when he stated:

The membership was committed overall to accomplishing any big or small thing that would benefit the [Chicana/o] community.... The RCAF would not have been so successful if it hadn't been for all the different spider organizations ... you have the Breakfast for Niños, the Barrio Art class, the high school art classes, the Cultural Affairs Committee.... The RCAF, it was the core group. And I think the fact that we were producing posters to help document our history and also celebrate our culture, it was something visible that people could see and appreciate.[48]

In a way, then, one could argue that the Chicana/o community dictated or at the very least influenced the agenda of the RCAF. To become a member of the RCAF was to lead a life committed to *la causa* and, especially, to *la gente*.

Notes

1 Ella Maria Diaz, *Flying Under the Radar with the Royal Chicano Air Force: Mapping a Chicano/a Art History* (University of Texas Press, 2017), 1, 8–9.

2 Lorena V. Márquez, *La Gente: Struggles for Empowerment and Community Self-Determination in Sacramento* (University of Arizona Press, 2020), 4.

3 The Sacramento Movimiento Chicano Oral History Project, "The Sacramento Chicano Movement: From Voiceless to Empowered," privately archived documentary, 2017, 10:27.

4 Stan Padilla, interview by David Rasul, October 15, 2015. Transcript from Sacramento Movimiento Chicano and Mexican American Education Oral History Project, Donald and Beverly Gerth Special Collections and University Archives, California State University Sacramento (hereafter, "Oral History Project"), 14.

5 Anne-Marie Angelo, "'Black Oppressed People All over the World Are One': The British Black Panthers' Grassroots Internationalism, 1969–1973," *Journal of Civil and Human Rights* 4, no. 1 (Spring/Summer 2018): 64–97.

6 Angelo, "Black Oppressed People," 78.

7 Brain D. Christens, Jyoti Gupta, and Paul W. Speer, "Community Organizing: Studying the Development and Exercise of Grassroots Power," *Journal of Community Psychology* 49, no. 8 (November 2021): 3002.

8 Sacramento Poderosas, "Juanita Polendo Ontiveros, Sacramento Poderosa 2022," https://sacpoderosas.org/juanita-polendo-ontiveros.

9 Obituary for Rosemary Rasul, "In Memoriam," *Sacramento Bee*, April 11, 2021.

10 Diaz, *Flying Under the Radar*, 9.

11 *The Mexican American Education Project: Final Report* (California State University Sacramento, Department of Special Collections and University Archives, 1973), 5.

12 *Mexican American Education Project*, 129.

13 Diaz, *Flying Under the Radar*, 9–10.

14 *Mexican American Education Project*, 19.

15 Luis C. González, interview by author, August 25, 2024.

16 Armed Forces of the United States Report of Transfer or Discharge, US Government, Box 1, MSS 2004/19:1, Joe Serna Jr. Papers, Donald and Beverly Gerth Special Collections and University Archives, California State University Sacramento (hereafter, "Serna Papers").

17 Lan-Chen Pao, "Out of the Fields," *Lodi News-Sentinel*, May 18, 1992, Box 1, "Gerenia Serna" folder, Serna Papers.

18 Susan Ferris and Ricardo Sandoval, *The Fight in the Fields: Cesar Chavez and the Farmworkers Movement* (Harcourt Brace, 1997), 19.

19 "Joe Serna Jr., Mayor of Sacramento," 1999, Box 1, Serna Papers.

20 Armed Forces of the United States Report of Transfer or Discharge.

21 Joe and Evelyn met while they were students at Lodi High School, near Sacramento. "Woodbridge Couple Serves with Guatemala Peace Corps," *Lodi News-Sentinel*, November 16, 1966, Box 1, "Scrapbook" folder, Serna Papers. Record of Military Status of Registrant, US Government, January 22, 1968, Box 1, Serna Papers.

22 Joe Serna Jr., Councilman, "Dear Friend Letter," Box 1, "Scrapbook" folder, Serna Papers.

23 Luis C. González, interview by author, June 9, 2024.

24 Serna, "Dear Friend Letter" and "Sacramento Mayor Joe Serna Jr. Dies: First Latino in the Job, Loyal Ally of Cesar Chavez," *San Francisco Chronicle*, November 8, 1999, Box 1, "Newspaper and Magazine Articles" Folder, Serna Papers.

25 "Joe Serna, Jr., Sacramento City Councilman, District 5," 1991, Box 1, Serna Papers.

26 Raymond P. Váldez, interview by Senón Valádez, June 25, 2015, Oral History Project.

27 Héctor González, interview by author, August 25, 2024.

28 "Los artistas [de RCAF] son, él [César Chávez] sabia, que nada se podía hacer en organizar cualquier movimiento, cualquier causa sin la ayuda de los artistas, porque sin los artistas no hay cartelones, no hay botones, no hay banderas, no hay nada de comunicación sin los artistas." Juanita Polendo Ontiveros, interview by Valeria García, May 31, 2014, Oral History Project.

29 Juanishi Orosco, quoted in Steve LaRosa and Toby Momtaz, producers, *Royal Chicano Air Force—Art and Activism*, aired September 15, 2021, KVIE, https://www.pbs.org/video/royal-chicano-air-force-art-and-activism-pgl7zg.

30 Juanita Polendo Ontiveros, interview by author, August 30, 2024.

31 Héctor González, interview by author, August 25, 2024.

32 Yes on 14 Flyer, "Farm Workers Ask You to Vote Yes on Prop. 14," University of California, San Diego Library, https://libraries.ucsd.edu/farmworkermovement/ufwarchives/RogeroPitt/04/Yes%20on%2014%20Flyers_001.pdf.

33 California Proposition 14, Agricultural Labor Relations Board Initiative (1976), Ballotpedia, accessed on September 22, 2024, https://ballotpedia.org/California_Proposition_14,_Agricultural_Labor_Relations_Board_Initiative_(1976).

34 David Rasul, interview by Nataly Figueroa and Jordon Nguyen, April 29, 2015, Oral History Project, 18–19.

35 Diaz, *Flying Under the Radar*, 102.

36 Joshua Bloom and Waldo E. Martin Jr., *Black Against Empire: The History and Politics of the Black Panther Party* (University of California Press, 2016), 181–82.

37 Quoted in Diaz, *Flying Under the Radar*, 103.

38 Diaz, *Flying Under the Radar*, 104. According to Diaz, RCAF members "Lupe Portillo, Gina Montoya, and Melinda Santana (Rasul) also served as program coordinators at various times."

39 "Request For Funds—Fiscal Year 1978–79," Royal Chicano Air Force Archives, CEMA 8, Box 10, Folder 18, Department of Special Collections, University Libraries, University of California, Santa Barbara (hereafter, "RCAF Archives").

40 "Washington Community Council Breakfast Program Agreement," November 3, 1975, RCAF Archives, CEMA 8, Box 8, Folder 7.

41 Melinda Santana Rasul, interviewed by Alejandra Romero, May 8, 2014, Oral History Project, 8.

42 Tim Quintero, interview by author, February 28, 2024.

43 Quintero interview.

44 *Alkali Review*, June 1990, 3. Courtesy of Tim Quintero, scan in author's possession.

45 *Alkali Review*, February–March, 1988, 1. Courtesy of Tim Quintero, scan in author's possession.

46 Quintero interview.

47 "Celebración de Día Del Maiz En Zapata Park," *El Hispano*, June 6, 1976.

48 Luis C. González interview, August 25, 2024.

Plates

Introduction

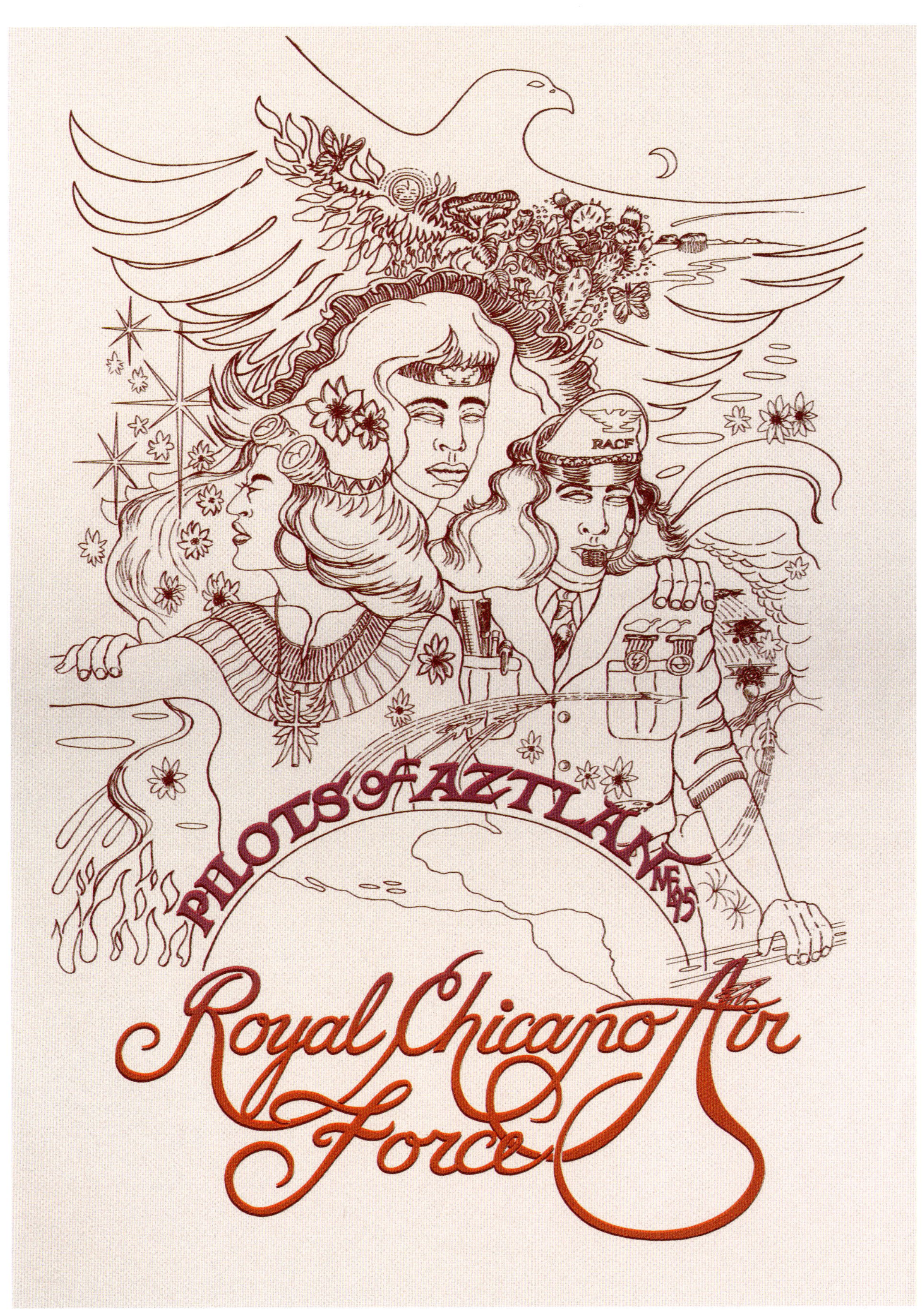

1 Max Garcia (1942–2020), *Pilots of Aztlan–Royal Chicano Air Force*, 1995. Screenprint, 19 × 30 in. Royal Chicano Air Force Poster Collection, Gerth Special Collections & University Archives, California State University, Sacramento.

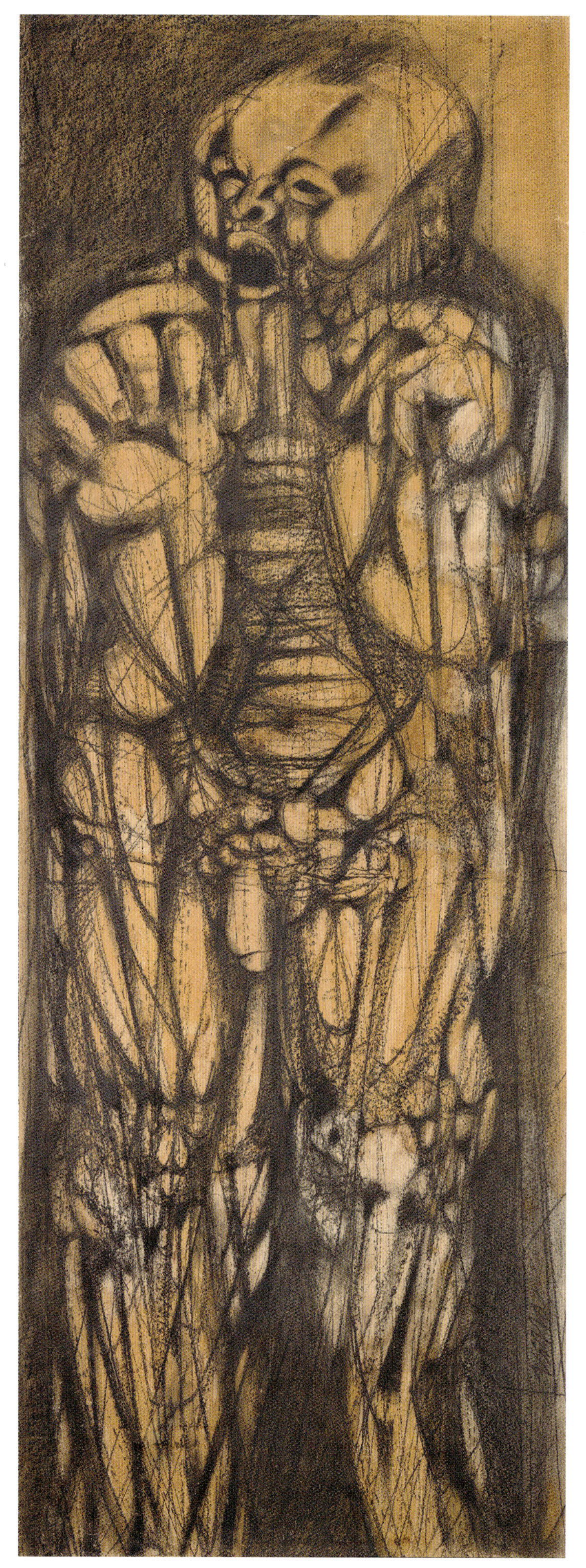

2 Esteban Villa (1930–2022), *Untitled*, c. 1966. Art crayon on board, 80 × 30 in. Villa Family Collection.

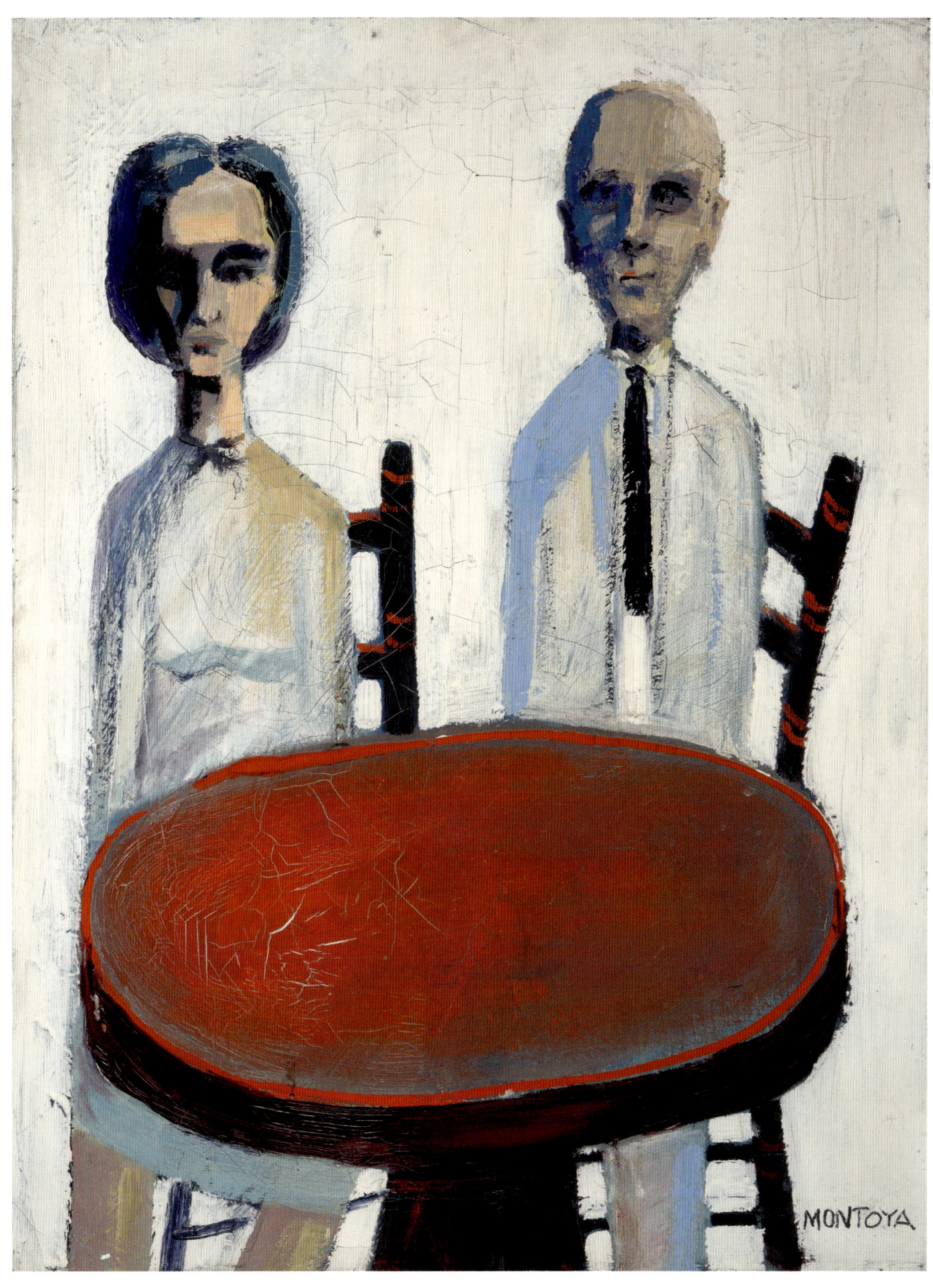

3 José Montoya (1932–2013), *The Visit*, 1965. Oil on canvas, 38 × 24 in. Stacy Paragary Collection.

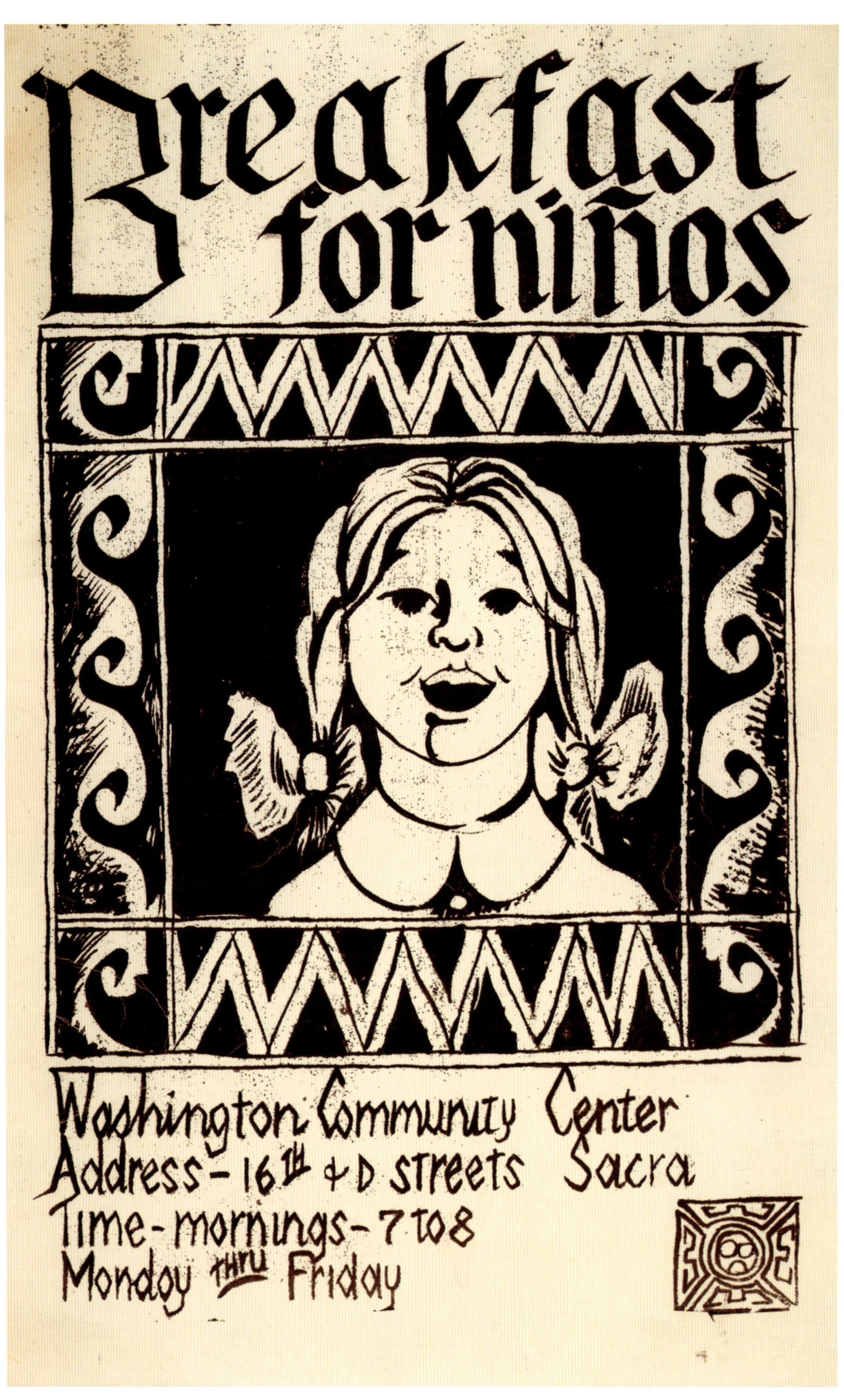

4 Esteban Villa (1930–2022), *Breakfast for Niños*, 1969. Screenprint, 22 × 14 in. Royal Chicano Air Force Archives, CEMA 8, University of California, Santa Barbara Library.

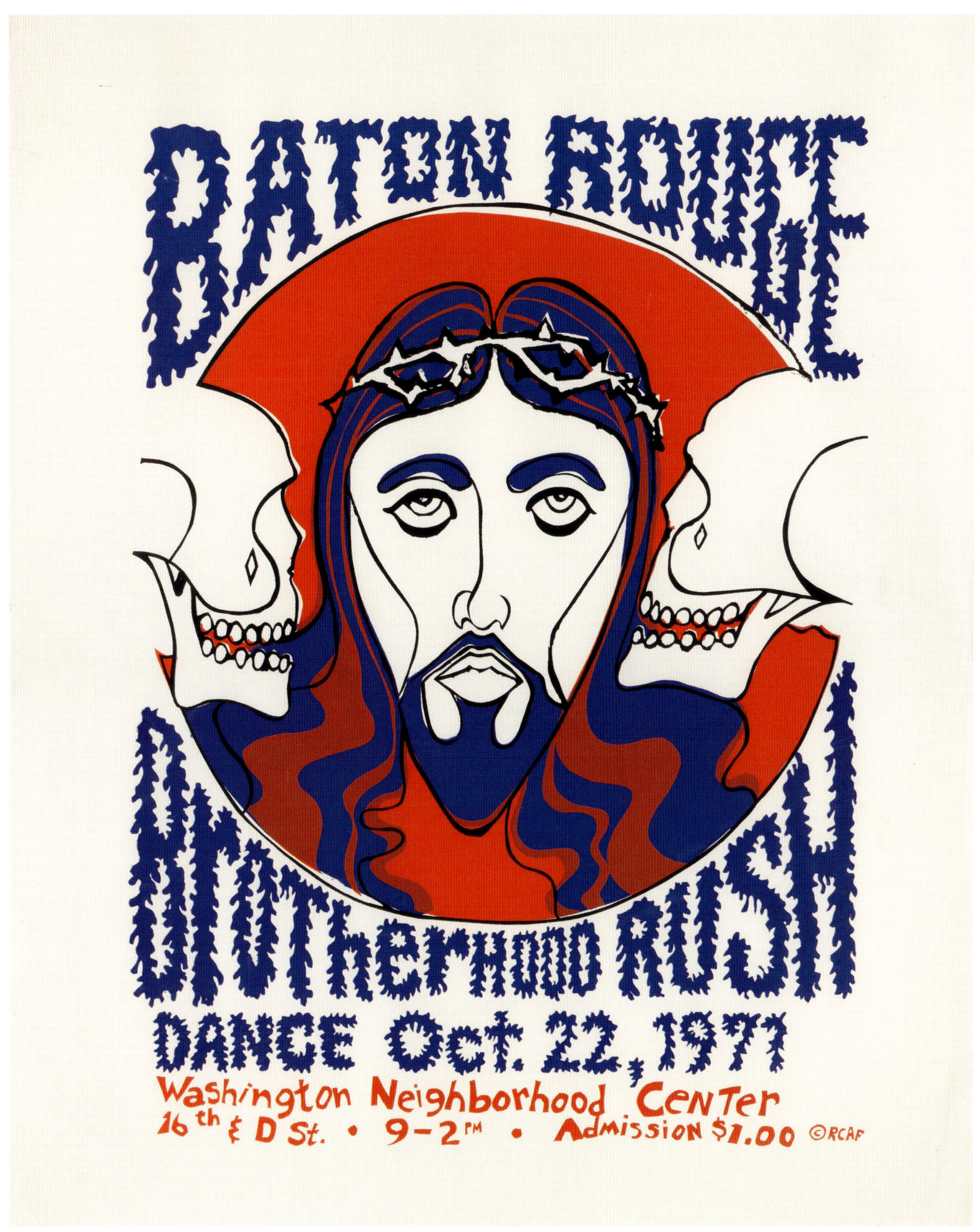

5 Max Garcia (1942–2020), *Baton Rouge*, 1971. Screenprint, 26 7/8 × 22 1/4 in. Rasul Chicano Art Collection.

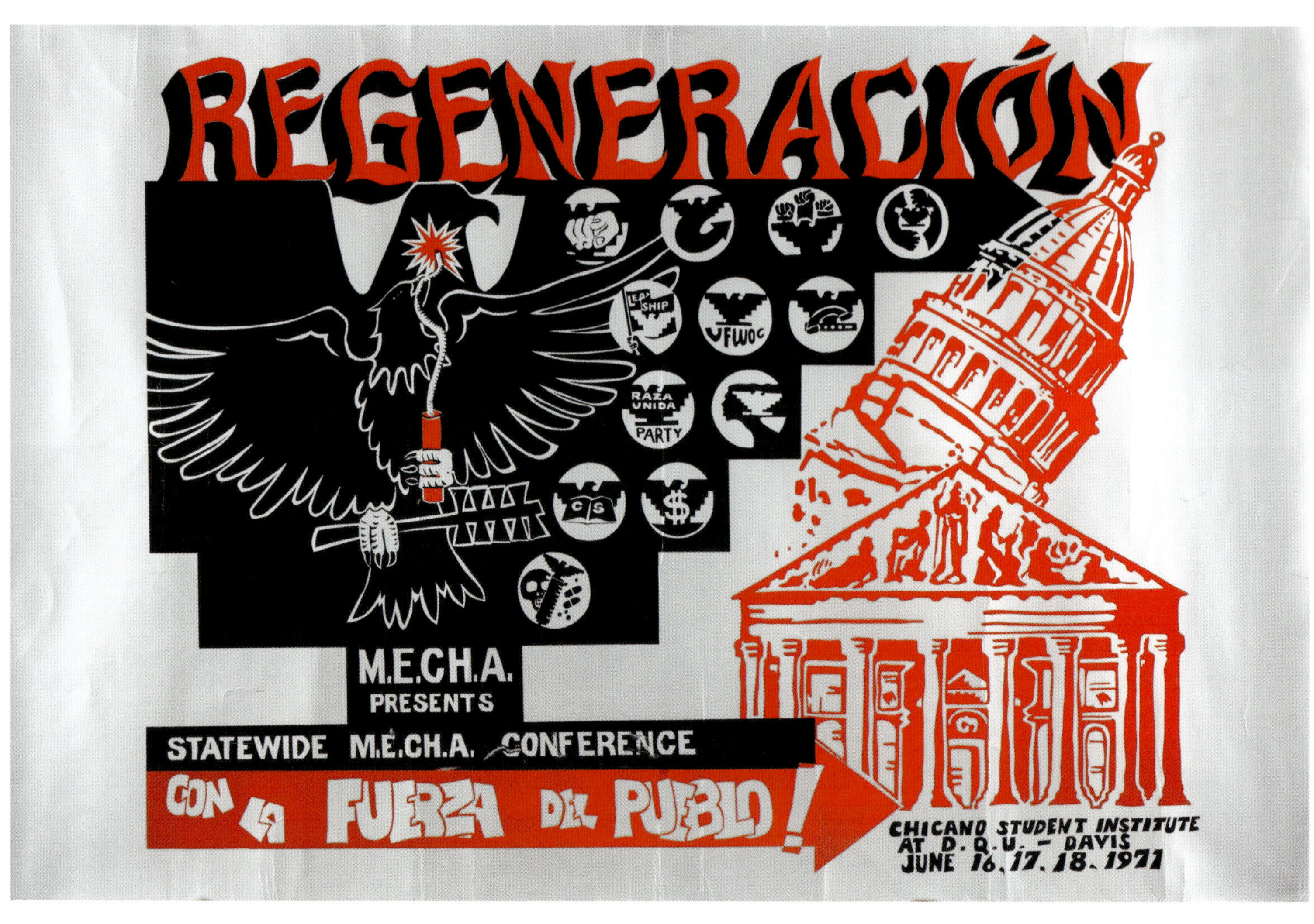

6 Max Garcia (1942–2020) and Ricardo Favela (1944–2007), *Regeneración,* 1971. Screenprint, 23 × 34 3/4 in. Oakland Museum of California, Gift of the Terrazas Martin Family on behalf of Margaret Terrazas-Santos, 2022.1.971.

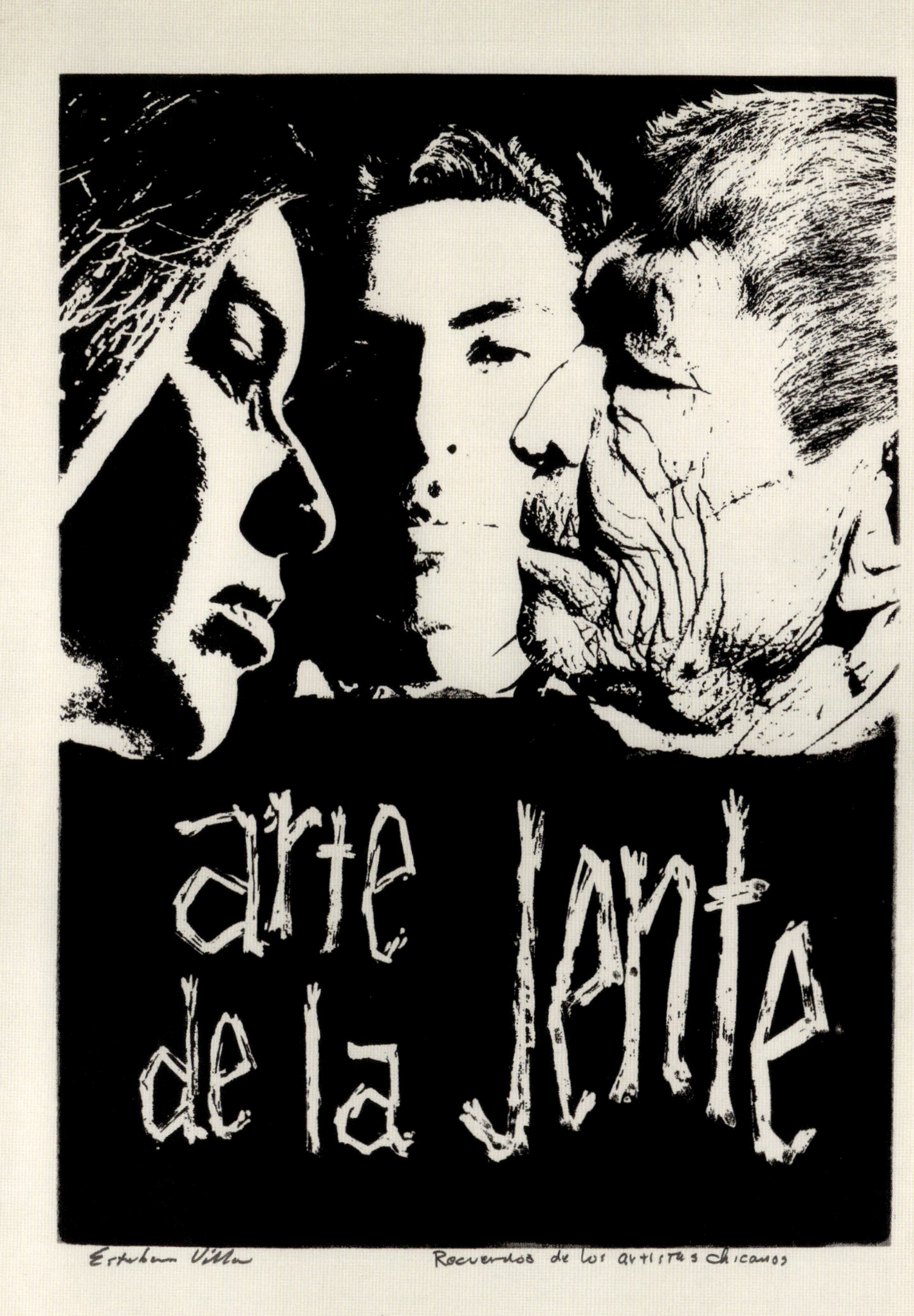

7 Esteban Villa (1930–2022), *Arte de la Jente*, 1970. Screenprint, 34 × 22⅛ in. Rasul Chicano Art Collection.

Centro de Artistas Chicanos

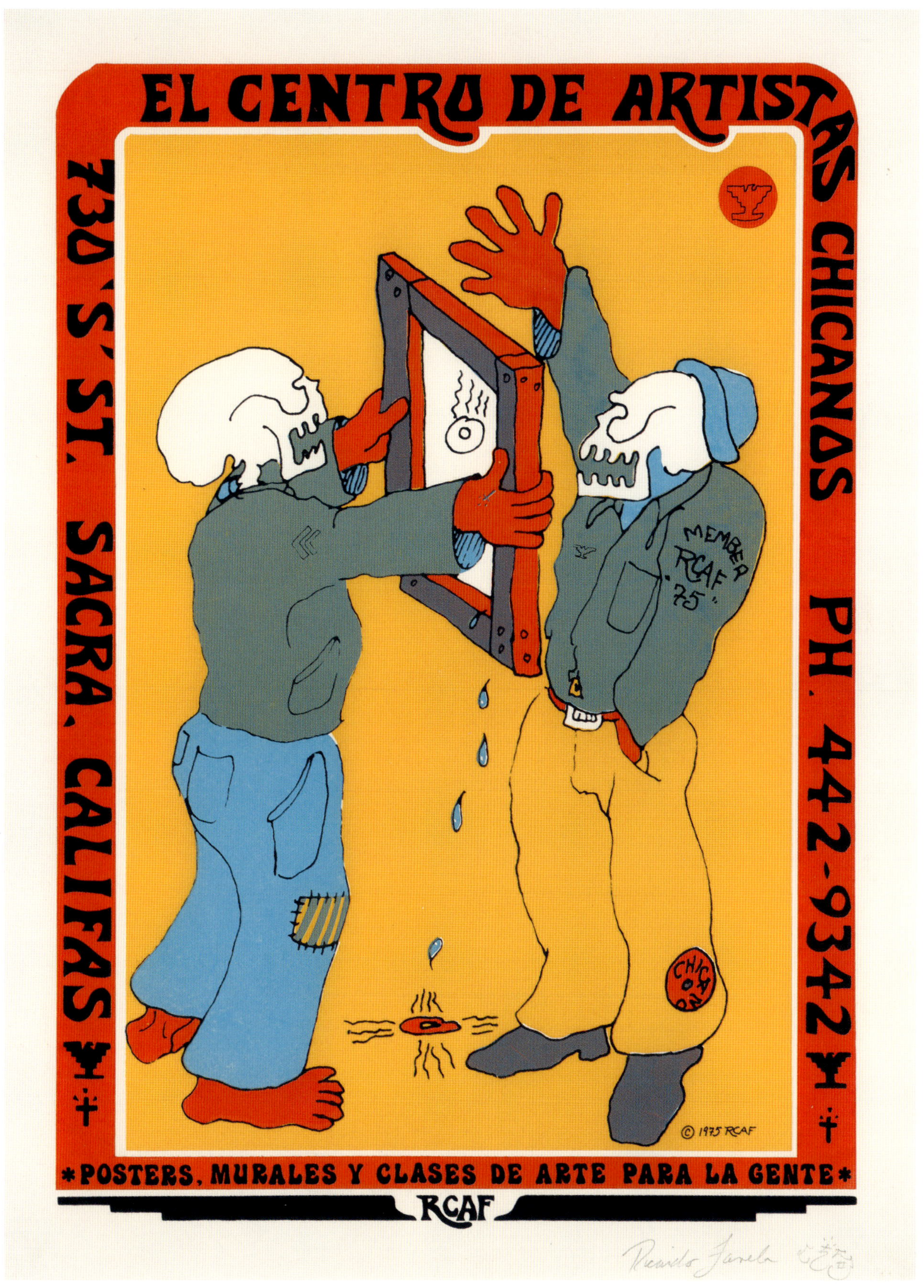

8 Ricardo Favela (1944–2007), *El Centro de Artistas Chicanos*, 1975. Screenprint, 25 × 19 in. RCAFavela Collection.

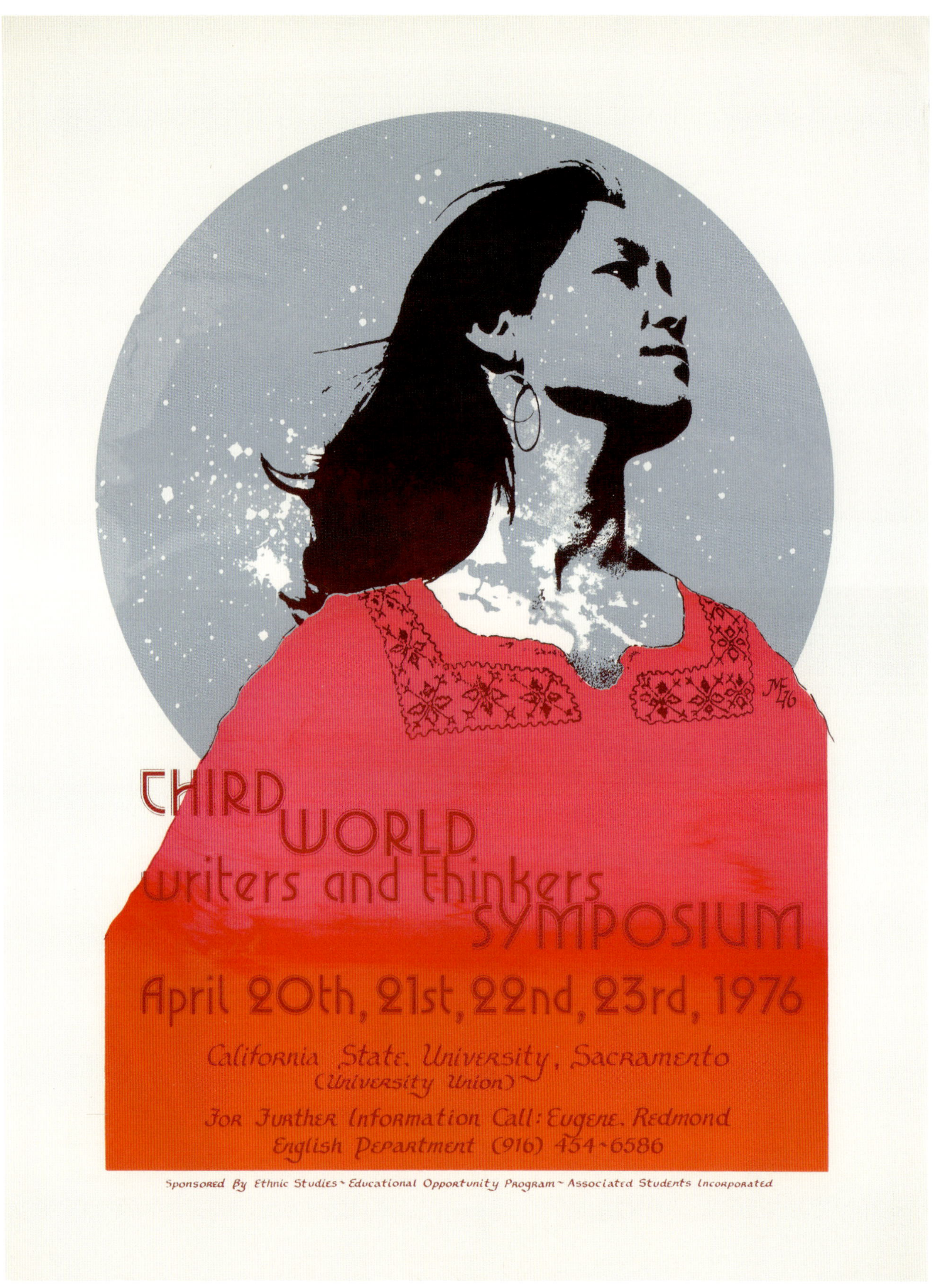

9 Max Garcia (1942–2020) and Héctor D. González (born 1945), *Third World Writers and Thinkers Symposium*, 1976. Screenprint, 25 × 19 in. Collection of Luis C. González.

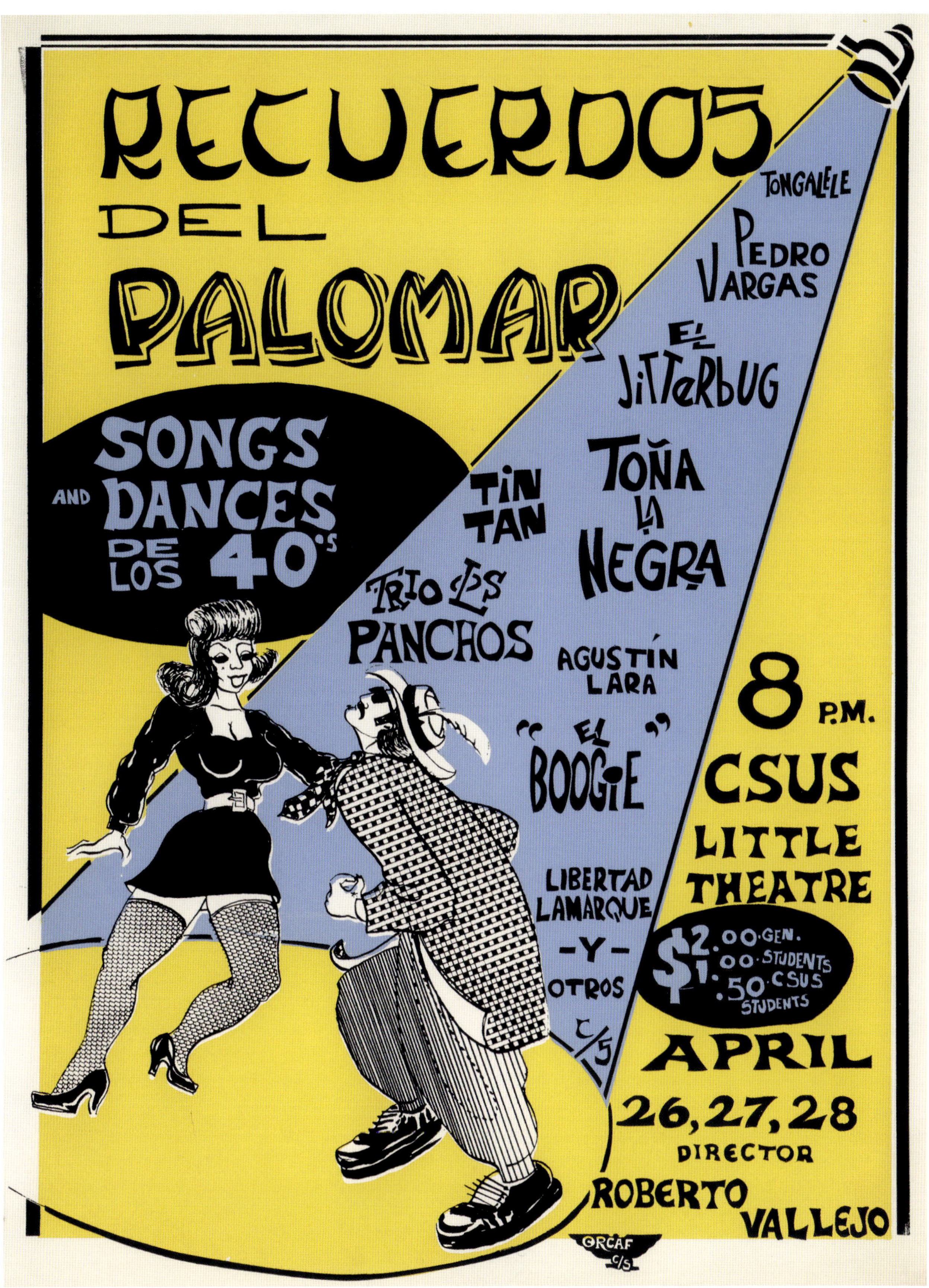

10 José Montoya (1932–2013), *Recuerdos del Palomar*, 1973. Screenprint, 25 × 19 in. Collection of Luis C. González.

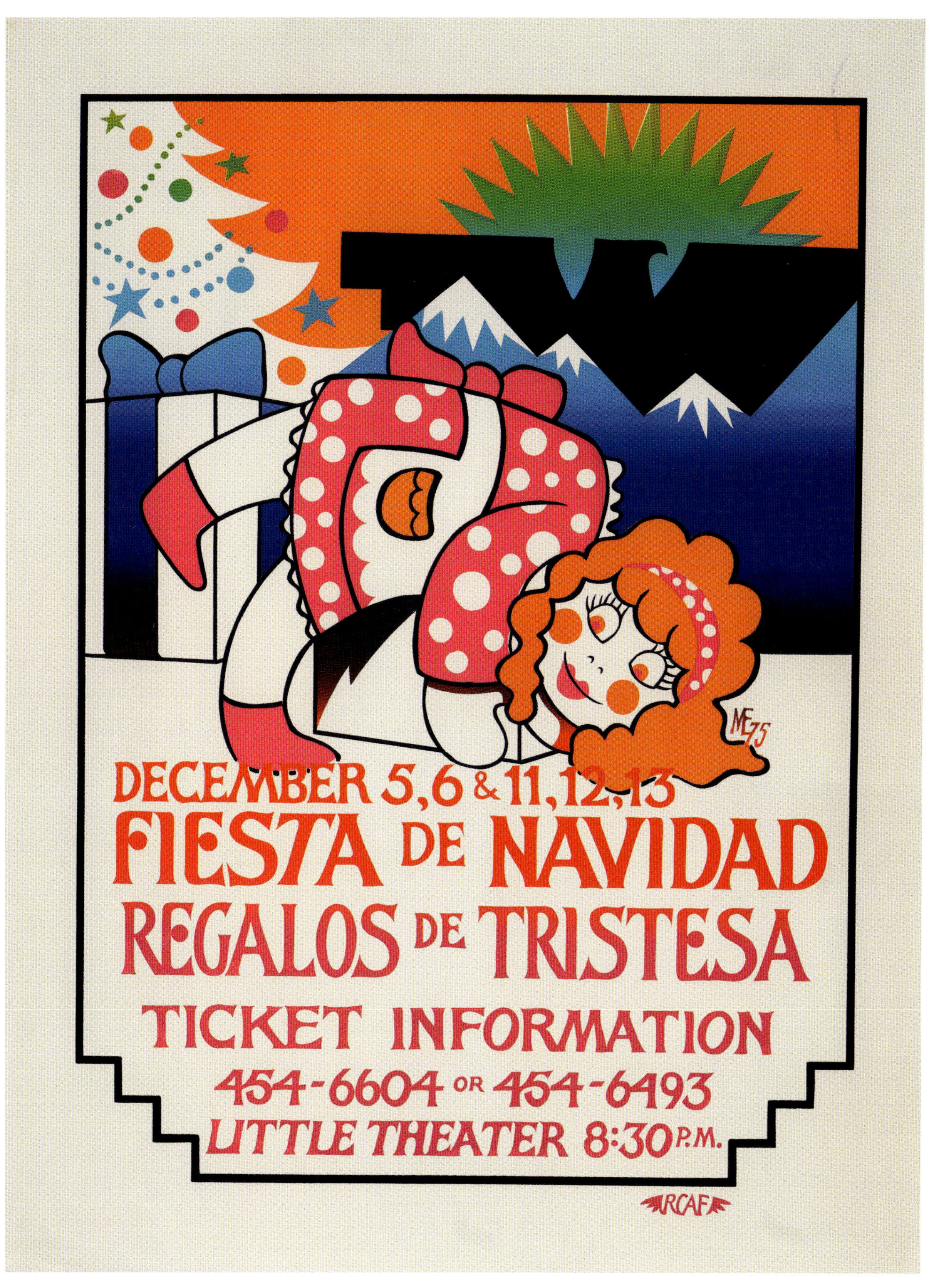

11 Max Garcia (1942–2020), *Fiesta de Navidad: Regalos de Tristesa*, 1975. Screenprint, 25 × 19 in. Royal Chicano Air Force Archives, CEMA 8, University of California, Santa Barbara Library.

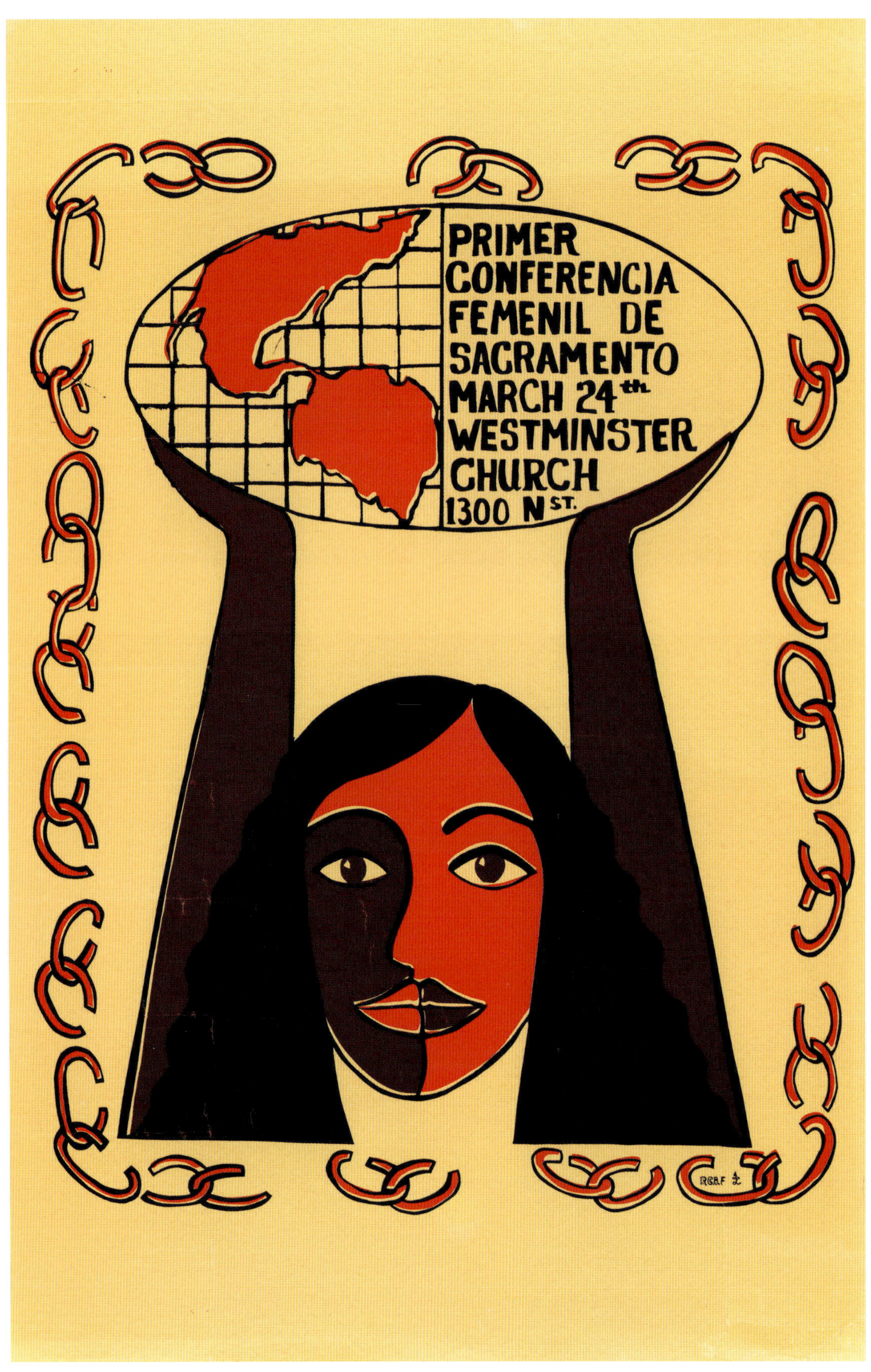

12 Irma Lerma Barbosa (born 1949), *Primer Conferencia Femenil de Sacramento,* 1973. Screenprint, 35 × 23 in. Royal Chicano Air Force Archives, CEMA 8, University of California, Santa Barbara Library.

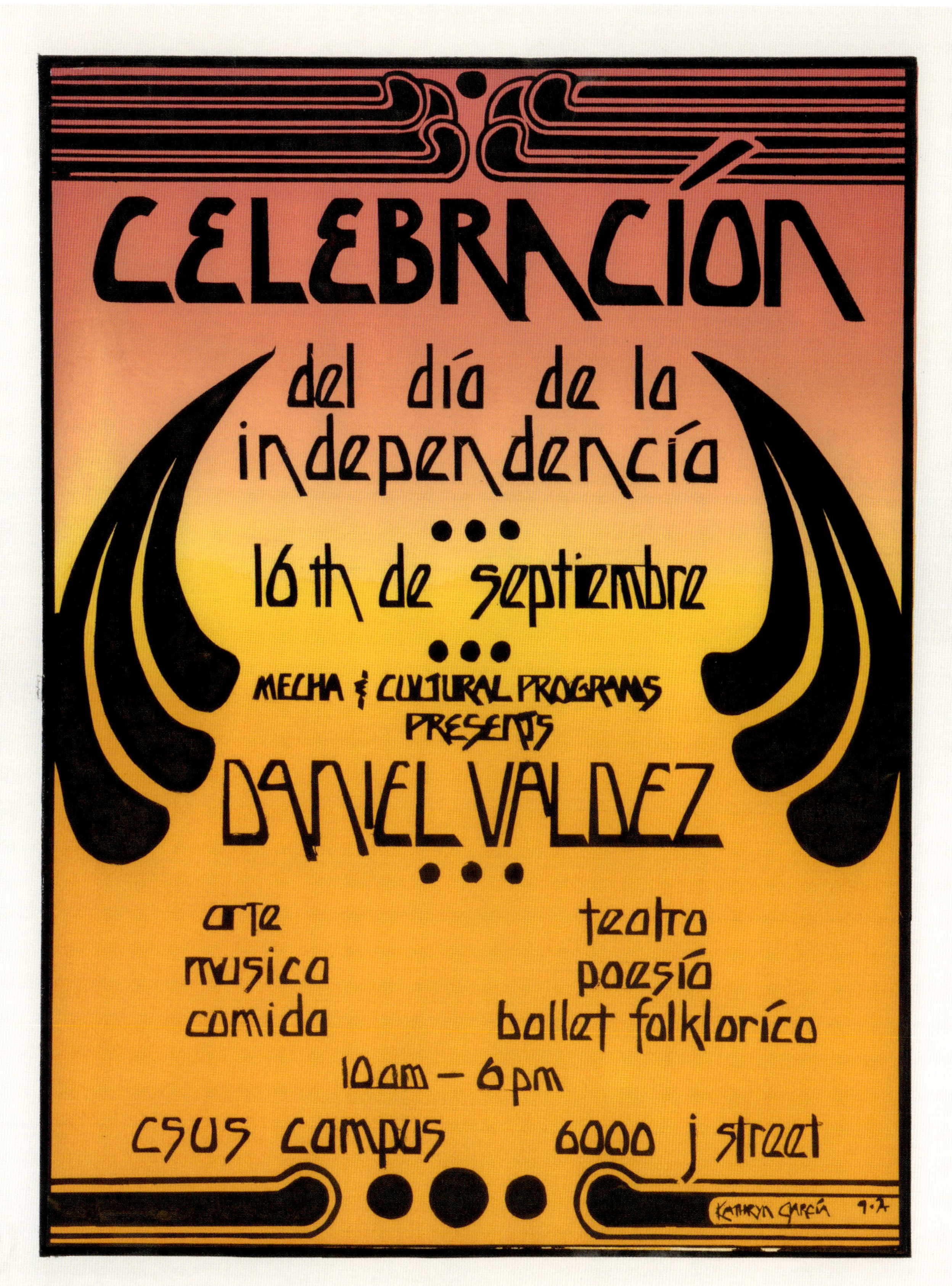

13 Kathryn Garcia (born 1952), *Celebración del Día de La Independencia*, 1974. Screen-print, 25 × 19 in. La Raza Galeria Posada Poster Collection, Gerth Special Collections & University Archives, California State University, Sacramento.

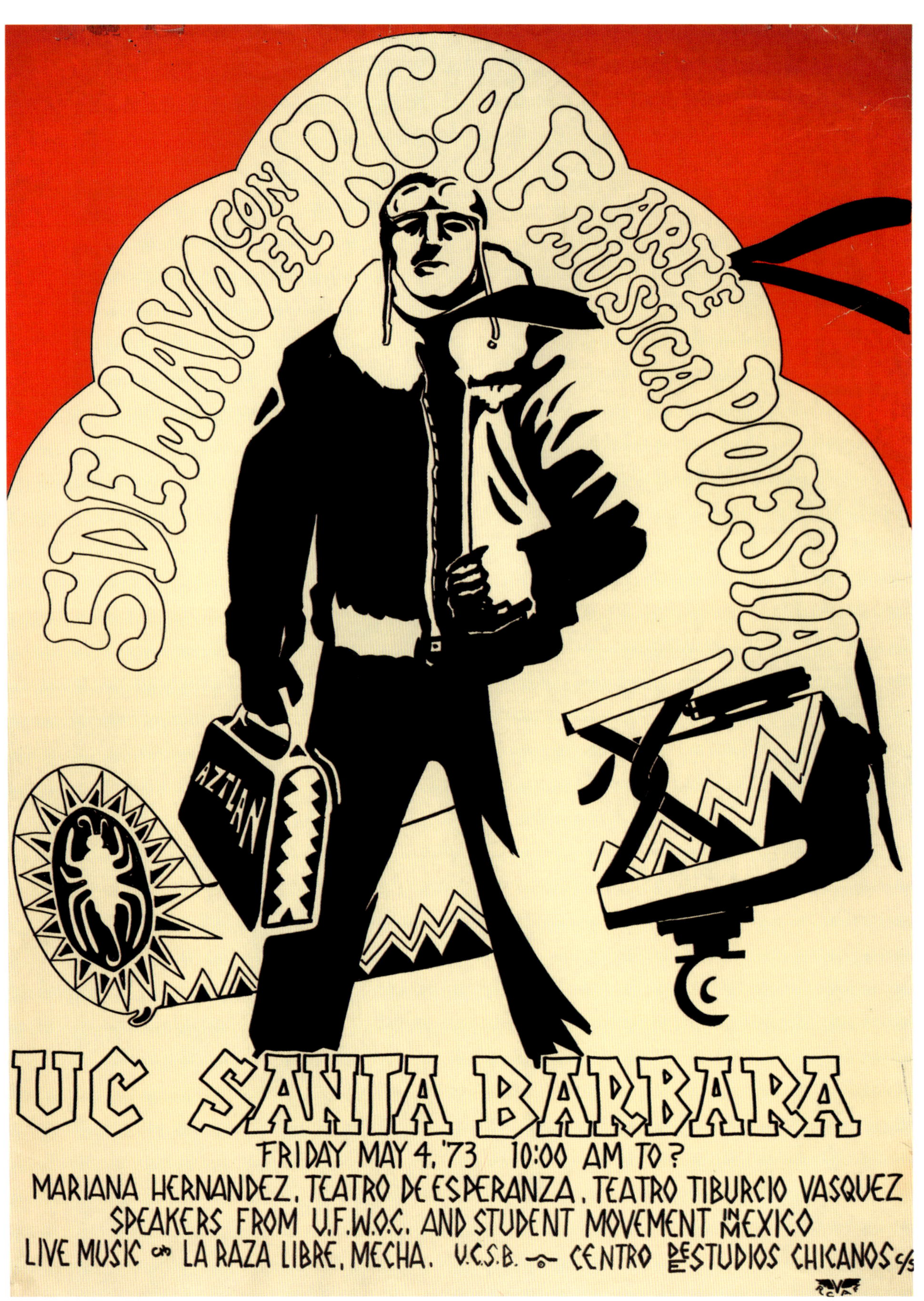

14 Esteban Villa (1930–2022), *5 de Mayo con el RCAF*, 1973. Screenprint, 28½ × 21 in. Royal Chicano Air Force Archives, CEMA 8, University of California, Santa Barbara Library.

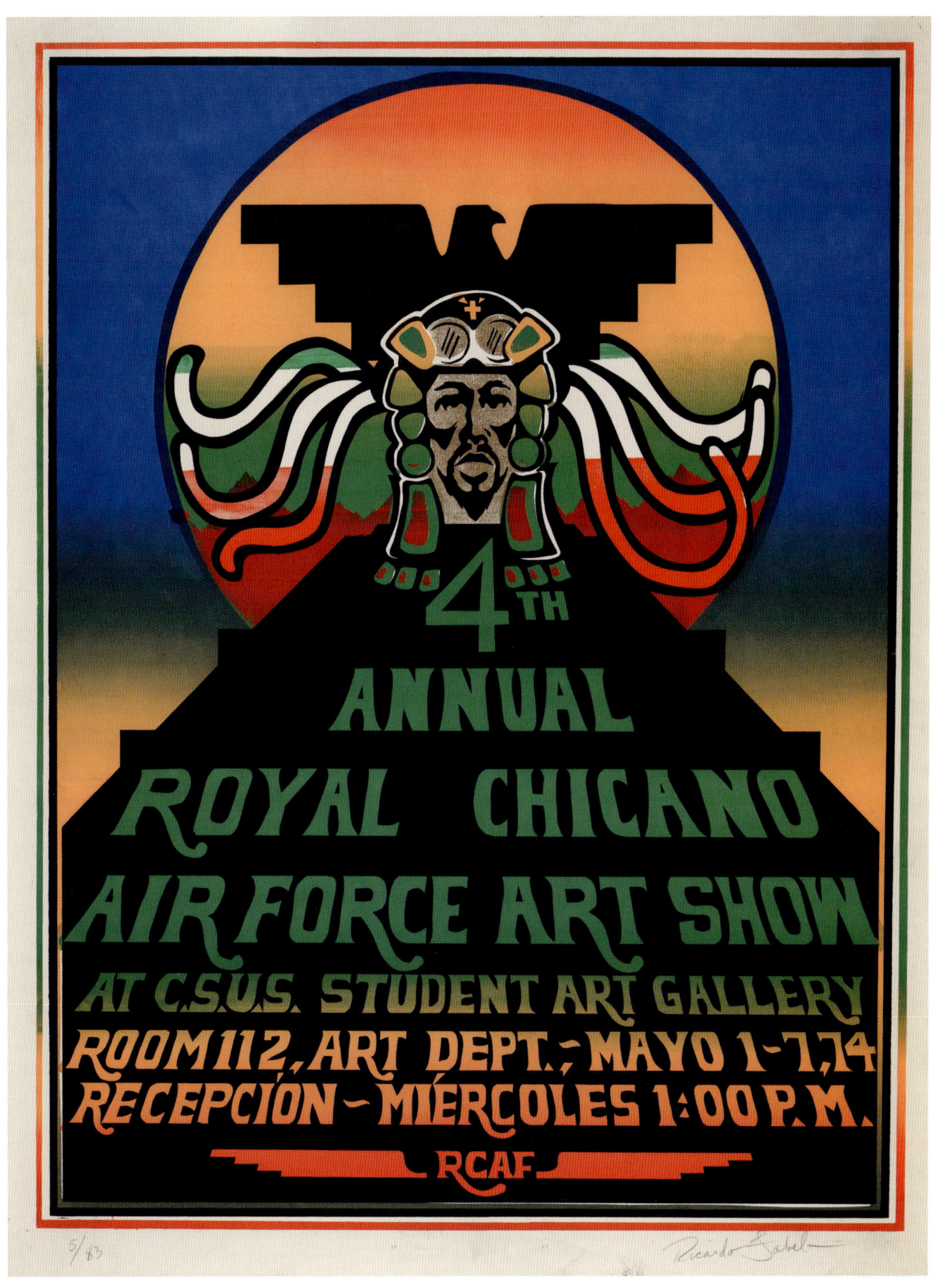

15 Ricardo Favela (1944–2007), *4th Annual Royal Chicano Air Force Art Show*, 1974. Screenprint, 25 × 19 in. Royal Chicano Air Force Archives, CEMA 8, University of California, Santa Barbara Library.

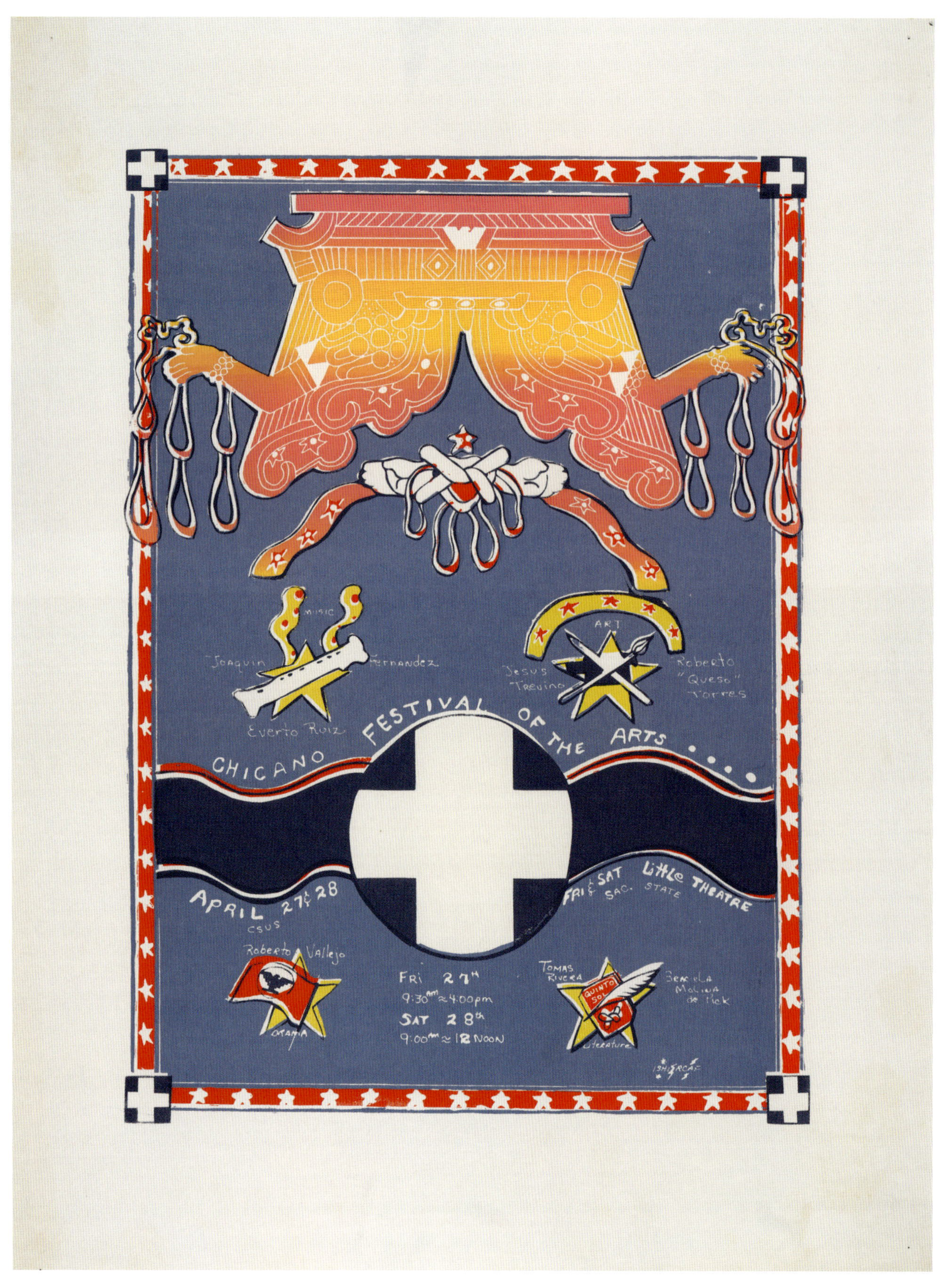

16 Juanishi Orosco (1945–2023), *Chicano Festival of the Arts*, 1973. Screenprint, 25 × 19 in. Royal Chicano Air Force Archives, CEMA 8. University of California, Santa Barbara Library.

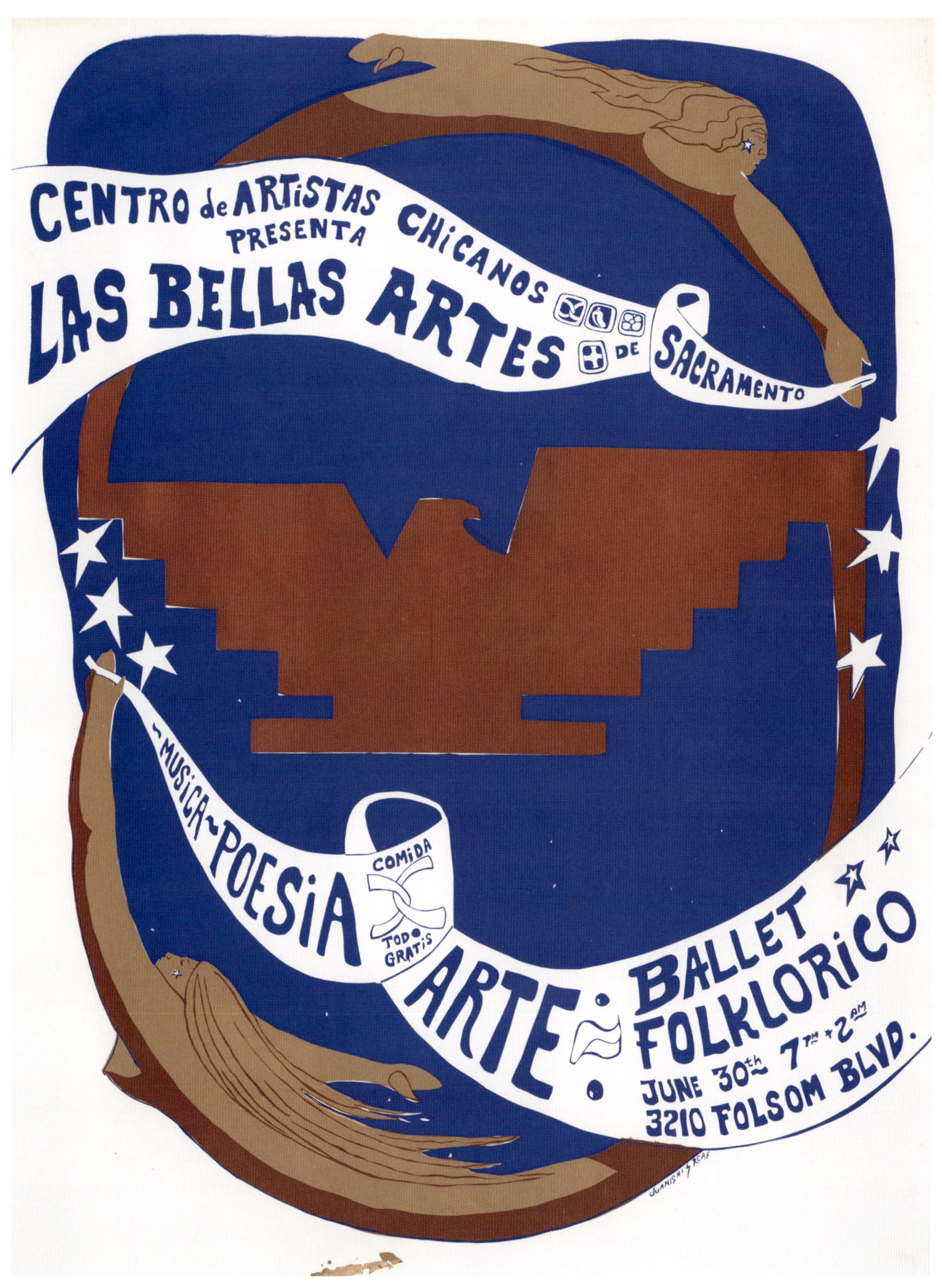

17 Juanishi Orosco (1945–2023), *Las Bellas Artes de Sacramento*, 1973. Screenprint, 25 × 19 in. Royal Chicano Air Force Archives, CEMA 8, University of California, Santa Barbara Library.

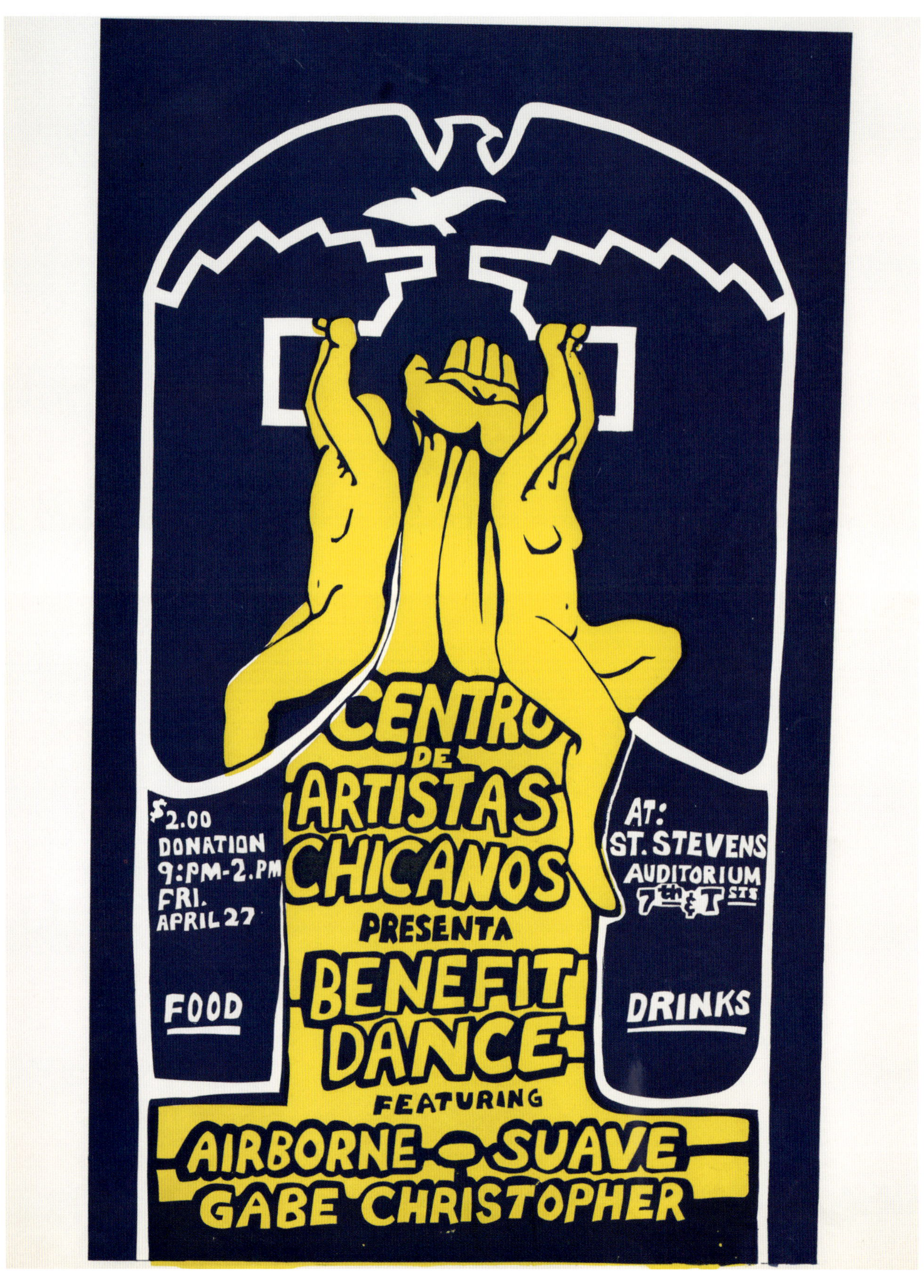

18 Rudy O. Cuellar (born 1950) and José Felix, *Centro de Artistas Chicanos Benefit Dance*, 1973. Screenprint, 35 × 23 in. Royal Chicano Air Force Archives, CEMA 8, University of California, Santa Barbara Library.

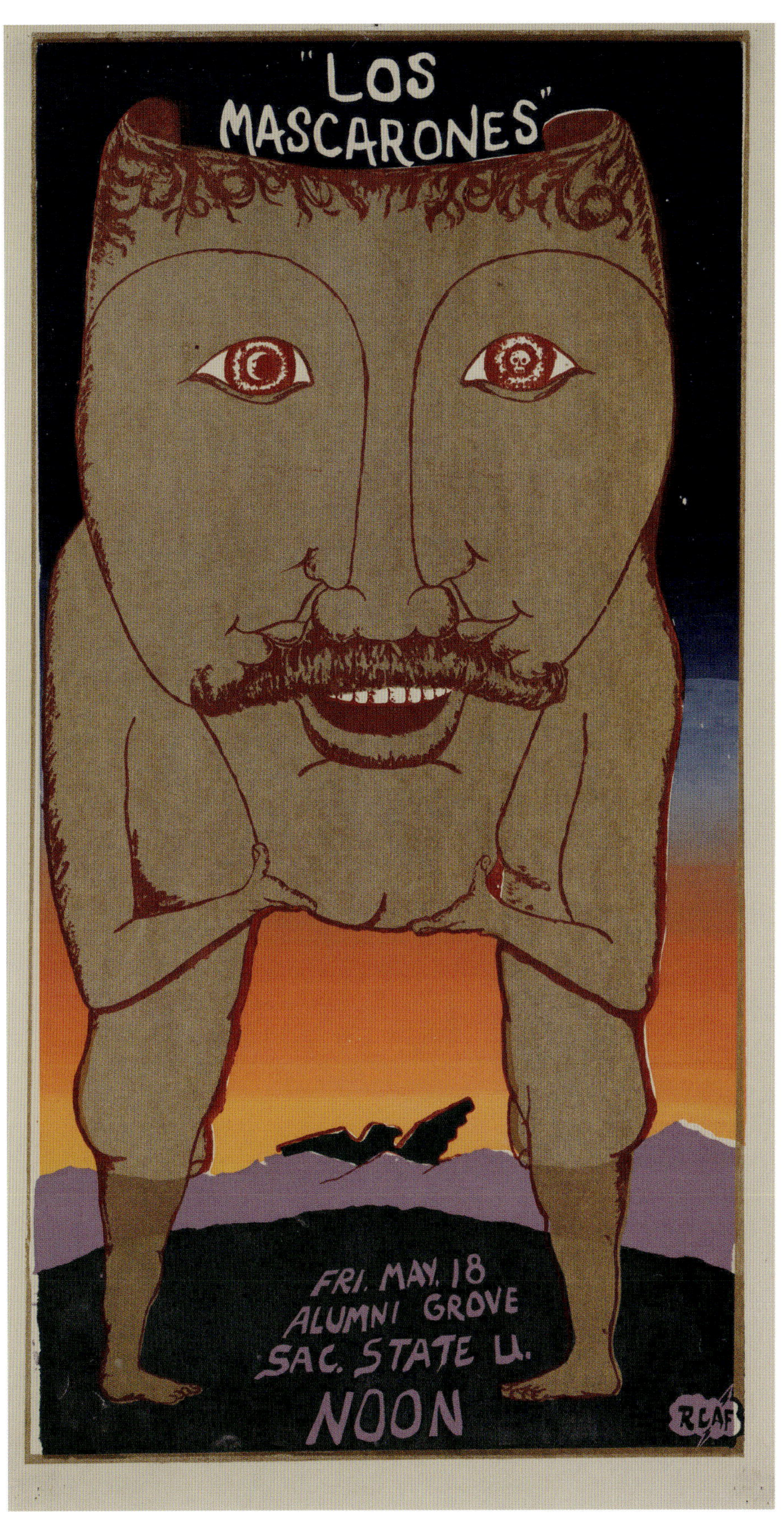

19 Rudy O. Cuellar (born 1950), *Los Mascarones*, 1973. Screenprint, 24 × 13 in. Royal Chicano Air Force Archives, CEMA 8, University of California, Santa Barbara Library.

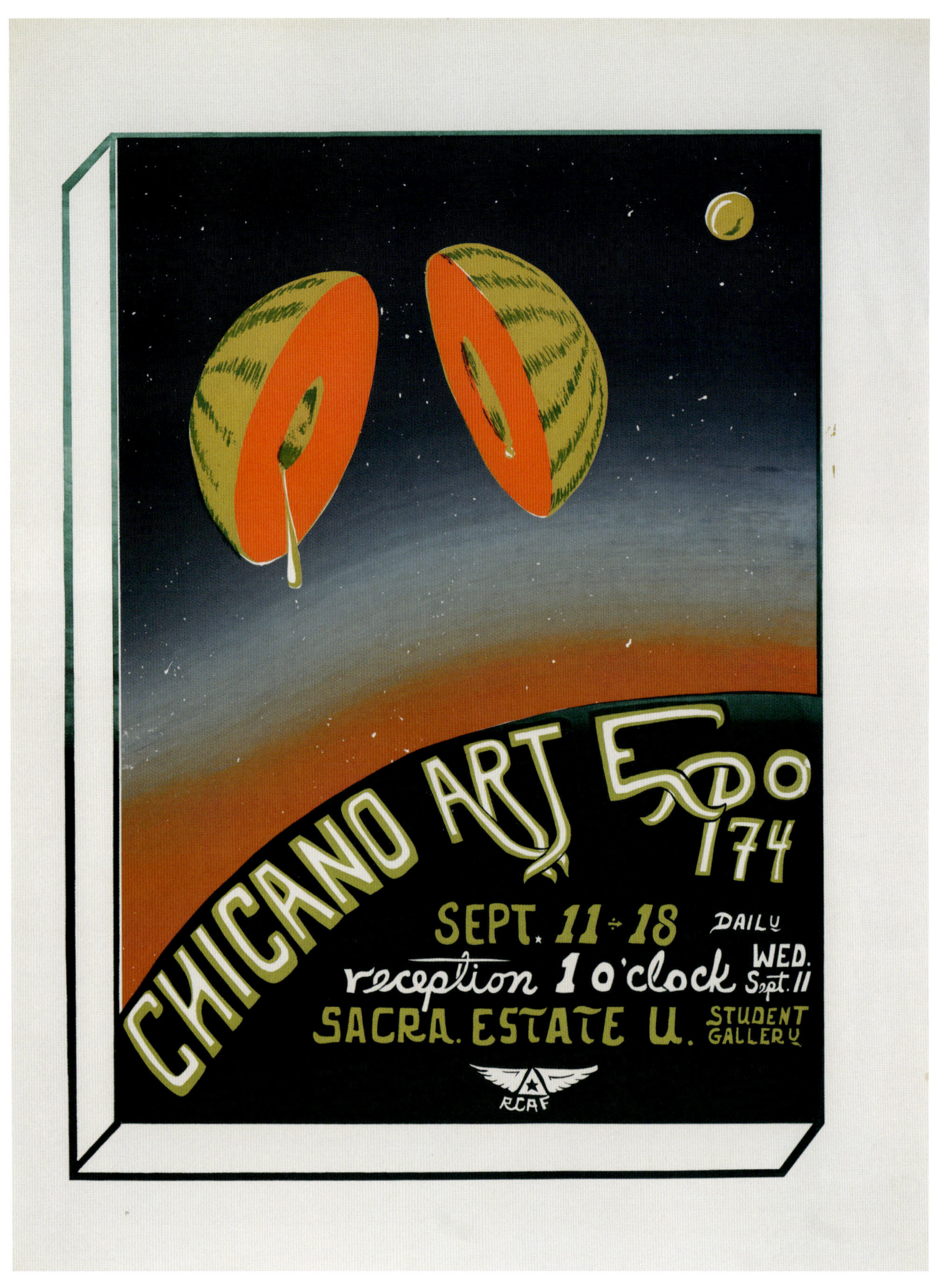

20 Rudy O. Cuellar (born 1950), *Chicano Art Expo*, 1974. Screenprint, 25 × 19 in. Royal Chicano Air Force Archives, CEMA 8, University of California, Santa Barbara Library.

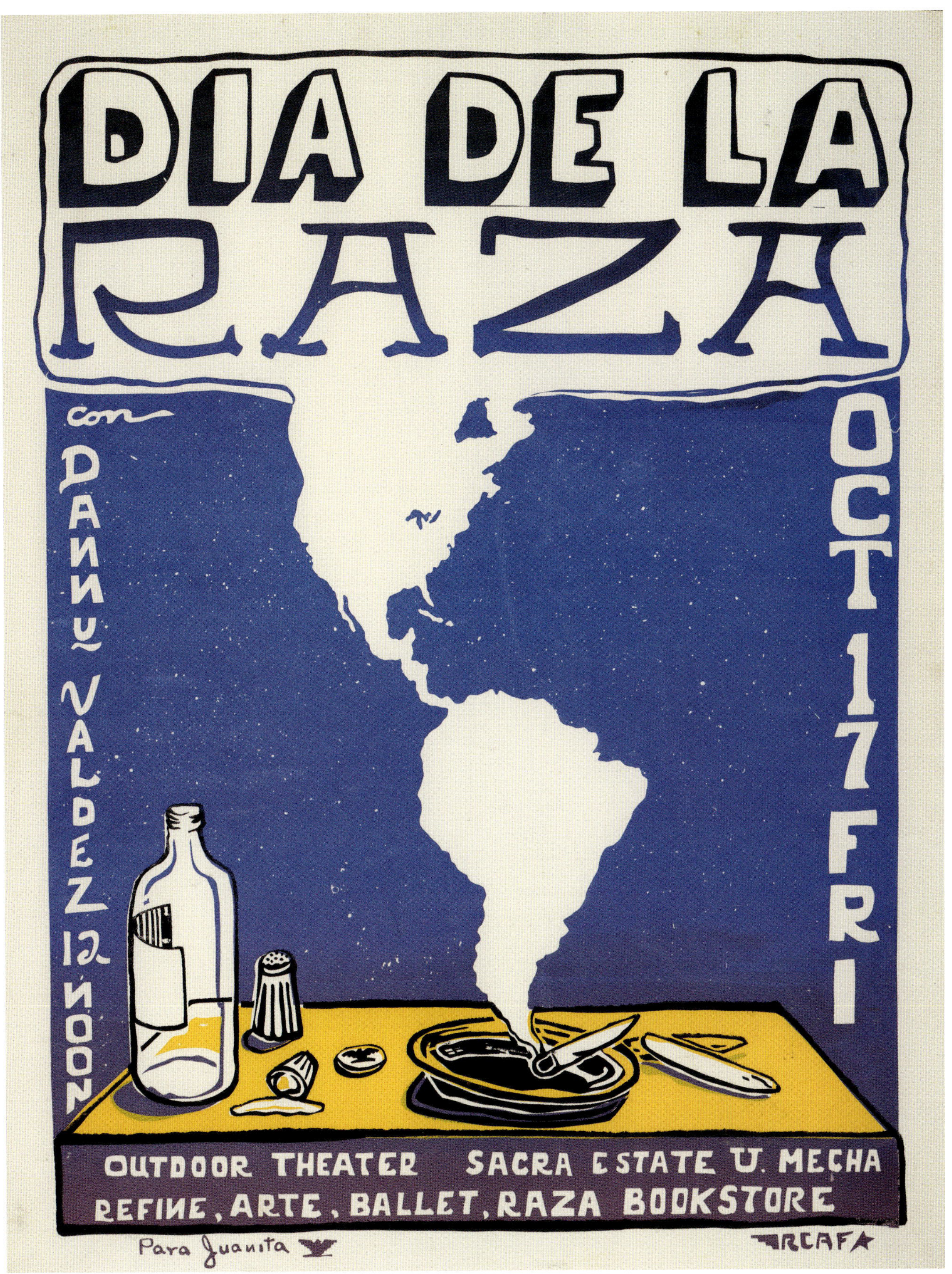

21 Rudy O. Cuellar (born 1950), *Día de la Raza*, 1975. Screenprint, 24 × 18½ in. Royal Chicano Air Force Archives, CEMA 8, University of California, Santa Barbara Library.

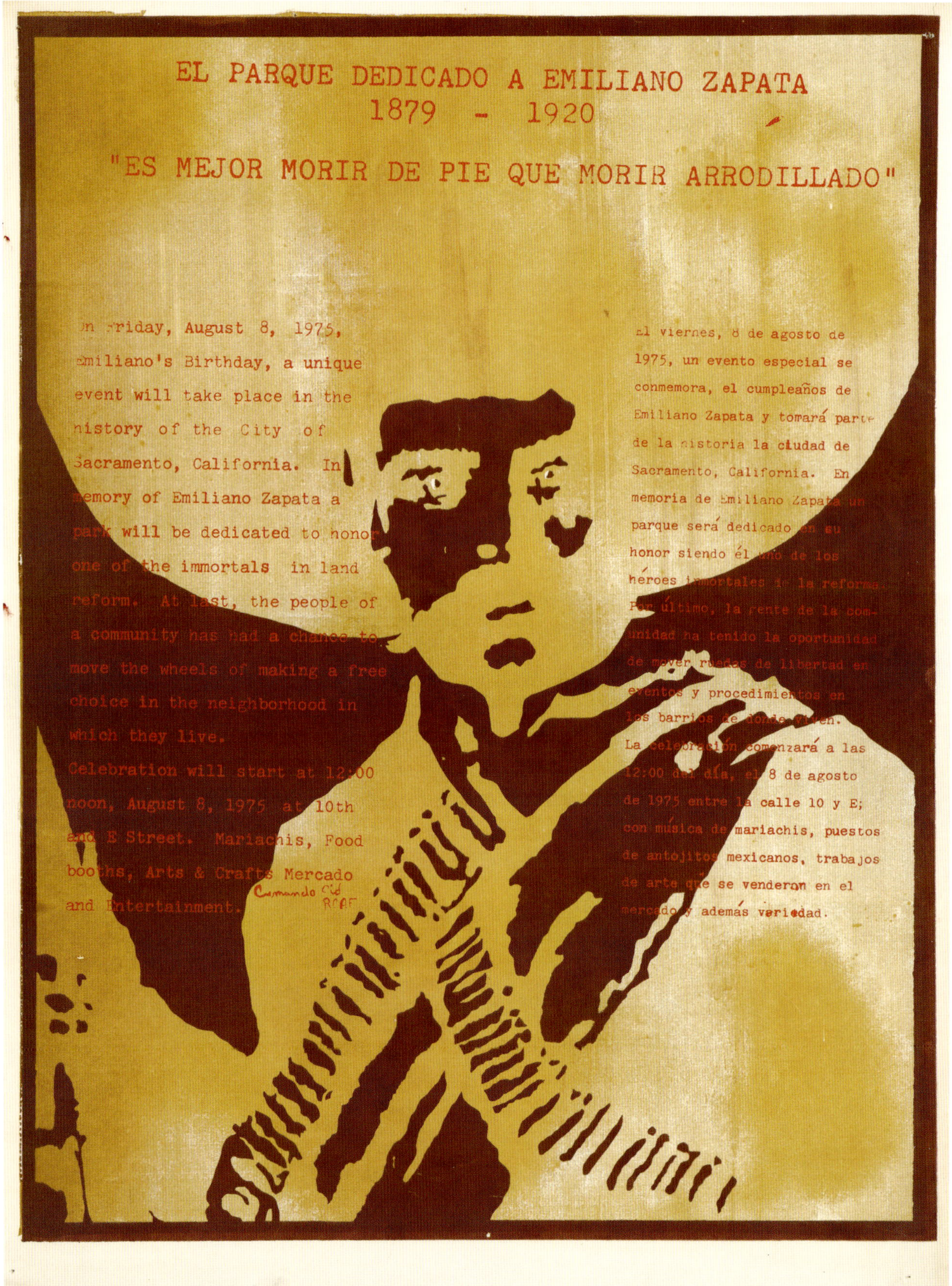

EL PARQUE DEDICADO A EMILIANO ZAPATA
1879 - 1920

"ES MEJOR MORIR DE PIE QUE MORIR ARRODILLADO"

On Friday, August 8, 1975, Emiliano's Birthday, a unique event will take place in the history of the City of Sacramento, California. In memory of Emiliano Zapata a park will be dedicated to honor one of the immortals in land reform. At last, the people of a community has had a chance to move the wheels of making a free choice in the neighborhood in which they live.
Celebration will start at 12:00 noon, August 8, 1975 at 10th and E Street. Mariachis, Food booths, Arts & Crafts Mercado and Entertainment.

El viernes, 8 de agosto de 1975, un evento especial se conmemora, el cumpleaños de Emiliano Zapata y tomará parte de la historia la ciudad de Sacramento, California. En memoria de Emiliano Zapata un parque será dedicado en su honor siendo él uno de los héroes inmortales de la reforma. Por último, la gente de la comunidad ha tenido la oportunidad de mover ruedas de libertad en eventos y procedimientos en los barrios de donde viven.
La celebración comenzará a las 12:00 del día, el 8 de agosto de 1975 entre la calle 10 y E; con música de mariachis, puestos de antojitos mexicanos, trabajos de arte que se venderon en el mercado y además variedad.

Armando Cid
RCAF

22 Armando Cid (1943–2009), *El Parque Dedicado a Emiliano Zapata*, 1975. Screenprint, 25 × 19 in. Rasul Chicano Art Collection.

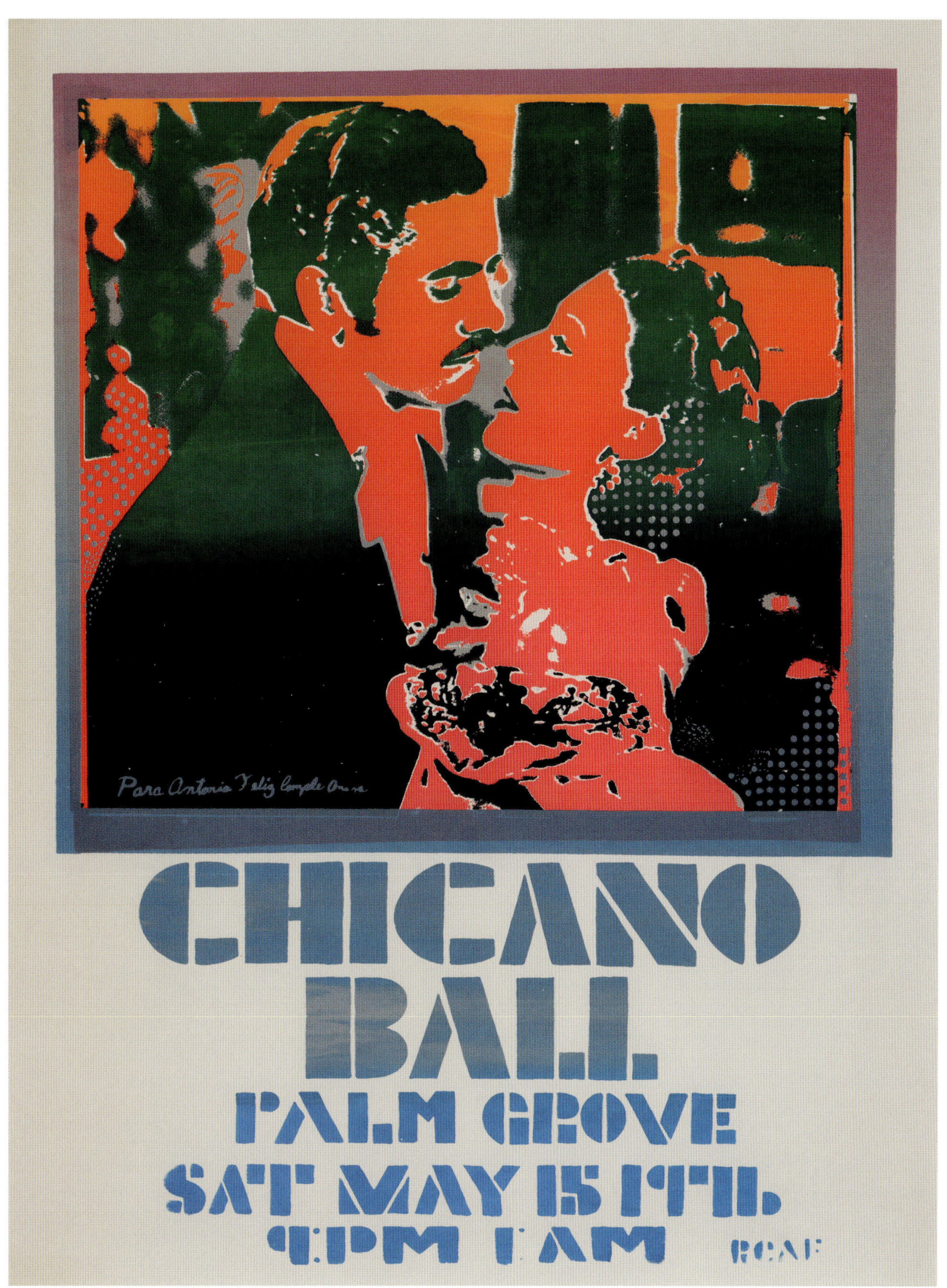

23 Armando Cid (1943–2009), *Chicano Ball*, 1976. Screenprint, 25 × 19 in. Royal Chicano Air Force Archives, CEMA 8, University of California, Santa Barbara Library.

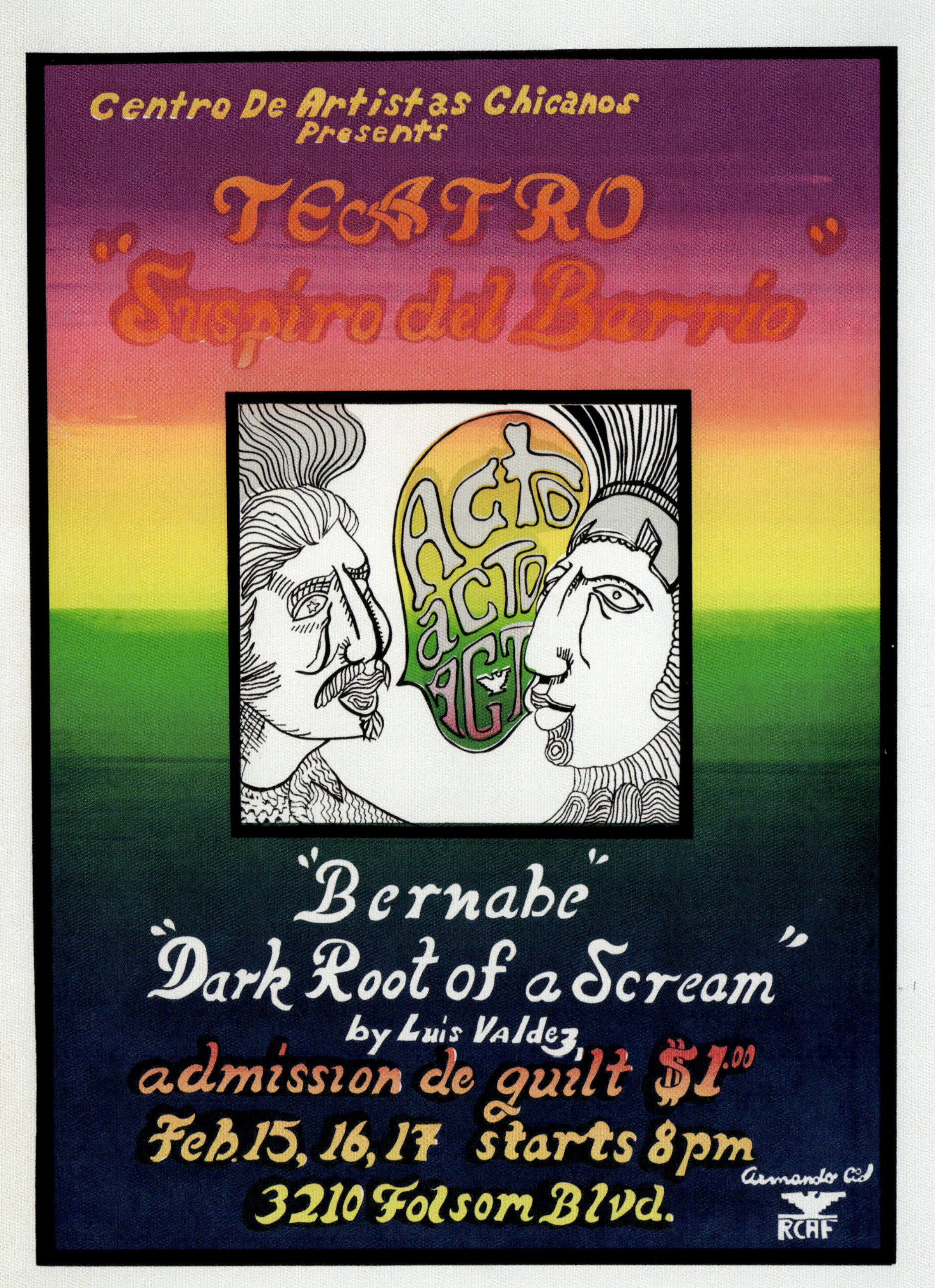

24 Armando Cid (1943–2009), *Teatro "Suspiro del Barrio,"* 1975. Screenprint, 25 × 19 in. Royal Chicano Air Force Archives, CEMA 8, University of California, Santa Barbara Library.

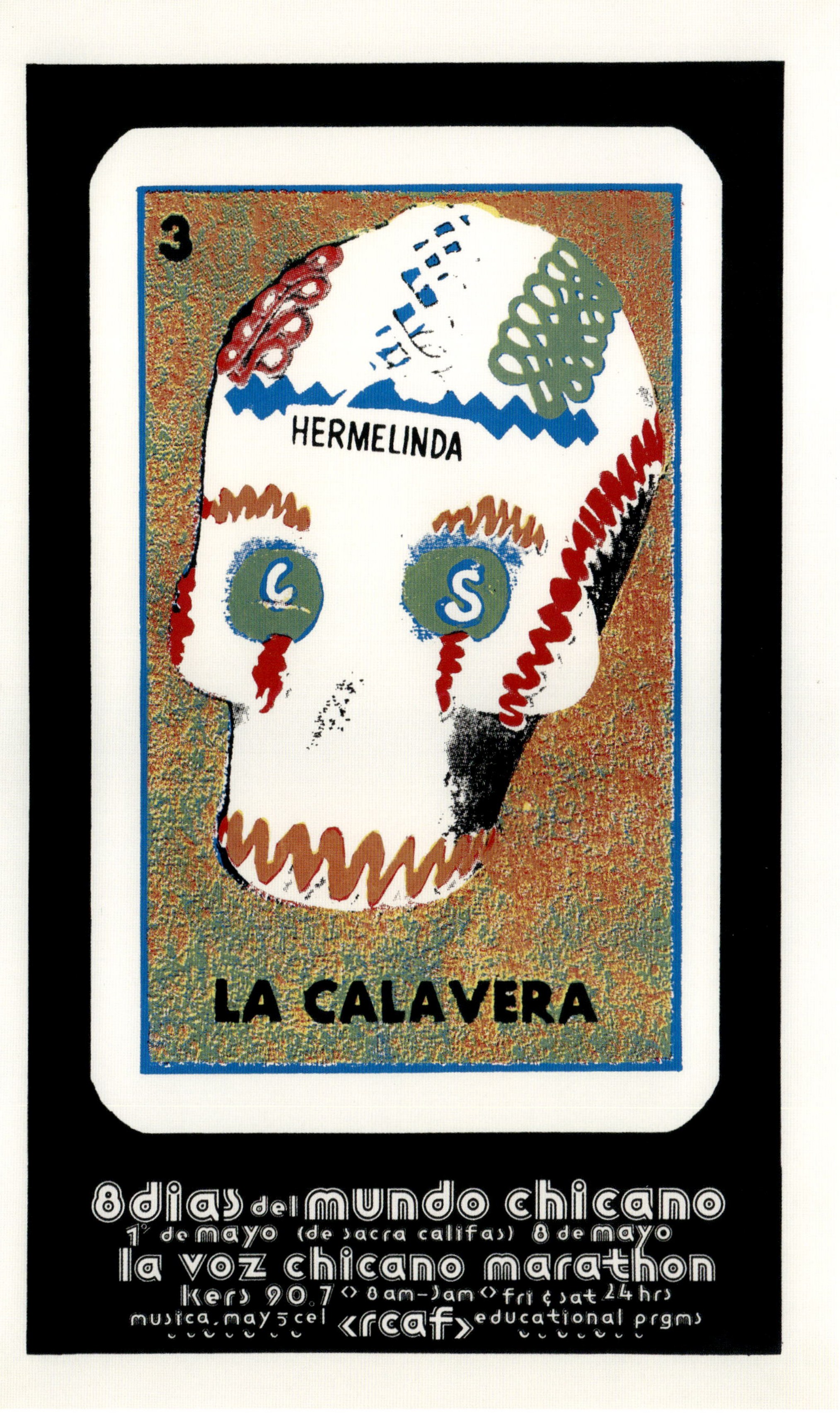

25 Luis C. González (born 1953), *8 Días del Mundo Chicano*, 1976. Screenprint, 25 × 16 in. Collection of Luis C. González.

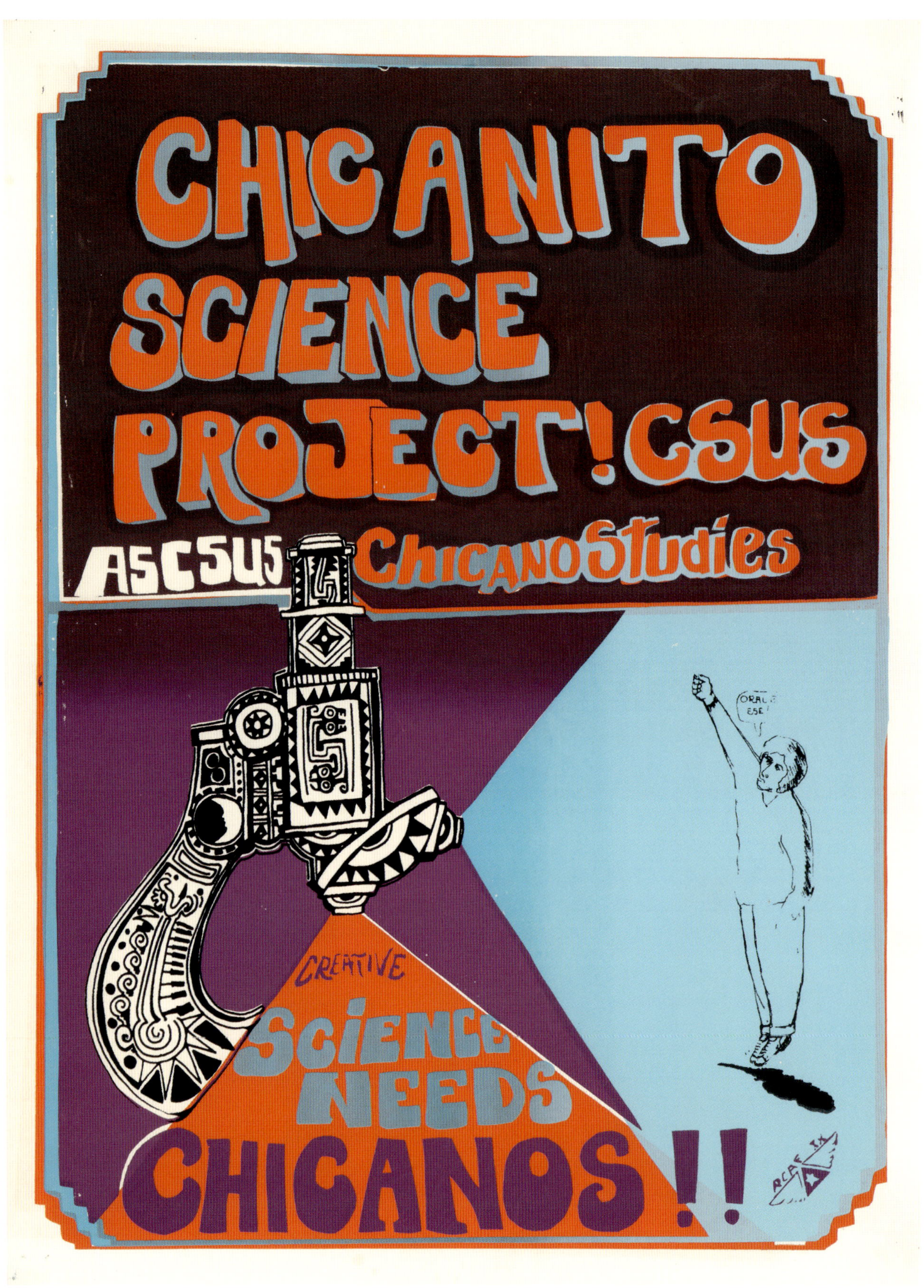

26 Juan Cervantes (1951–2014), *Chicanito Science Project*, mid-1970s. Screenprint, 25 × 19 in. Cervantes-Powell Family Collection.

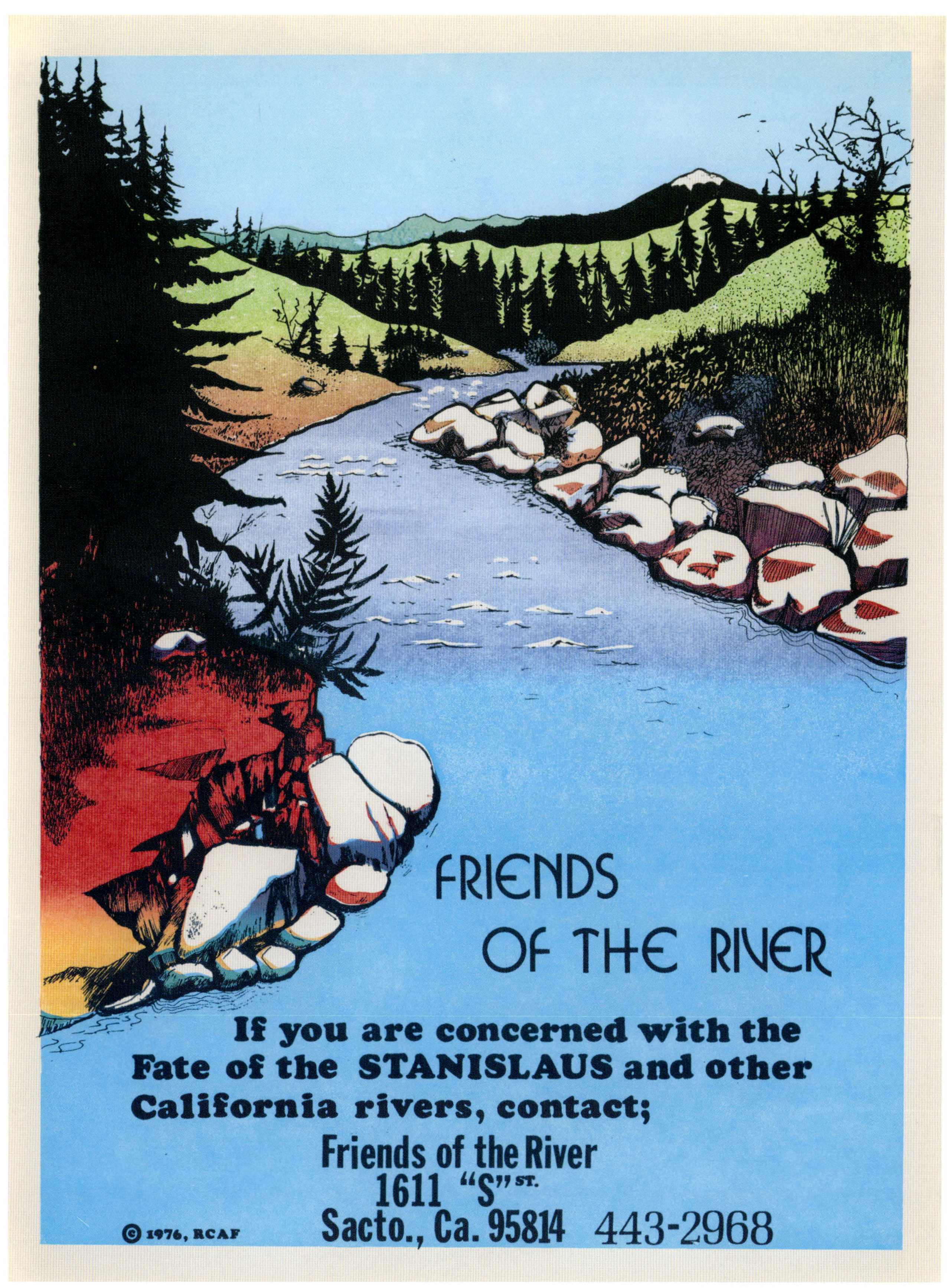

27 Juan Cervantes (1951–2014), *Friends of the River*, 1976. Screenprint, 25 × 19 in. Royal Chicano Air Force Archives, CEMA 8, University of California, Santa Barbara Library.

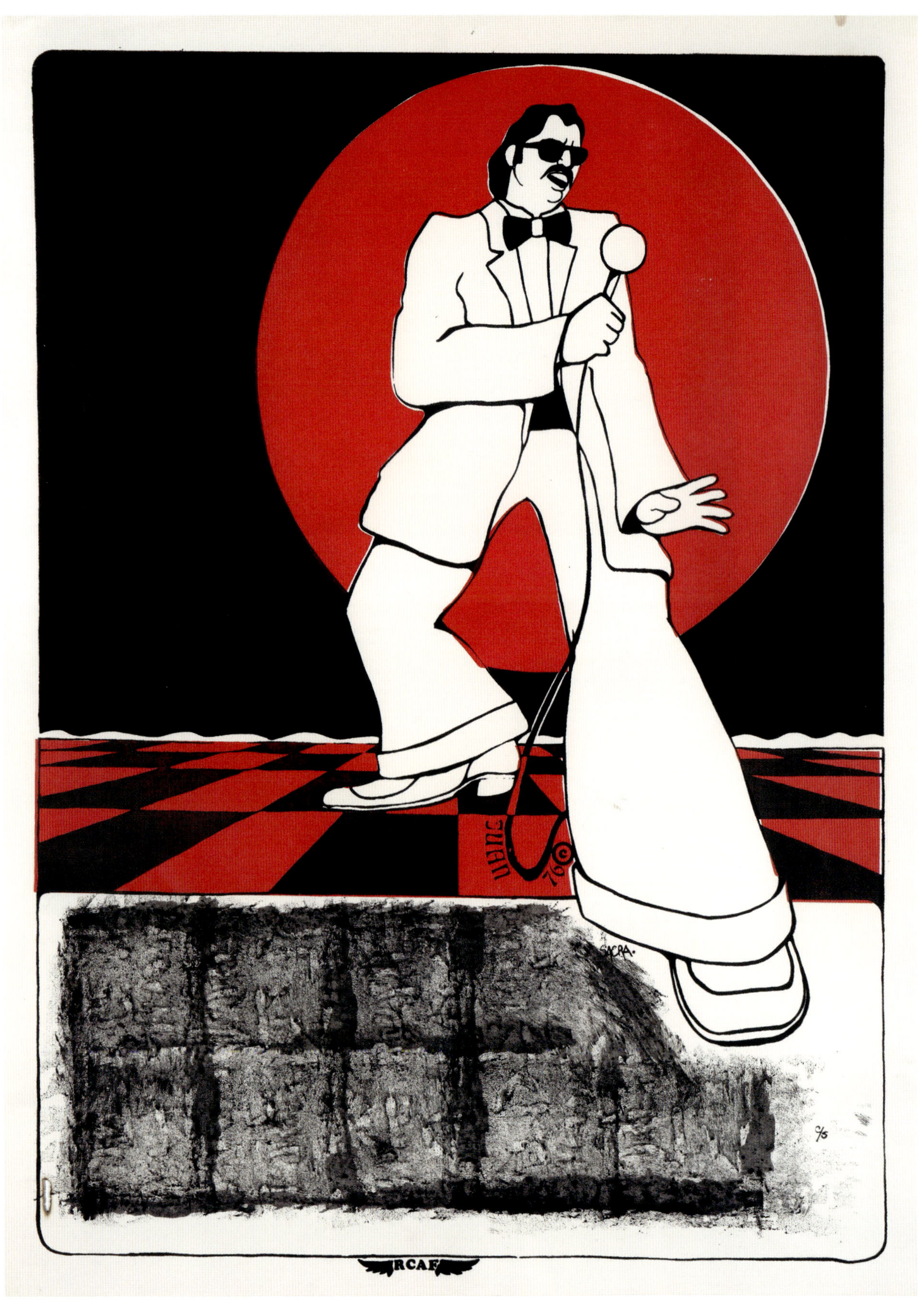

28 Juan Cervantes (1951–2014), *The Singer*, 1976. Screenprint, 25 × 19 in. Cervantes-Powell Family Collection.

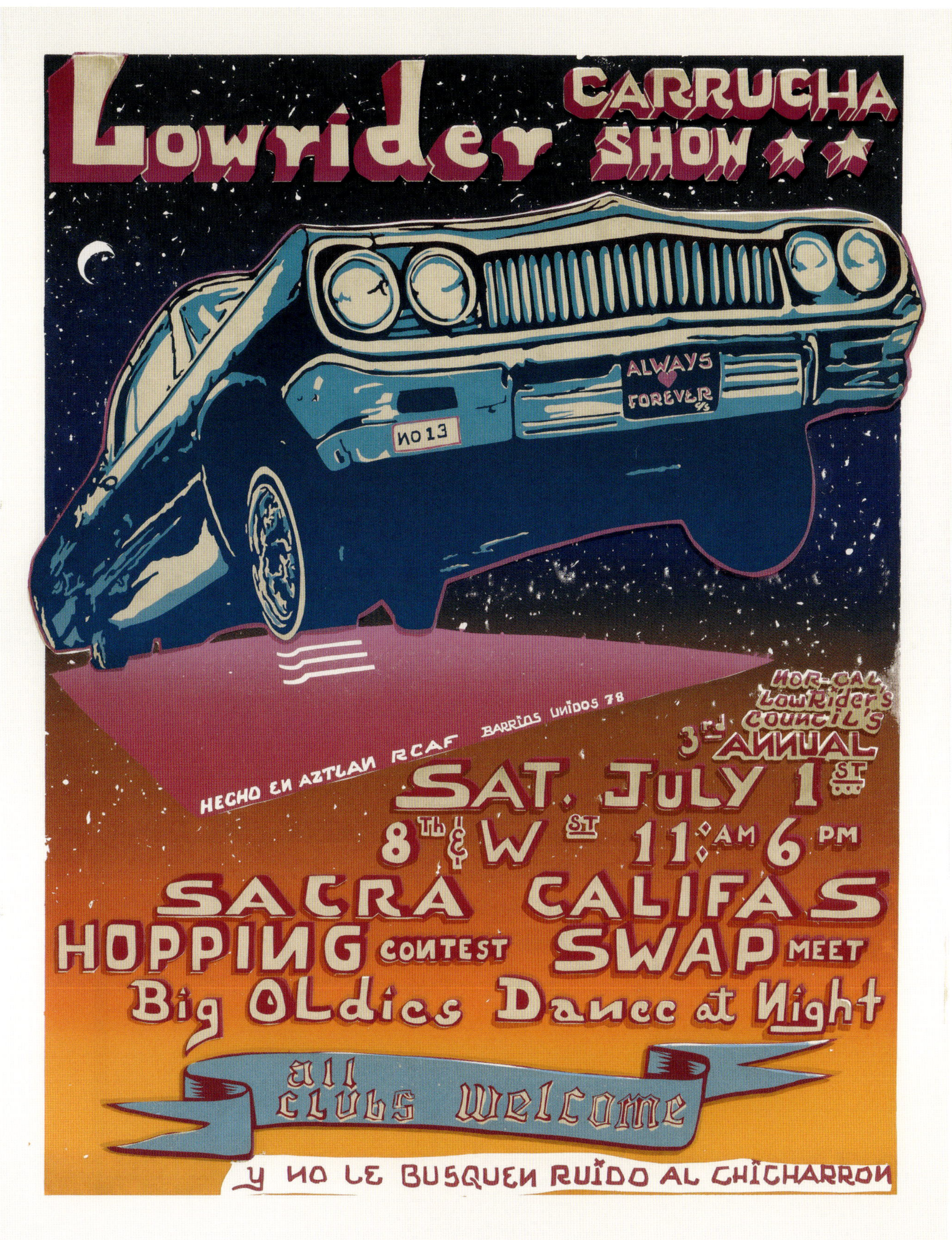

29 Rudy O. Cuellar (born 1950), *Lowrider Carrucha Show*, 1978. Screenprint, 29 ⅛ × 23 in. Collection of Rudy O. Cuellar.

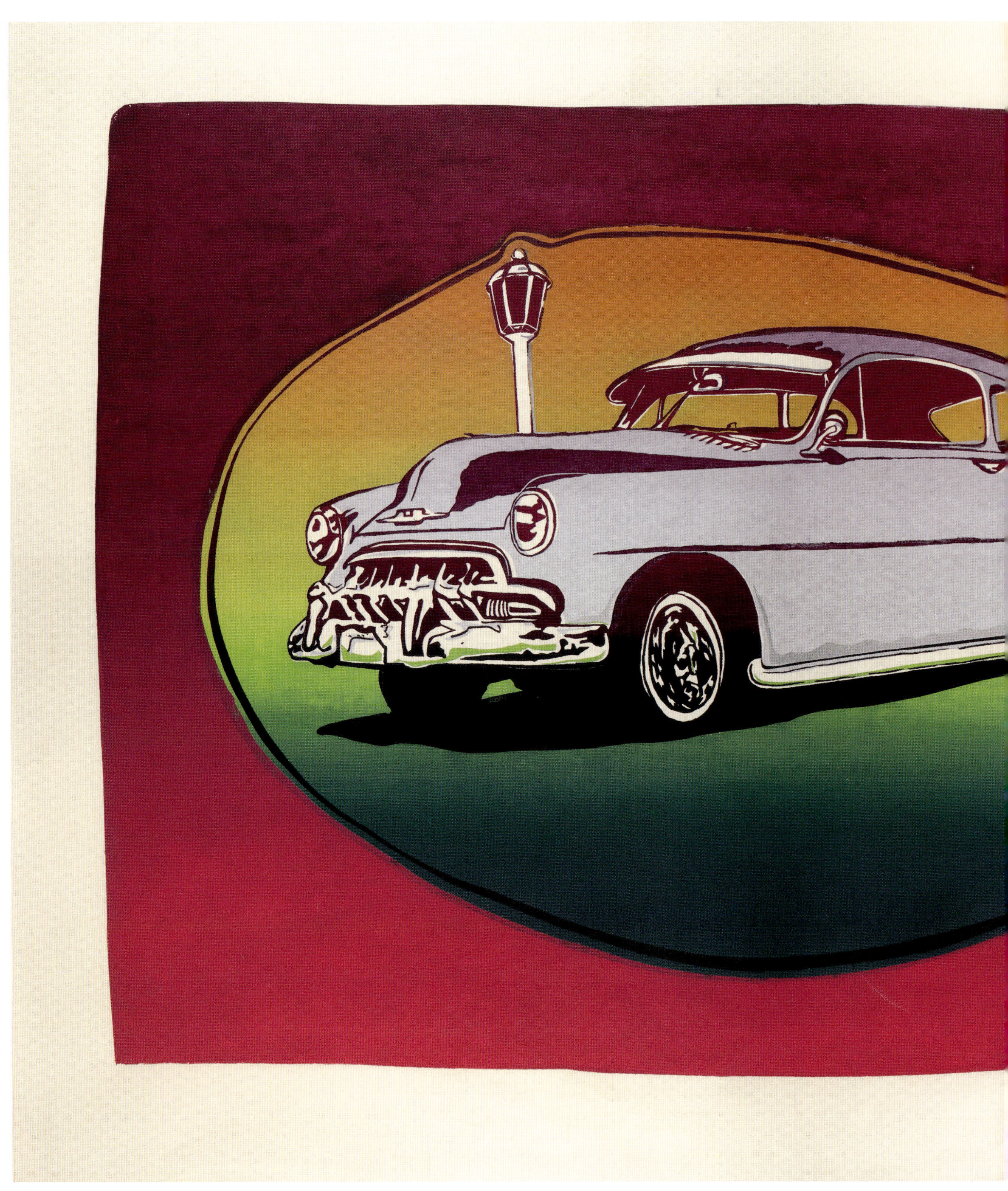

30 Rudy O. Cuellar (born 1950), *1951 Chevy Fastback*, 1982. Screenprint, 28½ × 40 in. Collection of Rudy O. Cuellar.

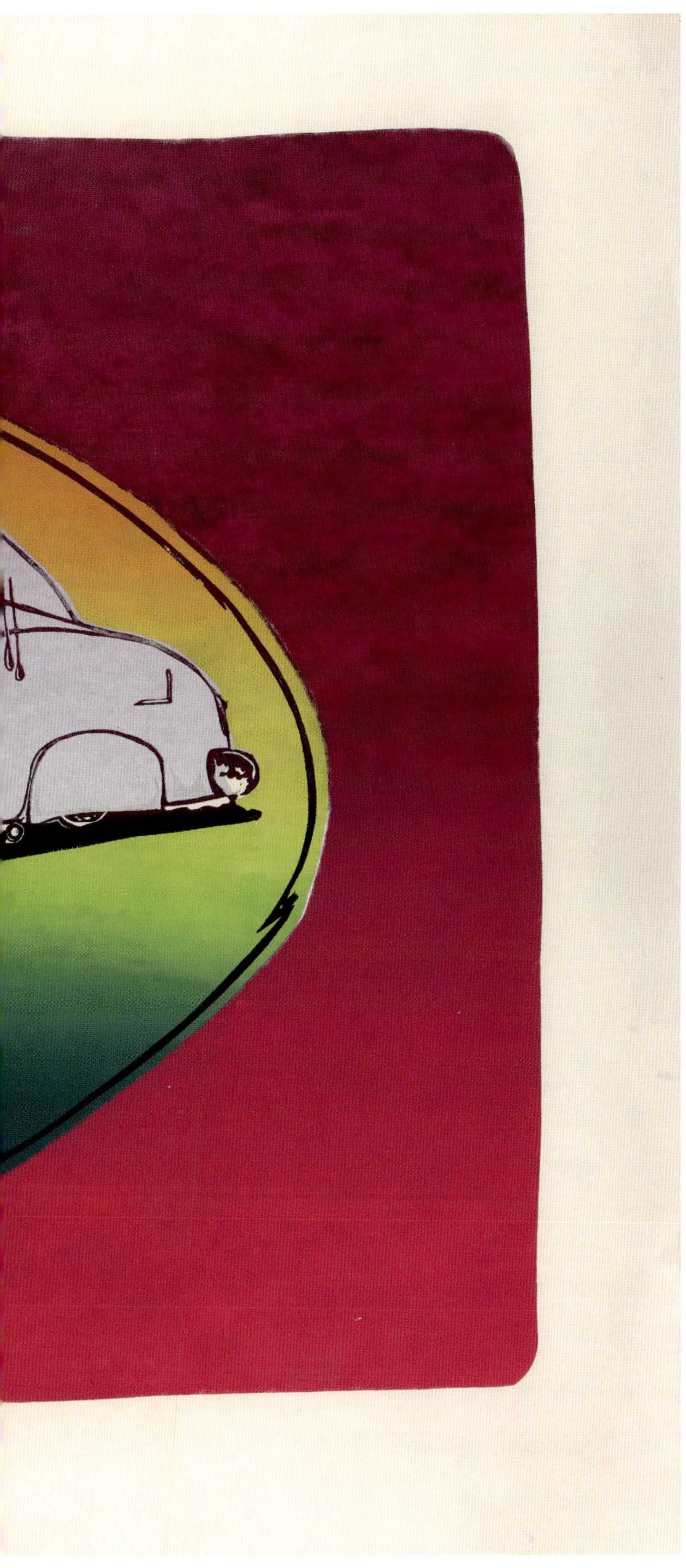

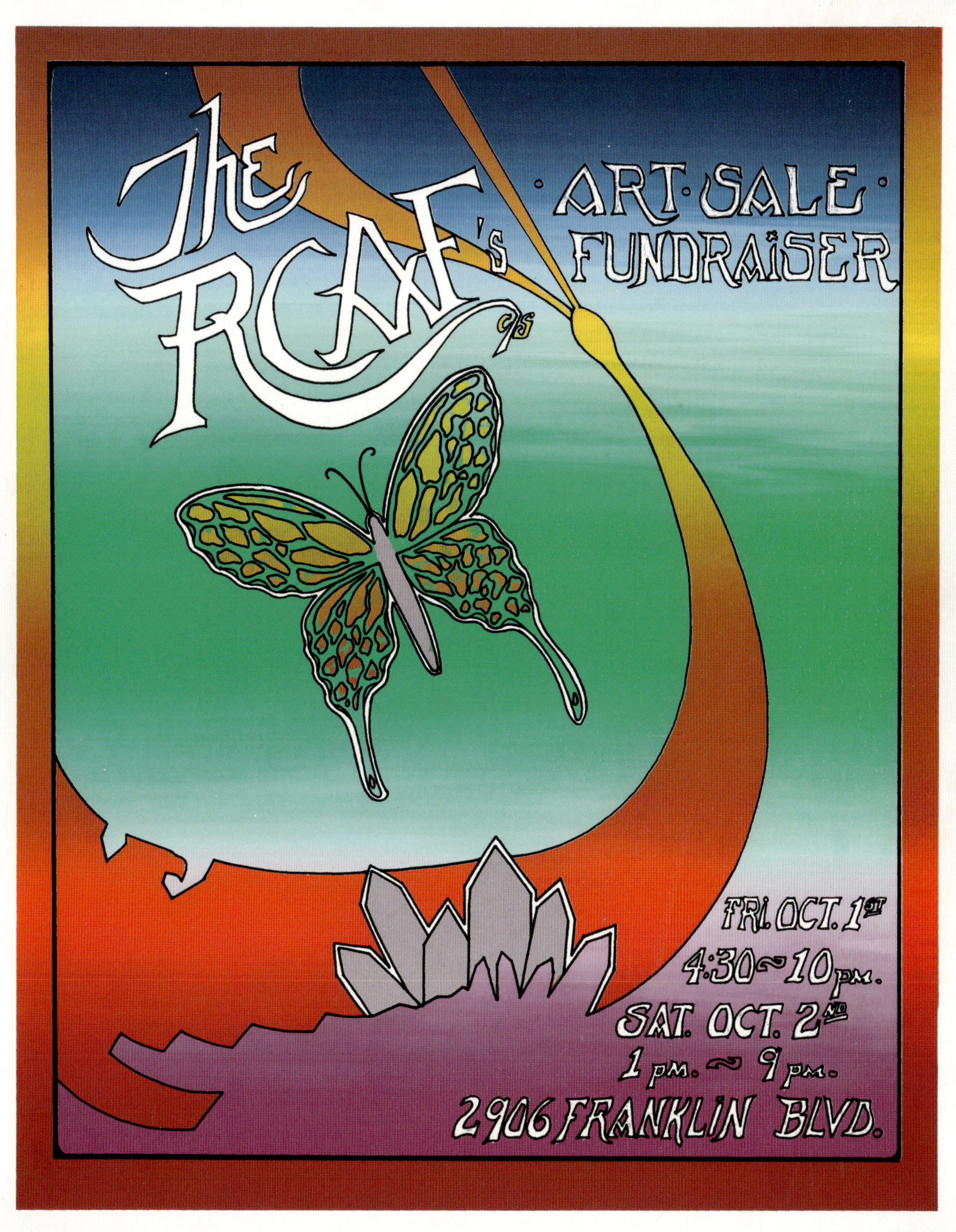

31 Juanishi Orosco (1945–2023), *The RCAF's Art Sale Fundraiser*, 1982. Screenprint, 19 ½ × 15 ¼ in. Royal Chicano Air Force Poster Collection, Gerth Special Collections & University Archives, California State University, Sacramento.

Luis "Louie the Foot" González's Poetry Prints

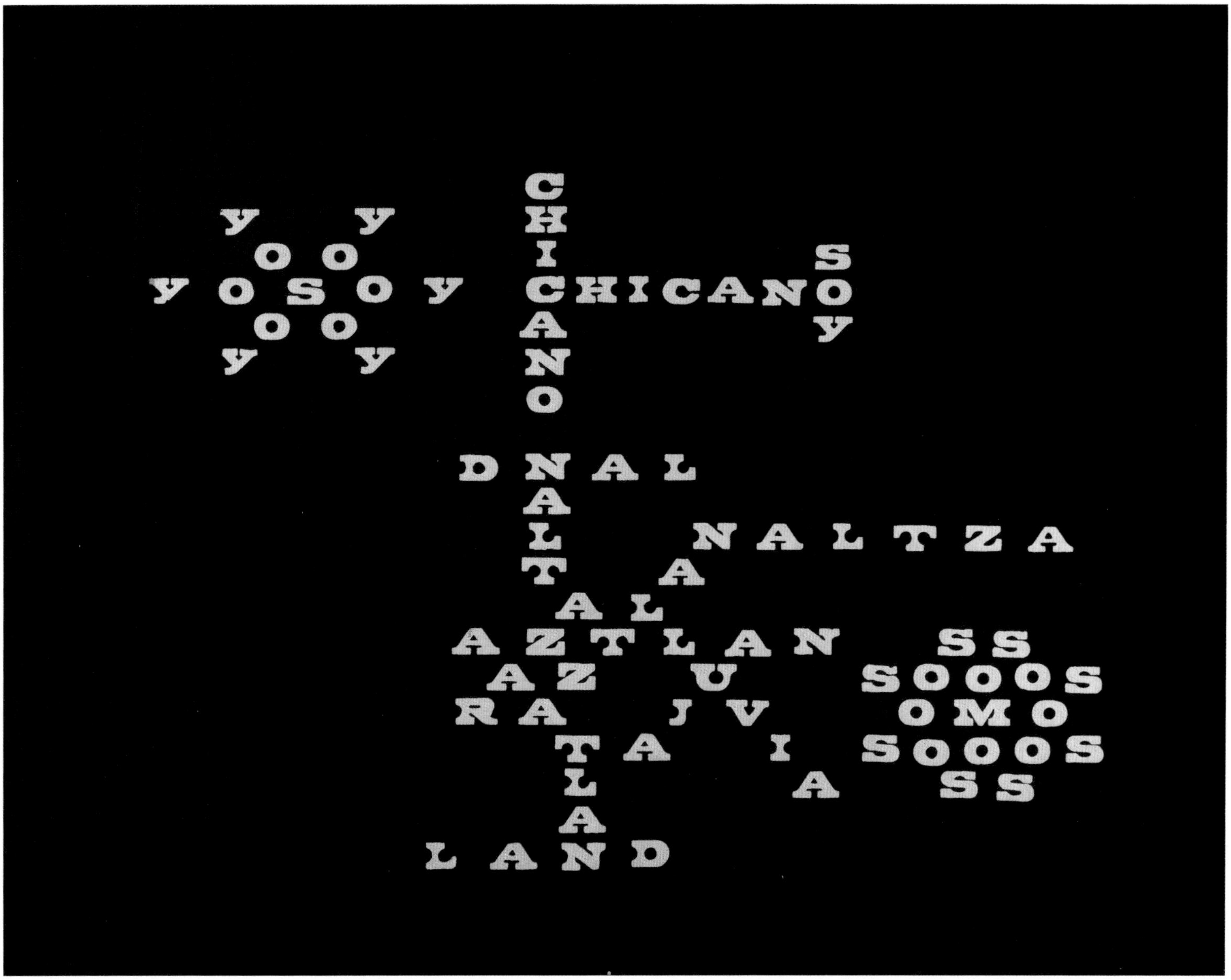

32 Luis C. González (born 1953), *Yo Soy Chicano*, 1975. Screenprint, 13 ¾ × 18 in. Collection of Luis C. González.

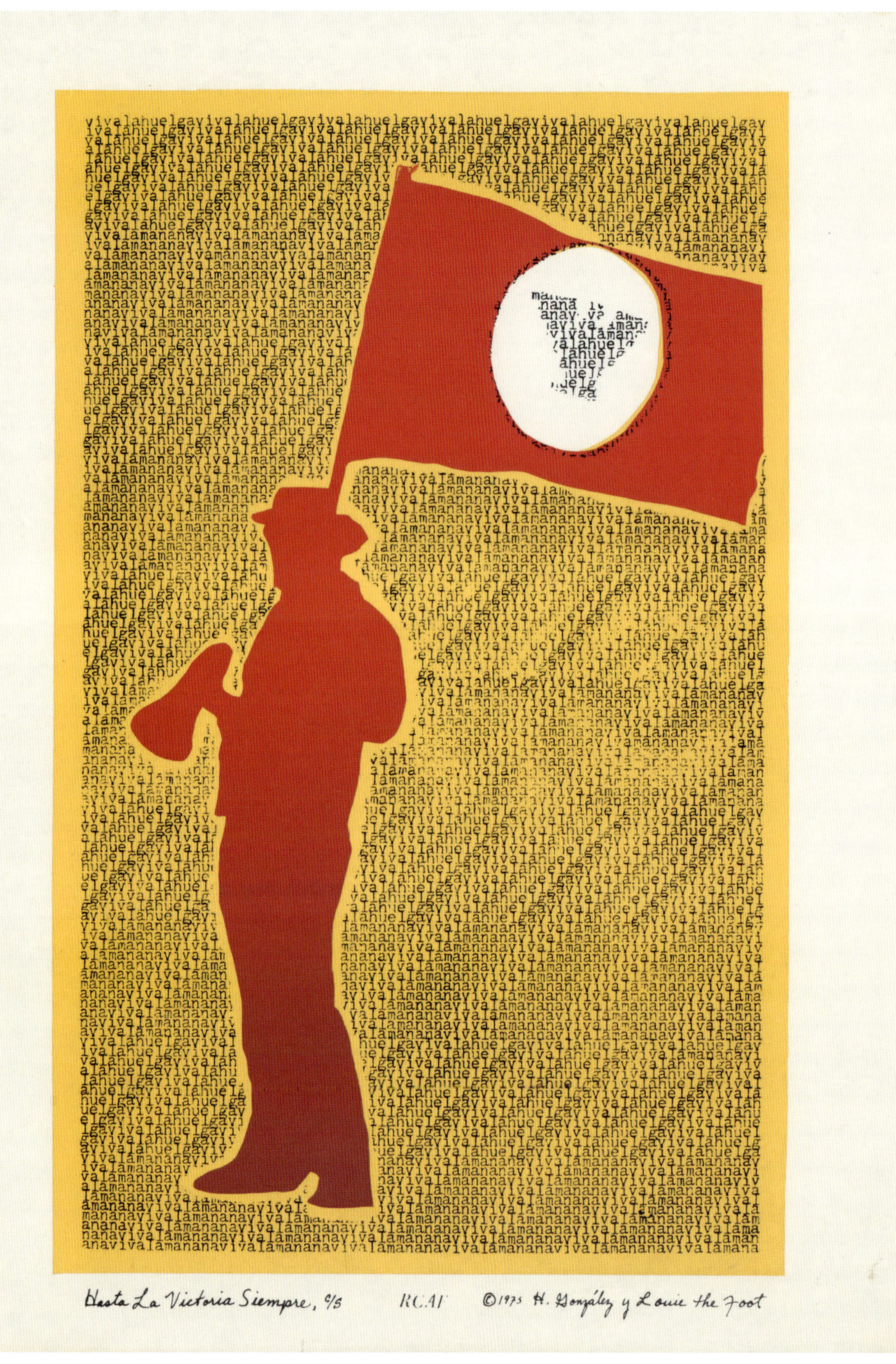

33 Luis C. González (born 1953) and Héctor D. González (born 1945), *Hasta La Victoria Siempre*, 1975. Screenprint, 25 × 17¼ in. Courtesy of the California History Room, California State Library.

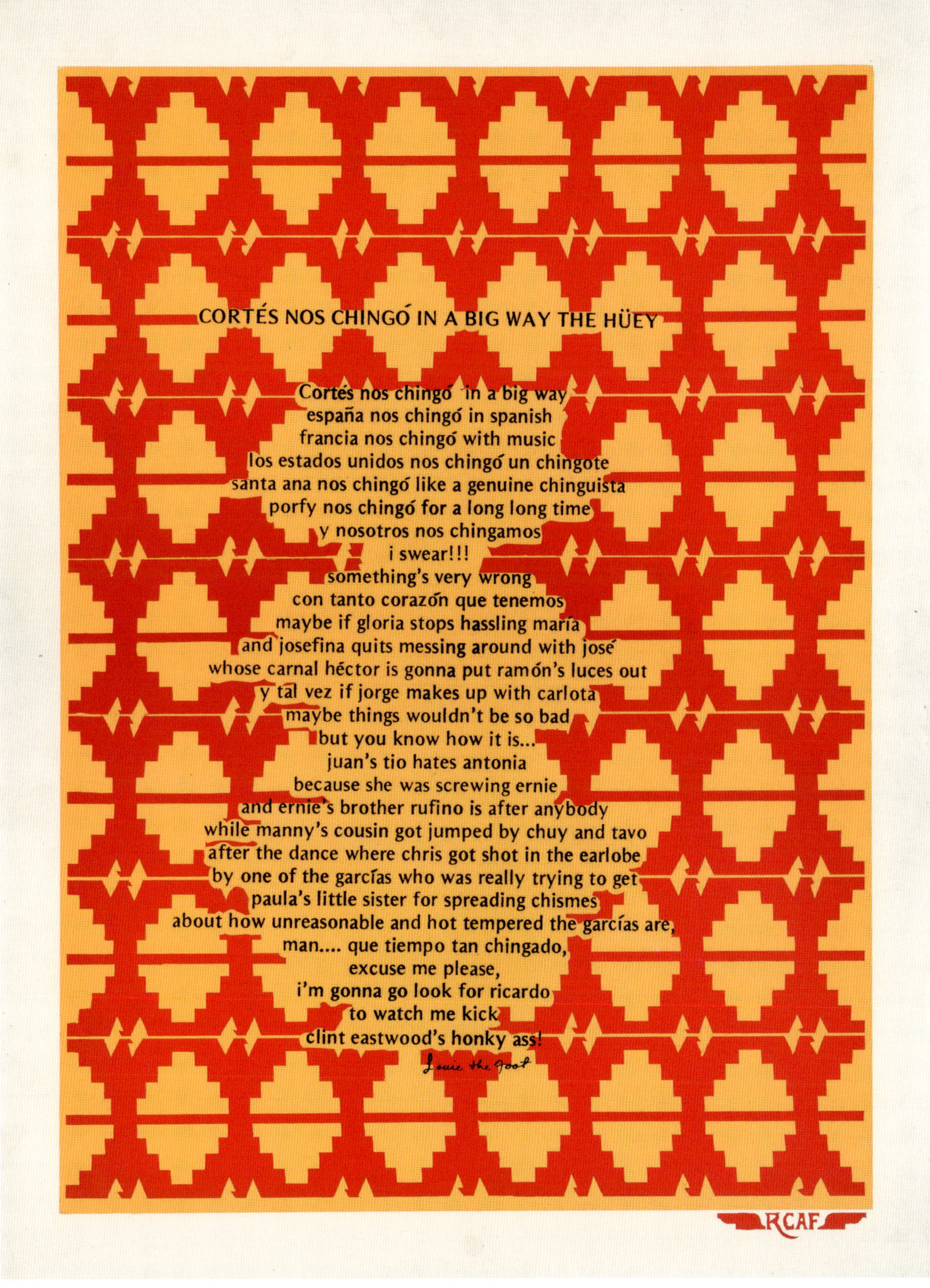

34 Luis C. González (born 1953) and Ricardo Favela (1944–2007), *Cortés Nos Chingó in a Big Way The Hüey*, 1976. Screenprint, 25 × 19 in. Collection of Luis C. González.

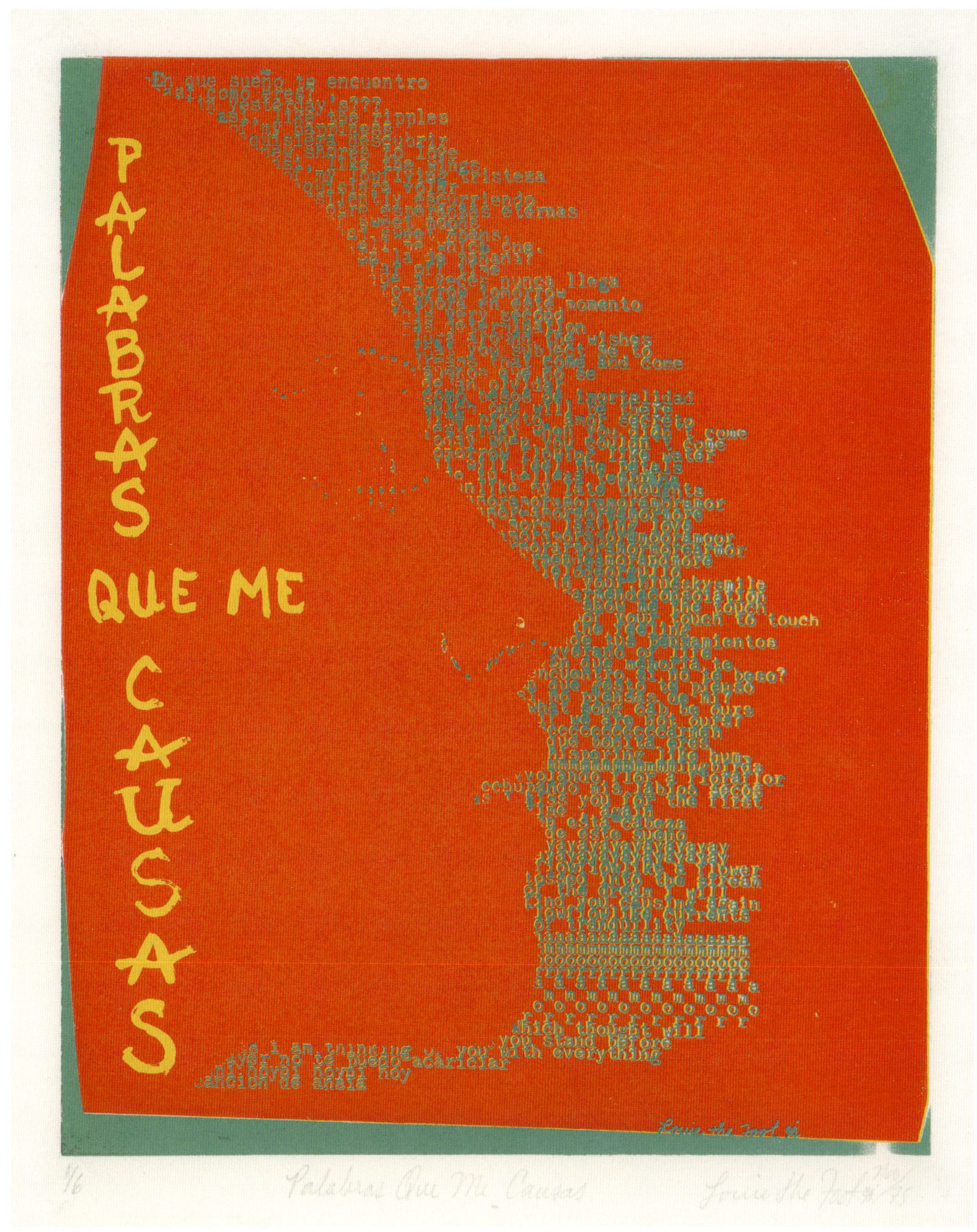

35 Luis C. González (born 1953), *Palabras Que Me Causas*, 1975. Screenprint, 14½ × 12 in. Collection of Luis C. González.

Cultural Affairs Committee

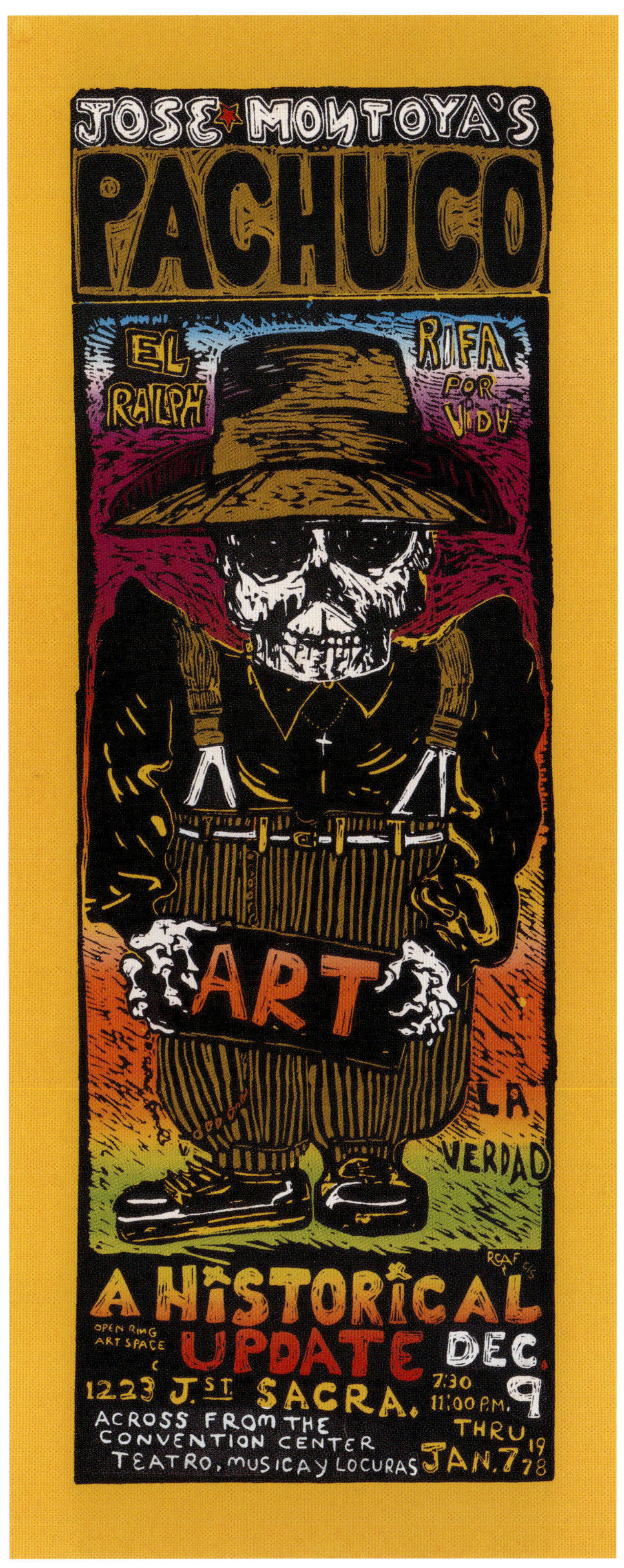

36 Rudy O. Cuellar (born 1950), Luis C. González (born 1953), and José Montoya (1932–2013), *José Montoya's Pachuco Art, A Historical Update*, 1977. Screenprint, 31 × 13 in. Collection of Luis C. González.

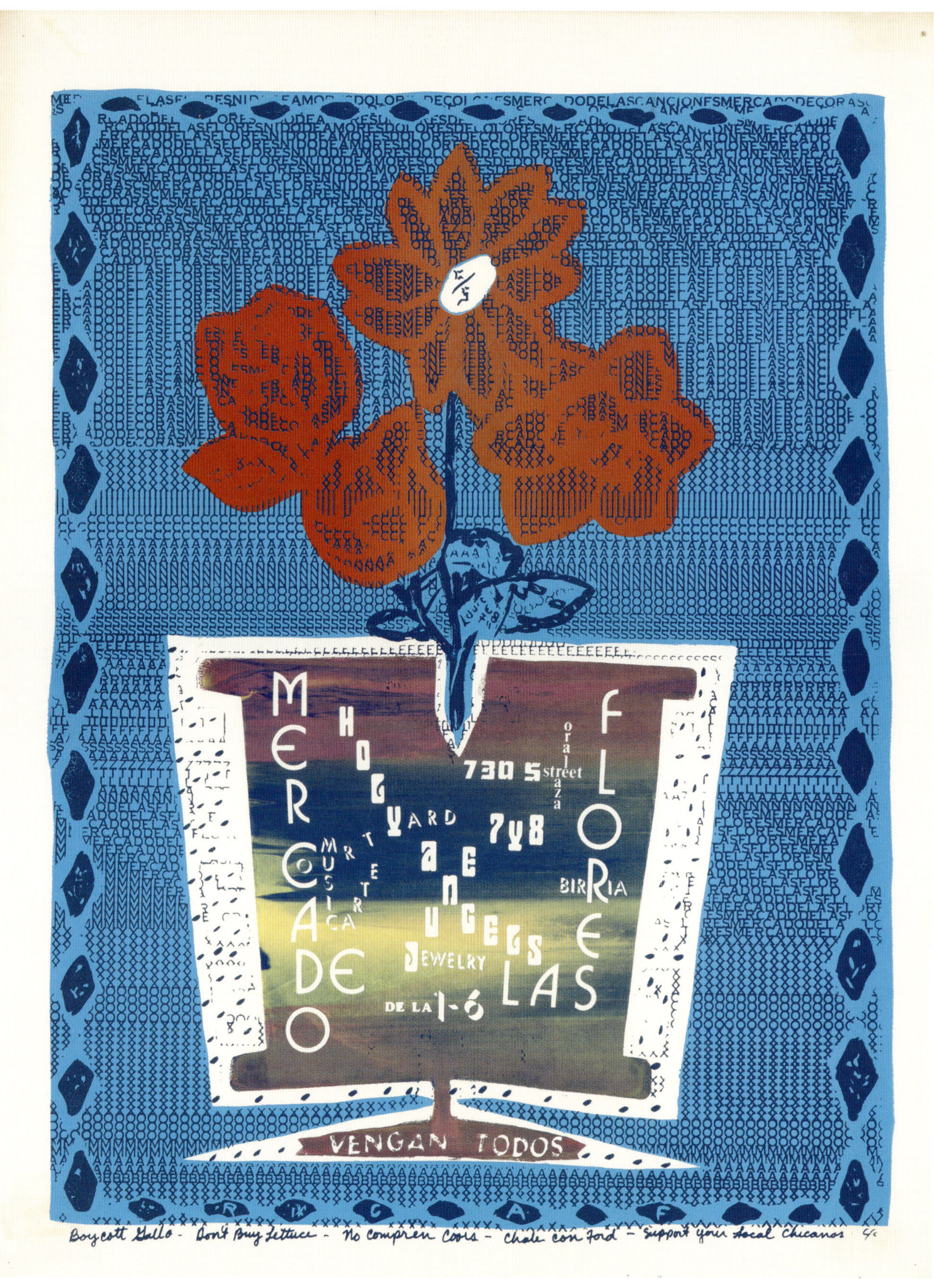

37 Luis C. González (born 1953), *Mercado de las Flores*, 1975. Screenprint, 25 × 19 in. Collection of Luis C. González.

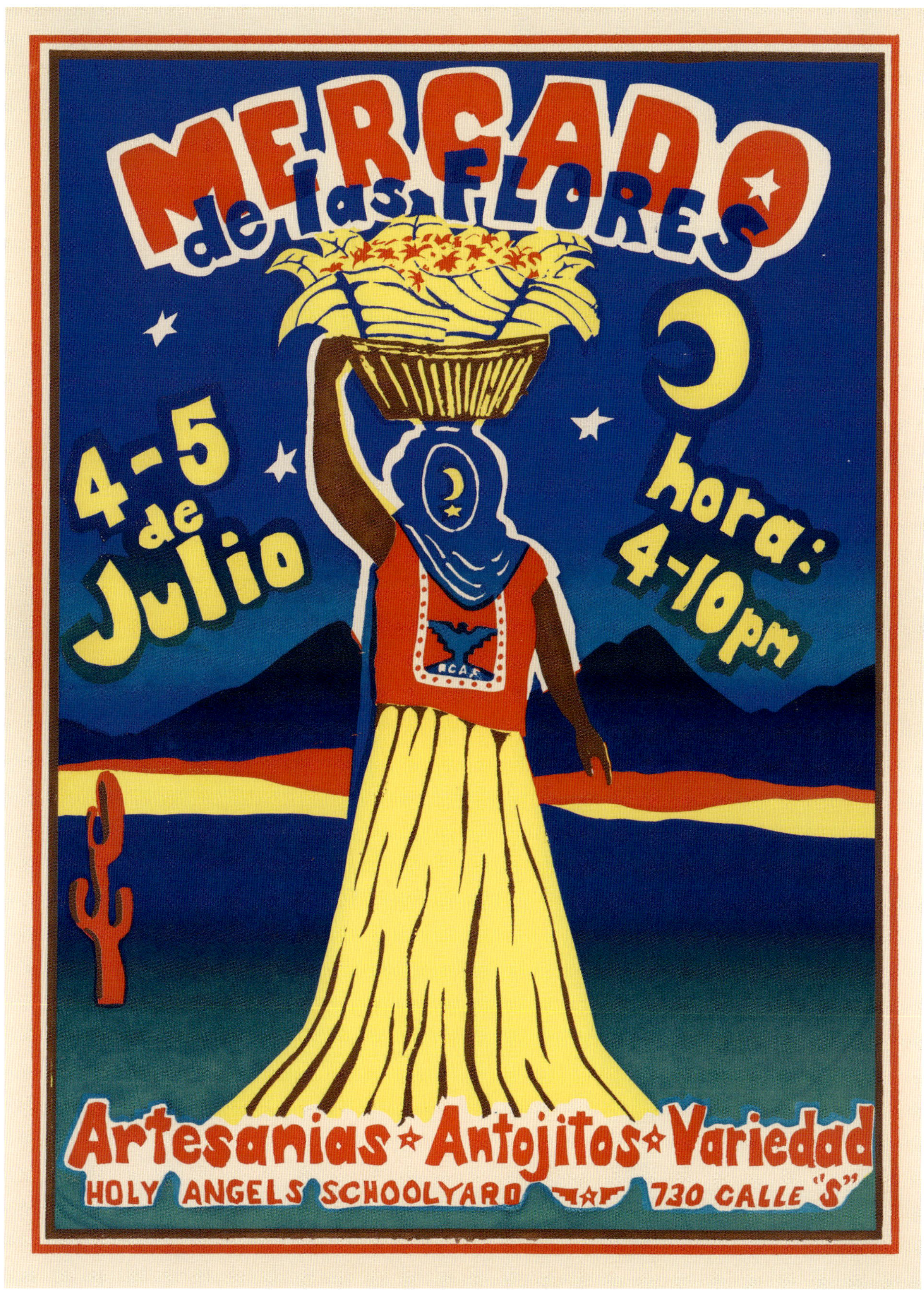

38 Juan Carrillo (born 1941), *Mercado de las Flores*, 1976. Screenprint, 24 ½ × 18 ⅛ in. Collection of Juan Manuel Carrillo.

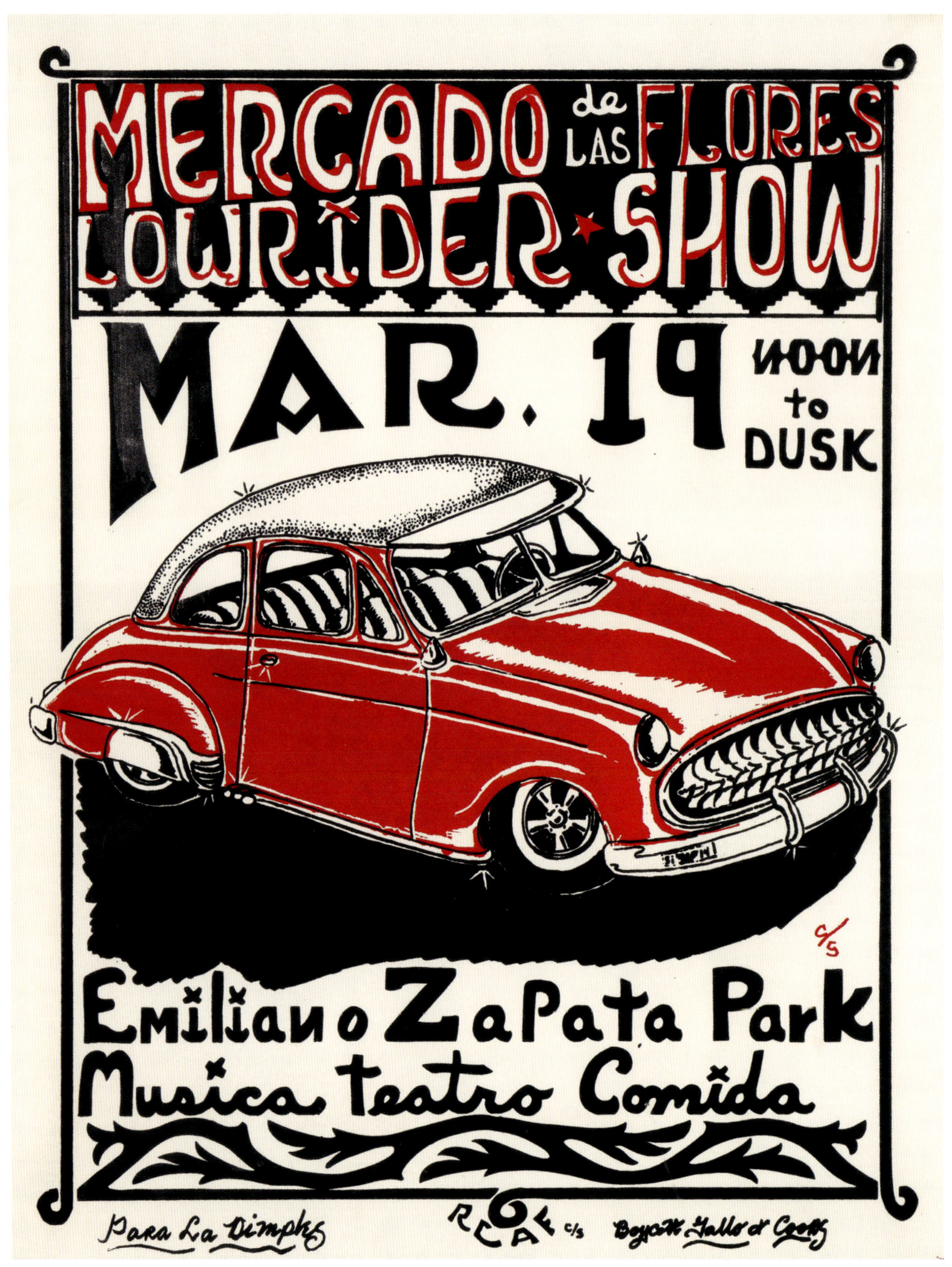

39 Rudy O. Cuellar (born 1950), *Mercado de las Flores Lowrider Show,* 1977. Screenprint, 22 ⅝ × 17 ½ in. Collection of Rudy O. Cuellar.

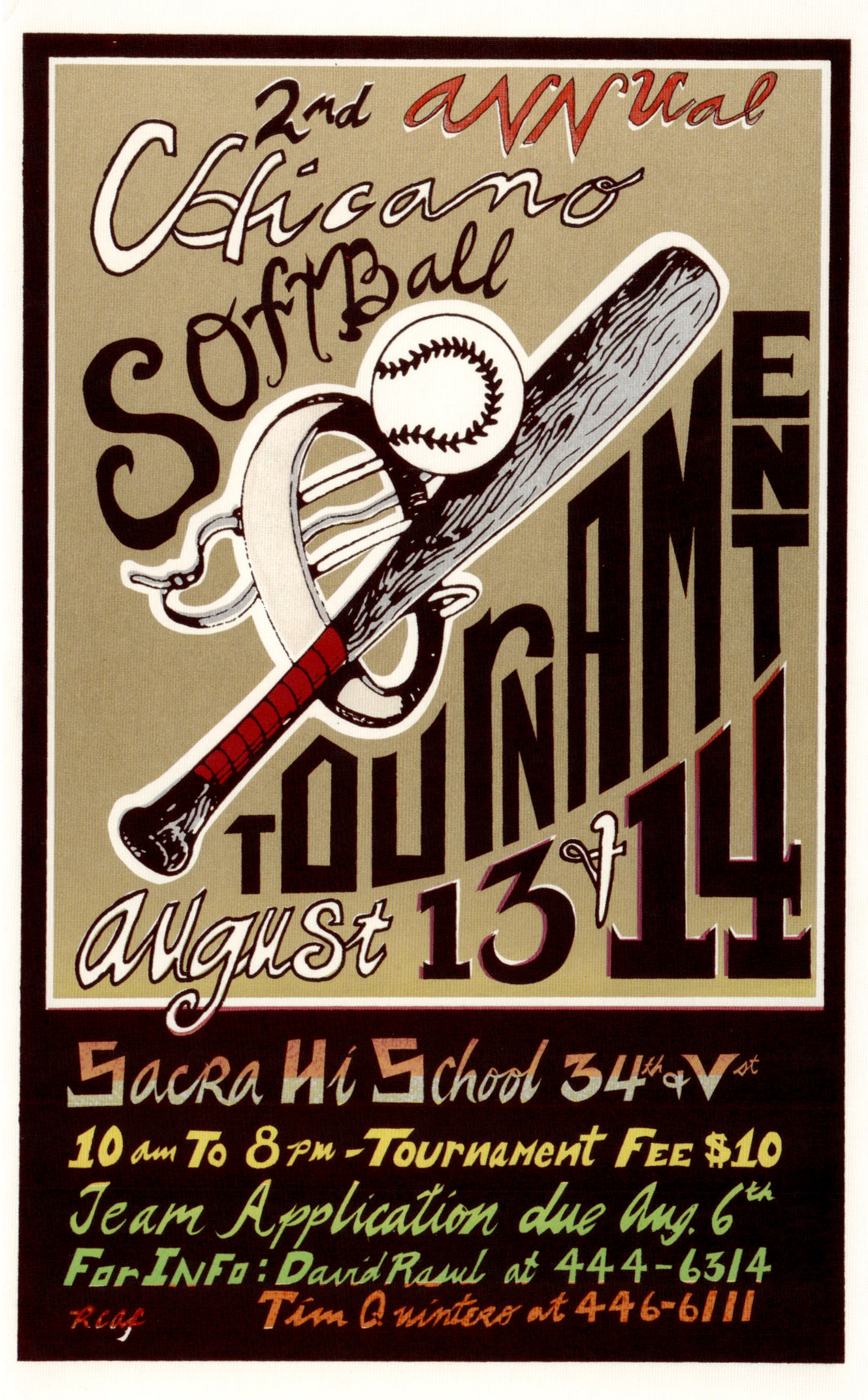

40 Luis C. González (born 1953), *2nd Annual Chicano Softball Tournament*, 1977. Screen-print, 17 ½ × 11 ⅜ in. Collection of Luis C. González.

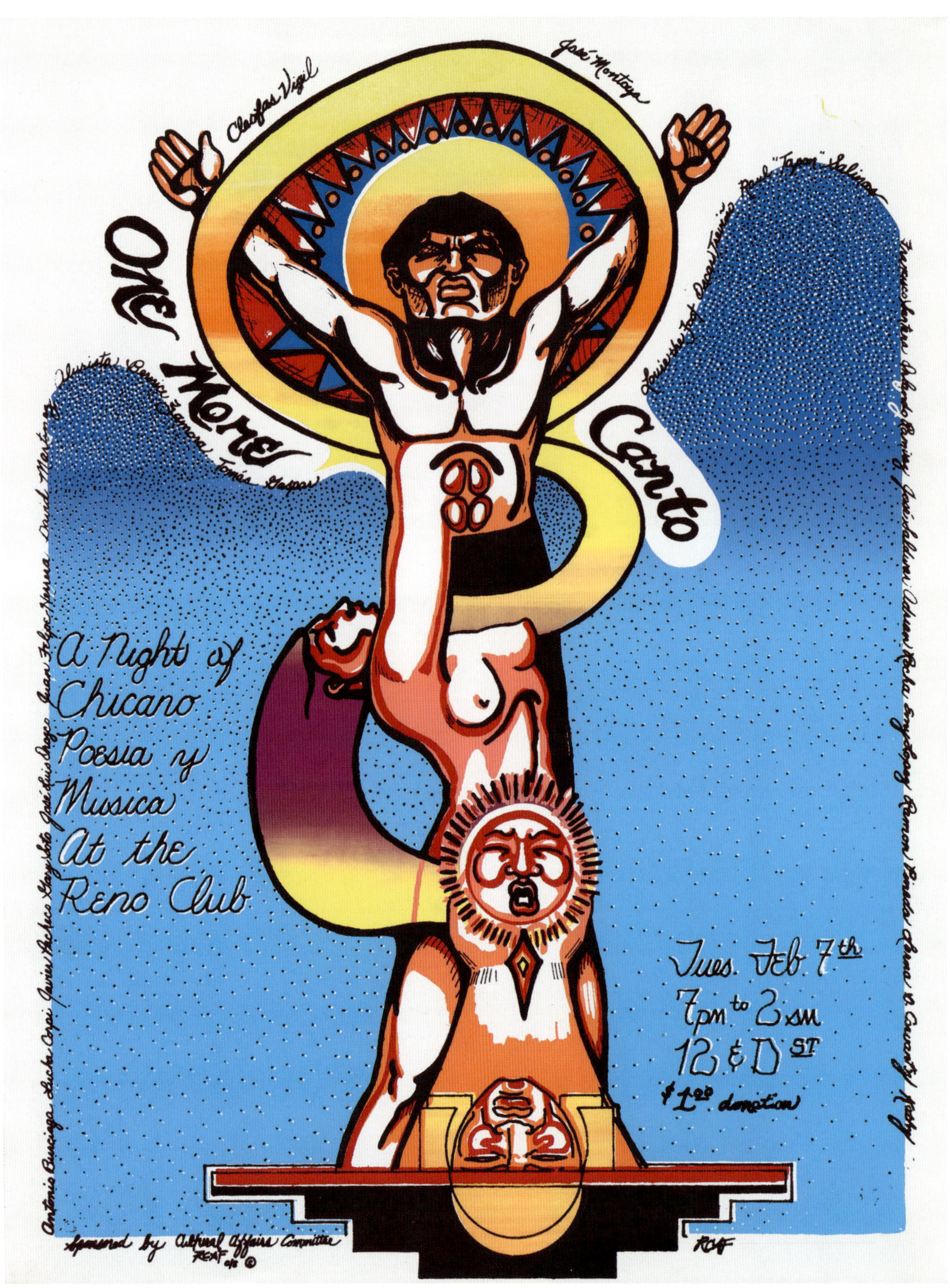

41 Juanishi Orosco (1945–2023), *One More Canto*, 1978. Screenprint, 22½ × 17 in. Courtesy of the California History Room, California State Library.

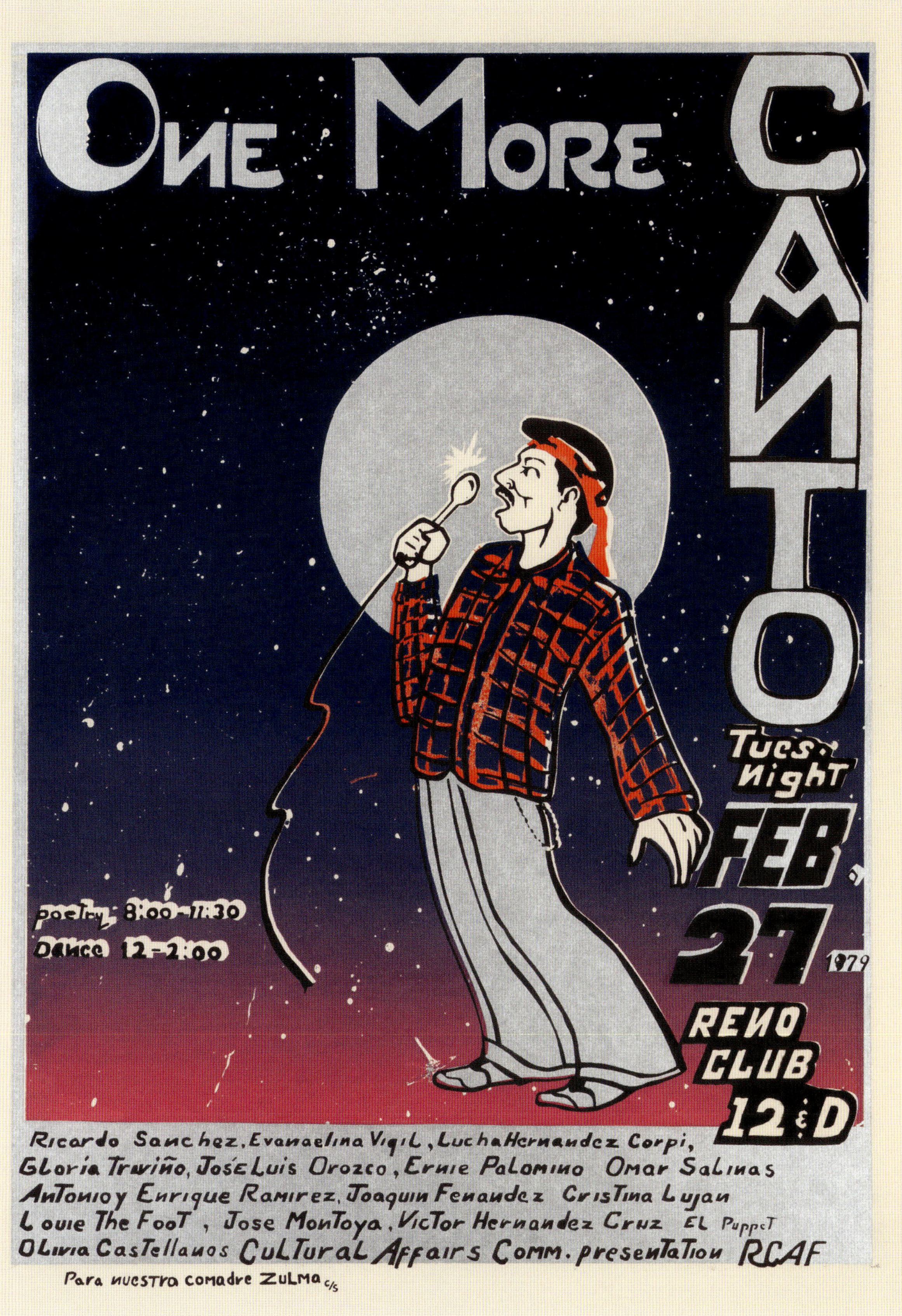

42 Rudy O. Cuellar (born 1950) and Juanishi Orosco (1945–2023), *One More Canto*, 1979. Screenprint, 23 × 17½ in. Collection of Rudy O. Cuellar.

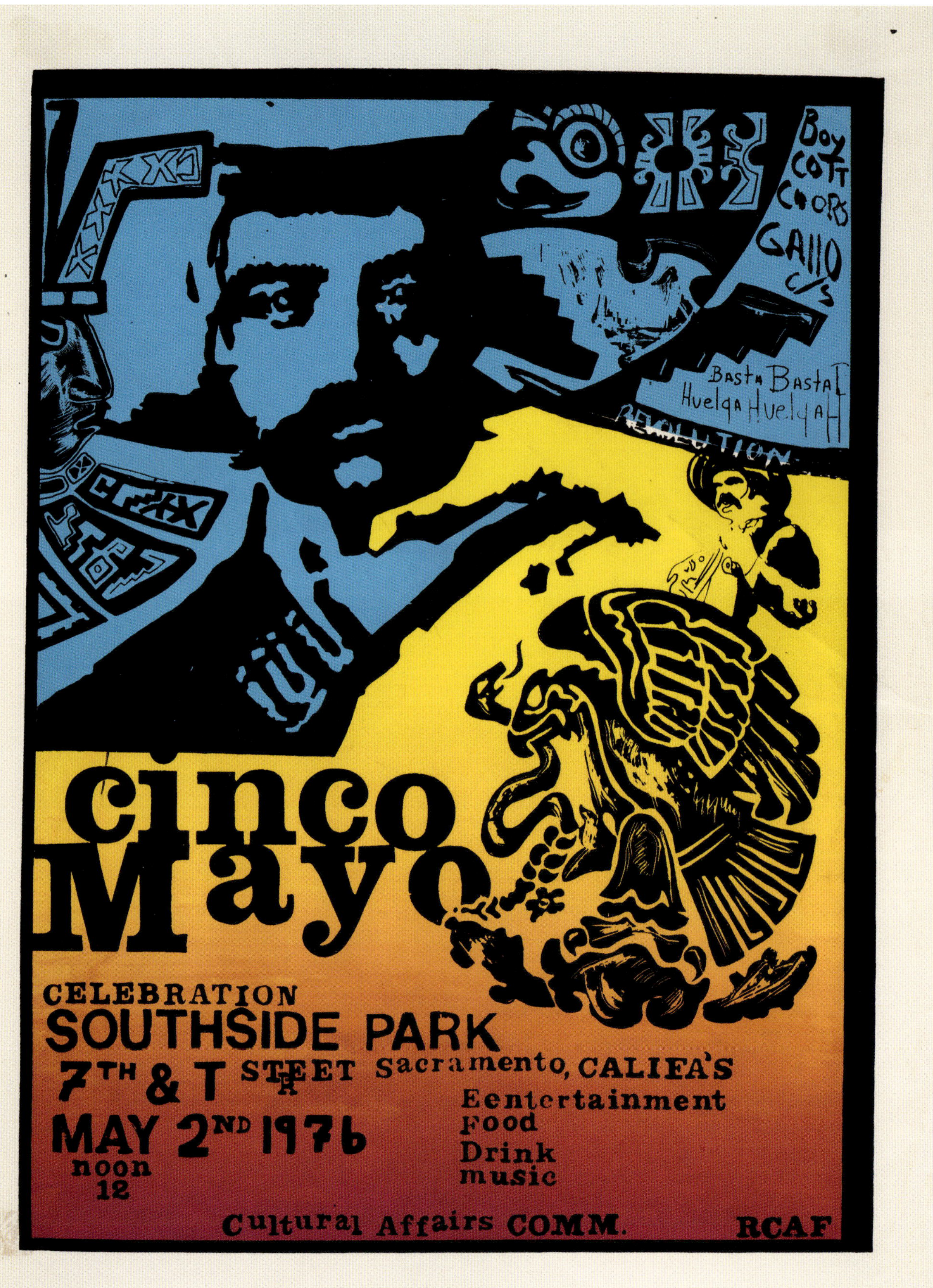

43 Armando Cid (1943–2009), *Cinco de Mayo*, 1976. Screenprint, 25 × 19 in. Royal Chicano Air Force Archives, CEMA 8, University of California, Santa Barbara Library.

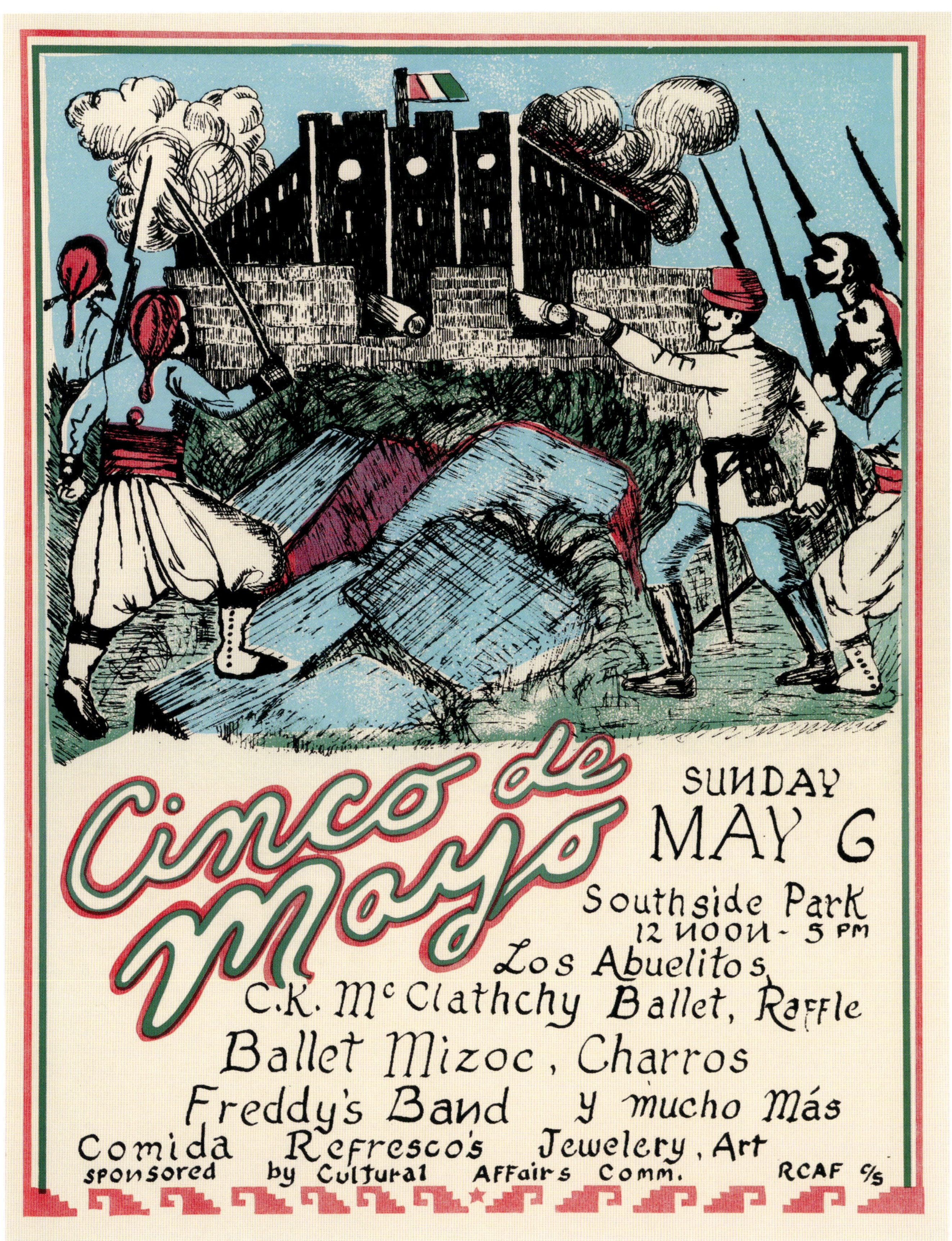

44 Rudy O. Cuellar (born 1950), *Cinco de Mayo*, 1979. Screenprint, 23 × 17 5/8 in. Royal Chicano Air Force Poster Collection, Gerth Special Collections & University Archives, California State University, Sacramento.

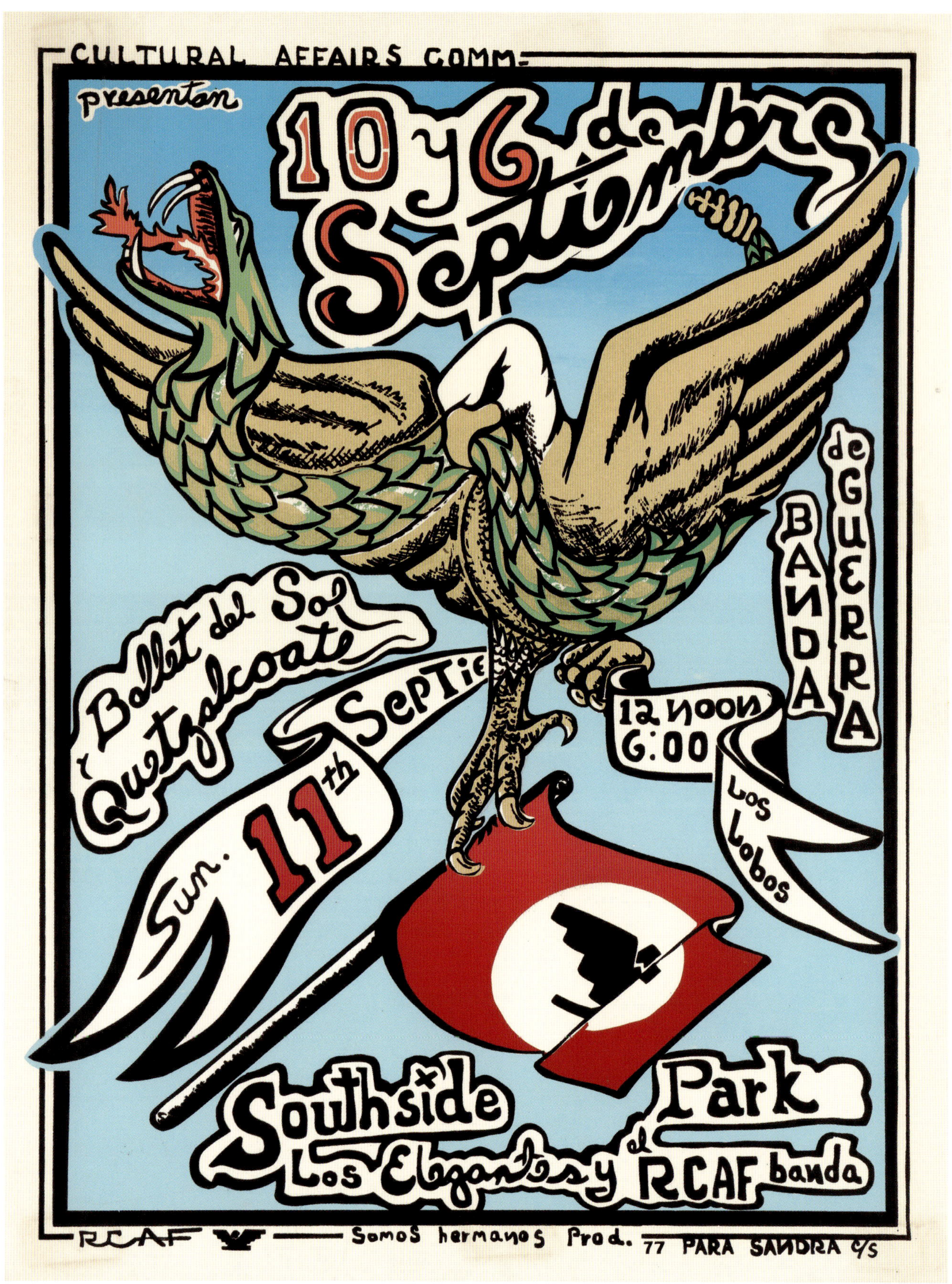

45 Rudy O. Cuellar (born 1950), *10 y 6 de Septiembre*, 1977. Screenprint, 22½ × 17½ in. Collection of Rudy O. Cuellar.

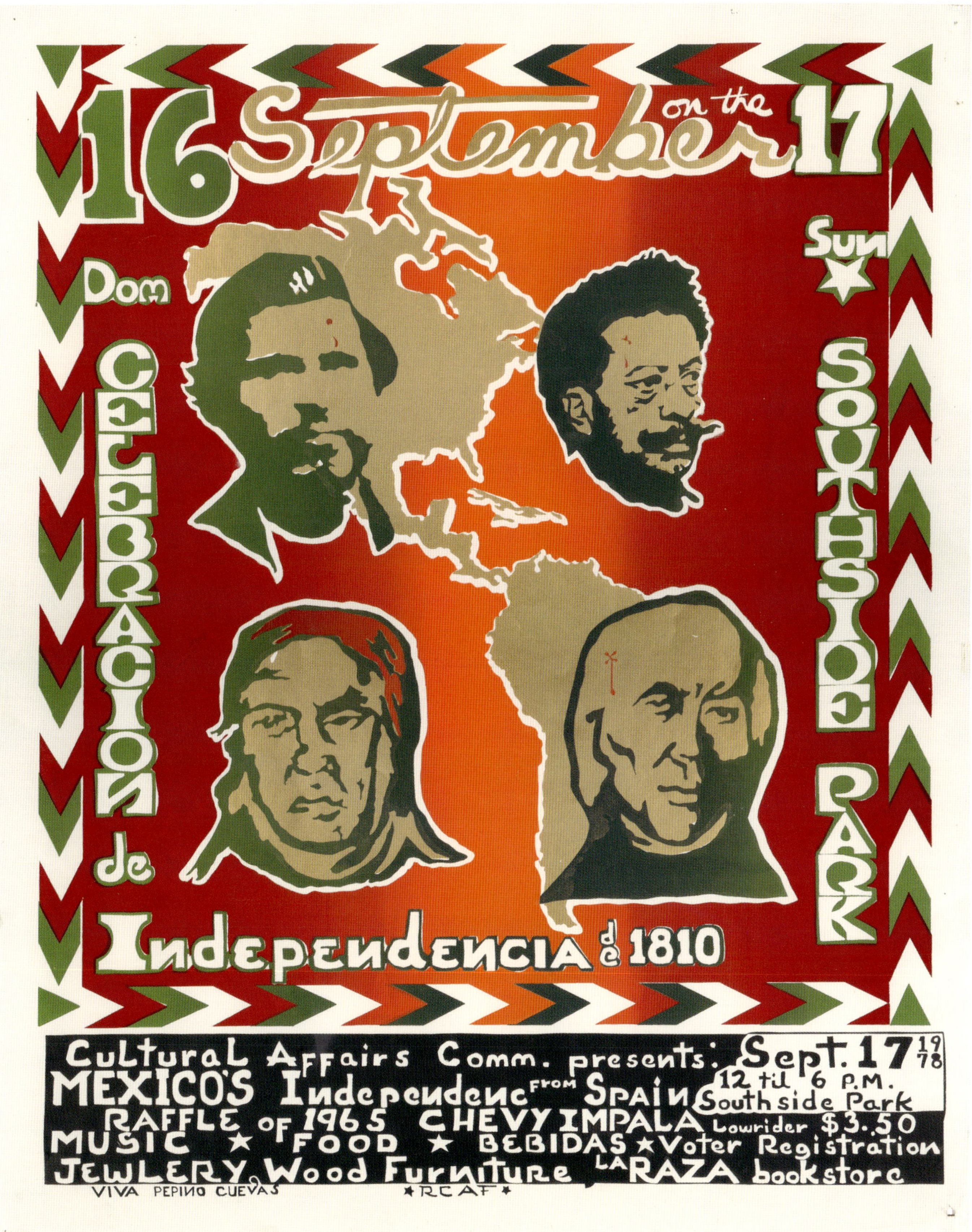

46 Rudy O. Cuellar (born 1950), *16 September on the 17*, 1978. Screenprint, 29 × 23 in. La Raza Galeria Posada Poster Collection, Gerth Special Collections & University Archives, California State University, Sacramento.

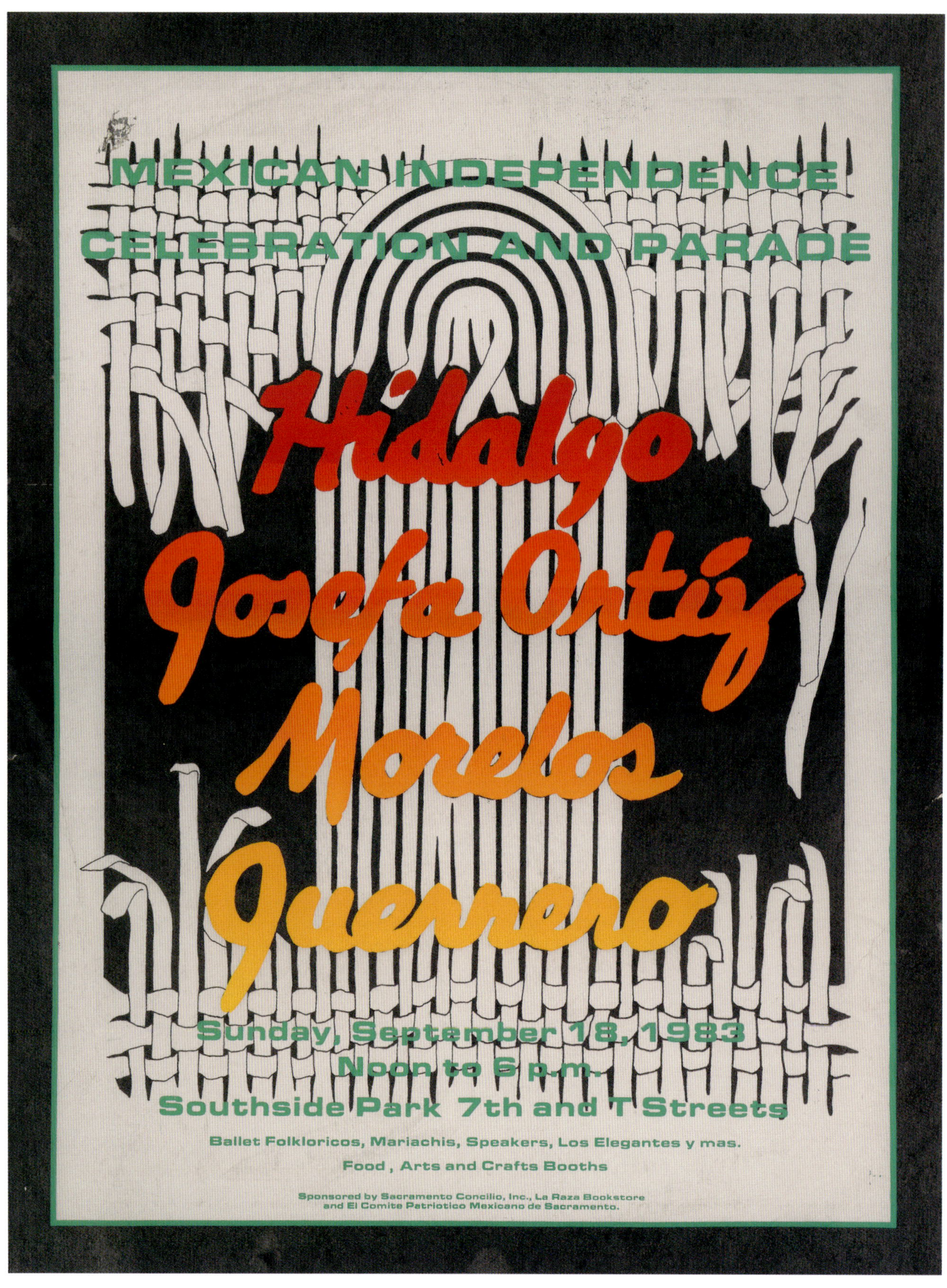

47 Lorraine García-Nakata (born 1950), *Mexican Independence Celebration and Parade*, 1983. Screenprint, 28 × 22 in. La Raza Galeria Posada Poster Collection, Gerth Special Collections & University Archives, California State University, Sacramento.

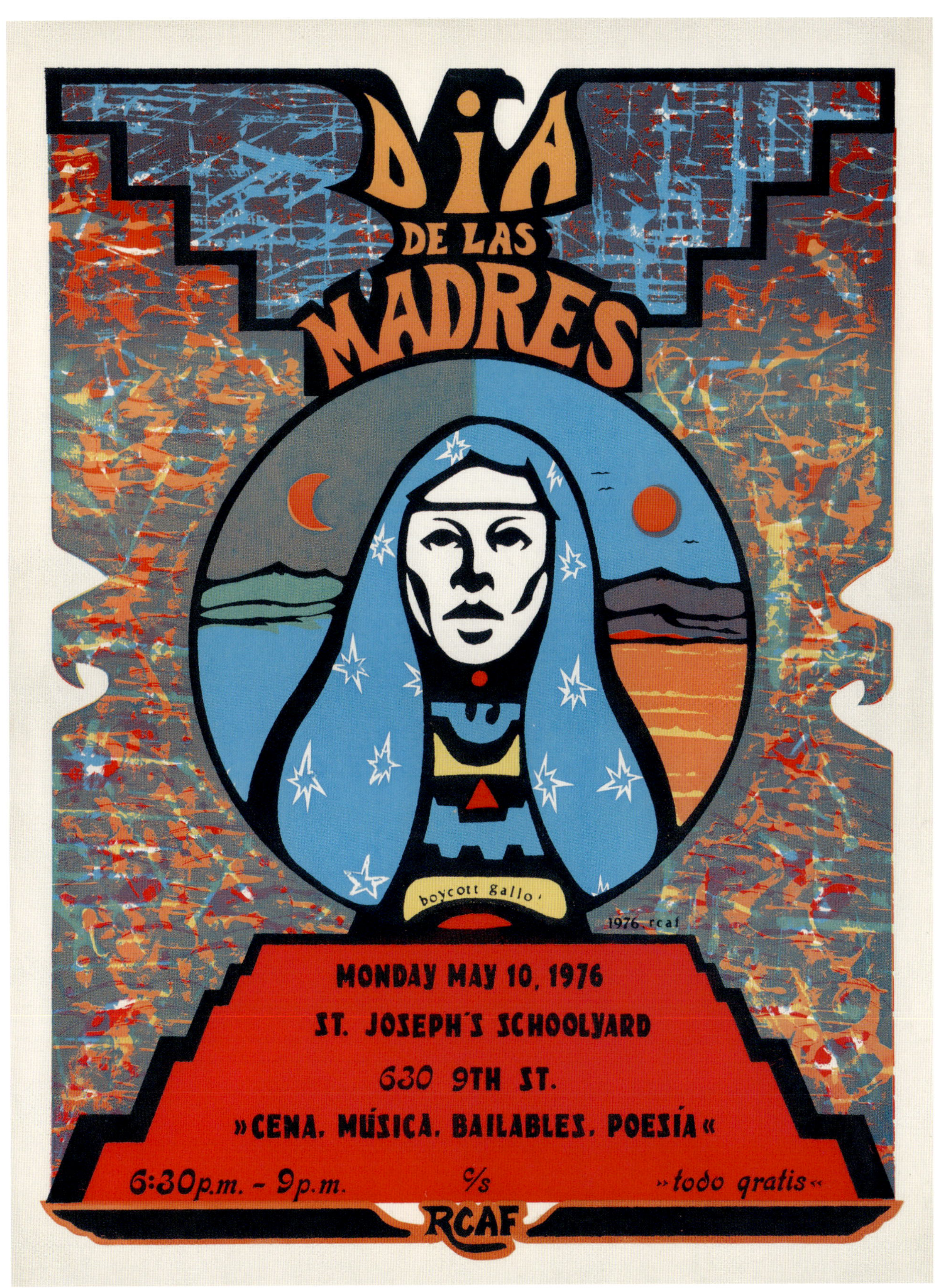

48 Ricardo Favela (1944–2007), *Día de las Madres*, 1976. Screenprint, 25 × 19 in. RCAFavela Collection.

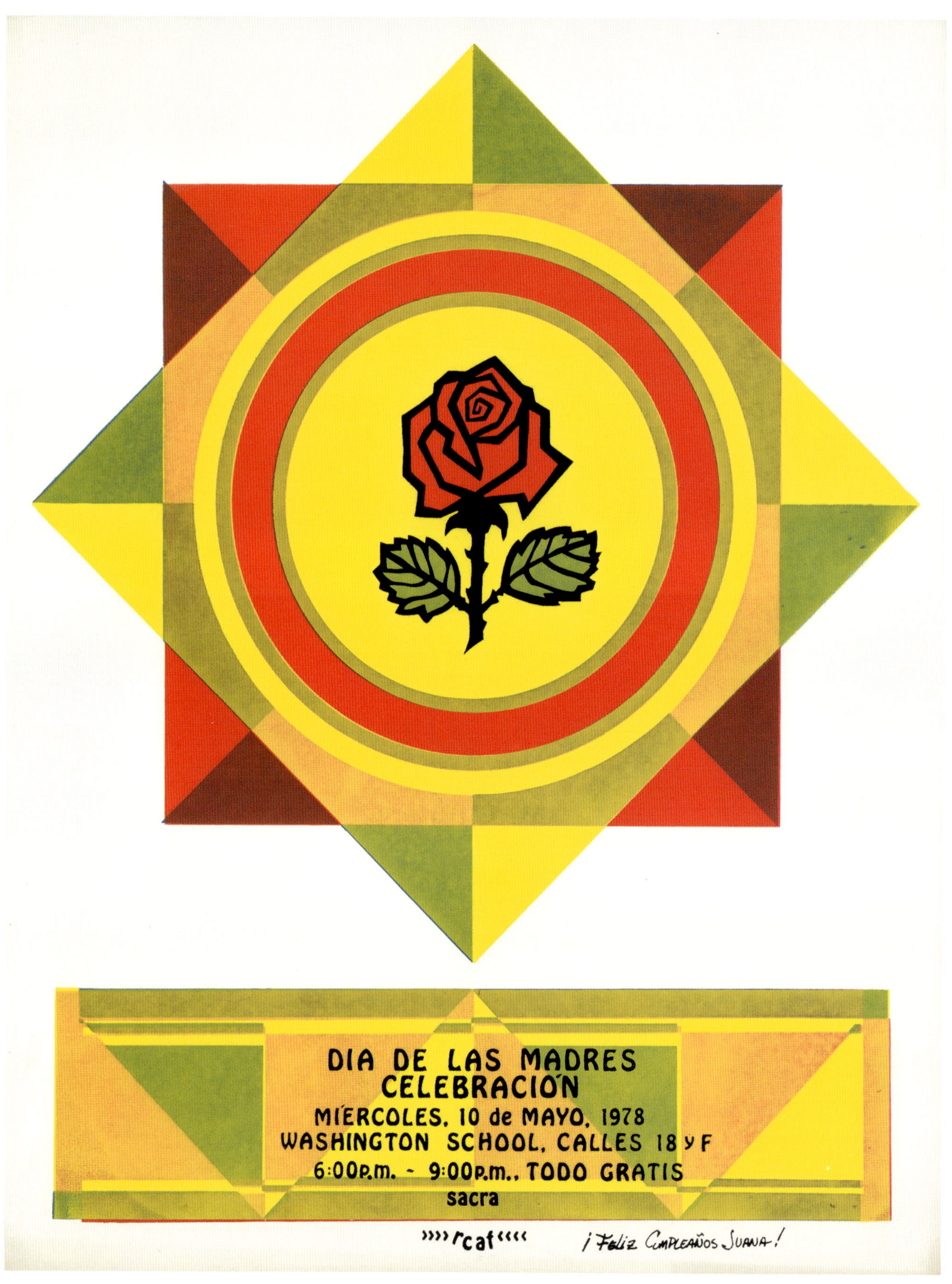

49 Ricardo Favela (1944–2007), *Día de las Madres Celebración*, 1978. Screenprint, 22 ¾ × 17 ⅝ in. RCAFavela Collection.

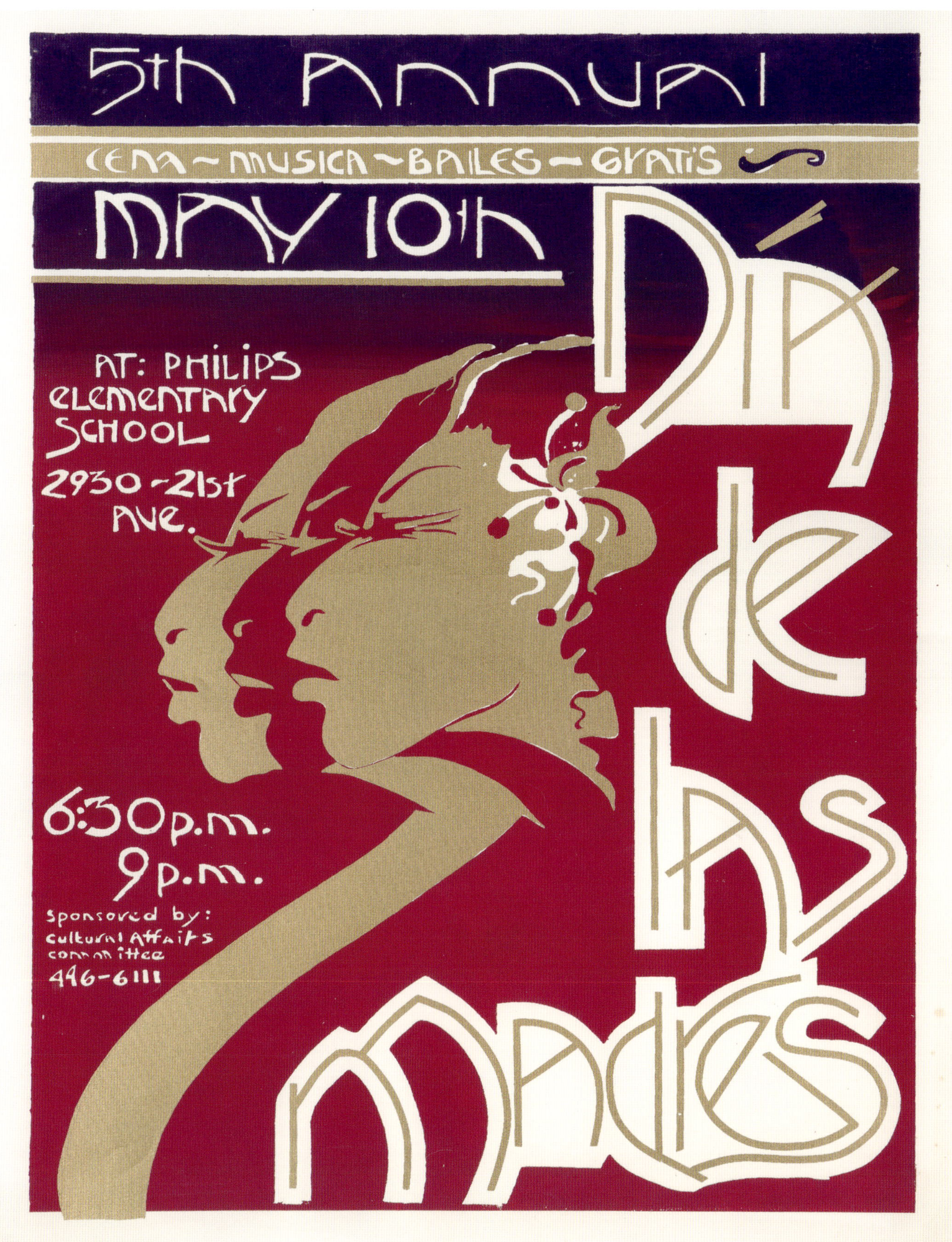

50 Eva Garcia (1949–1991), *5th Annual Día de las Madres,* 1979. Screenprint, 23 × 18 in. La Raza Galeria Posada Poster Collection, Gerth Special Collections & University Archives, California State University, Sacramento.

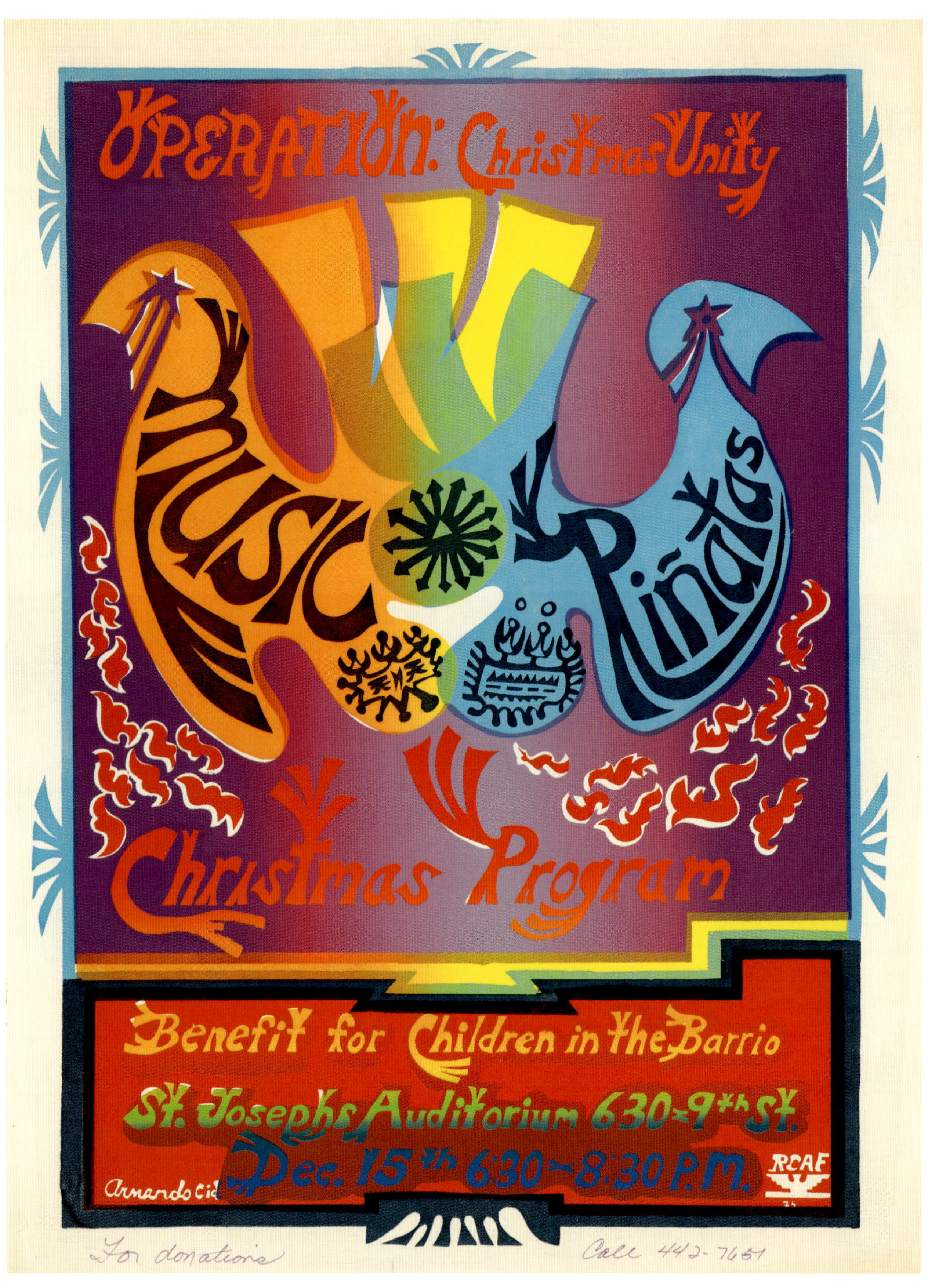

51 Armando Cid (1943–2009), *Operation Christmas Unity*, 1973. Screenprint, 25⅛ × 19 in. Rasul Chicano Art Collection.

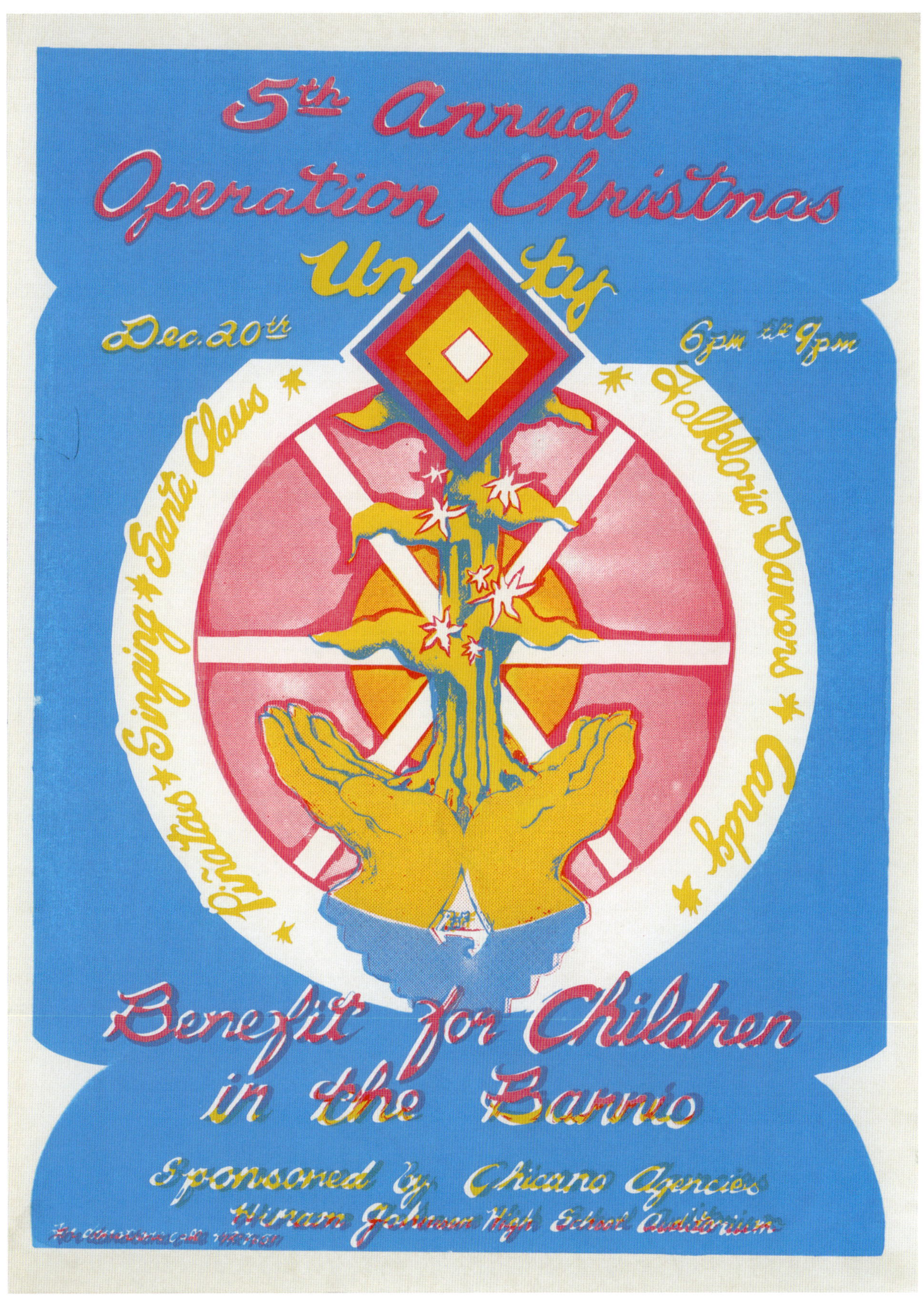

52 Juanishi Orosco (1945–2023), *5th Annual Operation Christmas Unity*, 1975. Screenprint, 24 × 18 in. Courtesy of the California History Room, California State Library.

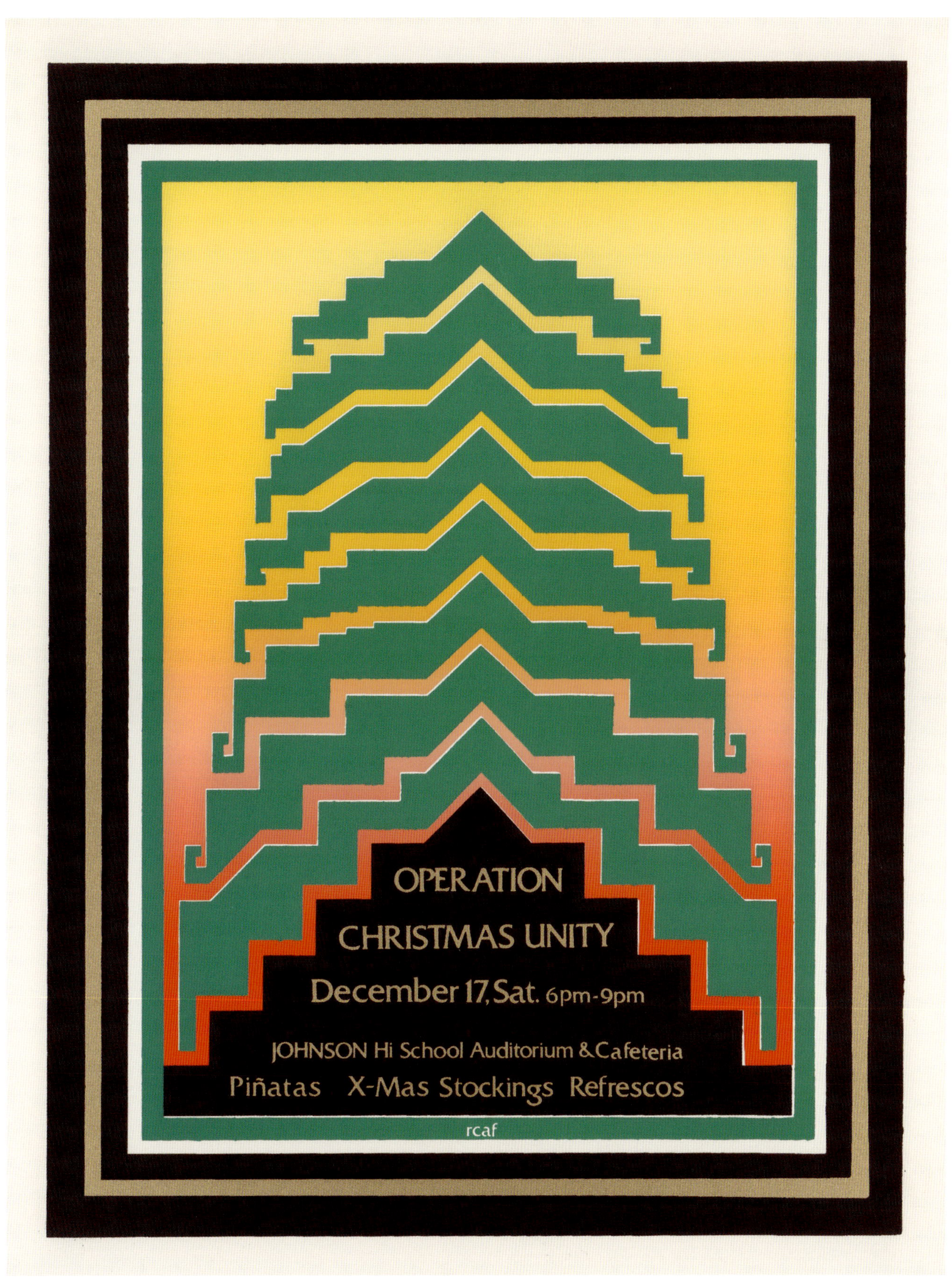

53 Luis C. González (born 1953), *Operation Christmas Unity*, 1977. Screenprint, 22½ × 17½ in. Collection of Luis C. González.

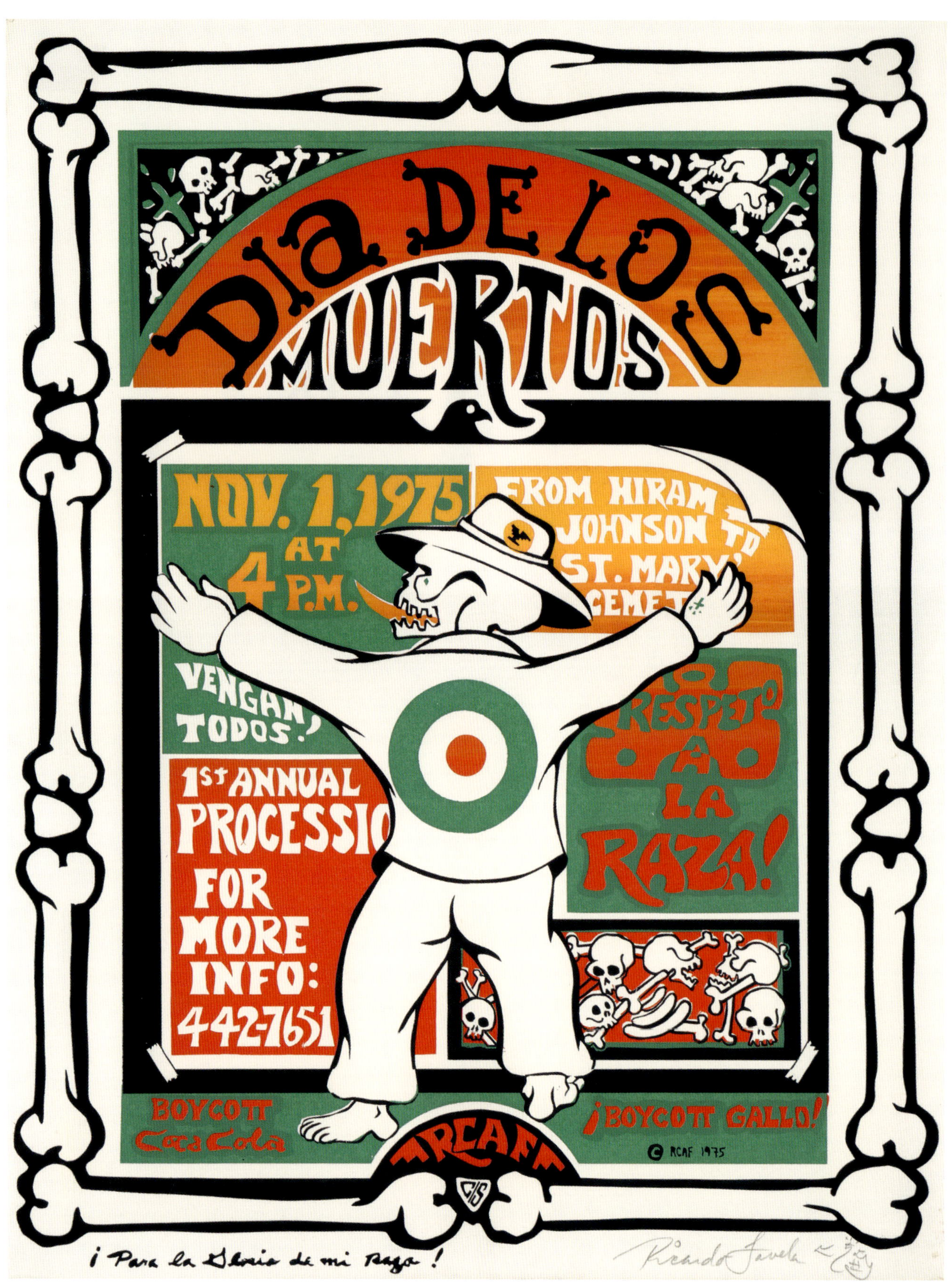

54 Ricardo Favela (1944–2007), *Día de los Muertos,* 1975. Screenprint, 25 × 19 in. RCAFavela Collection.

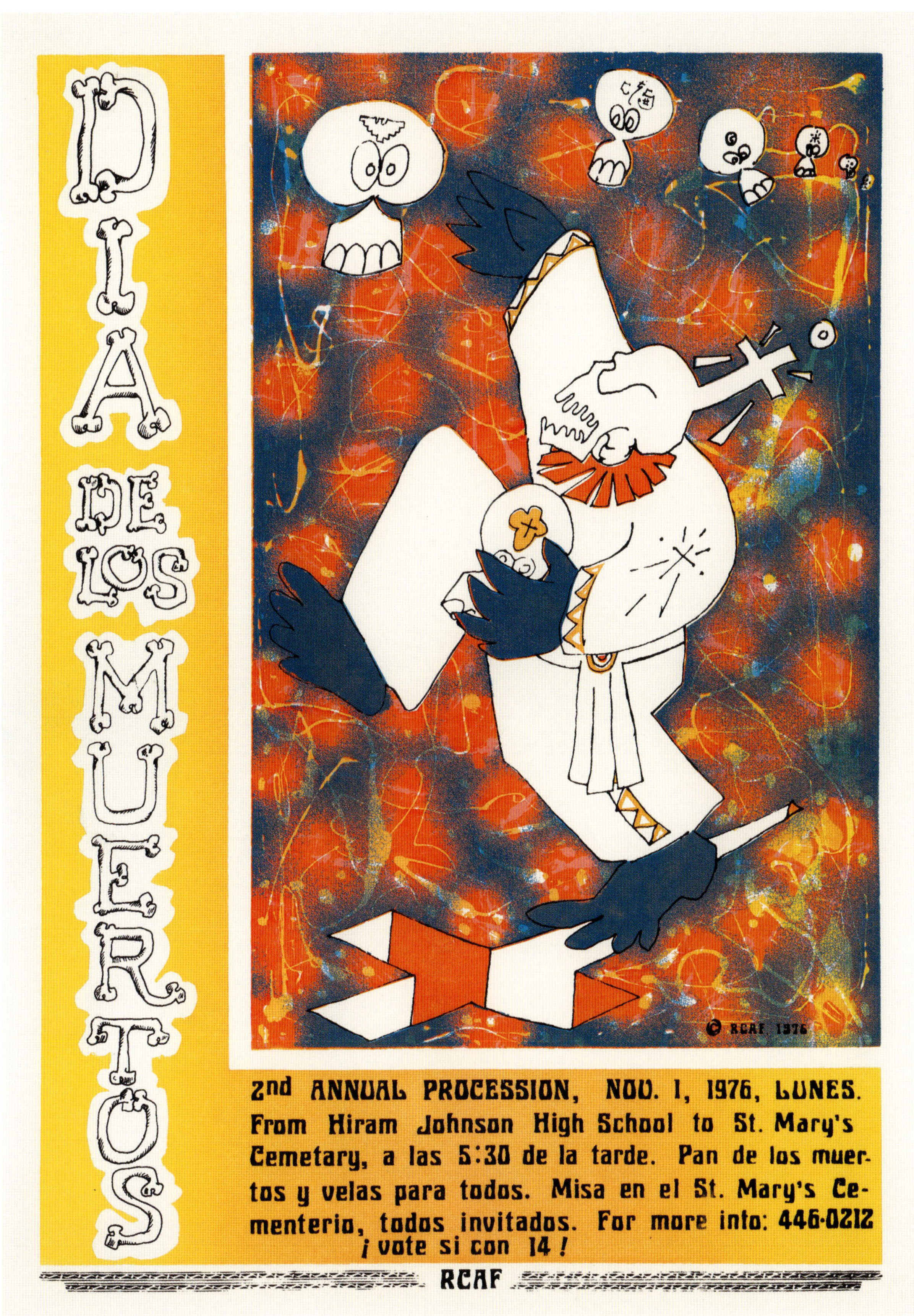

55 Ricardo Favela (1944–2007), *Día de los Muertos*, 1976. Screenprint, 25 × 19 in. RCAFavela Collection.

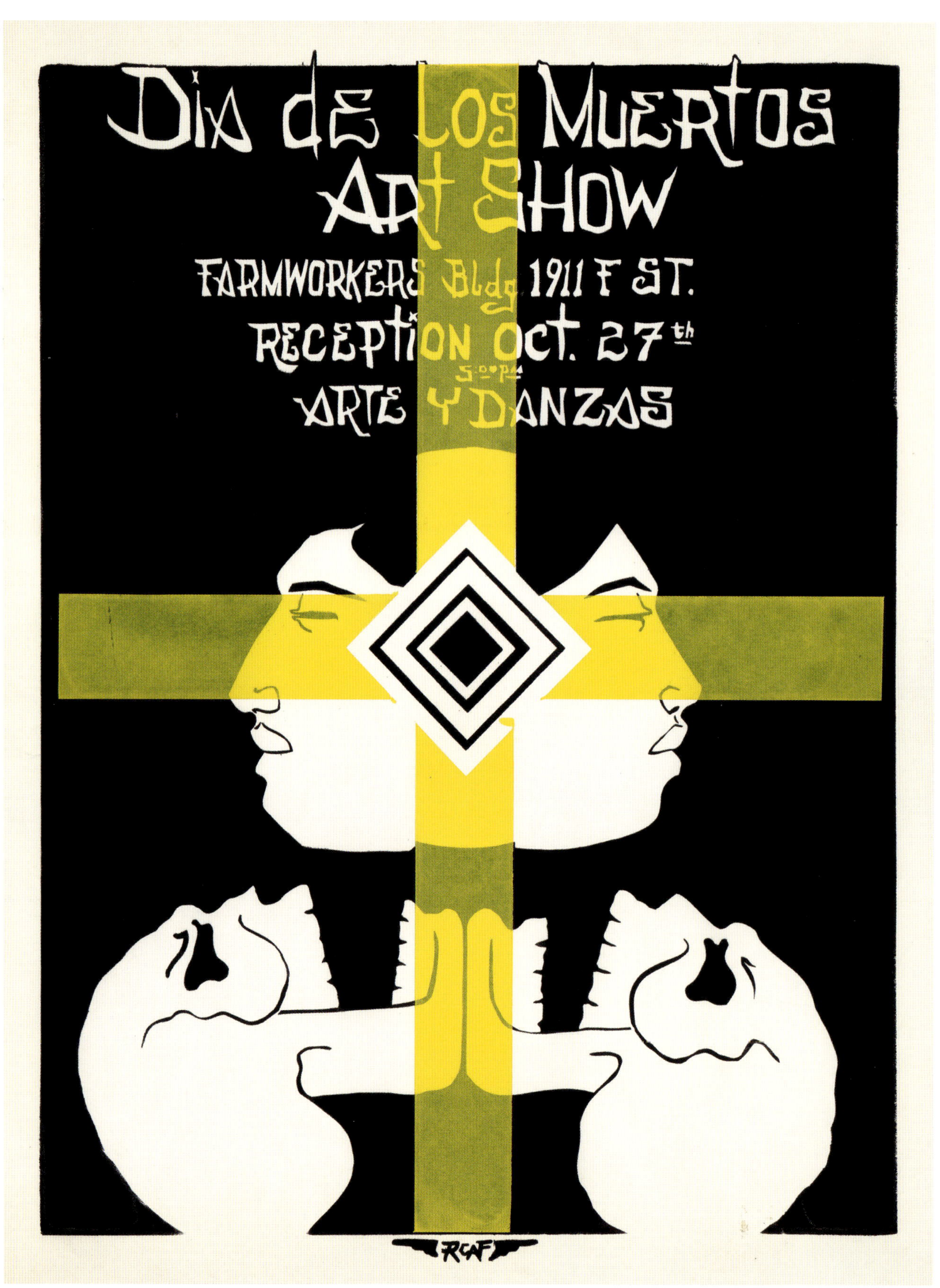

56 Juanishi Orosco (1945–2023), *Día de los Muertos Art Show*, 1979. Screenprint, 25 × 19 in. Collection of Luis C. González.

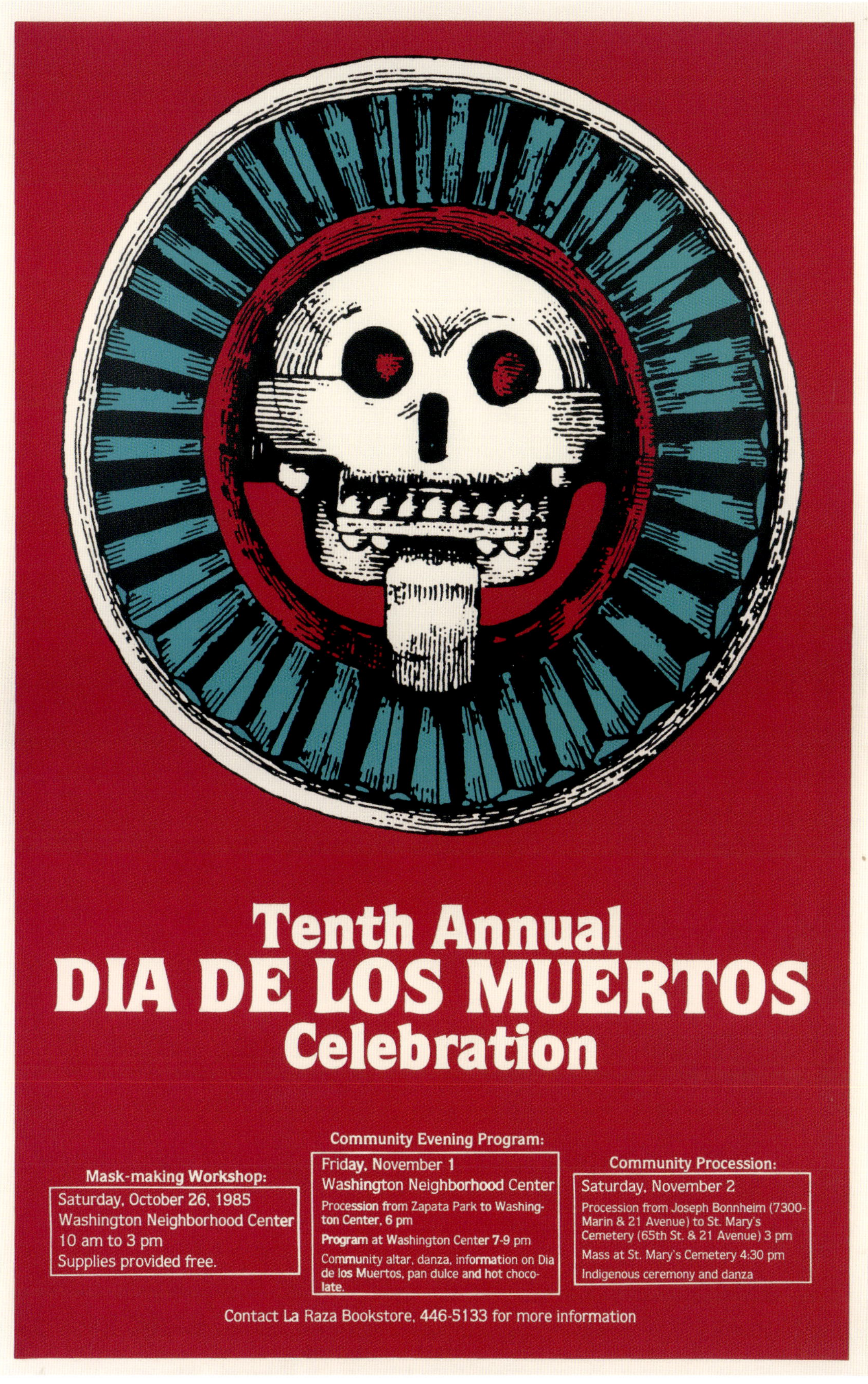

57 Luis C. González (born 1953), *Tenth Annual Día de los Muertos Celebration,* 1985. Screen-print, 35 × 23 in. Collection of Luis C. González.

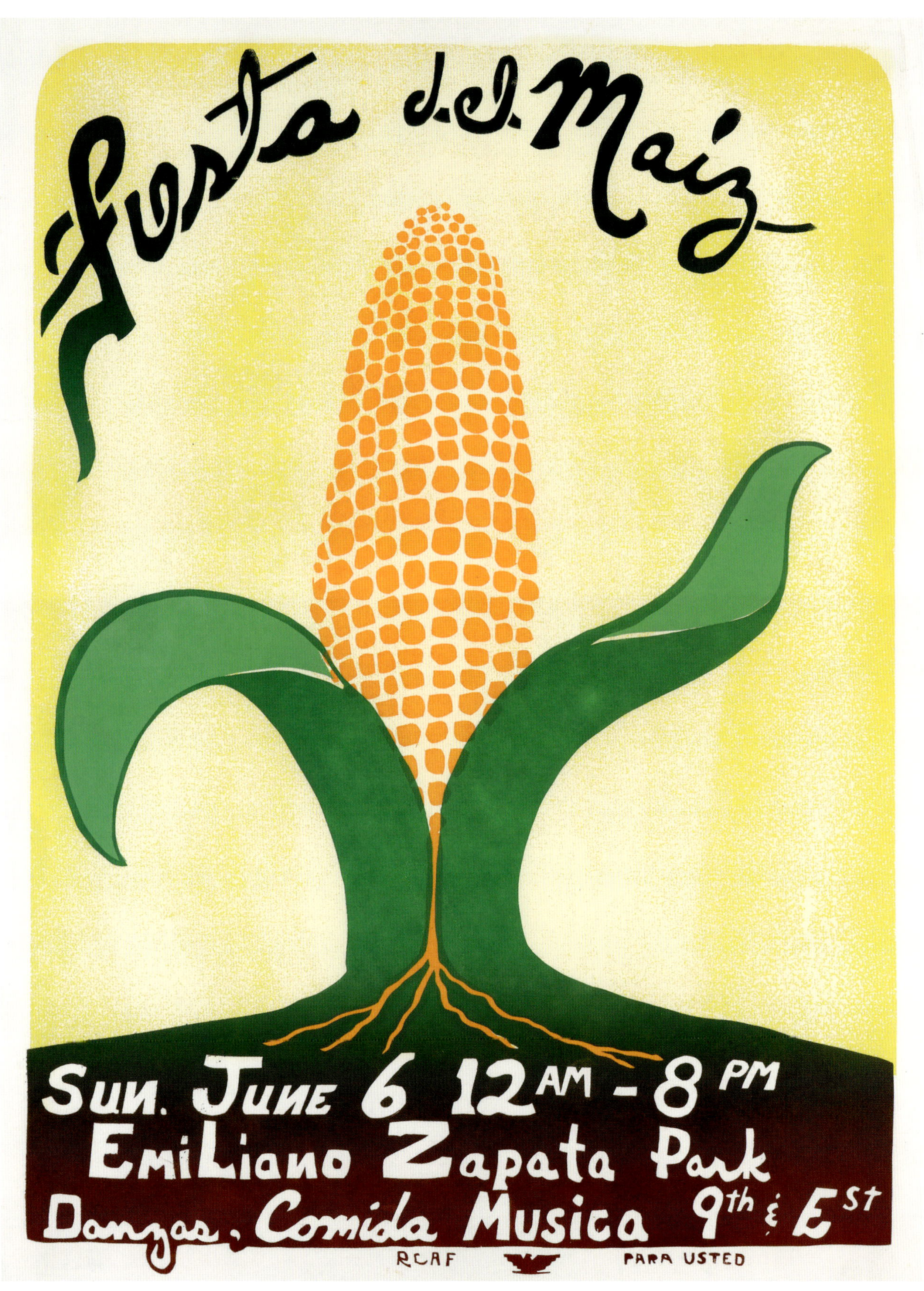

58 Rudy O. Cuellar (born 1950), *Fiesta del Maíz*, 1976. Screenprint, 23 7⁄8 × 18 in. Collection of Rudy O. Cuellar.

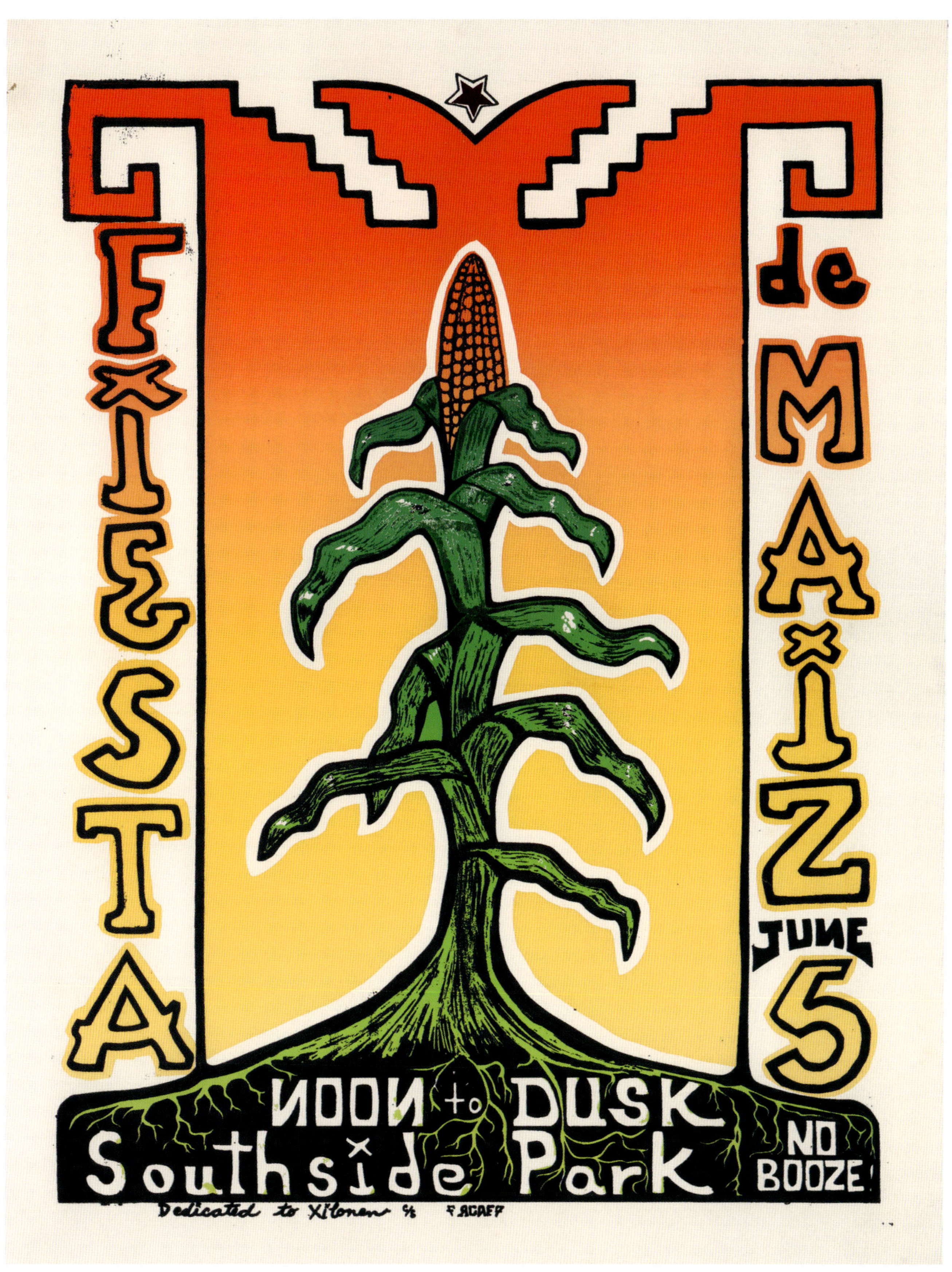

59 Rudy O. Cuellar (born 1950), *Fiesta de Maíz*, 1977. Screenprint, 22 5/8 × 17 1/2 in. Collection of Rudy O. Cuellar.

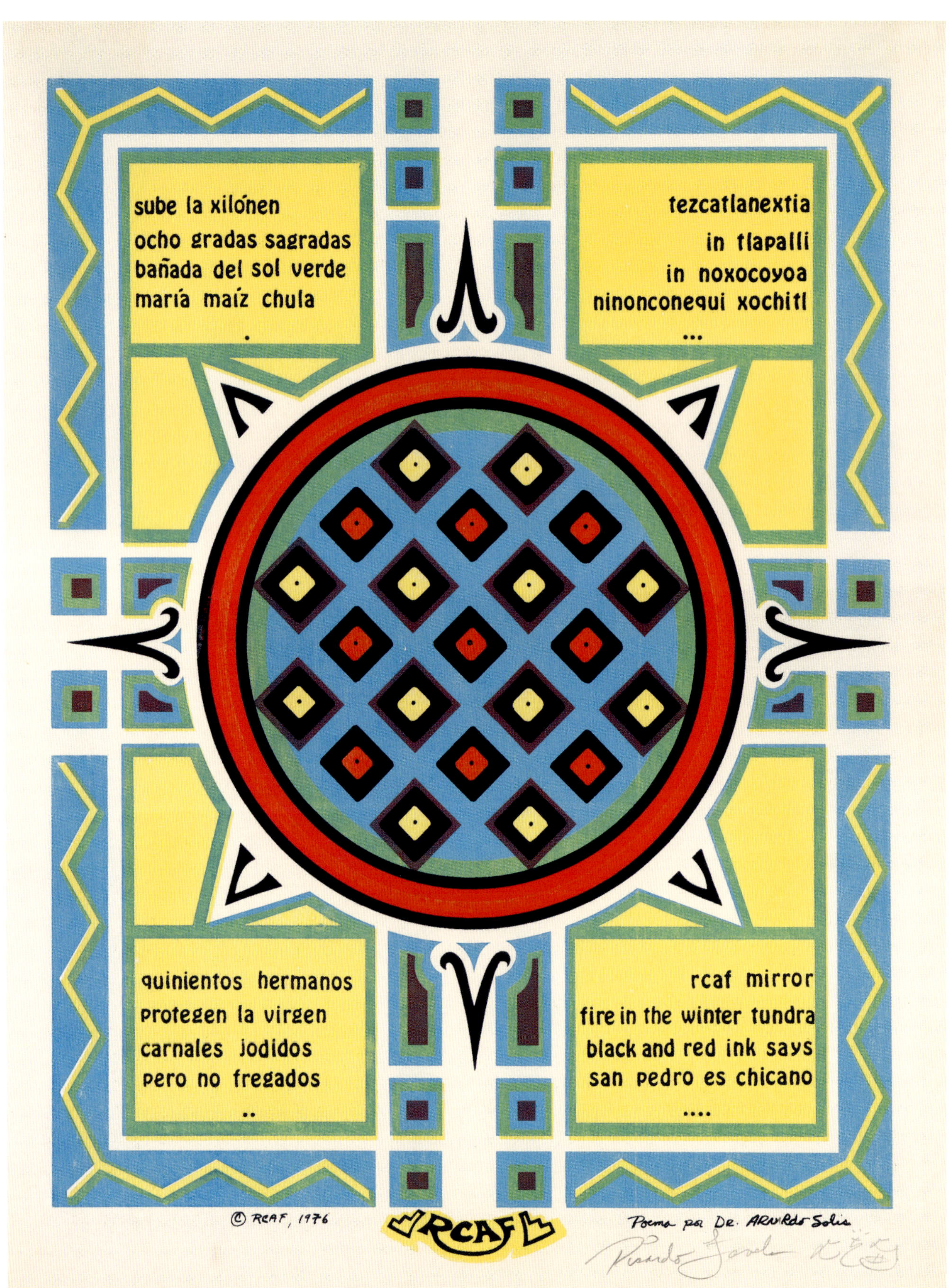

60 Ricardo Favela (1944–2007), *Sube La Xilónen*, 1976. Poem by Dr. Arnaldo Solis. Screenprint, 23 × 17½ in. RCAFavela Collection.

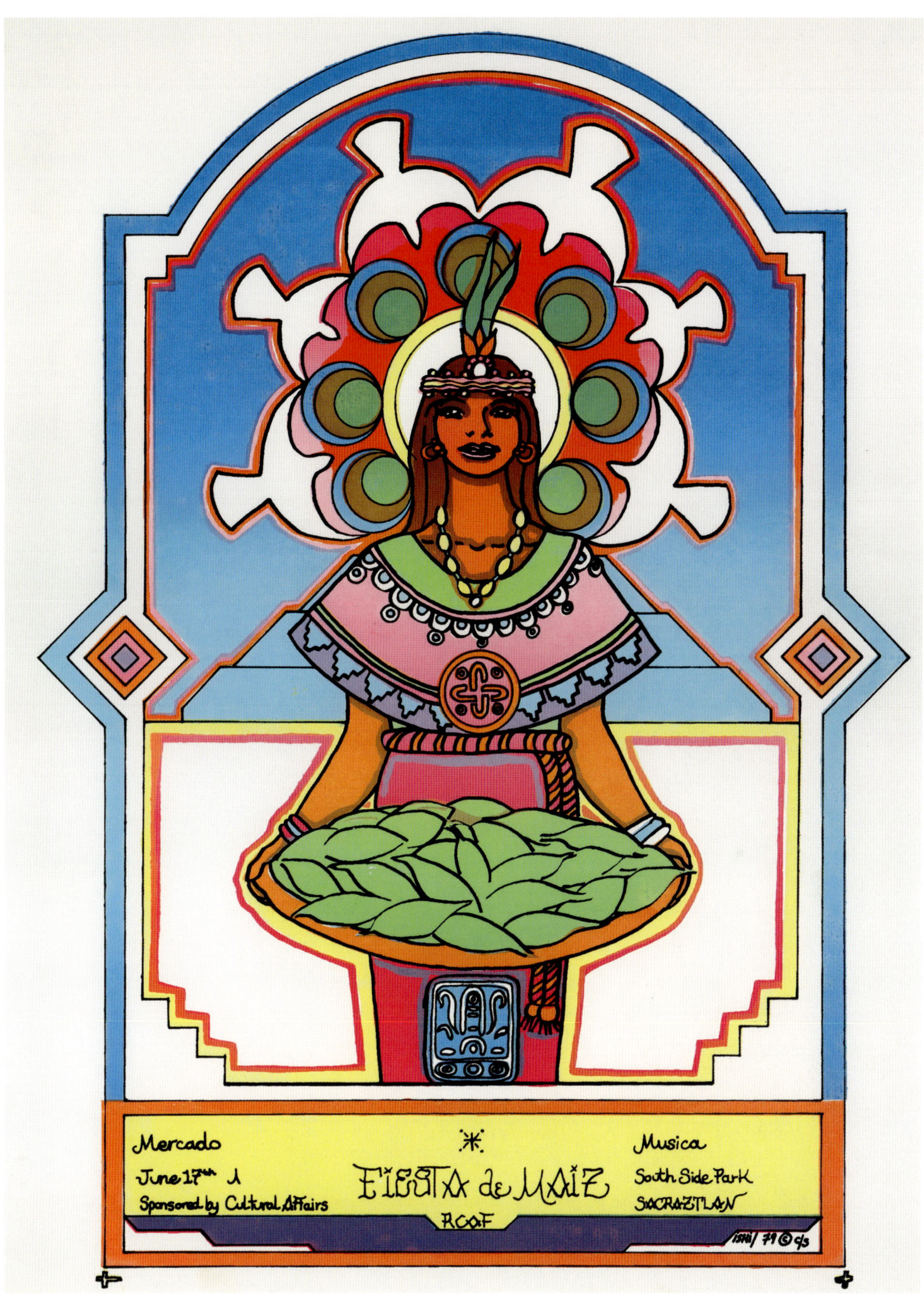

61 Juanishi Orosco (1945–2023), *Fiesta de Maíz*, 1979. Screenprint, 23 × 17 ⅛ in. Collection of Luis C. González.

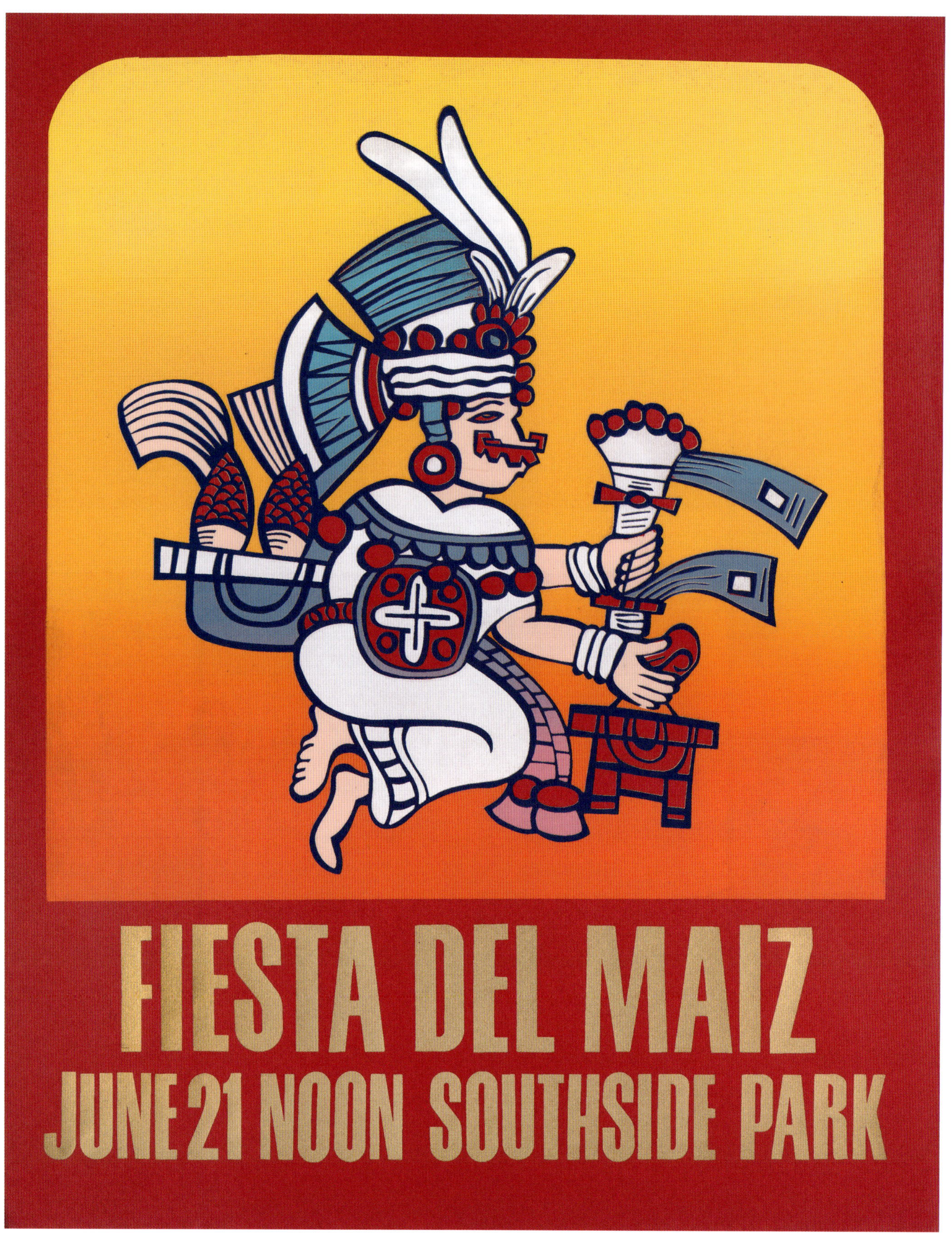

62 Luis C. González (born 1953), *Fiesta del Maíz*, 1981. Screenprint, 28½ × 22½ in. Collection of Luis C. González.

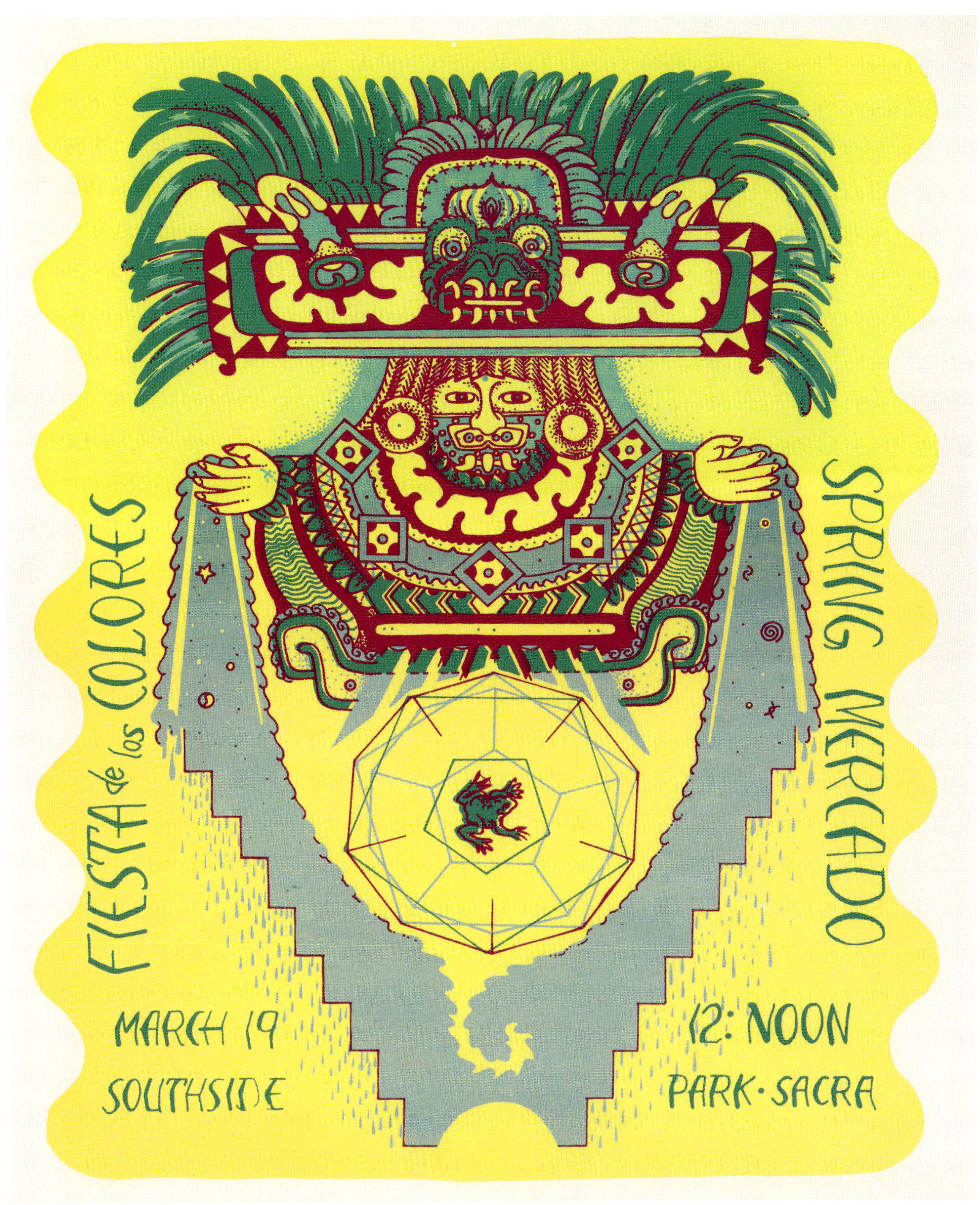

63 Stan Padilla (born 1945), *Fiesta de los Colores,* 1978. Screenprint, 22 ⅝ × 17 ⅝ in. Royal Chicano Air Force Poster Collection, Gerth Special Collections & University Archives, California State University, Sacramento.

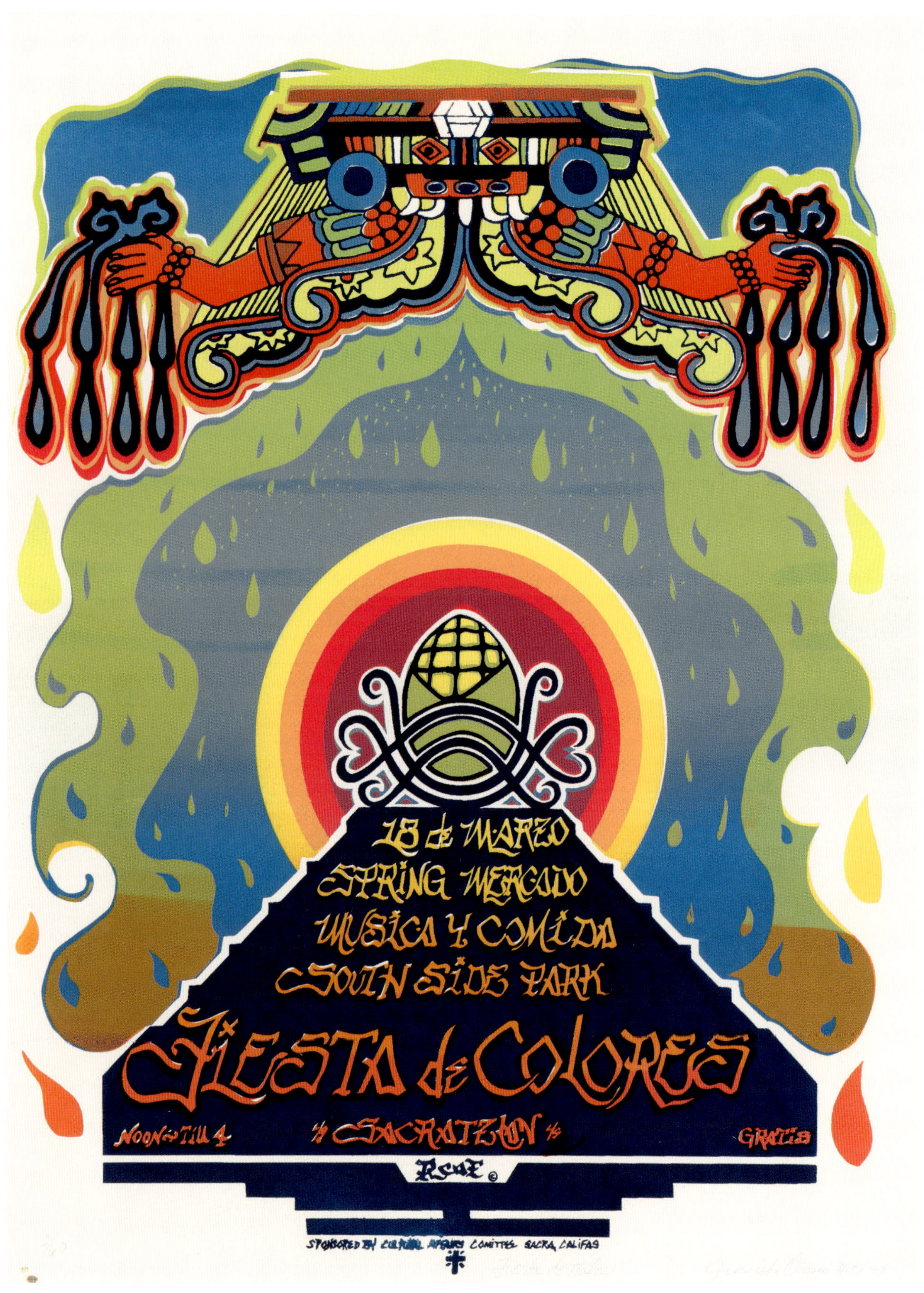

64 Juanishi Orosco (1945–2023), *Fiesta de Colores*, 1979. Screenprint, 23 × 17½ in. La Raza Galeria Posada Poster Collection, Gerth Special Collections & University Archives, California State University, Sacramento.

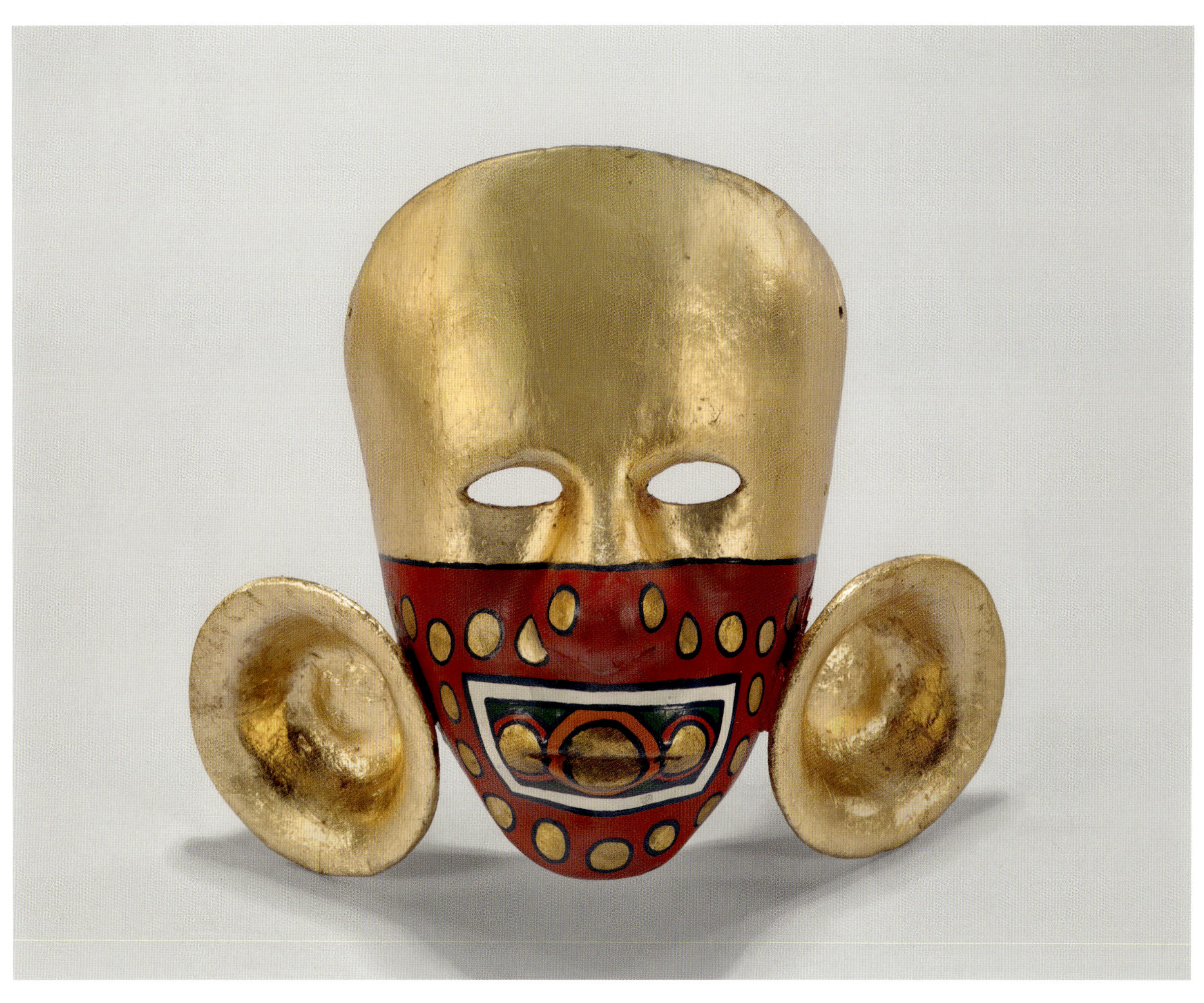

65 Enrique Ortiz Villegas (born 1944), *Tlaloc Mask from Fiesta de Colores*, 1979; restored 2024. Paris Craft, enamel paints, imitation gold-leaf foil, 9 ½ × 10 ¼ in. Collection of Enrique Ortiz Villegas.

Political Activism and Solidarity

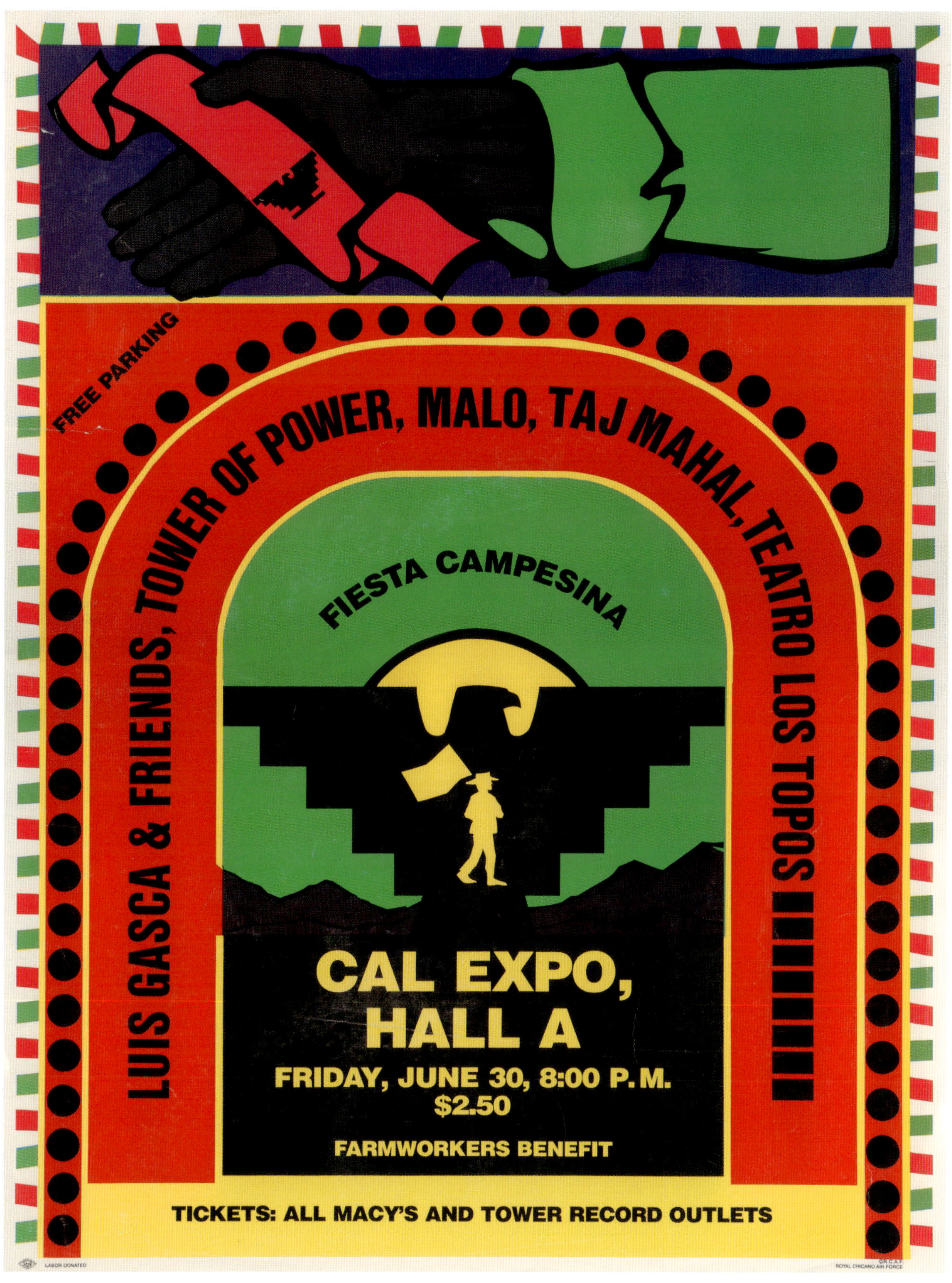

66 Esteban Villa (1930–2022), *Fiesta Campesina*, 1972. Offset lithograph, 30 × 22 in. La Raza Galeria Posada Poster Collection, Gerth Special Collections & University Archives, California State University, Sacramento.

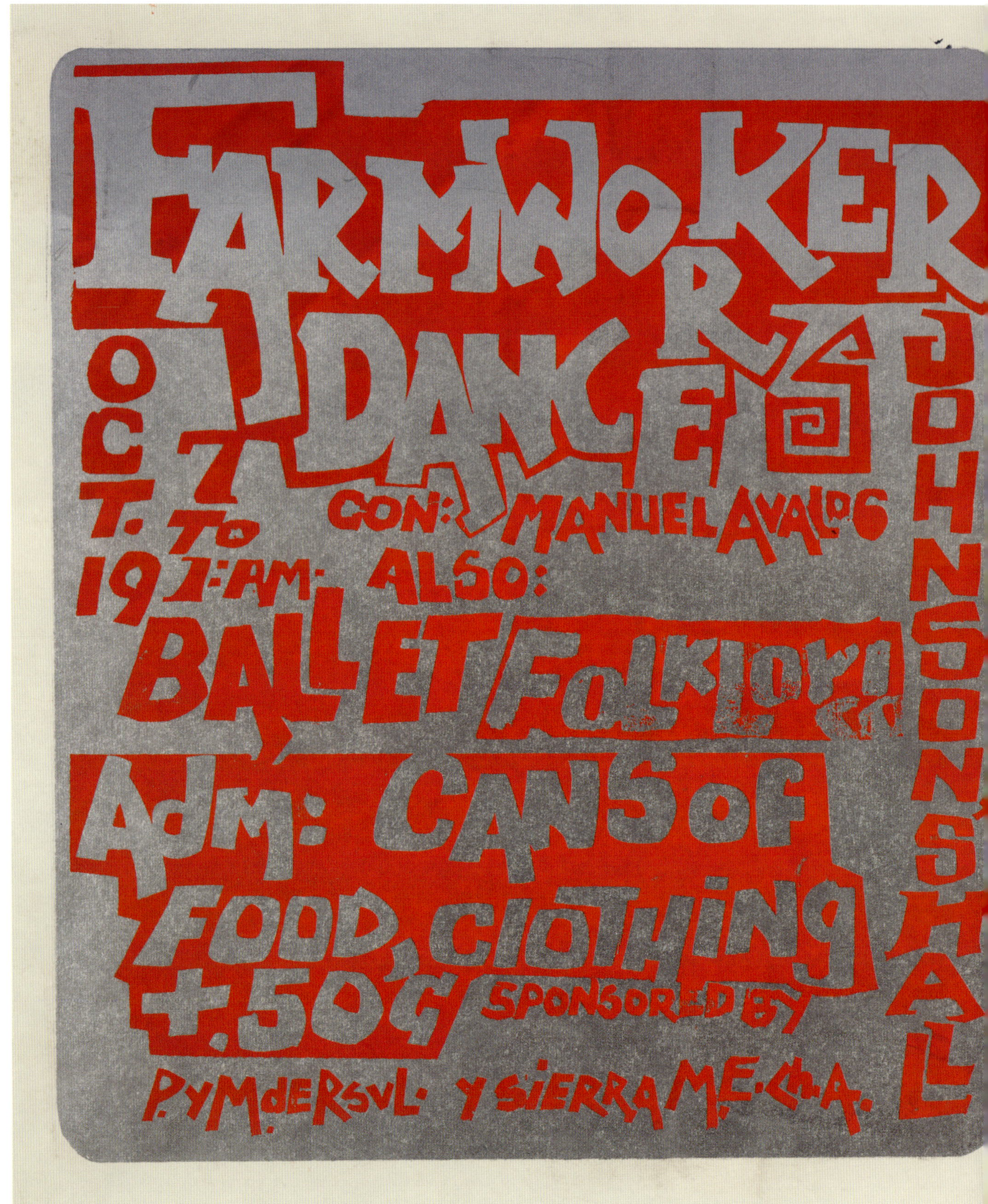

67 Armando Cid (1943–2009), *Farmworker Dance Benefit*, c. 1973. Screenprint, 13 × 21 in. Royal Chicano Air Force Archives, CEMA 8, University of California, Santa Barbara Library.

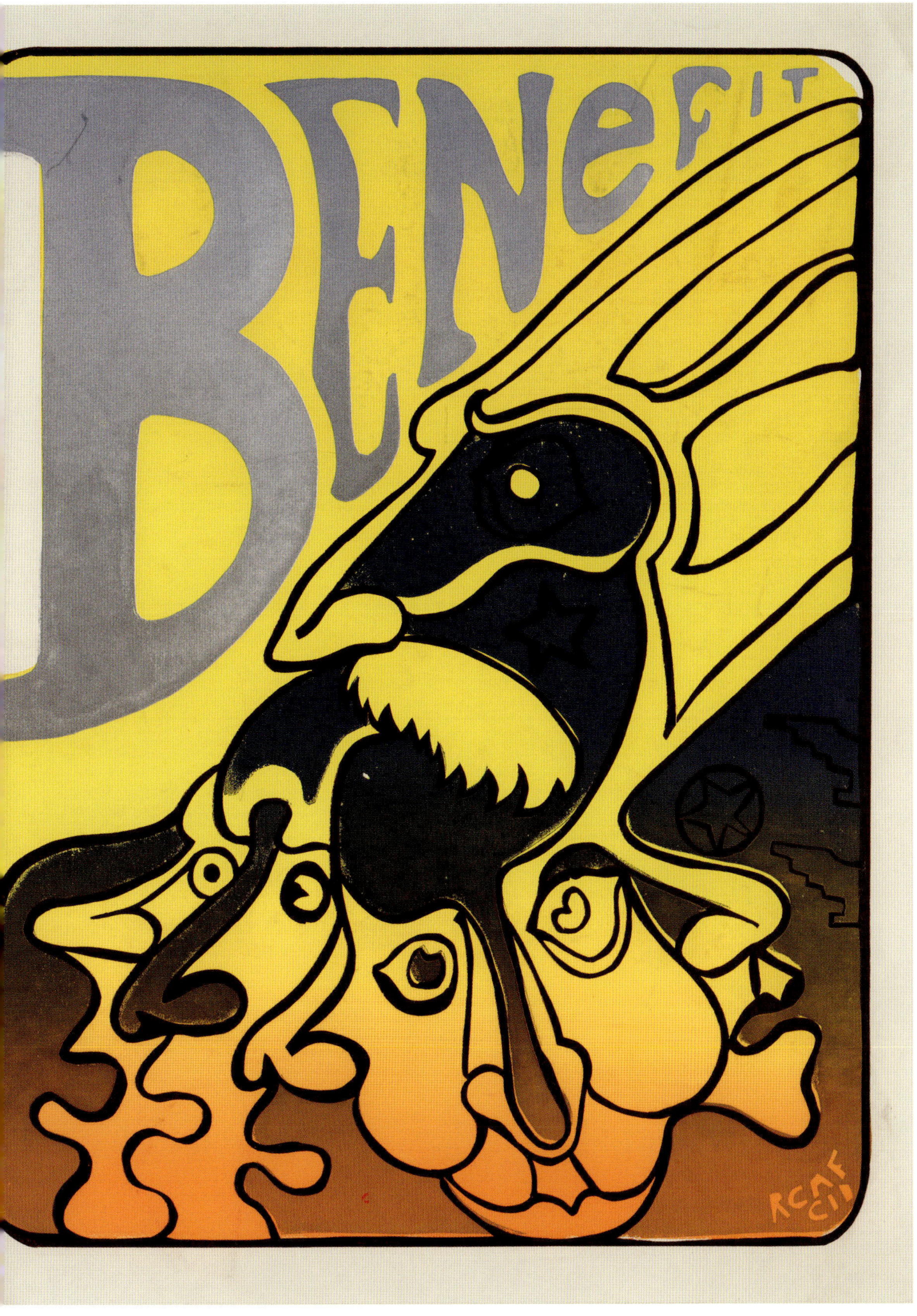
BENEFIT

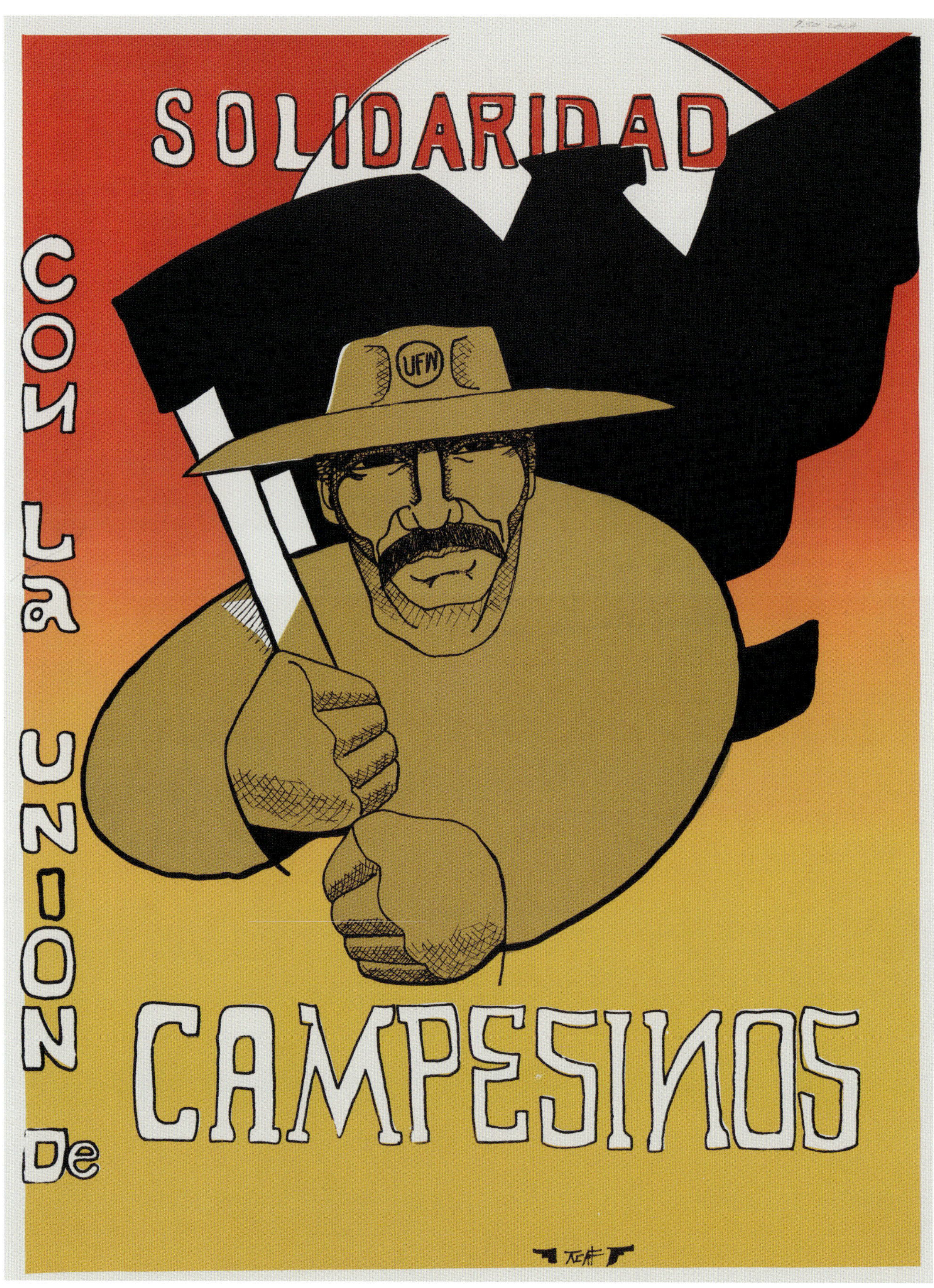

68 Juanishi Orosco (1945–2023), *Solidaridad con la Union de Campesinos*, early 1970s. Screenprint, 25 × 19 in. Courtesy of the California History Room, California State Library.

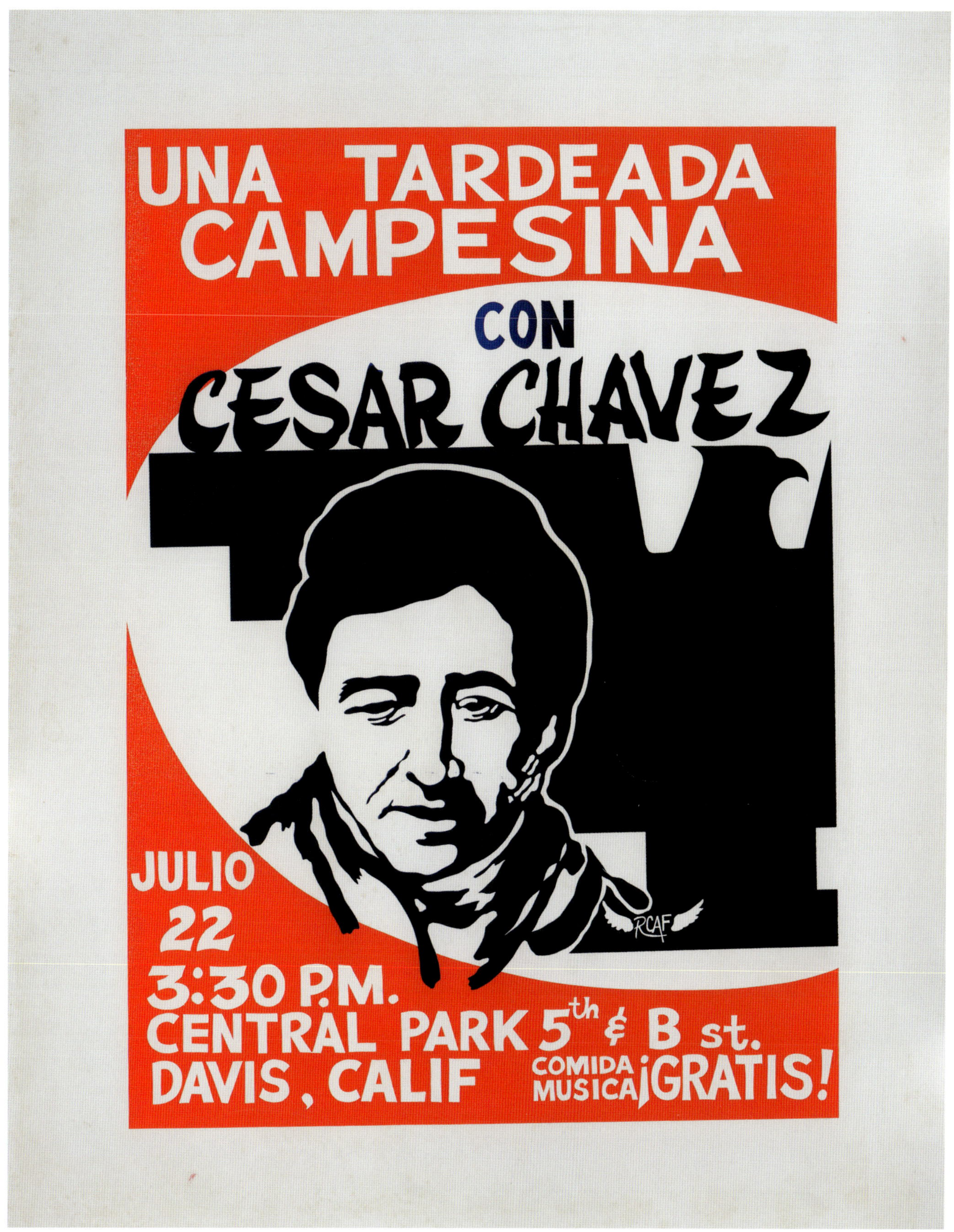

69 José Montoya (1932–2013) and Max Garcia (1942–2020), *Una Tardeada Campesina con Cesar Chavez*, 1972. Screenprint, 25 × 19 in. Royal Chicano Air Force Archives, CEMA 8, University of California, Santa Barbara Library.

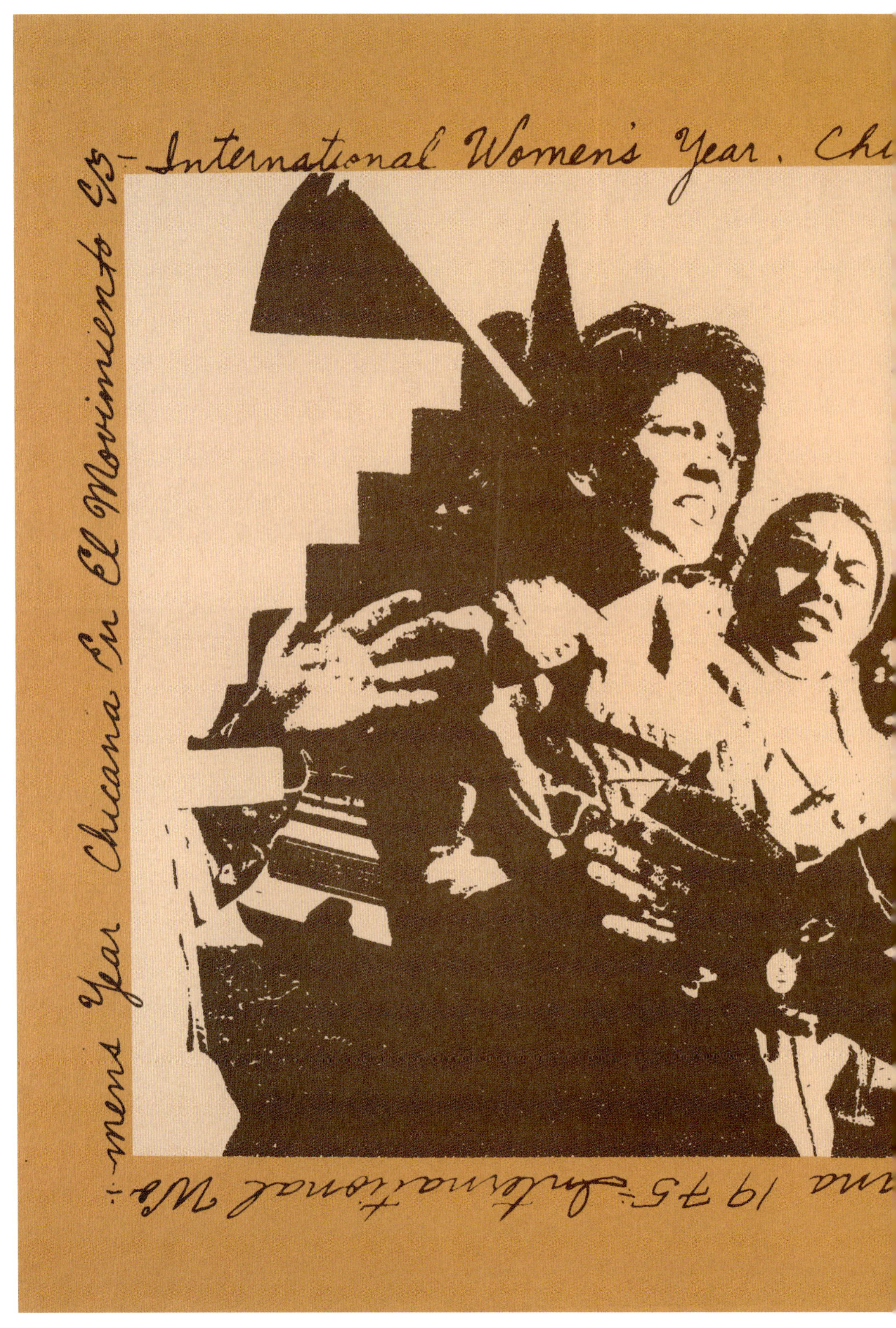

70 Luis C. González (born 1953) and Héctor D. González (born 1945), *International Women's Year, Chicana*, 1975. Screenprint, 15 × 22 in. Royal Chicano Air Force Archives, CEMA 8, University of California, Santa Barbara Library.

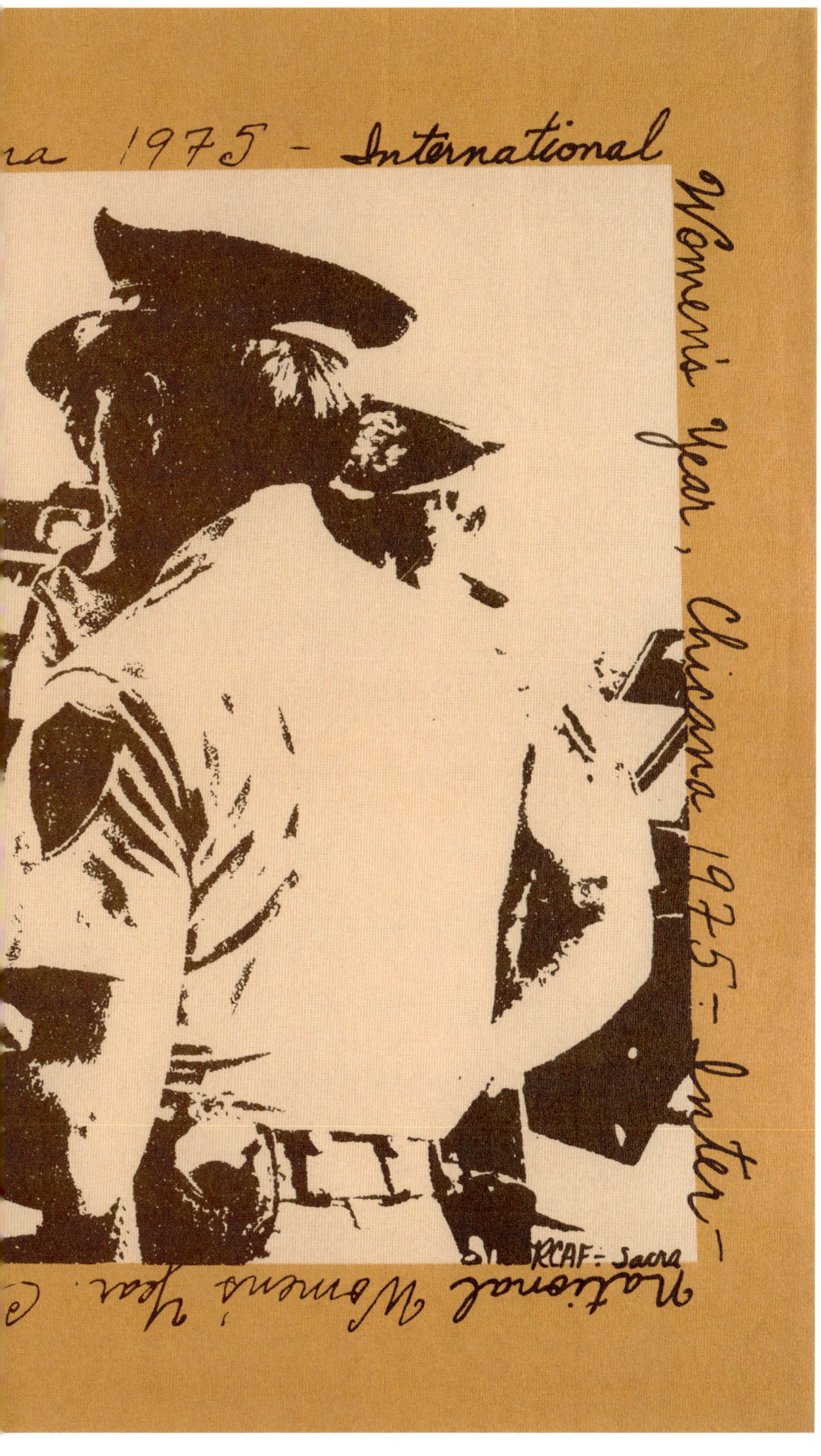
1975 - International
Women's Year, Chicana 1975 - International Women's Year.
RCAF - Sacra

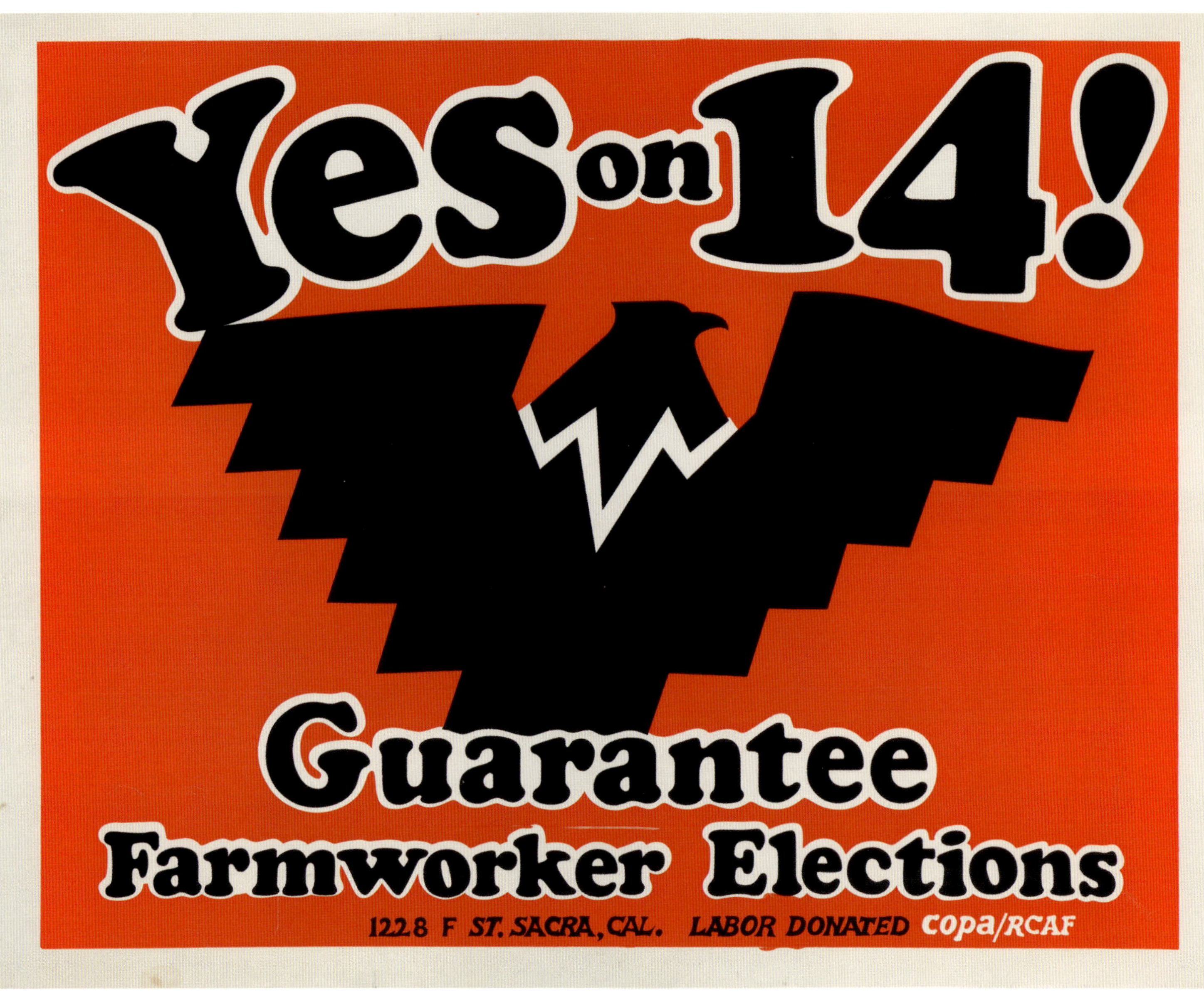

71 Max Garcia (1942–2020), *Yes on 14!*, 1976. Screenprint, 17½ × 22⅝ in. Rasul Chicano Art Collection.

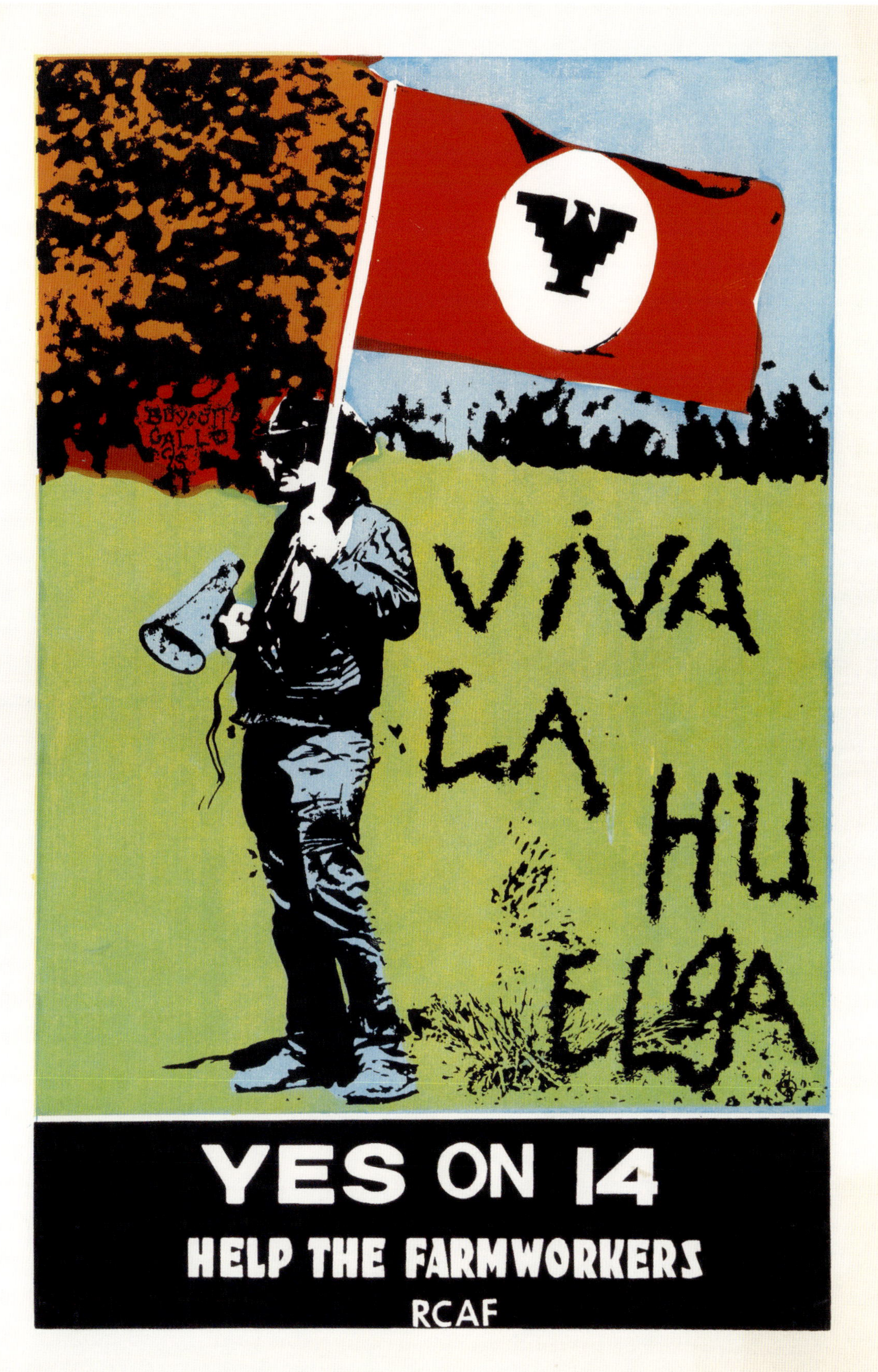

72 Luis C. González (born 1953), photograph by Héctor González, *Viva la Huelga*, 1976. Screenprint, 25 ½ × 16 ½ in. Royal Chicano Air Force Poster Collection, Gerth Special Collections & University Archives, California State University, Sacramento.

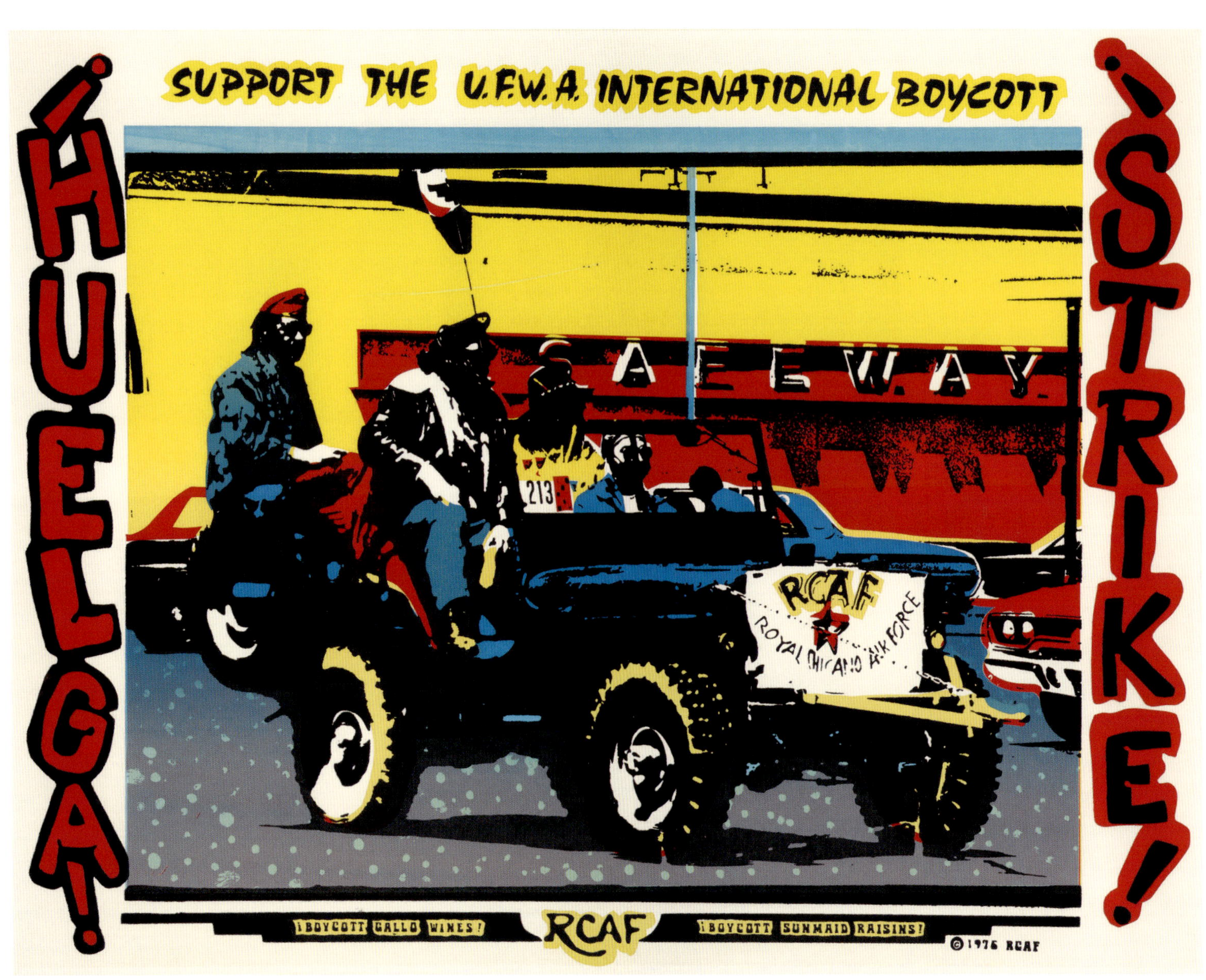

73 Ricardo Favela (1944–2007), photograph by Harold Nihei, *¡Huelga! ¡Strike!*, 1976. Screenprint, 19 × 25 in. RCAFavela Collection.

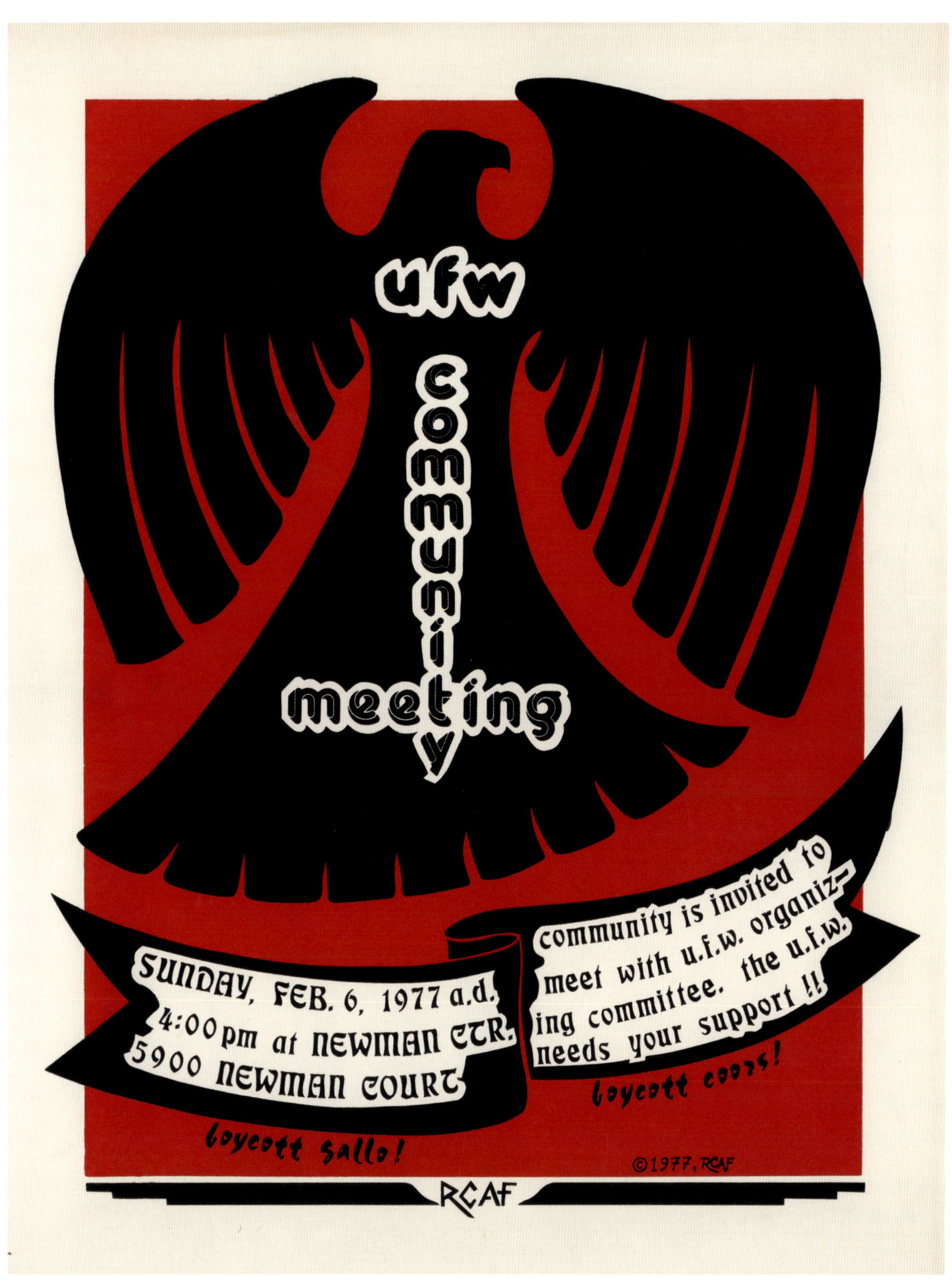

74 Ricardo Favela (1944–2007), *UFW Community Meeting*, 1977. Screenprint, 22 ¾ × 17 ⅝ in. RCAFavela Collection.

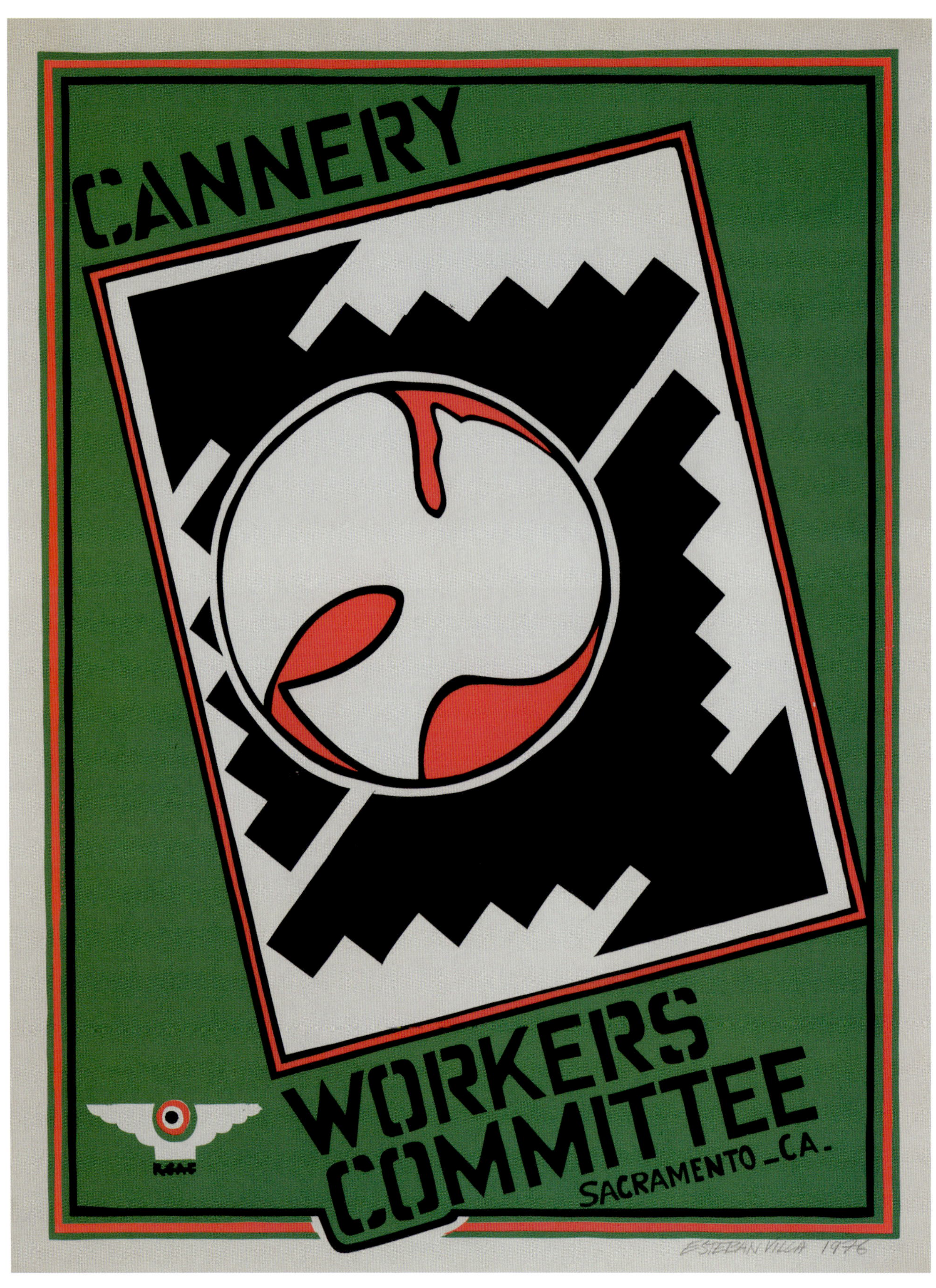

75 Esteban Villa (1930–2022), *Cannery Workers Committee*, 1976. Screenprint, 25 × 19 in. Royal Chicano Air Force Archives, CEMA 8, University of California, Santa Barbara Library.

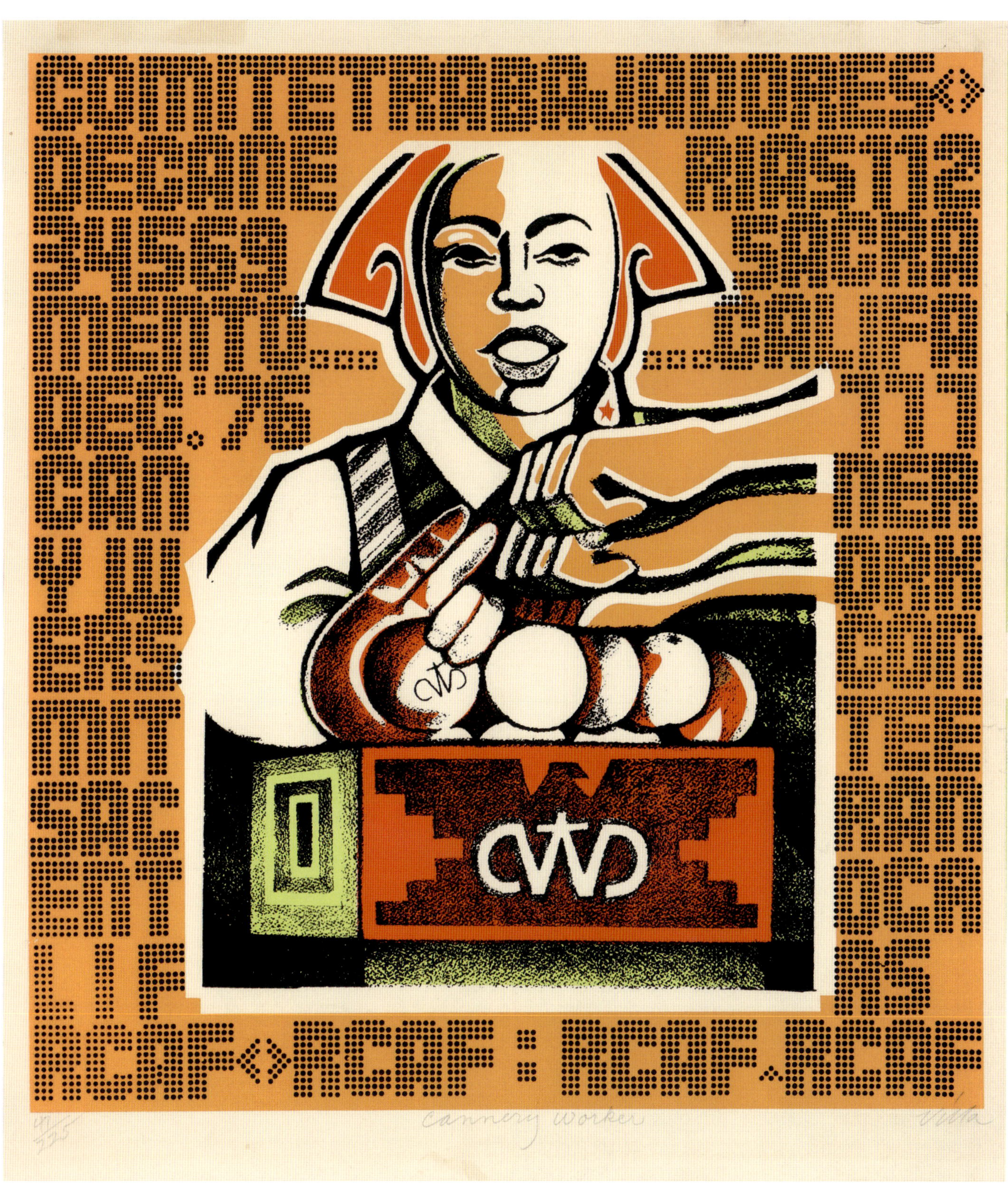

76 Esteban Villa (1930–2022), *Comite Trabajadores de Canerias*, 1976, Screenprint, 16 ½ × 14 ⅞ in. Villa Family Collection.

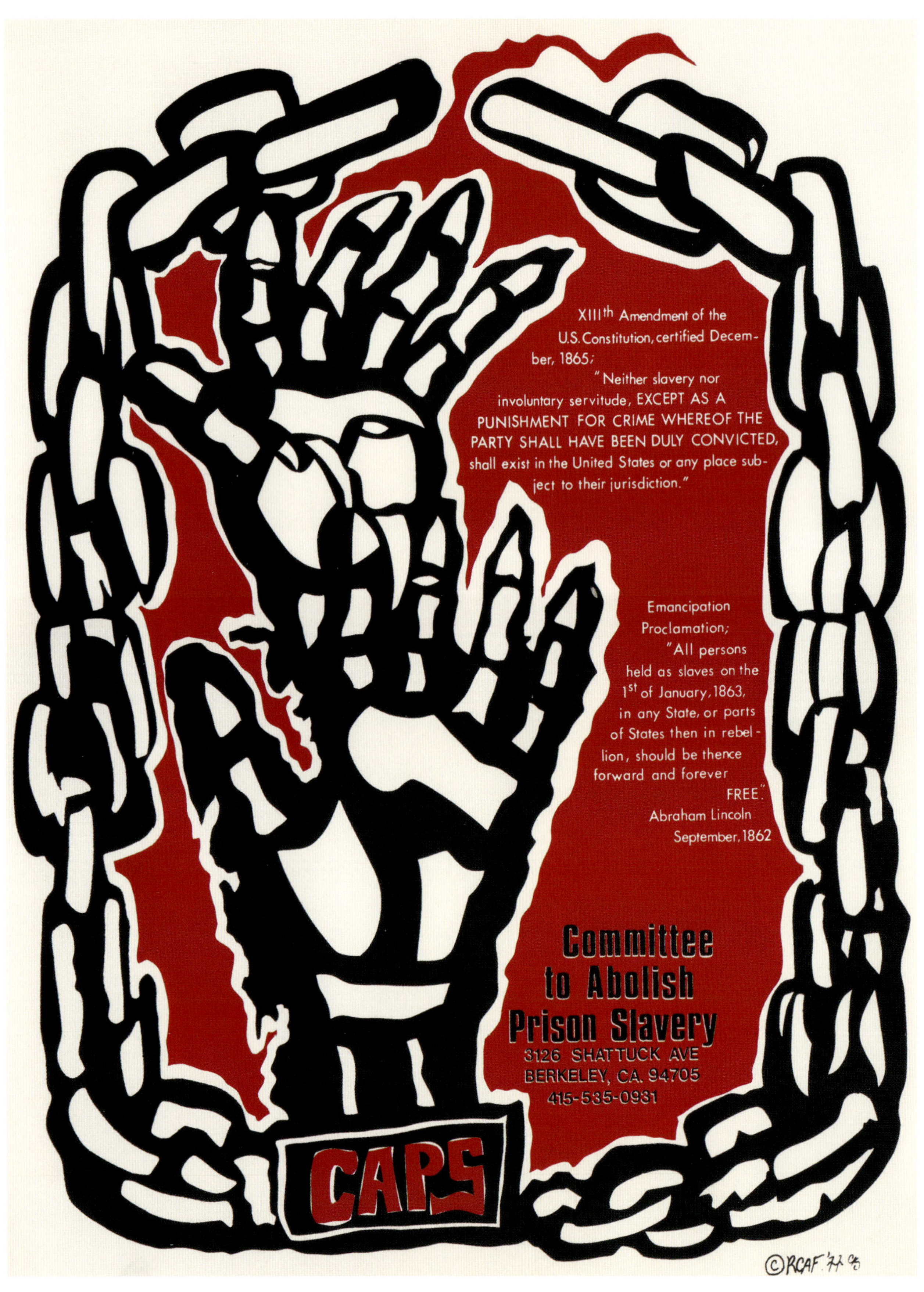

77 Juan Cervantes (1951–2014) and Luis C. González (born 1953), *Committee to Abolish Prison Slavery*, 1977. Screenprint, 22⅝ × 17⅜ in. Cervantes-Powell Family Collection.

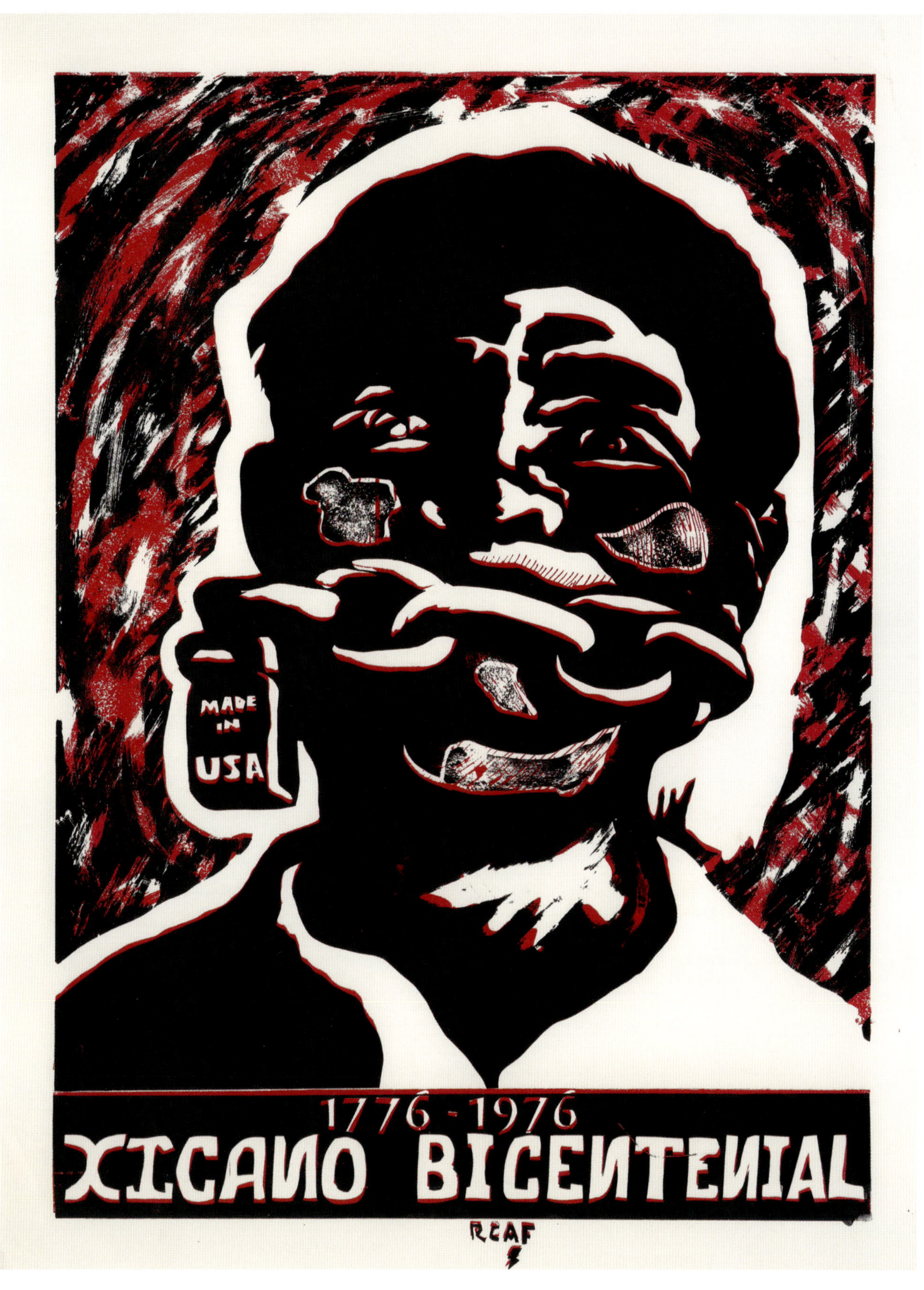

78 Rudy O. Cuellar (born 1950), *Xicano Bicentenial, 1776–1976*, 1976. Screenprint, 25 × 19 in. Collection of Rudy O. Cuellar.

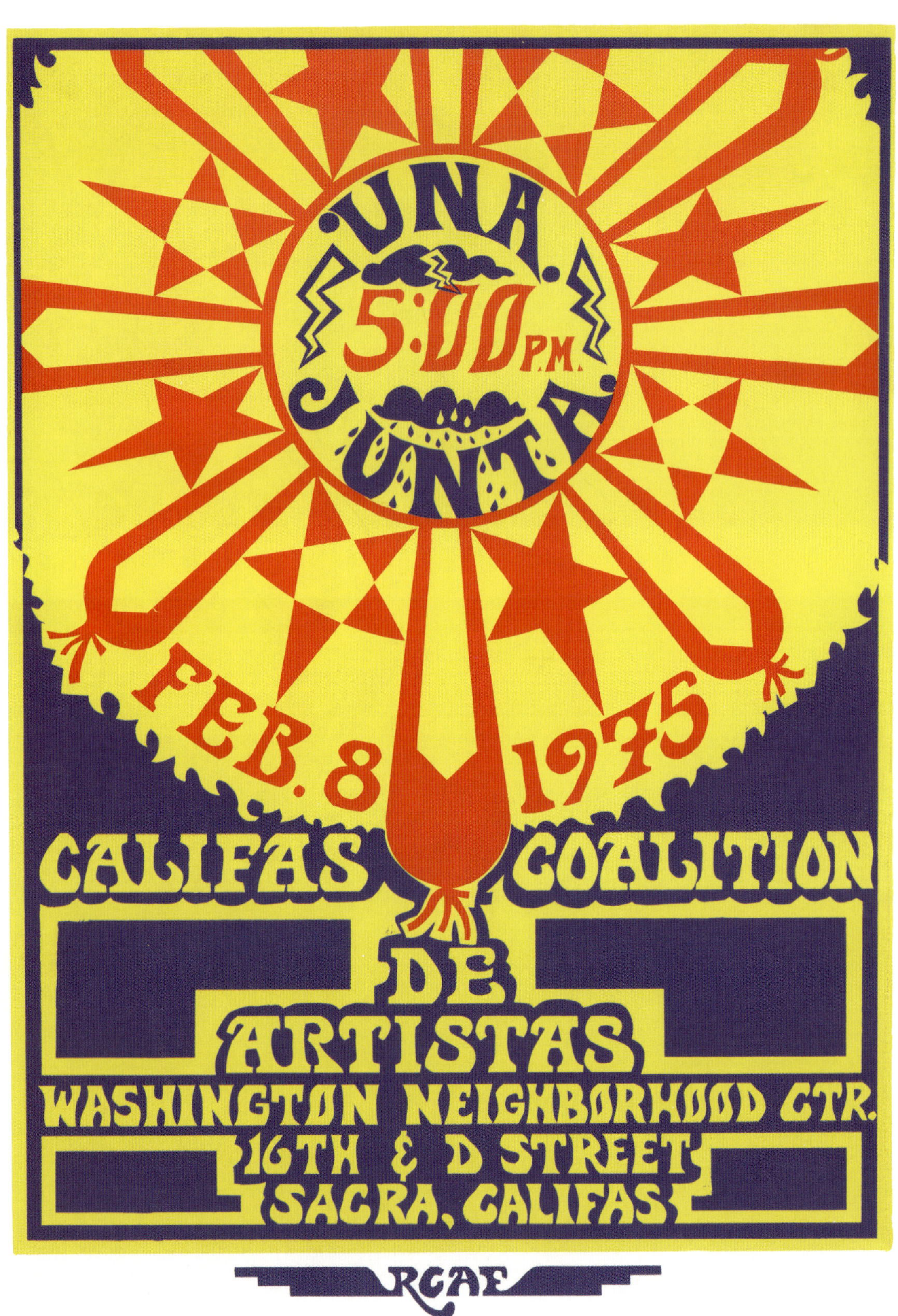

79 Ricardo Favela (1944–2007), *Califas Coalition de Artistas*, 1975. Screenprint, 25 × 19 in. Courtesy of the California History Room, California State Library.

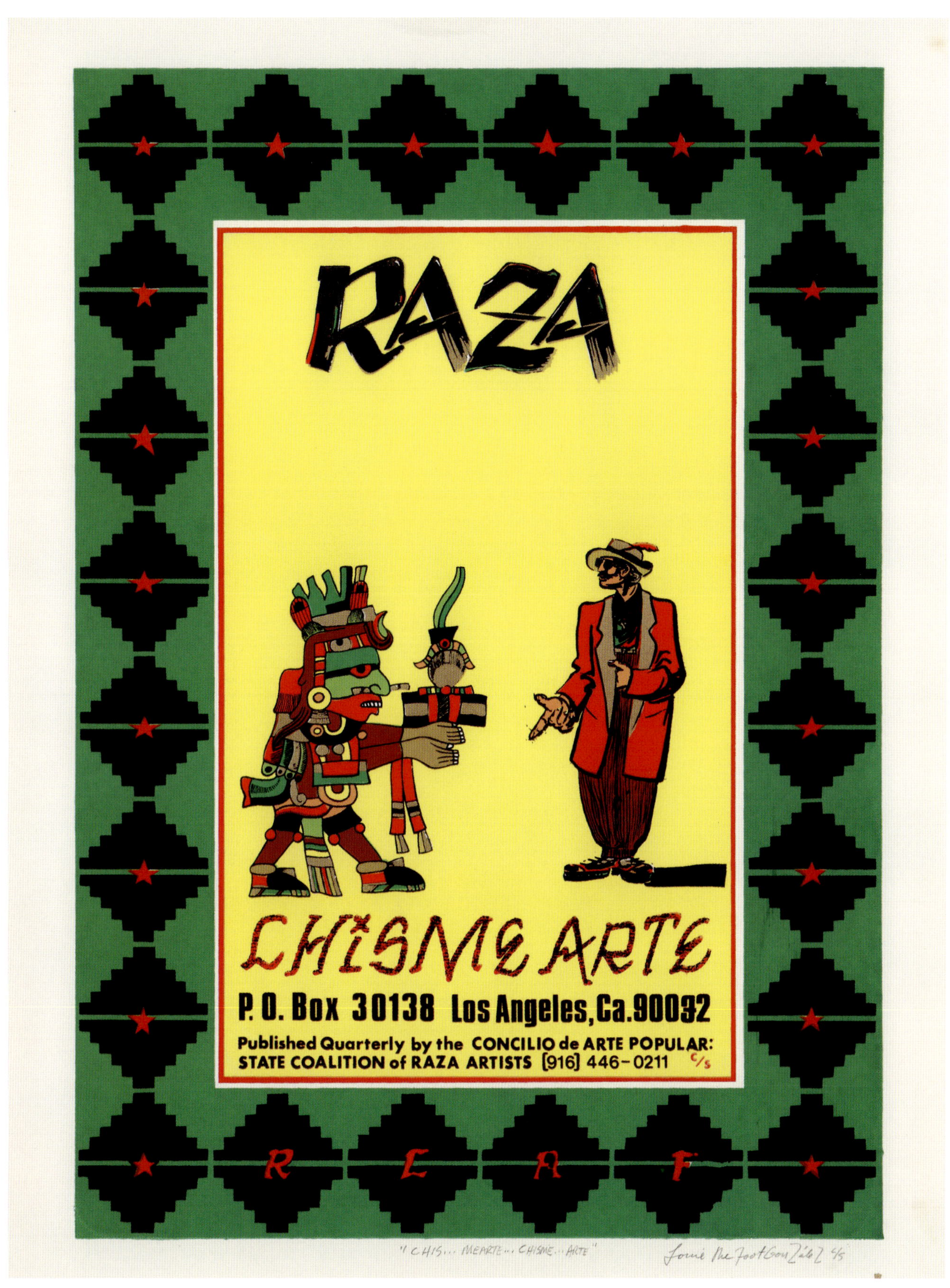

80 Luis C. González (born 1953) and José Montoya (1932–2013), *Raza Chisme Arte*, c. 1978. Screenprint, 22 ⅝ × 17 ½ in. Collection of Luis C. González.

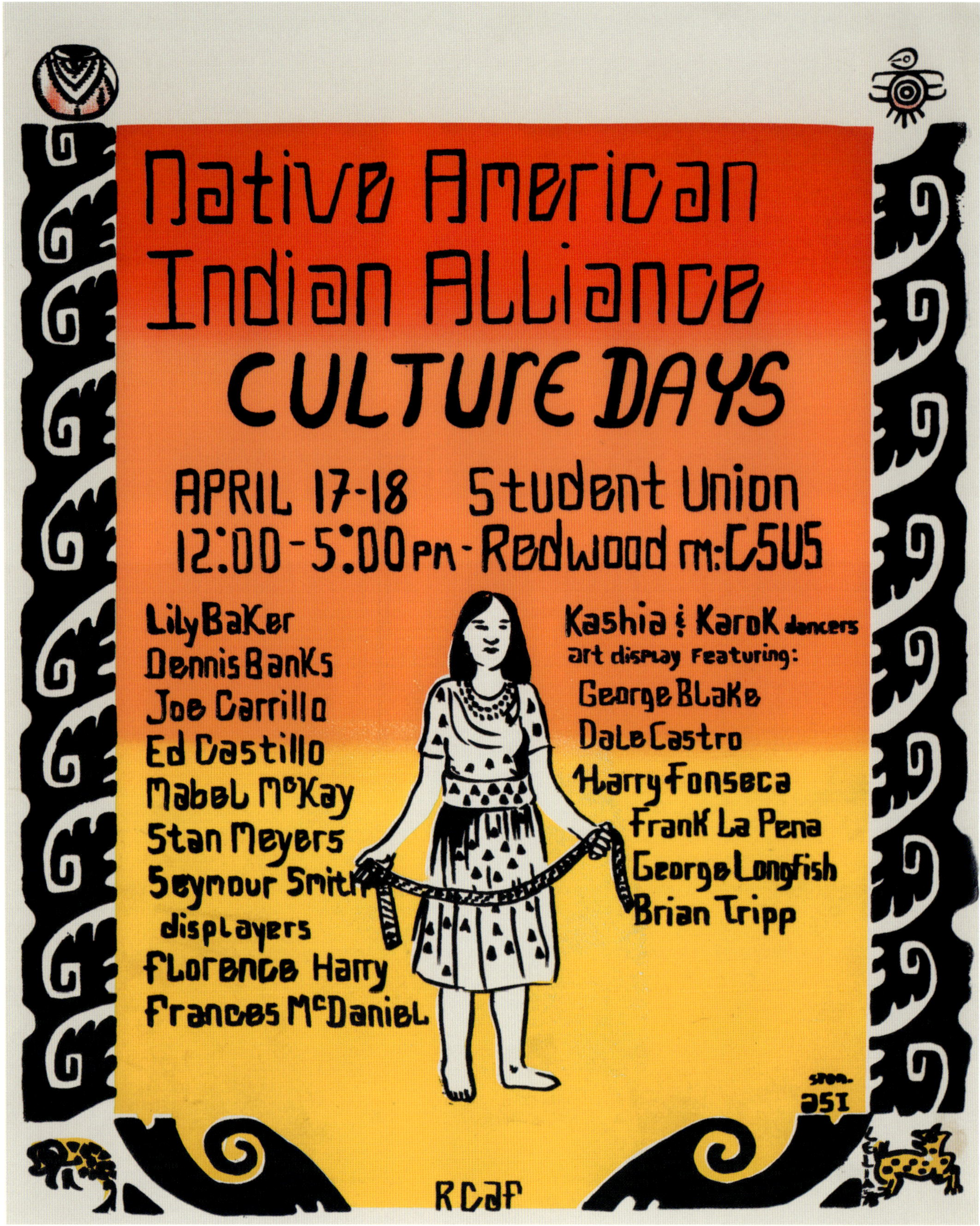

81 Celia Herrera Rodriguez (born 1952), Rudy O. Cuellar (born 1950), and Luis C. González (born 1953), *Native American Indian Alliance Culture Days*, 1975. Screenprint, 17 × 14 in. Royal Chicano Air Force Archives, CEMA 8, University of California, Santa Barbara Library.

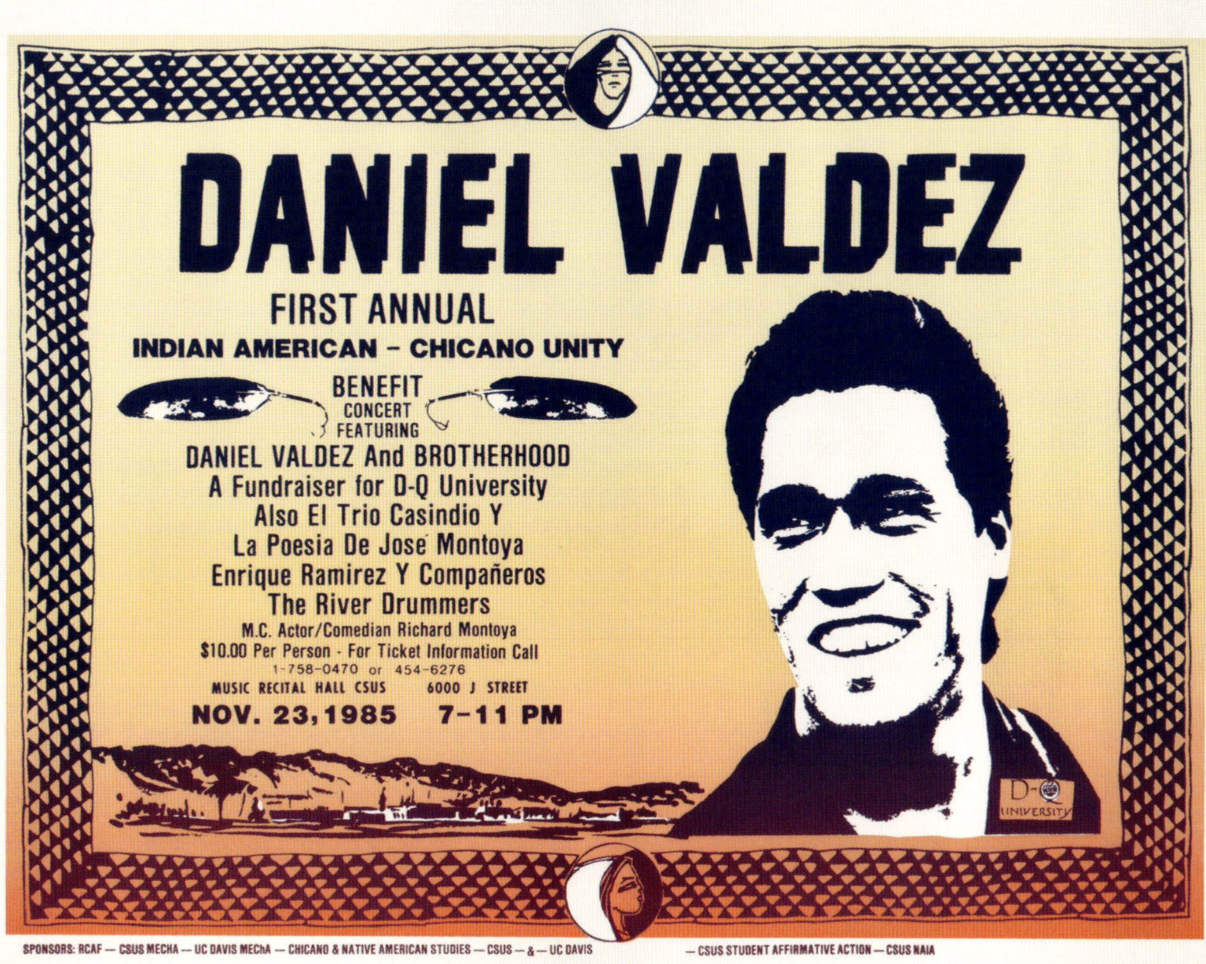

82 Rudy O. Cuellar (born 1950), Luis C. González (born 1953), and José Montoya (1932–2013), *First Annual Indian American-Chicano Unity*, 1985. Screenprint, 23 ⅛ × 29 in. Collection of Rudy O. Cuellar.

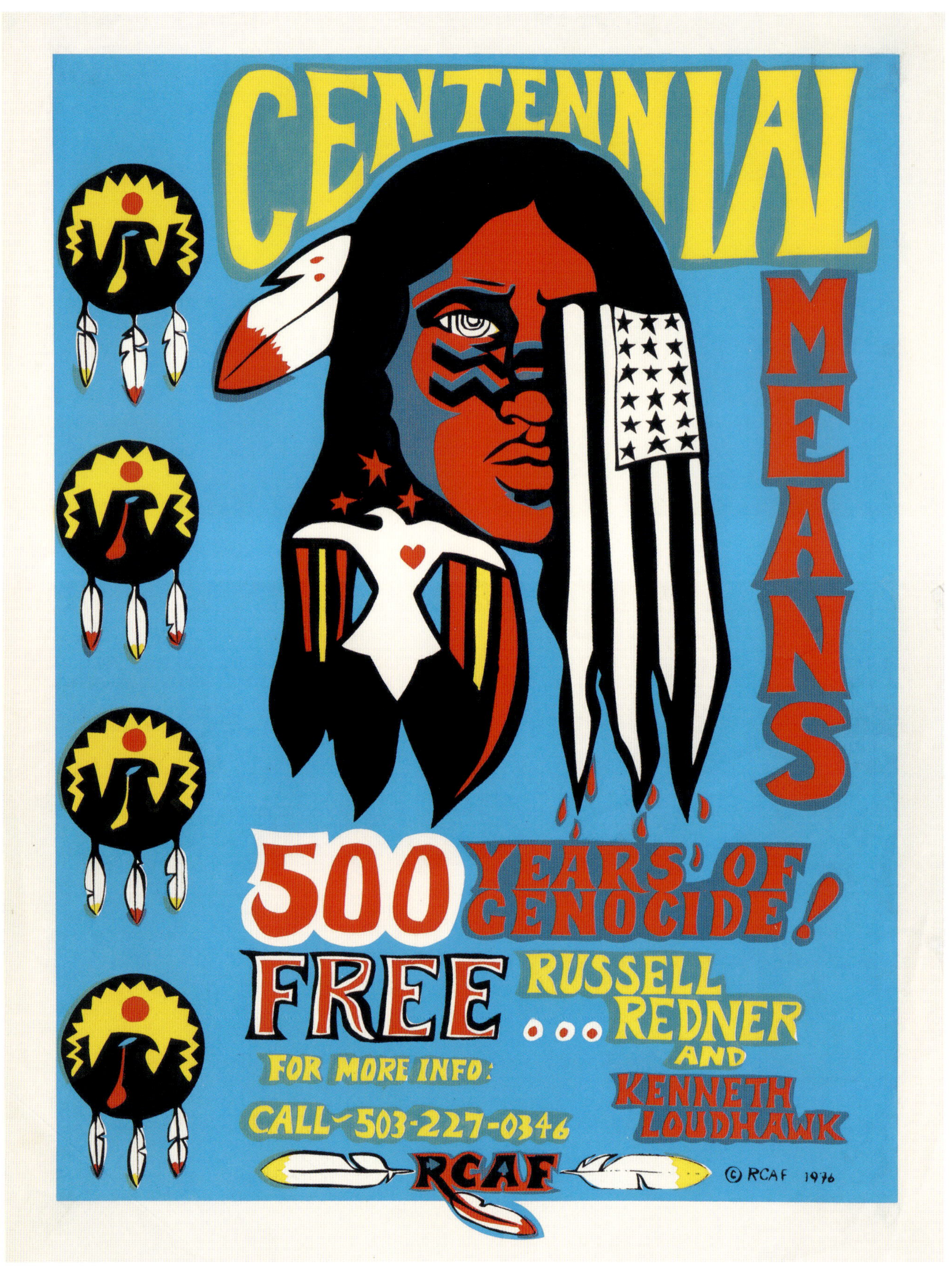

83 Ricardo Favela (1944–2007), *Centennial Means 500 Years of Genocide!*, 1976. Screenprint, 25 × 19 in. La Raza Galeria Posada Poster Collection, Gerth Special Collections & University Archives, California State University, Sacramento.

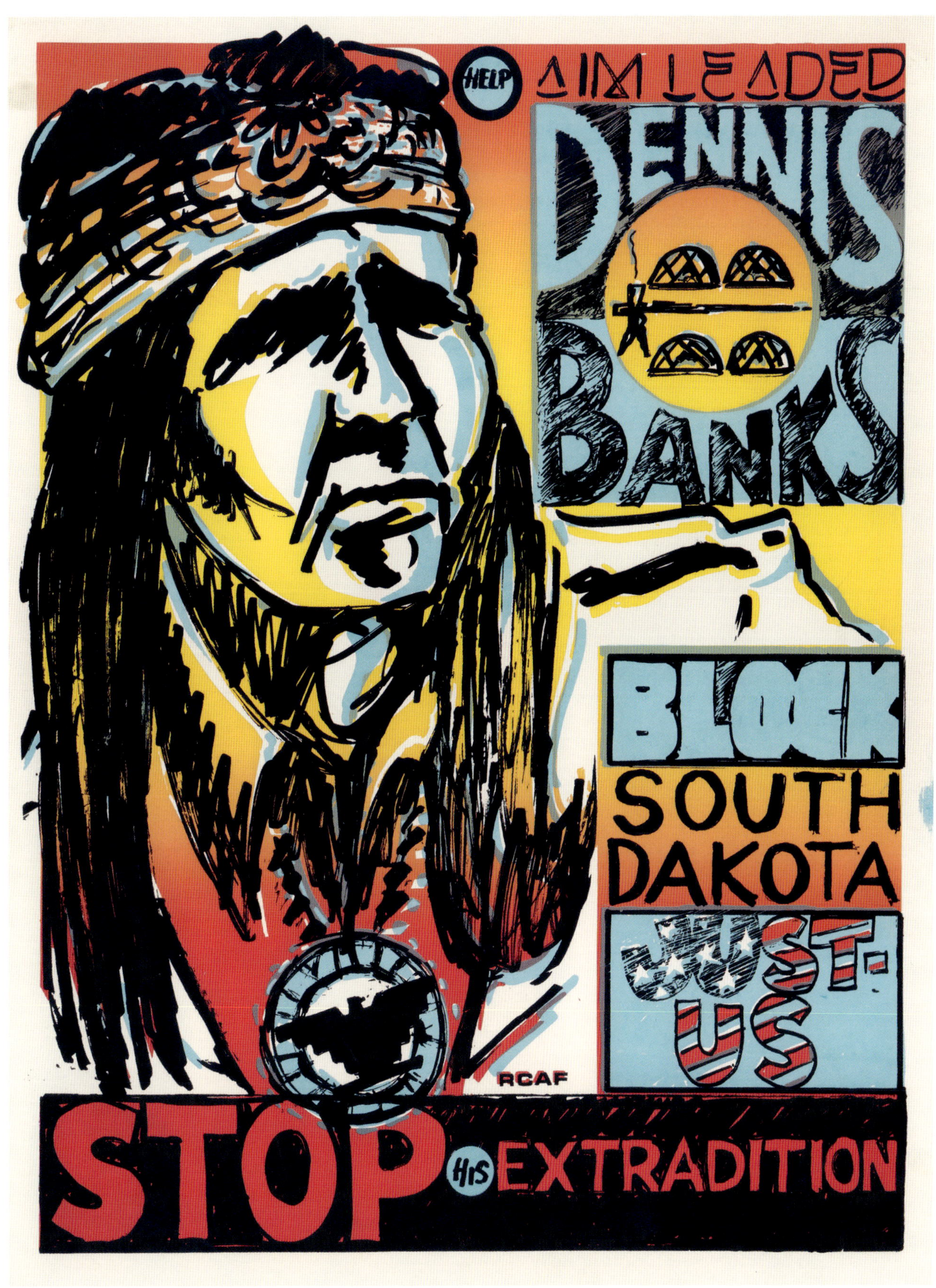

84 José Montoya (1932–2013), *Dennis Banks*, c. 1976. Screenprint, 22½ × 17½ in. La Raza Galeria Posada Poster Collection, Gerth Special Collections & University Archives, California State University, Sacramento.

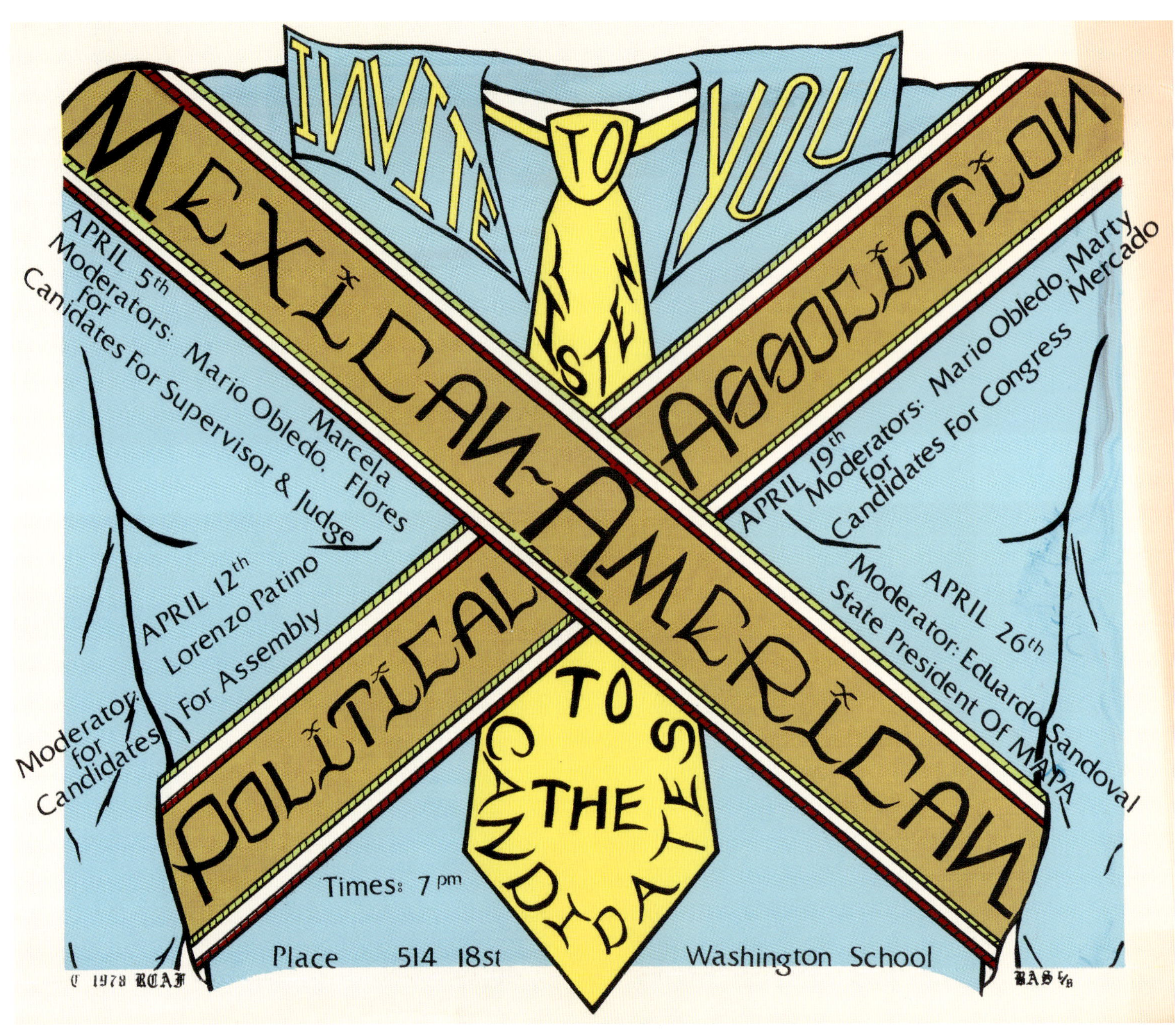

85 Raul Suarez, *Mexican-American Political Association*, 1978. Screenprint, 17½ × 22½ in. Royal Chicano Air Force Poster Collection, Gerth Special Collections & University Archives, California State University, Sacramento.

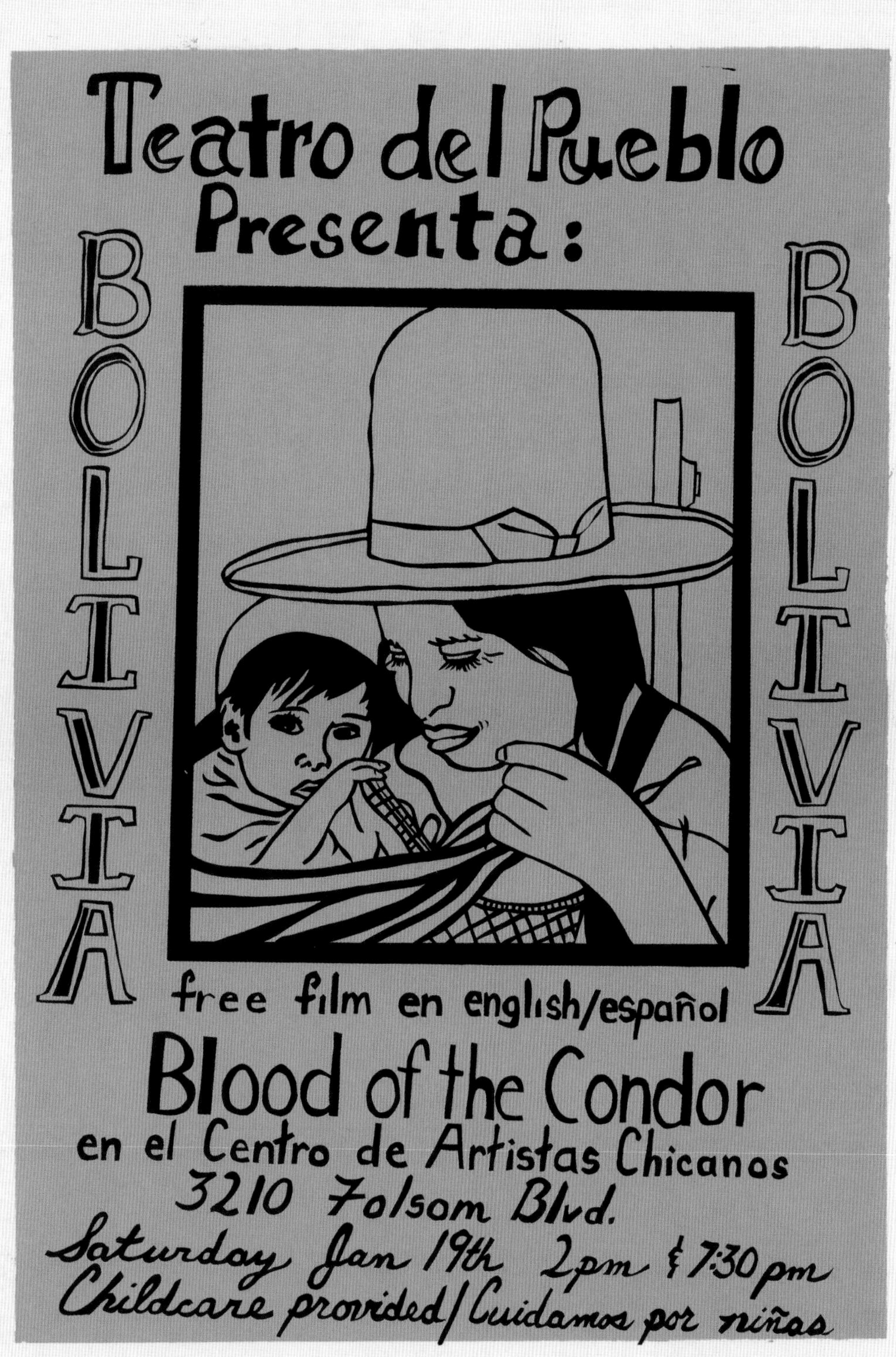

86 Irma Lerma Barbosa (born 1949), *Teatro del Pueblo Presenta: Bolivia*, 1974. Screenprint, 24 × 18 in. Villa Family Collection.

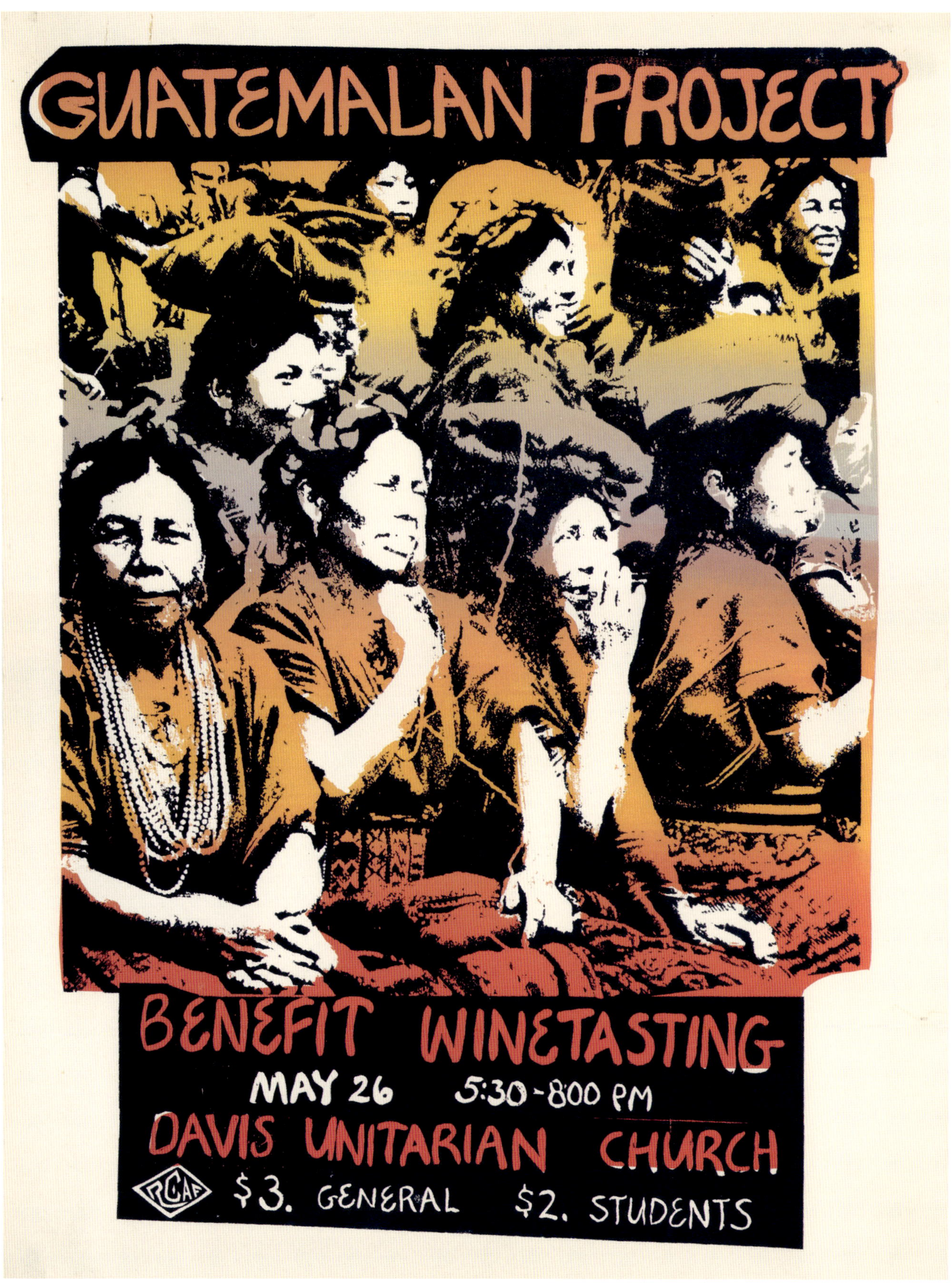

87 Rudy O. Cuellar (born 1953), *Guatemalan Project*, 1980. Screenprint, 22 ⅝ × 17 ½ in. Villa Family Collection.

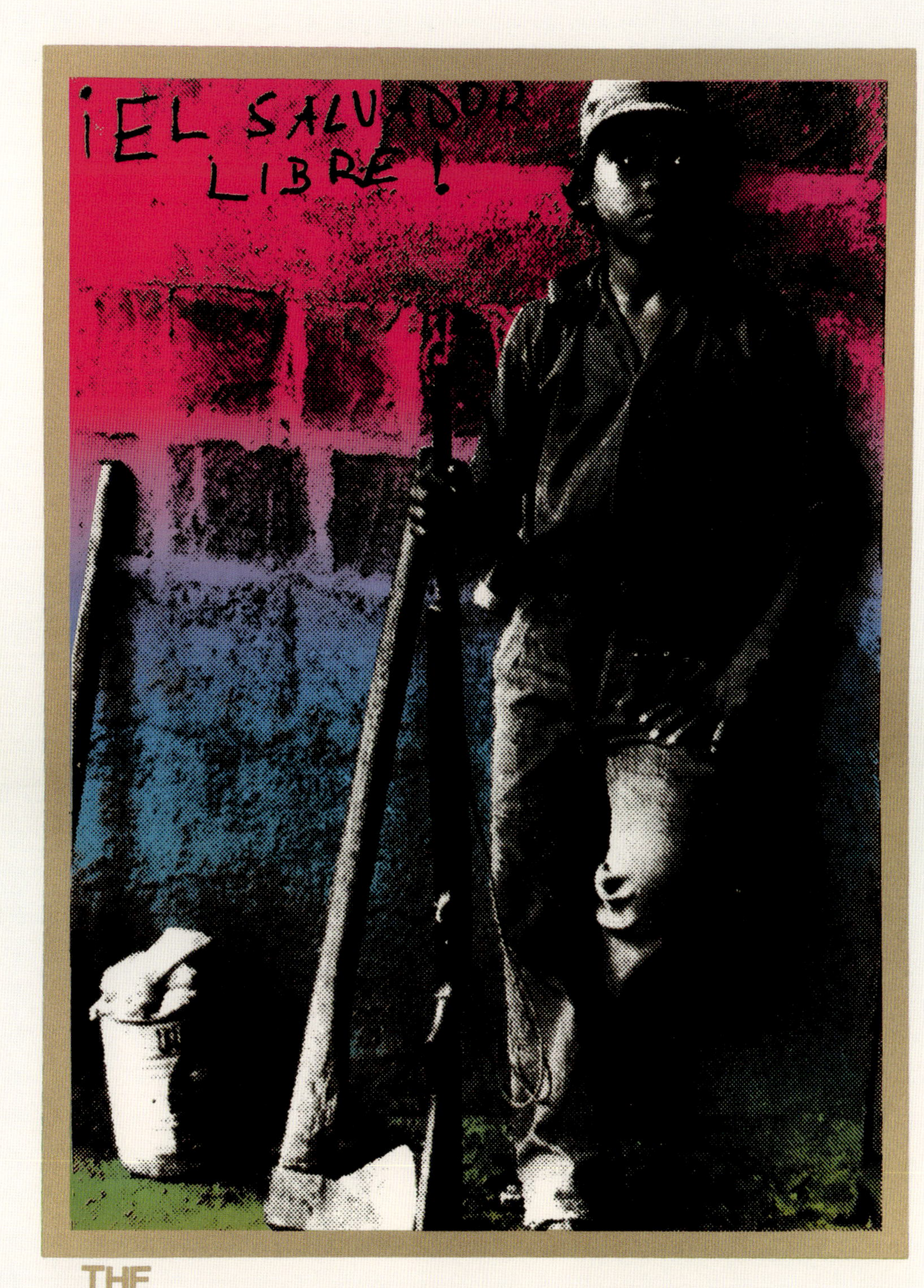

88 Luis C. González (born 1953), *The Salvadorean People's Support Committee*, 1981. Screenprint, 26 × 17 3/4 in. Collection of Luis C. González.

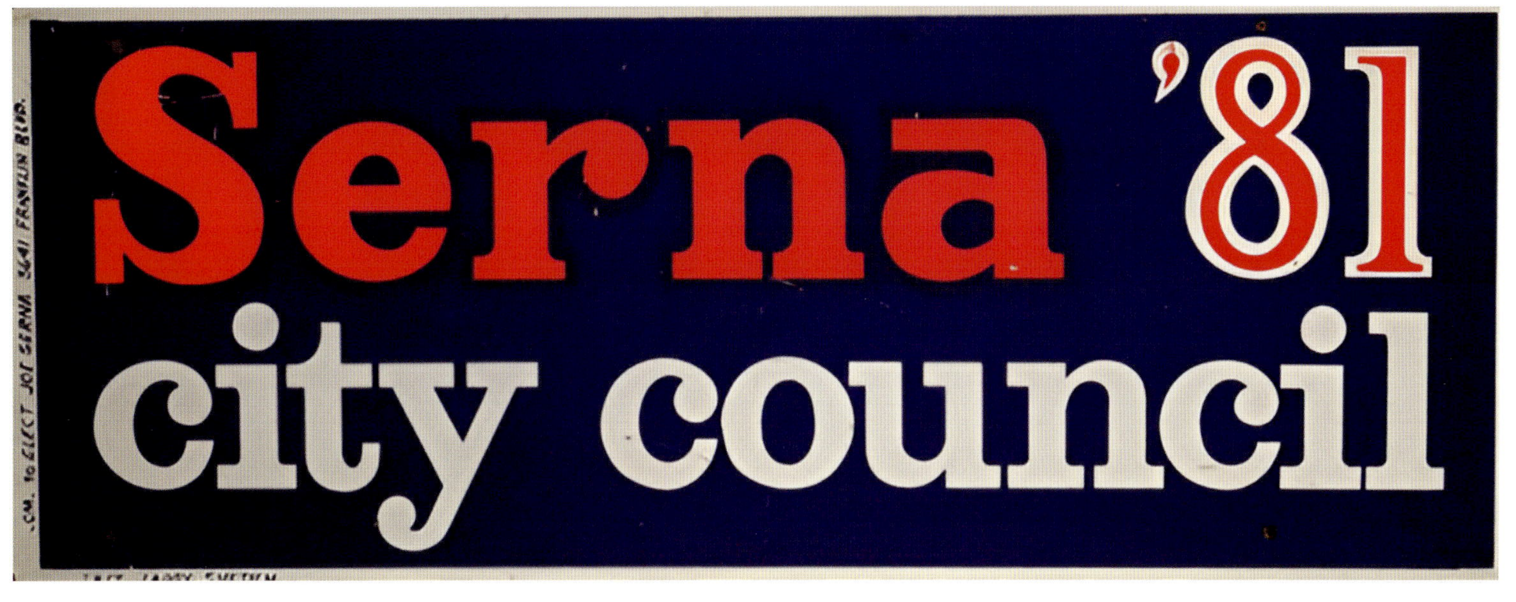

89 Evelyn Jenkins-Cronn (1940–1993), *Serna City Council Lawn Sign*, 1981. Screenprint, 12 x 32 in. Serna Family Collection. Photograph by Phil Serna.

La Raza Galeria Posada

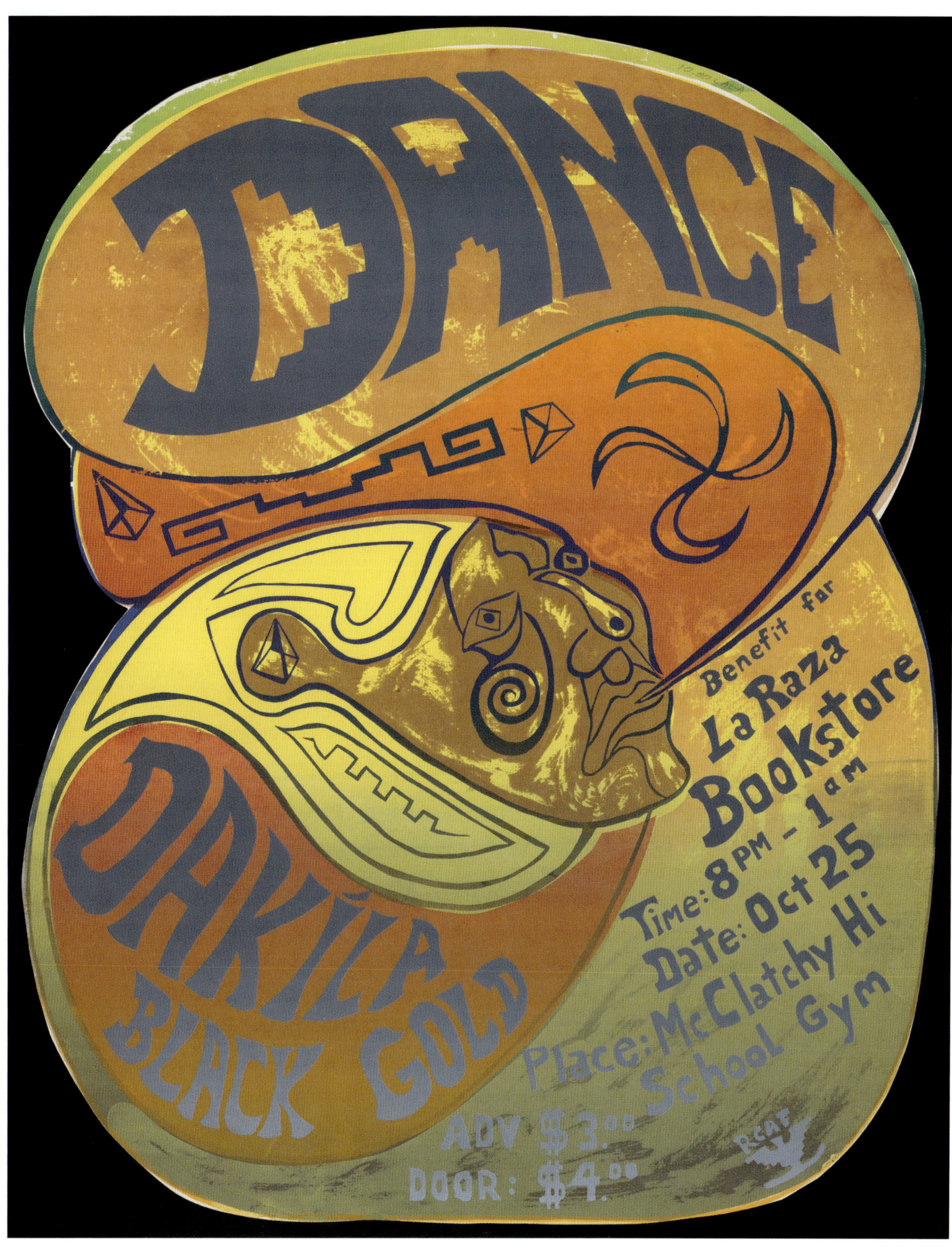

90 Armando Cid (1943–2009), *Dance Benefit for La Raza Bookstore*, 1974. Screenprint, 24 × 18 in. Courtesy of the California History Room, California State Library.

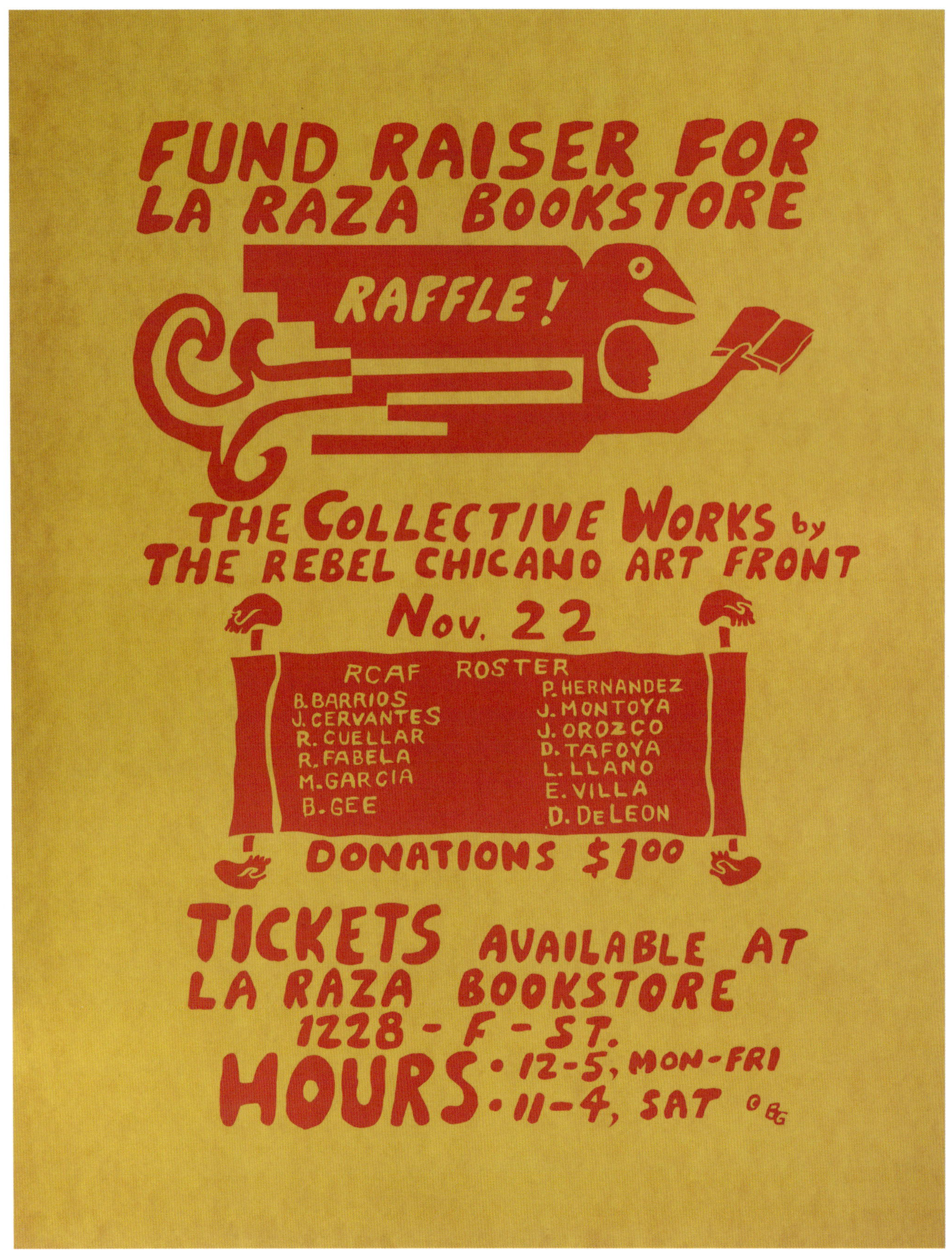

91 Bill Gee (born 1949), *Fund Raiser for La Raza Bookstore*, c. 1972. Screenprint on posterboard, 22 5/8 × 16 in. Royal Chicano Air Force Archives, CEMA 8, University of California, Santa Barbara Library.

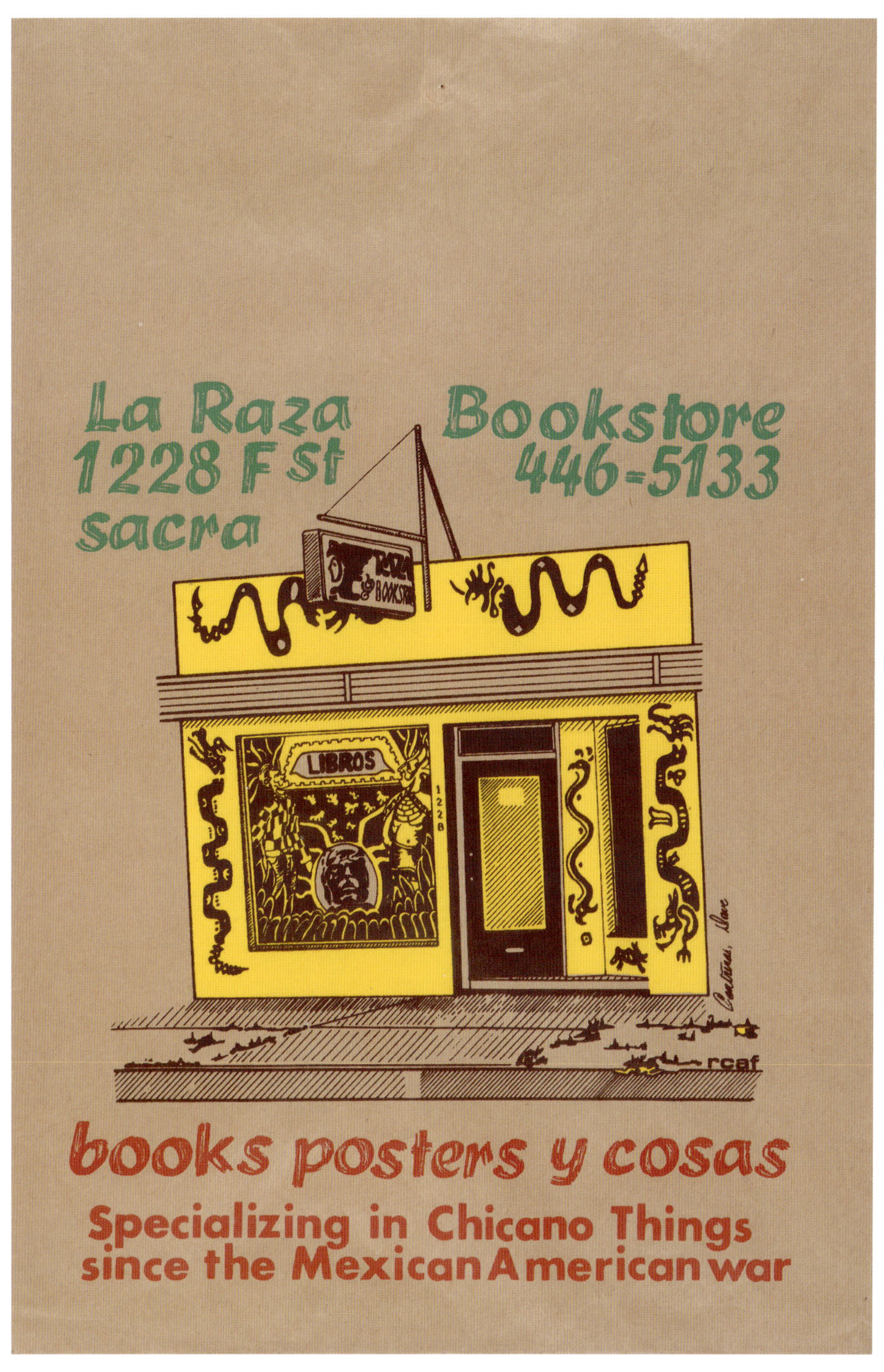

92 Luis C. González (born 1953), drawing by David Contreras, *La Raza Bookstore Bag*, c. 1978. Screenprint, 18 ½ × 12 in. Collection of Luis C. González.

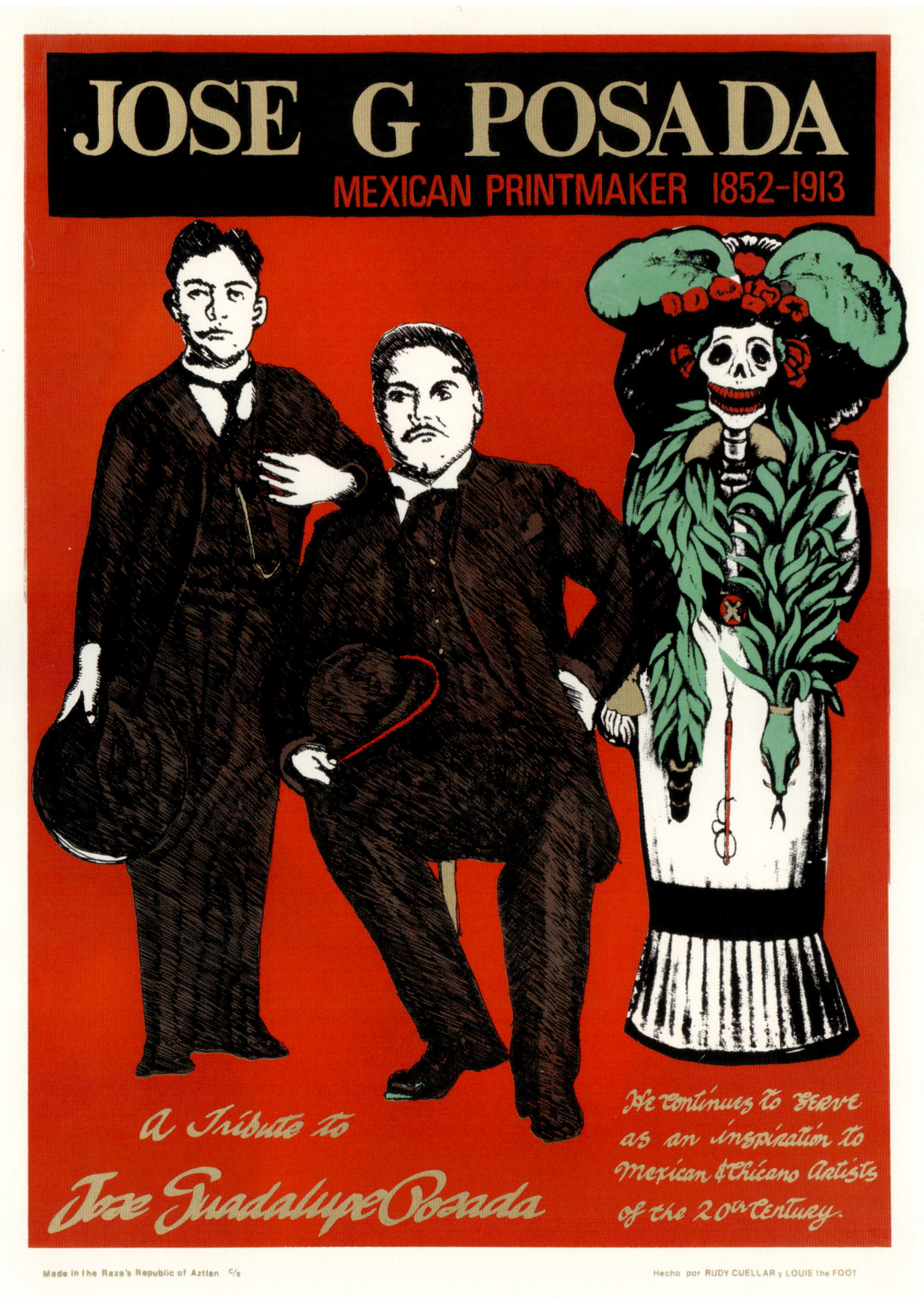

93 Rudy O. Cuellar (born 1950) and Luis C. González (born 1953), *José G. Posada*, 1980. Screenprint, 23 × 17¼ in. Collection of Luis C. González.

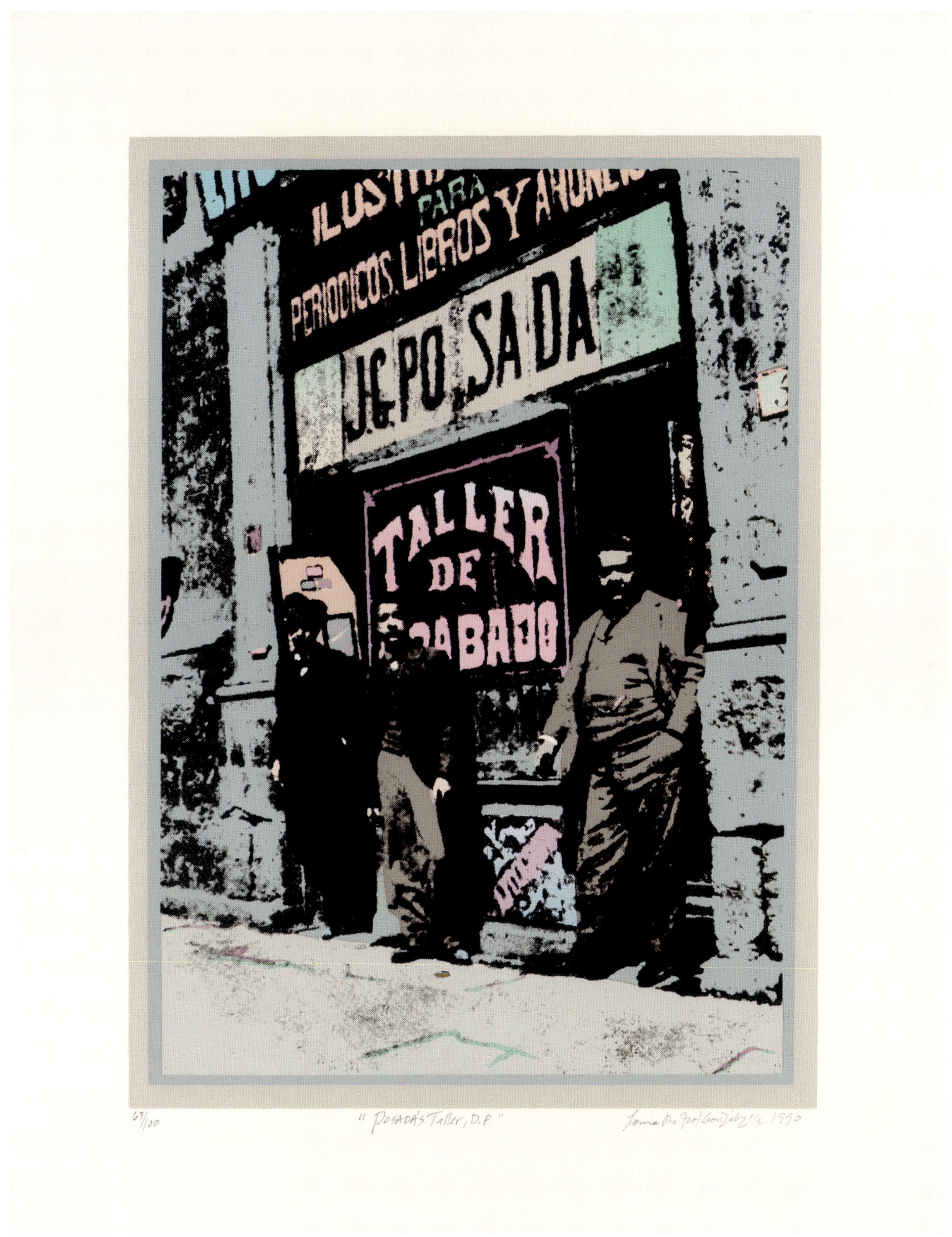

94 Luis C. González (born 1953), *Posada's Taller, D.F.*, 1990. Screenprint, 28 × 22⅛ in. Collection of Luis C. González.

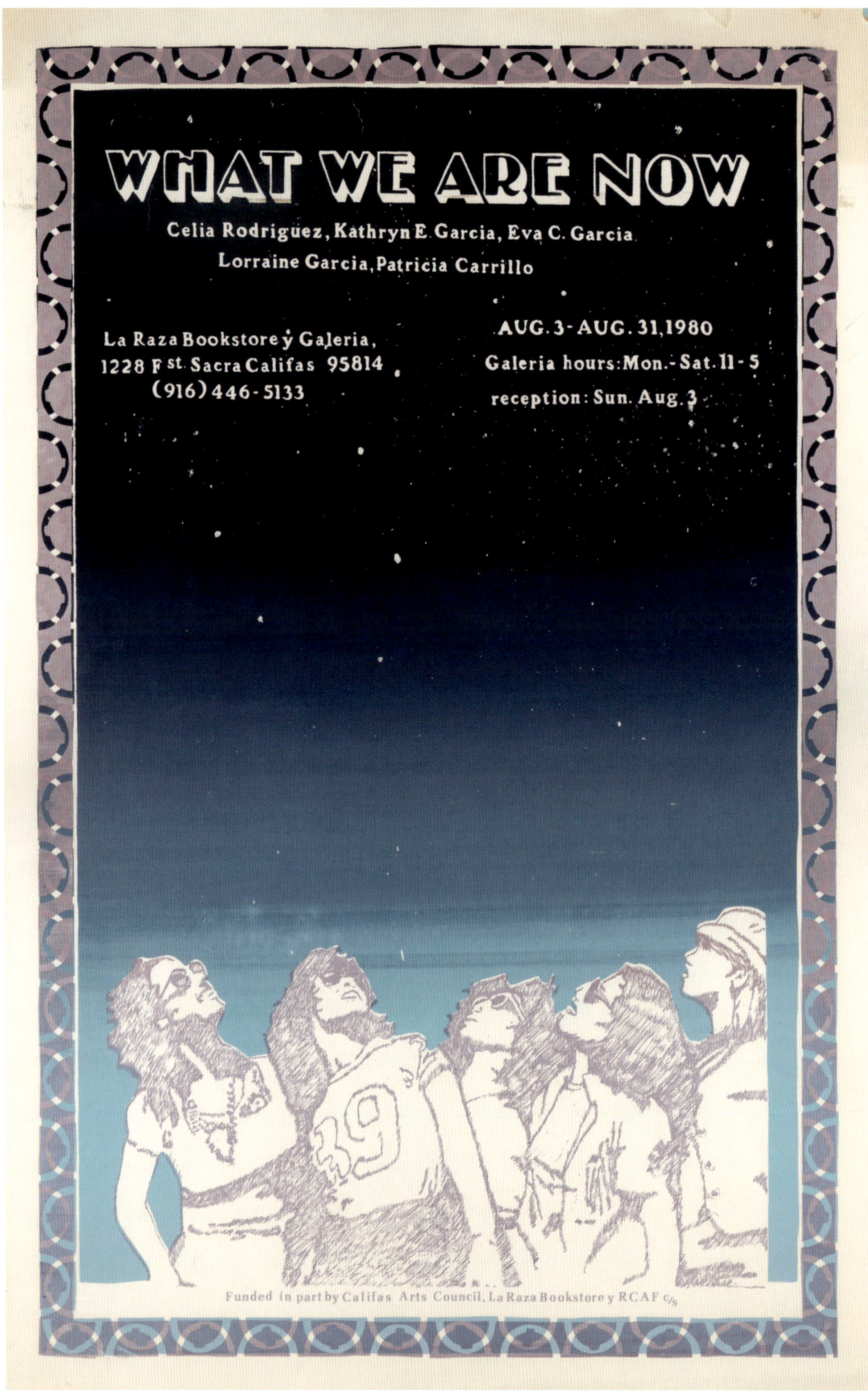

95 Rudy O. Cuellar (born 1950), *What We Are Now*, 1980. Screenprint, 35 × 23 in. Collection of Rudy O. Cuellar.

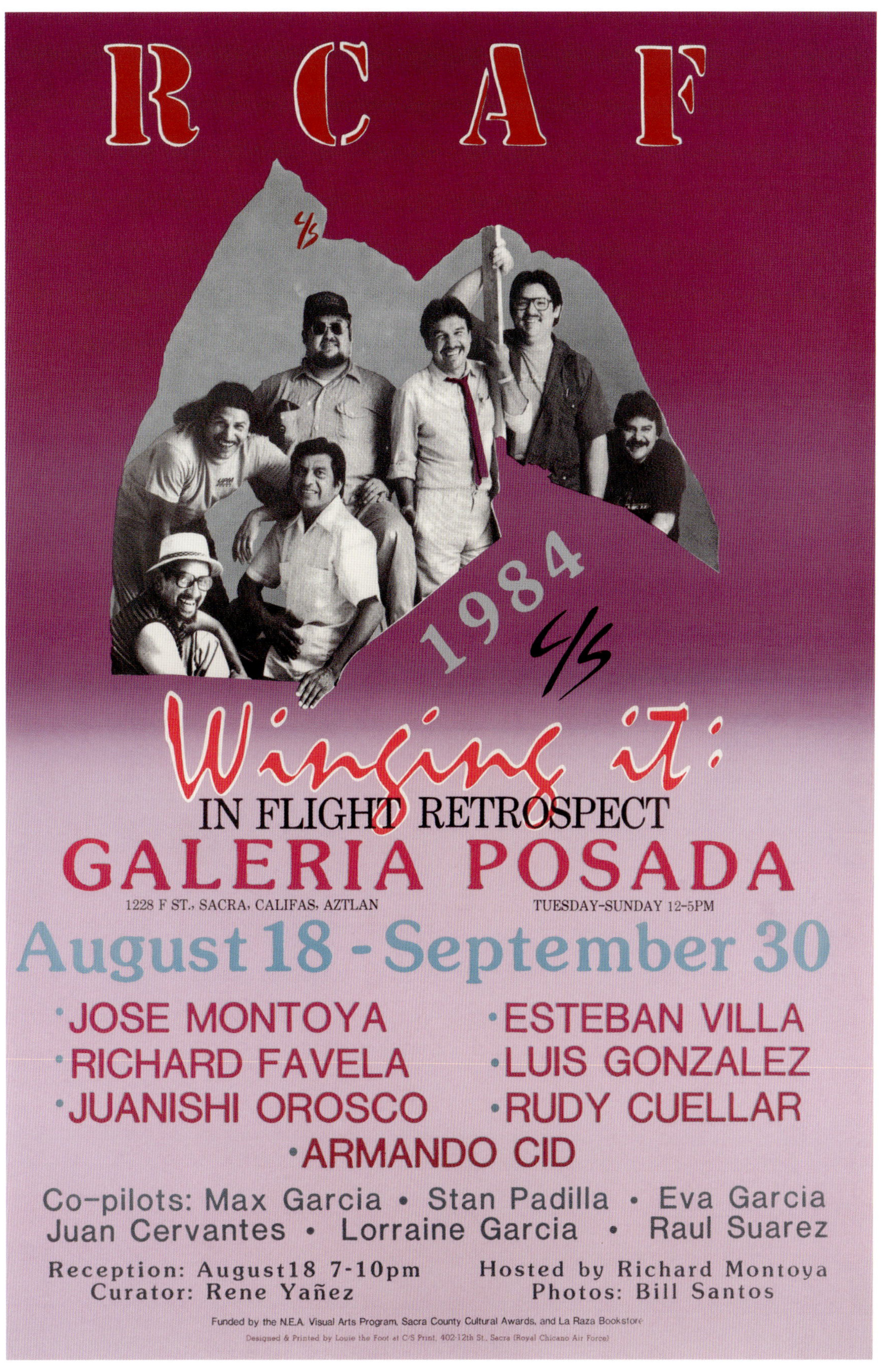

96 Luis C. González (born 1953), photograph by Bill Santos, *Winging It*, 1984. Screenprint, 44⅞ × 30⅛ in. Collection of Luis C. González.

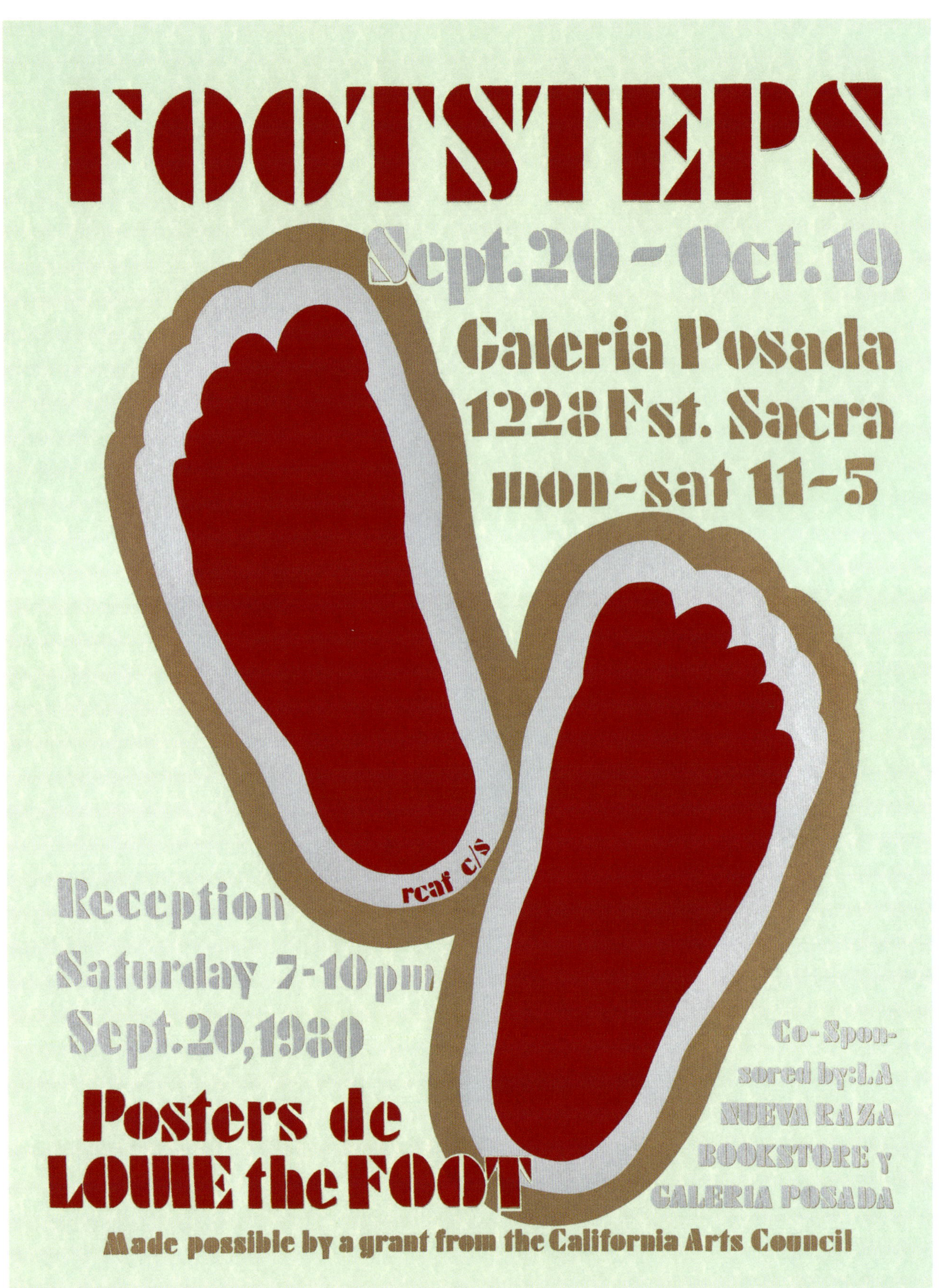

97 Luis C. González (born 1953), *Footsteps*, 1980. Screenprint, 23 × 17½ in. Collection of Luis C. González.

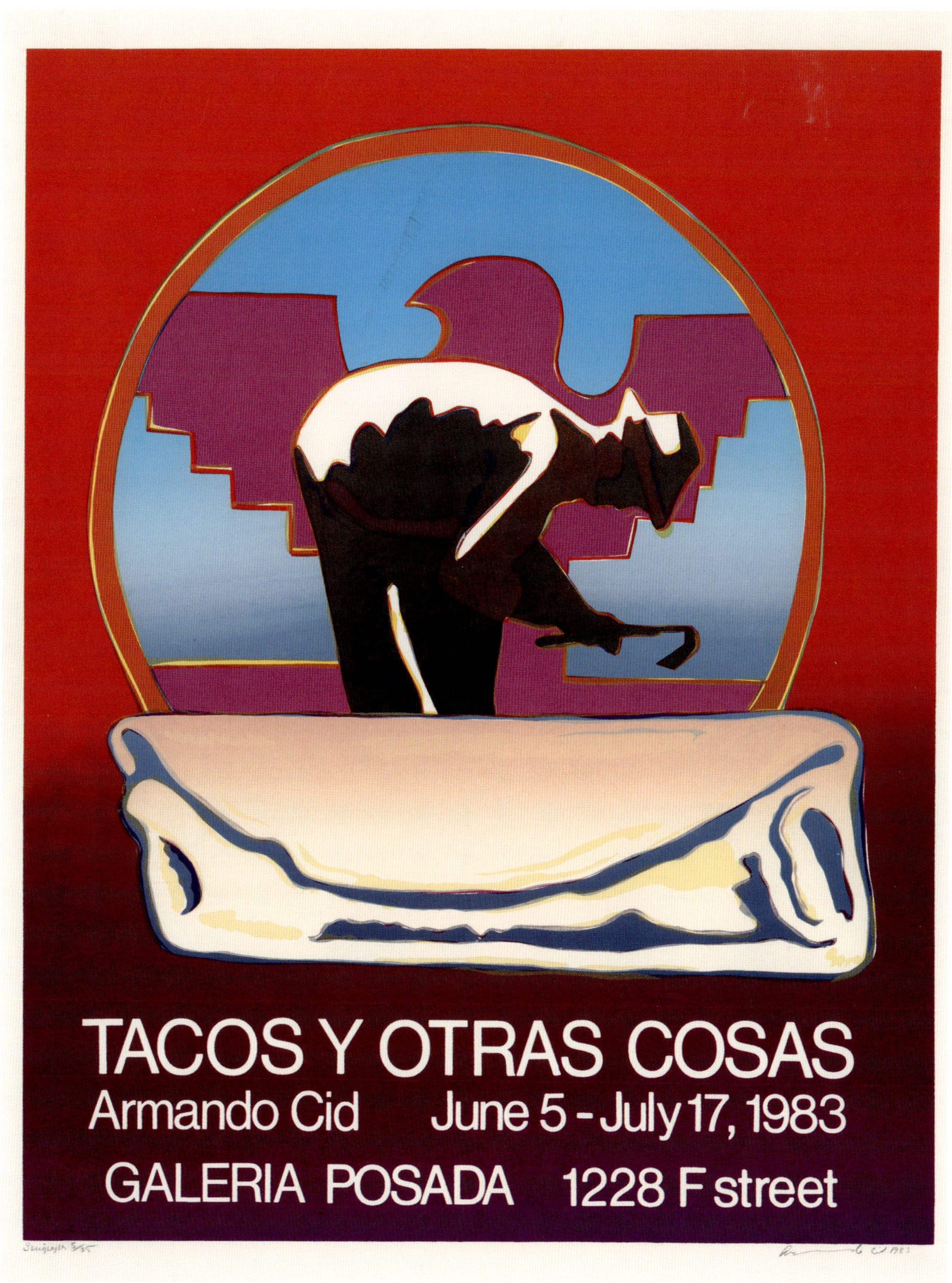

98 Armando Cid (1943–2009), *Tacos y Otras Cosas*, 1983. Screenprint, 23 × 17½ in. La Raza Galeria Posada Poster Collection, Gerth Special Collections & University Archives, California State University, Sacramento.

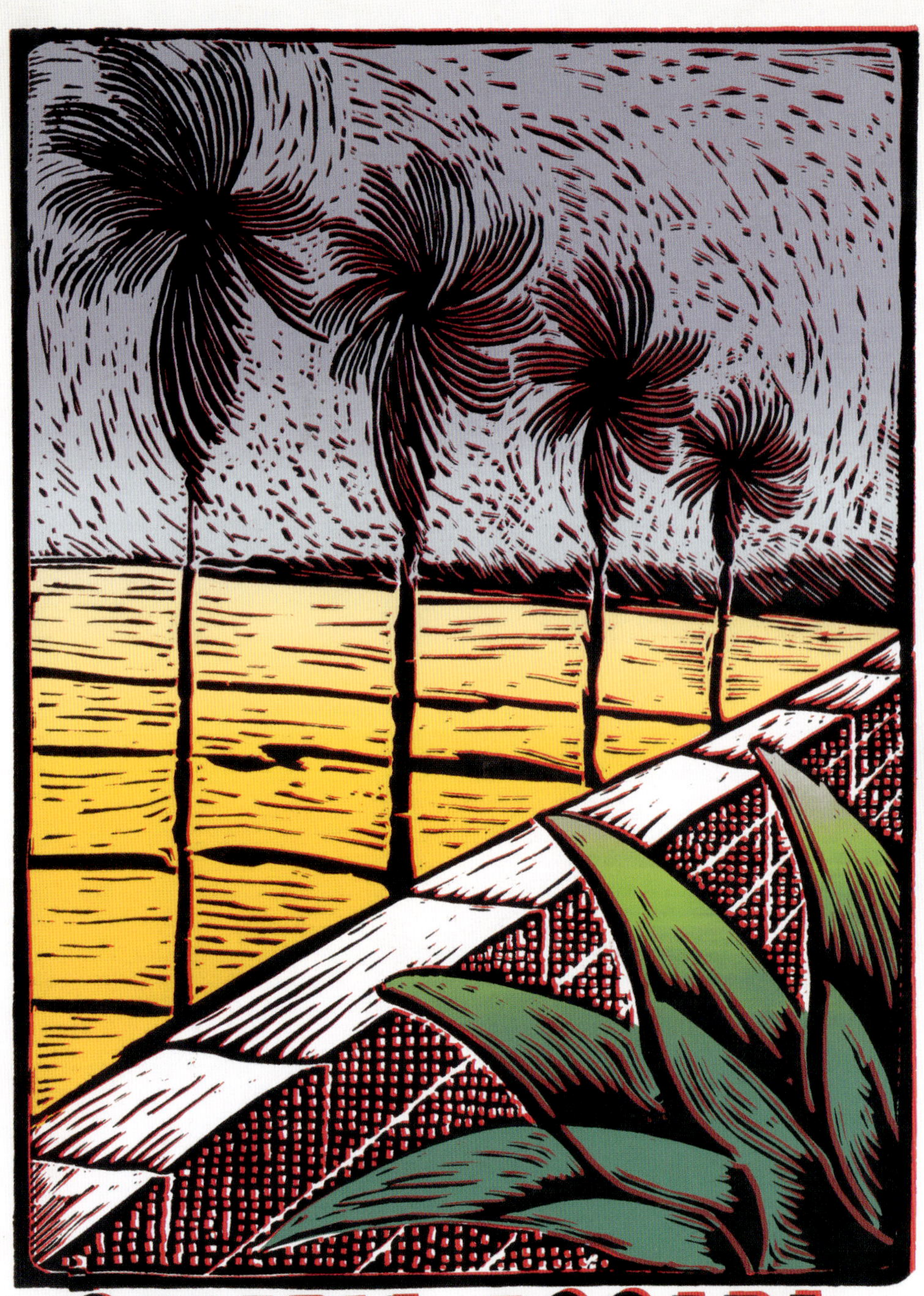

99 Esteban Villa (1930–2022) and Rudy O. Cuellar (born 1950), *Galeria Posada Sacra Prints*, 1981. Screenprint, 26 × 17 in. Collection of Rudy O. Cuellar.

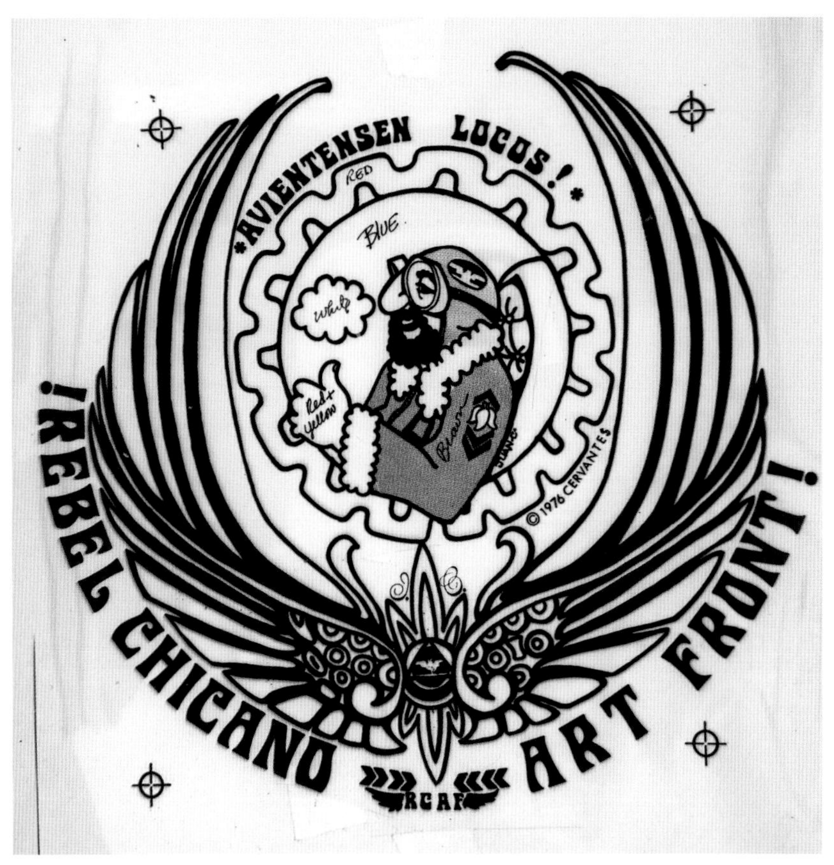

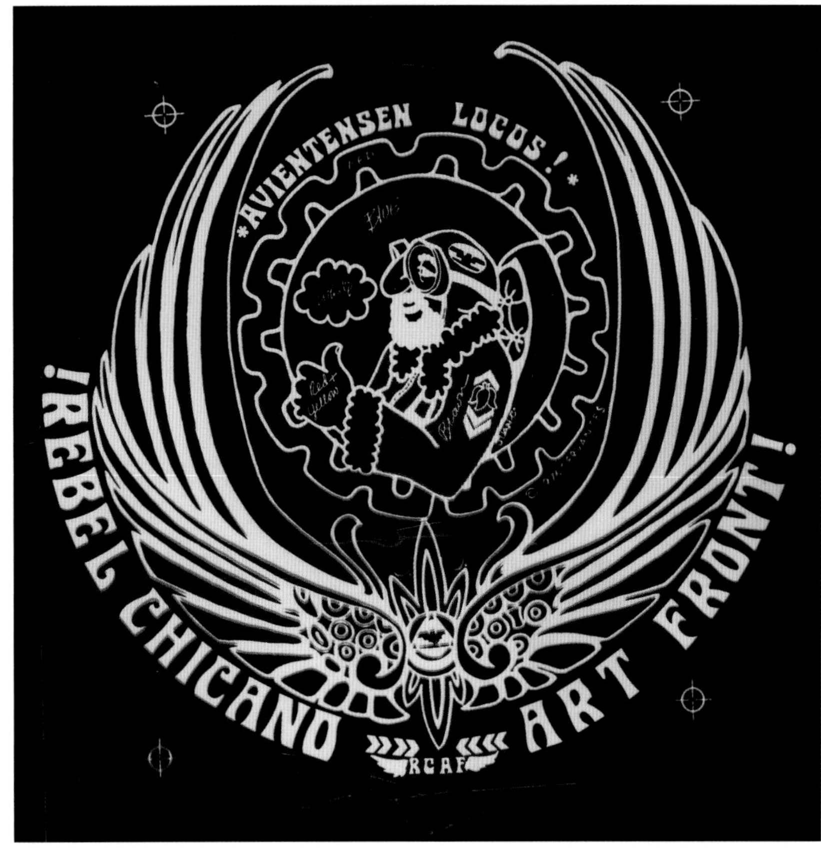

100 Juan Cervantes (1951–2014), *¡Rebel Chicano Art Front!*, 1976. Film negative and positive print, 6 × 6 in. Cervantes-Powell Family Collection.

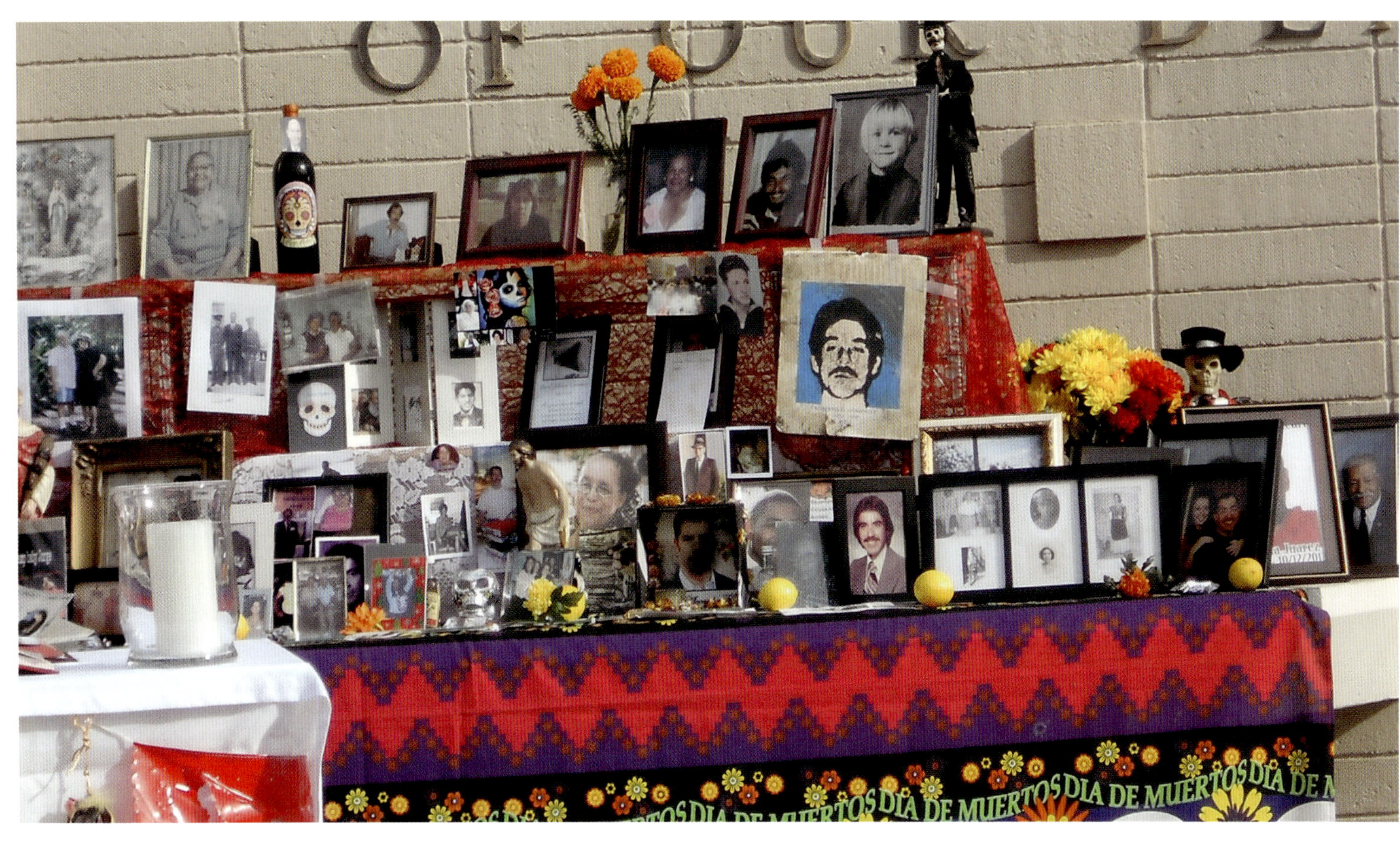

Alfred "Freddy" González (born 1945), *Detail of Dia de los Muertos Ofrenda by Guadalupe "Lupe" Portillo at St. Mary's Cemetery*, 2013. Collection of Alfred "Freddy" González.

Ofrenda (In Remembrance)

Angelo Alvarez
Jennie Baca
Anita Ramos Barnes
Joseph Camacho
Ada Carrillo
Rudy Carrillo
Juan Cervantes
Armando Cid
Rodolfo Cuellar Sr.
Ricardo Favela
Eva Garcia
Max Garcia
Francisco "Fox" Godina
Carlota Gutierrez
Isabel Hernandez Serna
Evelyn Jenkins-Cronn
Alberto "Beto" Mestas
José Montoya
Mary Ellen Montoya
Joe Nava
Elias Nuñez
Juan "Juanishi" Orosco
Jesse "Chuy" Ortiz
Ros Padilla
Carlos "Stubbo" Portillo
Sam Quiñones
Gloria Rangel
Olivia Rangel
Rosemary Rasul
Sam Ríos Jr.
Federico "Freddy" Rodriguez
Arturo "Turtle" Rodriguez
Manuela Serna
Joseph "Joe" Serna Jr.
Benny Trujillo
Esteban Villa
Helen Villa

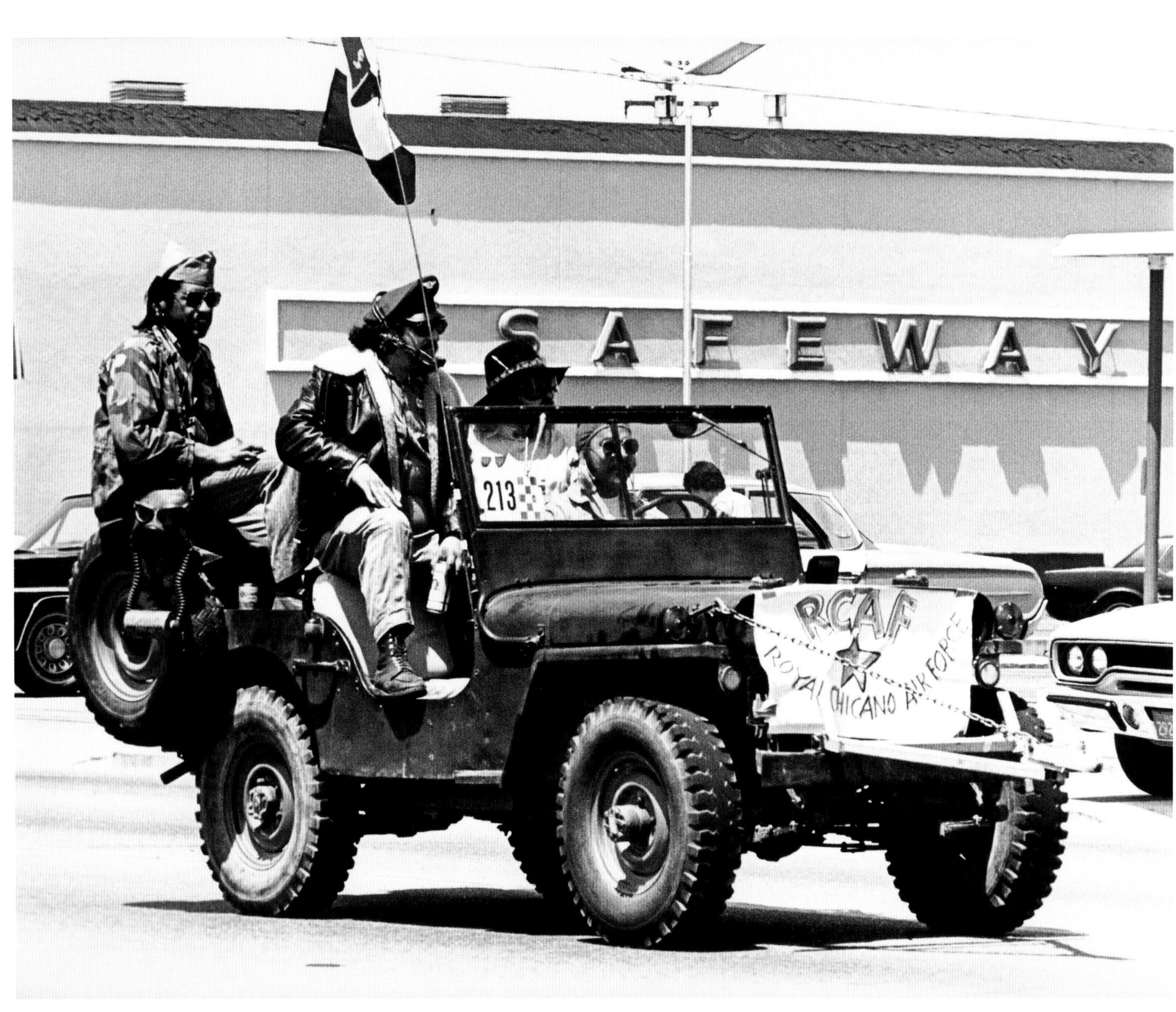

Harold Nihei (born 1939), *RCAF Accidentally Joins a Parade in Woodland*, 1976. [Esteban Villa, José Montoya, Ricardo Favela, and Pedro "Pete" Hernandez]. Collection of Harold Nihei.

Exhibition Checklist

Juan Carrillo (born 1941)

Mercado de las Flores, 1976
Screenprint, 24½ × 18⅛ in.
Collection of Juan Manuel Carrillo
Plate 38

Juan Cervantes (1951–2014)

Chicanito Science Project, mid-1970s
Screenprint, 25 × 19 in.
Cervantes-Powell Family Collection
Plate 26

Friends of the River, 1976
Screenprint, 25 × 19 in.
Royal Chicano Air Force Archives, CEMA 8.
University of California, Santa Barbara Library
Plate 27

¡Rebel Chicano Art Front!, 1976
Film negative, 6 × 6 in.
Cervantes-Powell Family Collection
Plate 100

The Singer, 1976
Screenprint, 25 × 19 in.
Cervantes-Powell Family Collection
Plate 28

Juan Cervantes (1951–2014) and Luis C. González (born 1953)

Committee to Abolish Prison Slavery, 1977
Screenprint, 22⅝ × 17⅜ in.
Cervantes-Powell Family Collection
Plate 77

Armando Cid (1943–2009)

Chicano Ball, 1976
Screenprint, 25 × 19 in.
Royal Chicano Air Force Archives, CEMA 8.
University of California, Santa Barbara Library
Plate 23

Cinco de Mayo, 1976
Screenprint, 25 × 19 in.
Royal Chicano Air Force Archives, CEMA 8.
University of California, Santa Barbara Library
Plate 43

Dance Benefit for La Raza Bookstore, 1974
Screenprint, 24 × 18 in.
Courtesy of the California History Room, California State Library
Plate 90

El Parque Dedicado a Emiliano Zapata, 1975
Screenprint, 25 × 19 in.
Rasul Chicano Art Collection
Plate 22

Farmworker Dance Benefit, ca. 1973
Screenprint, 13 × 21 in.
Royal Chicano Air Force Archives, CEMA 8.
University of California, Santa Barbara Library
Plate 67

Operation Christmas Unity, 1973
Screenprint, 25⅛ × 19 in.
Rasul Chicano Art Collection
Plate 51

Tacos y Otras Cosas, 1983
Screenprint, 23 × 17½ in.
La Raza Galeria Posada Poster Collection, Gerth Special Collections & University Archives. California State University, Sacramento
Plate 98

Teatro "Suspiro del Barrio," 1975
Screenprint, 25 × 19 in.
Royal Chicano Air Force Archives, CEMA 8.
University of California, Santa Barbara Library
Plate 24

Rudy O. Cuellar (born 1950)

10 y 6 de Septiembre, 1977
Screenprint, 22½ × 17½ in.
Collection of Rudy O. Cuellar
Plate 45

16 September on the 17, 1978
Screenprint, 29 × 23 in.
La Raza Galeria Posada Poster Collection, Gerth Special Collections & University Archives. California State University, Sacramento
Plate 46

1951 Chevy Fastback, 1982
Screenprint, 28½ × 40 in.
Collection of Rudy O. Cuellar
Plate 30

Chicano Art Expo, 1974
Screenprint, 25 × 19 in.
Royal Chicano Air Force Archives, CEMA 8.
University of California, Santa Barbara Library
Plate 20

Cinco de Mayo, 1979
Screenprint, 23 × 17⅝ in.
Royal Chicano Air Force Poster Collection, Gerth Special Collections & University Archives. California State University, Sacramento
Plate 44

Día de la Raza, 1975
Screenprint, 24 × 18½ in.
Royal Chicano Air Force Archives, CEMA 8.
University of California, Santa Barbara Library
Plate 21

Fiesta del Maíz, 1976
Screenprint, 23⅞ × 18 in.
Collection of Rudy O. Cuellar
Plate 58

Fiesta de Maíz, 1977
Screenprint, 22⅝ × 17½ in.
Collection of Rudy O. Cuellar
Plate 59

Guatemalan Project, 1980
Screenprint, 22⅝ × 17½ in.
Villa Family Collection
Plate 87

Los Mascarones, 1973
Screenprint, 24 × 13 in.
Royal Chicano Air Force Archives, CEMA 8.
University of California, Santa Barbara Library
Plate 19

Lowrider Carrucha Show, 1978
Screenprint, 29⅛ × 23 in.
Collection of Rudy O. Cuellar
Plate 29

Mercado de las Flores Lowrider Show, 1977
Screenprint, 22 5/8 × 17 1/2 in.
Collection of Rudy O. Cuellar
Plate 39

What We Are Now, 1980
Screenprint, 35 × 23 in.
Collection of Rudy O. Cuellar
Plate 95

Xicano Bicentenial, 1776–1976, 1976
Screenprint, 25 × 19 in.
Collection of Rudy O. Cuellar
Plate 78

Rudy O. Cuellar (born 1950) and José Felix

Centro de Artistas Chicanos Benefit Dance, 1973
Screenprint, 35 × 23 in.
Royal Chicano Air Force Archives, CEMA 8. University of California, Santa Barbara Library
Plate 18

Rudy O. Cuellar (born 1950) and Luis C. González (born 1953)

José G. Posada, 1980
Screenprint, 23 × 17 1/4 in.
Collection of Luis C. González
Plate 93

Rudy O. Cuellar (born 1950), Luis C. González (born 1953), and José Montoya (1932–2013)

José Montoya's Pachuco Art, A Historical Update, 1977
Screenprint, 31 × 13 in.
Collection of Luis C. González
Plate 36

First Annual Indian American–Chicano Unity, 1985
Screenprint, 23 1/8 × 29 in.
Collection of Rudy O. Cuellar
Plate 82

Rudy O. Cuellar (born 1950) and Juanishi Orosco (1945–2023)

One More Canto, 1979
Screenprint, 23 × 17 1/2 in.
Collection of Rudy O. Cuellar
Plate 42

Ricardo Favela (1944–2007)

4th Annual Royal Chicano Air Force Art Show, 1974
Screenprint, 25 × 19 in.
Royal Chicano Air Force Archives, CEMA 8. University of California, Santa Barbara Library
Plate 15

Califas Coalition de Artistas, 1975
Screenprint, 25 × 19 in.
Courtesy of the California History Room, California State Library
Plate 79

Centennial Means 500 Years of Genocide!, 1976
Screenprint, 25 × 19 in.
La Raza Galeria Posada Poster Collection, Gerth Special Collections & University Archives. California State University, Sacramento
Plate 83

Día de las Madres, 1976
Screenprint, 25 × 19 in.
RCAFavela Collection
Plate 48

Día de las Madres Celebración, 1978
Screenprint, 22 3/4 × 17 5/8 in.
RCAFavela Collection
Plate 49

Día de los Muertos, 1975
Screenprint, 25 × 19 in.
RCAFavela Collection
Plate 54

Día de los Muertos, 1976
Screenprint, 25 × 19 in.
RCAFavela Collection
Plate 55

El Centro de Artistas Chicanos, 1975
Screenprint, 25 × 19 in.
RCAFavela Collection
Plate 8

¡Huelga! ¡Strike!, 1976 (photograph by Harold Nihei)
Screenprint, 19 × 25 in.
RCAFavela Collection
Plate 73

Sube La Xilónen, 1976 (poem by Dr. Arnaldo Solis)
Screenprint, 23 × 17 1/2 in.
RCAFavela Collection
Plate 60

UFW Community Meeting, 1977
Screenprint, 22 3/4 × 17 5/8 in.
RCAFavela Collection
Plate 74

Eva Garcia (1949–1991)

5th Annual Día de las Madres, 1979
Screenprint, 23 × 18 in.
La Raza Galeria Posada Poster Collection, Gerth Special Collections & University Archives. California State University, Sacramento
Plate 50

Kathryn Garcia (born 1952)

Celebración del Día de La Independencia, 1974
Screenprint, 25 × 19 in.
La Raza Galeria Posada Poster Collection, Gerth Special Collections & University Archives. California State University, Sacramento
Plate 13

Max Garcia (1942–2020)

Baton Rouge, 1971
Screenprint, 26 7/8 × 22 1/4 in.
Rasul Chicano Art Collection
Plate 5

Fiesta de Navidad: Regalos de Tristesa, 1975
Screenprint, 25 × 19 in.
Royal Chicano Air Force Archives, CEMA 8. University of California, Santa Barbara Library
Plate 11

Pilots of Aztlan–Royal Chicano Air Force, 1995
Screenprint, 19 × 30 in.
Royal Chicano Air Force Poster Collection, Gerth Special Collections & University Archives. California State University, Sacramento
Plate 1

Yes on 14!, 1976
Screenprint, 17 1/2 × 22 5/8 in.
Rasul Chicano Art Collection
Plate 71

Max Garcia (1942–2020) and Ricardo Favela (1944–2007)

Regeneración, 1971
Screenprint, 23 × 34 3/4 in.
Collection of the Oakland Museum of California. Gift of the Terrazas Martin Family on behalf of Margaret Terrazas-Santos
Plate 6

Max Garcia (1942–2020) and Héctor D. González (born 1945)

Third World Writers and Thinkers Symposium, 1976
Screenprint, 25 × 19 in.
Collection of Luis C. González
Plate 9

Lorraine García-Nakata (born 1950)

Mexican Independence Celebration and Parade, 1983
Screenprint, 28 × 22 in.
La Raza Galeria Posada Poster Collection, Gerth Special Collections & University Archives. California State University, Sacramento
Plate 47

Bill Gee (born 1949)

Fund Raiser for La Raza Bookstore, c. 1972
Screenprint on posterboard, 22 5/8 × 16 in.
Royal Chicano Air Force Archives, CEMA 8. University of California, Santa Barbara Library
Plate 91

Luis C. González (born 1953)

2nd Annual Chicano Softball Tournament, 1977
Screenprint, 17 1/2 × 11 3/8 in.
Collection of Luis C. González
Plate 40

8 Días del Mundo Chicano, 1976
Screenprint, 25 × 16 in.
Collection of Luis C. González
Plate 25

Fiesta del Maíz, 1981
Screenprint, 28 1/2 × 22 1/2 in.
Collection of Luis C. González
Plate 62

Footsteps, 1980
Screenprint, 23 × 17 1/2 in.
Collection of Luis C. González
Plate 97

La Raza Bookstore Bag, ca. 1978 (drawing by David Contreras)
Screenprint, 18 1/2 × 12 in.
Collection of Luis C. González
Plate 92

Mercado de las Flores, 1975
Screenprint, 25 × 19 in.
Collection of Luis C. González
Plate 37

Operation Christmas Unity, 1977
Screenprint, 22 1/2 × 17 1/2 in.
Collection of Luis C. González
Plate 53

Palabras Que Me Causas, 1975
Screenprint, 14 1/2 × 12 in.
Collection of Luis C. González
Plate 35

Posada's Taller, D.F., 1990
Screenprint, 28 × 22 1/8 in.
Collection of Luis C. González
Plate 94

The Salvadorean People's Support Committee, 1981
Screenprint, 26 × 17 3/4 in.
Collection of Luis C. González
Plate 88

Tenth Annual Día de los Muertos Celebration, 1985
Screenprint, 35 × 23 in.
Collection of Luis C. González
Plate 57

Winging It, 1984 (photograph by Bill Santos)
Screenprint, 44 7/8 × 30 1/8 in.
Collection of Luis C. González
Plate 96

Yo Soy Chicano, 1975
Screenprint, 13 3/4 × 18 in.
Collection of Luis C. González
Plate 32

Luis C. González (born 1953) and Ricardo Favela (1944–2007)

Cortés Nos Chingó in a Big Way The Hüey, 1976
Screenprint, 25 × 19 in.
Collection of Luis C. González
Plate 34

Luis C. González (born 1953) and Héctor D. González (born 1945)

Hasta La Victoria Siempre, 1975
Screenprint, 25 × 17 1/4 in.
Courtesy of the California History Room, California State Library
Plate 33

International Women's Year, Chicana, 1975
Screenprint, 15 × 22 in.
Royal Chicano Air Force Archives, CEMA 8. University of California, Santa Barbara Library
Plate 70

Viva la Huelga, 1976
Screenprint, 25 1/2 × 16 1/2 in.
Royal Chicano Air Force Poster Collection, Gerth Special Collections & University Archives. California State University, Sacramento
Plate 72

Luis C. González (born 1953) and José Montoya (1932–2013)

Raza Chisme Arte, ca. 1978
Screenprint, 22 5/8 × 17 1/2 in.
Collection of Luis C. González
Plate 80

Irma Lerma Barbosa (born 1949)

Primer Conferencia Femenil de Sacramento, 1973
Screenprint, 35 × 23 in.
Royal Chicano Air Force Archives, CEMA 8. University of California, Santa Barbara Library
Plate 12

Teatro del Pueblo Presenta: Bolivia, 1974
Screenprint, 24 × 18 in.
Villa Family Collection
Plate 86

José Montoya (1932–2013)

Dennis Banks, ca. 1976
Screenprint, 22 1/2 × 17 1/2 in.
La Raza Galeria Posada Poster Collection, Gerth Special Collections & University Archives. California State University, Sacramento
Plate 84

Recuerdos del Palomar, 1973
Screenprint, 25 × 19 in.
Collection of Luis C. González
Plate 10

The Visit, 1965
Oil on canvas, 38 × 24 in.
Stacy Paragary Collection
Plate 3

José Montoya (1932–2013) and Max Garcia (1942–2020)

Una Tardeada Campesina con Cesar Chavez, 1972
Screenprint, 25 × 19 in.
Royal Chicano Air Force Archives, CEMA 8. University of California, Santa Barbara Library
Plate 69

Juanishi Orosco (1945–2023)

5th Annual Operation Christmas Unity, 1975
Screenprint, 24 × 18 in.
Courtesy of the California History Room, California State Library
Plate 52

Chicano Festival of the Arts, 1973
Screenprint, 25 × 19 in.
Royal Chicano Air Force Archives, CEMA 8, University of California, Santa Barbara Library
Plate 16

Día de los Muertos Art Show, 1979
Screenprint, 25 × 19 in.
Collection of Luis C. González
Plate 56

Fiesta de Colores, 1979
Screenprint, 23 × 17½ in.
La Raza Galeria Posada Poster Collection, Gerth Special Collections & University Archives. California State University, Sacramento
Plate 64

Fiesta de Maíz, 1979
Screenprint, 23 × 17⅛ in.
Collection of Luis C. González
Plate 61

Las Bellas Artes de Sacramento, 1973
Screenprint, 25 × 19 in.
Royal Chicano Air Force Archives, CEMA 8. University of California, Santa Barbara Library
Plate 17

One More Canto, 1978
Screenprint, 22½ × 17 in.
Courtesy of the California History Room, California State Library
Plate 41

The RCAF's Art Sale Fundraiser, 1982
Screenprint, 19½ × 15¼ in.
Royal Chicano Air Force Poster Collection, Gerth Special Collections & University Archives. California State University, Sacramento
Plate 31

Solidaridad con la Union de Campesinos, early 1970s
Screenprint, 25 × 19 in.
Courtesy of the California History Room, California State Library
Plate 68

Stan Padilla (born 1945)

Fiesta de los Colores, 1978
Screenprint, 22⅝ × 17⅝ in.
Royal Chicano Air Force Poster Collection, Gerth Special Collections & University Archives. California State University, Sacramento
Plate 63

Celia Herrera Rodriguez (born 1952), Rudy O. Cuellar (born 1950), and Luis C. González (born 1953)

Native American Indian Alliance Culture Days, 1975
Screenprint, 17 × 14 in.
Royal Chicano Air Force Archives, CEMA 8, University of California, Santa Barbara Library
Plate 81

Evelyn Jenkins-Cronn (1940–1993)

Serna City Council Lawn Sign, 1981
Screenprint, 12 × 32 in.
Serna Family Collection
Plate 89

Raul Suarez

Mexican-American Political Association, 1978
Screenprint, 17½ × 22½ in.
Royal Chicano Air Force Poster Collection, Gerth Special Collections & University Archives. California State University, Sacramento
Plate 85

Esteban Villa (1930–2022)

5 de Mayo con el RCAF, 1973
Screenprint, 28½ × 21 in.
Royal Chicano Air Force Archives, CEMA 8. University of California, Santa Barbara Library
Plate 14

Arte de la Jente, 1970
Screenprint, 34 × 22⅛ in.
Rasul Chicano Art Collection
Plate 7

Breakfast for Niños, 1969
Screenprint, 22 × 14 in.
Royal Chicano Air Force Archives, CEMA 8. University of California, Santa Barbara Library
Plate 4

Cannery Workers Committee, 1976
Screenprint, 25 × 19 in.
Royal Chicano Air Force Archives, CEMA 8. University of California, Santa Barbara Library
Plate 75

Comite Trabajadores de Canerias, 1976
Screenprint, 16½ × 14⅞ in.
Villa Family Collection
Plate 76

Fiesta Campesina, 1972
Offset lithograph, 30 × 22 in.
La Raza Galeria Posada Poster Collection, Gerth Special Collections & University Archives. California State University, Sacramento
Plate 66

Untitled, ca. 1966
Art crayon on board, 80 × 30 in.
Villa Family Collection
Plate 2

Esteban Villa (1930–2022) and Rudy O. Cuellar (born 1950)

Galeria Posada Sacra Prints, 1981
Screenprint, 26 × 17 in.
Collection of Rudy O. Cuellar
Plate 99

Enrique Ortiz Villegas (born 1944)

Tlaloc Mask from Fiesta de Colores, 1979; restored 2024
Paris Craft, enamel paints, imitation gold-leaf foil, 9½ × 10¼ in.
Collection of Enrique Ortiz Villegas
Plate 65

Selected Bibliography

Angelo, Anne-Marie. "'Black Oppressed People All over the World Are One': The British Black Panthers' Grassroots Internationalism, 1969–1973." *Journal of Civil and Human Rights* 4, no. 1 (Spring/Summer 2018): 64–97.

Anzaldúa, Gloria. *Light in the Dark/Luz en lo Oscuro: Rewriting Identity, Spirituality, Reality*. Duke University Press, 2015.

Avella, Steve M. *Sacramento: Indomitable City*. Arcadia, 2003.

Bann, Stephen, ed. *Concrete Poetry: An International Anthology*. London Magazine, 1967.

Barnett, Alan W. *Community Murals: The People's Art*. Cornwall Books, 1984.

Belt, Debra J. "A Conversation with Louie the Foot Gonzalez." *Artweek* 24, no. 3 (February 4, 1993): 21.

Beverley, John. "The Margin at the Center: On Testimonio (Testimonial Narrative)." *Modern Fiction Studies* 35, no. 1 (Spring 1989): 11–28.

Binnie, Mari Rodríguez. *The São Paulo Neo-Avant-Garde: Radical Art and Mass Print Media in Cold War Brazil*. University of Texas Press, 2024.

Bloom, Joshua, and Waldo E. Martin Jr. *Black Against Empire: The History and Politics of the Black Panther Party*. University of California Press, 2016.

Burg, William. *Sacramento Renaissance: Art, Music, and Activism in California's Capital City*. History Press, 2013.

Christens, Brian D., Jyoti Gupta, and Paul W. Speer. "Community Organizing: Studying the Development and Exercise of Grassroots Power." *Journal of Community Psychology* 49, no. 8 (November 2021): 3001–16.

Cockcroft, Eva, and Holly Barnet-Sanchez, eds. *Signs from the Heart: California Chicano Murals*. Social and Public Resource Center, 1990.

Coleman, Floyd. "Keeping Hope Alive: The Story of African American Murals." In *Walls of Heritage/Walls of Pride: African American Murals*, edited by James Prigoff and Robin J. Dunitz. Pomegranate Communications, 2000.

Curreri-Chadwick, Dyana. "Centro de Artistas Chicanos: Progressive Mural Installation and Poster Exhibition (1969–80), Exhibition dates: May 14–June 26, 1983." Exhibition files, Crocker Art Museum.

Davalos, Karen Mary. "Centro de Arte Público/Public Art Center." *Aztlán* 36, no. 2 (2011): 171–78.

Diaz, Ella Maria. "The Art of Telling: Toward a Genealogy of Testimoniadoras." *Label Me Latina/o* 13 (2023): 1–19.

Diaz, Ella Maria. *Flying Under the Radar with the Royal Chicano Air Force: Mapping a Chicano/a Art History*. University of Texas Press, 2017.

Diaz, Ella Maria. "The Necessary Theater of the Royal Chicano Air Force." *Aztlán* 38, no. 2 (2013): 41–70.

del Castillo, Richard Griswold, Teresa McKenna, and Yvonne Yarbro-Bejarano. "APPENDIX: Catalog of Grupos, Centros, and Teatros." In *Chicano Art: Resistance and Affirmation, 1965–1985*. Wight Art Gallery, University of California, Los Angeles, 1991.

"El Plan Espiritual de Aztlán." In *Aztlan: An Anthology of Mexican American Literature*, edited by Luis Valdez and Stan Steiner. Vintage, 1972.

Enciso, Jorge. *Design Motifs of Ancient Mexico*. Dover, 1953.

Ferreira, Jason. "With the Soul of a Human Rainbow: Los Siete, Black Panthers, and Third Worldism in San Francisco." In *Ten Years that Shook the City: San Francisco 1968–1978*, edited by Chris Carlsson. City Lights Foundation Books, 2011.

Ferris, Susan, and Ricardo Sandoval. *The Fight in the Fields: Cesar Chavez and the Farmworkers Movement*. Harcourt Brace, 1997.

Finch, Peter, ed. *Typewriter Poems*. Something Else Press, 1972.

Frank-Cardenas, Joshua. "The Rise and Fall of D-Q University: Foundations." *Tribal College Journal of American Indian Higher Education* 31, no. 2 (November 8, 2019). http://tribalcollegejournal.org/the-rise-and-fall-of-d-q-university-foundations.

Galarza, Ernesto. *Barrio Boy*. University of Notre Dame Press, 1971.

Garnier, Pierre. *Spatialisme et poésie concrète*. Gallimard, 1968.

Goldman, Shifra. *Dimensions of the Americas: Art and Social Change in Latin America and the United States*. University of Chicago Press, 1994.

Goldman, Shifra. "A Public Voice: Fifteen Years of Chicano Posters." *Art Journal* 44, no. 1 (1984): 50–57.

Gomringer, Eugen. *The Book of Hours, and Constellations*. Translated by Jerome Rothenberg. Something Else Press, 1968.

Harris, Michael D. "Urban Totems: The Communal Spirit of Black Murals." In *Walls of Heritage, Walls of Pride: African American Murals*, edited by James Prigoff and Robin J. Dunitz. Pomegranate Communications, 2000.

Heins, Marjorie. "Public Art, Censorship, and the Constitution." *Public Art Review* 6, no. 1 (1994): 10–12.

Hilder, Jamie. *Designed Words for a Designed World: The International Concrete Poetry Movement, 1955–1971*. McGill-Queen's University Press, 2016.

Keppel, Ben, Eva Sperling Cockcroft, John Pitman Weber, and James Cockcroft. *Toward a People's Art: The Contemporary Mural Movement*. 2nd ed. University of New Mexico Press, 1998.

Jackson, Carlos Francisco. *Chicana and Chicano Art: ProtestArte*. University of Arizona Press, 2009.

Josten, Jennifer. "Goeritz y la poesía concreta." In *Artecorreo*. PRM Editorial, 2011.

Latorre, Guisela. *Walls of Empowerment: Chicana/o Indigenist Murals of California*. University of Texas Press, 2008.

Lippard, Lucy. *Mixed Blessings: New Art in a Multicultural America*. Pantheon Books, 1990.

Marchi, Regina. *Day of the Dead in the USA: The Migration and Transformation of a Cultural Phenomenon*. 2nd ed. Rutgers University Press, 2022.

Márquez, Lorena V. *La Gente: Struggles for Empowerment and Community Self-Determination in Sacramento*. University of Arizona Press, 2020.

Mesa-Bains, Amalia. "Spiritual Geographies." In *The Road to Aztlan: Art from a Mythic Homeland*, edited by Virginia Fields and Victor Zamudio-Taylor. Los Angeles County Museum of Art, 2001.

Montejano, David. *Sancho's Journal: Exploring the Political Edge with the Brown Berets*. University of Texas Press, 2012.

Monteverde, Mildred. *Chicanos Gráficos . . . California*. Southern Colorado State College, 1971.

Montoya, José. *In Search of Mr. Con Safos: RCAF Retrospective Poster Art Exhibit*. Lankford & Cook Gallery, Rancho Cordova, CA, 1989. Exhibition brochure.

Montoya, José, and Juan M. Carrillo. "Posada: The Man and His Art: A Comparative Analysis of José Guadalupe Posada and the Current Chicano Art Movement as They Apply Toward Social and Cultural Change: A Visual Resource Unit for Chicano Education." Master's thesis, California State University, Sacramento, 1975.

Negrón-Muntaner, Frances. "The Look of Sovereignty: Politics and Style in the Young Lords." *Centro Journal* 27, no. 1 (Spring 2015): 4–33.

Noriega, Chon. "Postmodernism or Why This is Just Another Poster." In *Just Another Poster? Chicano Graphic Arts in California*. University Art Museum, University of California, Santa Barbara, 2001.

Ontiveros, Randy J. *In the Spirit of a New People: The Cultural Politics of the Chicano Movement*. New York University Press, 2014.

Pérez-Torres, Rafael. *Movements in Chicano Poetry: Against Myths, Against Margins*. Cambridge University Press, 1995.

Pieratos, N. A., S. S. Manning, and N. Tilsen. "Land Back: A Meta Narrative to Help Indigenous People Show Up as Movement Leaders." *Leadership* 17, no. 1 (2021): 47–61.

Quirarte, Jacinto. *Mexican American Artists*. University of Texas Press, 1973.

Ramos, E. Carmen. "Printing and Collecting the Revolution: The Rise and Impact of Chicano Graphics, 1965 to Now." In *Printing the Revolution! The Rise and Impact of Chicano Graphics, 1965 to Now*. Smithsonian American Art Museum, 2020.

Riojas, Mirasol. *The Accidental Arts Supporter: An Assessment of the Comprehensive Employment and Training Act (CETA)*. UCLA Chicano Studies Research Center, 2006.

Rios, Herminio, and Octavio Romano, eds. *La Voz Poética del Chicano*. El Grito Quarterly Book Series. Quinto Sol Publications, 1974.

Romo, Terezita. "Aesthetics of the Message: Chicana/o Posters, 1965–1987." In *Printing the Revolution! The Rise and Impact of Chicano Graphics, 1965 to Now*, edited by E. Carmen Ramos. Smithsonian American Art Museum, 2020.

Romo, Terezita. "Chicana/o Art: 1965–1975." In *A Companion to Modern and Contemporary Latin American and Latina/o Art*, edited by Alejandro Anreus, Robin Adele Greeley, and Megan A. Sullivan. Wiley-Blackwell, 2001.

Romo, Terezita, ed. *Chicanos en Mictlán: Día de los Muertos in California*. Mexican Museum, 2000.

Romo, Terezita. *Malaquias Montoya*. UCLA Chicano Studies Research Center Press, 2011.

Romo, Terezita. "Points of Convergence: The Iconography of the Chicano Poster." In *Just Another Poster? Chicano Graphic Arts in California*. University Art Museum, University of California, Santa Barbara, 2001.

Romo, Terezita. "*¡Presente!* Chicano Posters and Latin American Politics." In *Latin American Posters: Public Aesthetics and Mass Politics*, edited by Russ Davidson. Museum of New Mexico Press, 2006.

Romo, Terezita. "Two Compas on a Mission: The Emergence of the Royal Chicano Air Force." Master's thesis, California State University, Sacramento, 1996.

Romo, Terezita. "The Visual Poetry of Luis Gonzalez." In *The Second Coming of Con Safos*. C.N. Gorman Museum, 1993. Exhibition brochure.

Sacramento Poderosas. "Juanita Polendo Ontiveros, Sacramento Poderosa 2022." https://sacpoderosas.org/juanita-polendo-ontiveros.

Senie, Harriet F. *The Tilted Arc Controversy: Dangerous Precedent?* University of Minnesota Press, 2001.

Serra, Richard. "Art and Censorship." In *Writings/Interviews*. University of Chicago Press, 1994.

Solt, Mary Ellen, ed. *Concrete Poetry: A World View*. Indiana University Press, 1968.

Sontag, Susan. "Posters: Advertisement, Art, Political Artifact, Commodity." In *The Art of Revolution, Castro's Cuba: 1959–1970*. McGraw-Hill, 1970.

Sorell, Victor Alejandro. "The Persuasion of Art—The Art of Persuasion: Emanuel Martinez Creates a Pulpit for El Movimiento." In *Emanuel Martinez: A Retrospective*, edited by Teddy Dewalt. Museo de las Américas, 1995.

Stern, Kenneth S. *Loud Hawk*. University of Oklahoma Press, 2002.

Thompson, Ruthe. "Centro Screenprinting: Architects of the Chicano Renaissance." *ScreenPrinting* (August 1987): 114–117, 136.

Torres, Ricardo, Lupe Castellano, and Luis C. González. *Poemasomenos de Sacra*. Taller de Poesía and RCAF, 1973.

Treviño, Jesús Salvador. *Visions of Aztlán*. Barrio Dog Productions Inc., 2010.

Vasconcelos, José. "The Cosmic Race." In *Modern Art in Africa, Asia, and Latin America: An Introduction to Global Modernisms*, edited by Elaine O'Brien. Wiley-Blackwell, 2013.

Villa, Raúl. *Barrio Logos: Space and Place in Urban Chicano Literature and Culture*. University of Texas Press, 2000.

Ybarra-Frausto, Tomás. "*Califas*: California Chicano Art and Its Social Background." Unpublished manuscript. Prepared for Califas Seminar at Mary Porter Sesnon Gallery, University of California, Santa Cruz, April 16–18, 1982.

Ybarra-Frausto, Tomás. "The Chicano Movement/The Movement of Chicano Art." In *Exhibiting Cultures: The Poetics and Politics of Museum Display*, edited by Ivan Karp and Steven D. Lavine. Smithsonian Institution Press, 1991.

Affiliated Organizations

Aeronaves de Aztlán Auto Co-op
Alkali Flat Project Area Committee
Aztlan Dance Company
Breakfast for Niños
Centro de Artistas Chicanos
Chicanos Organization for Political Awareness/COPA
Danza Quetzalcoatl-Citlalli/Grupo Citlalli
Freddy's Band/RCAF Band
La Raza Bookstore/La Raza Galeria Posada
Teatro de la Calle

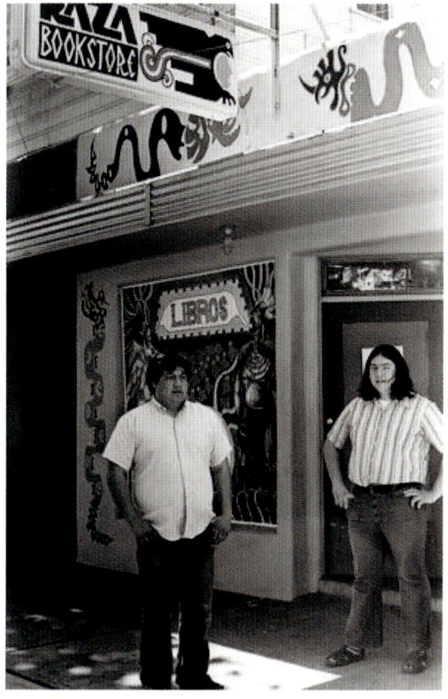

Héctor D. González (born 1945), *Philip Santos and Luis C. González in front of La Raza Bookstore*, circa 1973. Collection of Héctor D. González.

Selected Exhibitions

The following entries reflect the institution names at the times of the exhibition. Many have since changed.

1972

Royal Chicano Art Exhibition, Student Art Gallery, California State University, Sacramento

1973

Chicano Art Show, Student Art Gallery, California State University, Sacramento

Chicano Art, The Oakland Museum (now Oakland Museum of California)

Chicano Art, University of California, Santa Barbara

1974

Fourth Annual Royal Chicano Air Force Art Show, Student Art Gallery, California State University, Sacramento

1975

Posters and Society, San Francisco Museum of Modern Art, California

Chicanarte: Statewide Exposicion of Chicano Art, Los Angeles Municipal Art Gallery, California

Chicano Art, California Governor's Office, California State Capitol, Sacramento

Chicano Poster Show, Stanford University, Stanford, California

1977

Locuras y Curadas, Chicano Art Show, Sierra College, Rocklin, California

The Fifth Sun: Contemporary/Traditional Chicano and Latino Art, University Art Museum, University of California, Berkeley

1984

Winging It: In Flight Retrospective of RCAF Posters, La Raza Galeria Posada, Sacramento, California

1989

In Search of Mr. Con Safos: RCAF Retrospective Poster Art Exhibit, Lankford and Cook Gallery, Rancho Cordova, California

1990

Oro de Aztlan: El Arte del RCAF, Robert Else Gallery, California State University, Sacramento

1990–93

Chicano Art: Resistance and Affirmation (CARA), Wight Art Gallery, University of California, Los Angeles [Traveled to Denver Art Museum, Colorado; Albuquerque Museum of Art and History, New Mexico; San Francisco Museum of Modern Art, California; Fresno Art Museum, California; Tucson Museum of Art, Arizona; National Museum of American Art, Washington, DC; El Paso Museum of Art, Texas; and San Antonio Museum of Art, Texas]

1991

The State of Chicano Art, Galeria de la Raza, San Francisco, California

1992

RCAF Posters, Sacramento History Museum, California

1993

En el Ojo de Ollin: RCAF Posters, Crocker Art Museum, Sacramento, California

2000–3

Just Another Poster? Chicano Graphic Arts in California, University Art Museum, University of California, Santa Barbara [Traveled to Jack S. Blanton Museum of Art, University of Texas, Austin; Fowler Museum of Cultural History, University of California, Los Angeles; Oakland Museum of California; Jersey City Museum, New Jersey; and co-presented by Crocker Art Museum and La Raza Galeria Posada, Sacramento, California]

2005

RCAF: 37 Years of Culture con Cultura, La Raza Galeria Posada, Sacramento, California

2007

The RCAF Goes to College, University Library Gallery, California State University, Sacramento

2009

Sacrachicano: A Remembrance and Renewal of a Seminal Art Force—The RCAF, Sacramento Public Library, Central Branch, California

2014

Look to the Sky: The RCAF Posters of the 1970s and '80s, James Kaneko Gallery, American River College, Sacramento, California

2019

The Royal Chicano Air Force Lands at the Capitol, California State Capitol, Sacramento

Corazón, Archival Gallery, Sacramento

2020–25

¡Printing the Revolution! The Rise and Impact of Chicano Graphics, 1965 to Now, Smithsonian American Art Museum, Washington, DC [Traveled to Amon Carter Museum of American Art, Fort Worth, Texas; Hood Museum of Art, Dartmouth College, Hanover, New Hampshire; Frist Art Museum, Nashville, Tennessee; and Rollins Museum of Art, Winter Park, Florida]

2025

Chicanismo and the Art of Resistance: The Legacy of Ricardo Favela and the RCAF, Chicano Park Museum and Cultural Center, San Diego, California

Index